Very Near to You

Very Near to You

Human Readings of the Torah

Avraham Burg

Translated by J.J. Goldberg

Copyright © Avraham Burg
Jerusalem 2012/5772

All rights reserved. No part of this publication may be translated, reproduced, stored in a retrieval system or transmitted, in any form or by any means, electronic, mechanical, photocopying, recording or otherwise, without express written permission from the publishers.

Cover Design: Studio Paz
Typesetting: David Yehoshua

Originally published in Hebrew as *Belashon Bnei Adam*
by Kinneret Zmora-Bitan Dvir Publishing House, Ltd., 2009.

Biblical translations are based on the JPS 1917 version (public domain). Babylonian Talmud text is drawn from the Soncino Babylonian Talmud, edited by Rabbi Dr. Isidore Epstein (copyright 2007, Soncino Press, Ltd.). Saul Tchernichovsky's "Credo" ("Laugh") translated from Hebrew by Maurice Samuel. Natan Alterman's "On the Road to No-Amon" translated from Hebrew by Ilana Kurshan. Other translations, except where noted in the text, are by J. J. Goldberg. Certain translations from traditional text rely on online commentators, credited where possible.

ISBN: 978-965-229-564-4

1 3 5 7 9 8 6 4 2

Gefen Publishing House Ltd.
6 Hatzvi Street
Jerusalem 94386, Israel
972-2-538-0247
orders@gefenpublishing.com

Gefen Books
11 Edison Place
Springfield, NJ 07081, USA
516-593-1234
orders@gefenpublishing.com

www.gefenpublishing.com

Printed in Israel

Send for our free catalogue

Library of Congress Cataloging-in-Publication Data

Burg, Avraham.
   [Parashat ha-shavu'a bi-leshon bene adam. English.]
   Very near to you: human readings of the Torah / by Avraham Burg.
   p. cm.
ISBN 978-965-229-564-4
1. Bible. O.T. Pentateuch--Commentaries. I. Title.
BS1225.53.B86513 2012
222'.107--dc23
                              2011045779

In memory of my mother and teacher, Rivka née Slonim, and my father and teacher, Shlomo Yosef Burg.
May their memory be a blessing.

For the loves of my life, Yael, Itay and Noa, Roni and Ariel, Natan and Tamara, Dan and Daniella, Avital and Yonatan, Noam.

For the community of my life in Nataf in the Judean Hills at the approaches of Jerusalem.

Contents

Foreword .... *xi*

Avraham Burg's Portion .... *xv*

Preface .... *xix*

Genesis

Week 1: **Bereshit – In the Beginning** *3*

Week 2: **Noach – Noah Was a Righteous Man** *11*

Week 3: **Lech Lecha – Get Thee Out** *18*

Week 4: **Vayera – He Appeared** *25*

Week 5: **Chayei Sarah – The Life of Sarah** *33*

Week 6: **Toledot – These Are the Generations** *40*

Week 7: **Vayetze – Jacob Left** *48*

Week 8: **Vayishlach – Jacob Sent** *56*

Week 9: **Vayeshev – And Jacob Dwelt** *65*

Week 10: **Miketz – At the End of Two Years** *74*

Week 11: **Vayigash – Then He Came Near** *85*

Week 12: **Vayechi – And He Lived** *93*

Encore: **Genesis** *101*

Exodus

Week 13: **Shemot – Names** 107

Week 14: **Va'era – And I Appeared** 116

Week 15: **Bo – Go In** 125

Week 16: **Beshalach – When He Had Let the People Go** 136

Week 17: **Yitro – Jethro, the Priest of Midian** 147

Week 18: **Mishpatim – The Ordinances** 156

Week 19: **Terumah – Offering** 163

Week 20: **Tetzaveh – Thou Shalt Command** 173

Week 21: **Ki Tissa – When Thou Takest** 181

Week 22: **Vayakhel/Pekudei – And Moses Assembled/
These Are the Accounts** 190

Encore: **Exodus** 199

Leviticus

Week 23: **Vayikra – And the Lord Called** 205

Week 24: **Tzav – Command** 215

Week 25: **Shemini – On the Eighth Day** 224

Week 26: **Tazria/Metzora – If a Woman Be Delivered/
The Law of the Leper** 234

Week 27: **Acharei Mot/Kedoshim – After the Death/
Ye Shall Be Holy** 243

Week 28: **Emor – Speak Unto the Priests** 255

Week 29: **Behar/Bechukotai – At Mount Sinai/In My Statutes** 264

Encore: **Leviticus** 272

Numbers

Week 30: **Bamidbar – In the Wilderness** *279*

Week 31: **Naso – Take the Sum of the Sons** *289*

Week 32: **Beha'alotecha – When Thou Lightest the Lamps** *296*

Week 33: **Shelach Lecha – Send Thou Men** *306*

Week 34: **Korach – And They Rose Up** *315*

Week 35: **Chukkat – This Is the Statute** *323*

Week 36: **Balak – Balak Saw** *332*

Week 37: **Pinchas – Phinehas the Zealot** *338*

Week 38: **Mattot/Masei – The Tribes/The Stages** *343*

Encore: **Numbers** *352*

Deuteronomy

Week 39: **Devarim – These Are the Words Which Moses Spoke** *359*

Week 40: **Va'etchanan – And I Besought** *367*

Week 41: **Ekev – Because Ye Hearken** *379*

Week 42: **Re'eh – Behold** *387*

Week 43: **Shoftim – Judges** *395*

Week 44: **Ki Tetzeh – When Thou Goest Forth** *404*

Week 45: **Ki Tavo – When Thou Art Come In** *413*

Week 46: **Nitzavim/Vayelech – You Are Standing/
And Moses Went** *424*

Week 47: **Ha'azinu – Give Ear** *429*

Week 48: **Vezot Haberachah – And This Is the Blessing** *435*

Encore: **Deuteronomy** *438*

Foreword

MORE THAN A CENTURY AGO, the great Hebrew essayist Asher Ginsberg, better known as Ahad Ha'am, imagined a Jewish homeland in the land of Israel. This homeland, he dreamed, would nourish a bold new Jewish culture, utilizing a revived Hebrew language. It would be deeply rooted in the traditional rhythms of the Jewish home and street, yet vigorous and pioneering. It would, he hoped, produce intellectual, religious and artistic innovation that would inspire and enrich the daily lives of Jews throughout the Diaspora.

This book is what Ahad Ha'am had in mind. Avraham Burg has crafted a yearly cycle of biblical homilies, modeled on the traditional *dvar Torah*, the sermon that follows the weekly Torah reading in synagogue. Unlike too many sermons in today's synagogues, though, Burg does not simply reinforce his readers' preconceived notions of what the Torah has to say. He reaches into traditional Jewish sources and finds meanings that are both original and challenging, meanings that force conservatives and liberals alike to confront and reconsider their assumptions about Jewish moral and religious tradition.

Burg's challenge is at the heart of Ahad Ha'am's vision. Ahad Ha'am's cultural Zionism was a radical challenge to the political Zionist movement launched by Theodor Herzl. Herzl's Zionism aimed to end the Diaspora by gathering all Jews in one country. Ahad Ha'am's Zionism, by contrast, was meant not to end the Diaspora but to strengthen it. The Jewish state that Herzl described in his writings was essentially a Middle Eastern version of his own Mittel-European Vienna, from the opera and cafes down to the German language. Ahad Ha'am, by contrast, saw the renewed Jewish homeland as a place from which cultural and theological experiments would emerge to form the basis for a renewed worldwide Jewish culture.

More than eighty years after Ahad Ha'am's death, and more than sixty years after the birth of the Jewish state, that goal remains largely unmet, especially when it comes to the world's largest Diaspora community, the

Jews of the United States. The failure is clearest among secular Jews. Once upon a time, the culture of Eastern Europe offered secular Ashkenazi Jews in Israel and America a common idiom. When American Jewish leaders met Prime Minister Levi Eshkol in the 1960s, he teased them in Yiddish. Into the 1970s, young American Jews whose parents belonged to labor unions went to work on kibbutzim fired by the same socialist or social democratic ideals on which they had been raised. Most of that is now gone. Few outside the ultra-Orthodox now speak Yiddish. In Israel, the Labor party that represented the ideals of the kibbutz is now a skeleton of its former self. Its American Jewish cousin, the Jewish labor movement, which once shaped political discourse in the Jewish community, is a distant memory. Among secular Jews, what remains of the ideological link between Israel and American Jewry is a cluster of Jewish organizations, dominated by a wealthy few, which tend to define fidelity to Israel as fidelity to the Israeli government, irrespective of what values that government upholds.

In the Orthodox world, the bonds of peoplehood are stronger. Most American Orthodox Jews now spend a year in Israel after high school, develop some facility with Hebrew, have friends and family who have made *aliyah*, and bring back with them a set of practices and tastes that shape Orthodox life in the United States. American Orthodox Jews now frequently begin their *Kabbalat Shabbat* services on Friday evening with the song *Yedid Nefesh*, and their Shabbat meals with hummus, both imports from Israel. In at least one prominent American modern Orthodox school, the clocks in the front hall show the time in Israel alongside the time in the United States.

But for all the beauty of the ties between Orthodox America and Orthodox Israel, they are spawning a politics that is often indifferent, if not hostile, to the liberal values inscribed in both nations' declarations of independence. If *Yedid Nefesh* represents one form of American-Israeli Orthodox cross-fertilization, Baruch Goldstein, the murderer of Hebron, represents another. In both communities, fear of Palestinians and Muslims all too often descends into hatred of Palestinians and Muslims. And as Orthodoxy increasingly becomes the connective tissue between American Jewry and the Jewish state, pushing both Israeli and American Jewish politics further to the right, the mass of secular, left-leaning, American Jews drift further away.

Against that backdrop, Avraham Burg is a rare and crucial figure. He is a religious Jew deeply versed in classic texts. But he exemplifies Dr. Micha Goodman's call for a way of learning in which people do "not subjugate our subjective world to the text" but "bring our world to it." Burg does not only use Torah to challenge contemporary values; he uses contemporary values to challenge Torah, all the while revering that with which he argues. For young American Jews, often caught between an Orthodox world that demands submission and a non-Orthodox world in which traditional Jewish sources remain largely hidden, this will be a stirring combination.

Yet if that were all Burg offered, it could be replicated in the United States, where this spirit of intellectual openness and textual rigor informs efforts at religious renewal like the independent minyan movement. What makes Burg unique is that he offers us this combination as an Israeli deeply involved in the struggle for the soul of the Jewish state. Many American Jews wrestle with biblical texts, but that wrestling has little bearing on the affairs of state. Burg, by contrast, is a former speaker of the Knesset, a once and perhaps future politician enmeshed in a conversation about the Jewish state that is, inevitably, also a conversation about Judaism itself. Who else but an Israeli could see in the pragmatic, dexterous, taciturn Noah an echo of the Zionist pioneers? Who else would see in Simeon and Levi, the sons of Jacob who massacred the men of Shechem, a forerunner of the tribe of Kahane that threatens Israel today?

This is the kind of experiment in thought and vision that a Jewish state makes possible and the kind that we badly need today, not only to bridge the gulf between religious and secular in Jewish Israel and in Jewish America, but to bridge the gulf between Jewish Israel and Jewish America. Because if Judaism represents one necessary link between the two largest Jewish communities in the world, democracy represents another. If liberal-minded young American Jews fall in love with Israel again, it will be because they fall in love not merely with Israel as an experiment in Jewish life, but with Israel as an experiment in democratic values. In this book, Avraham Burg calls on American Jews to make Judaism relevant to that democratic experiment. In this age in which the Knesset outlaws settlement boycotts and rabbis circulate letters demanding that Jews not rent to Arabs, it is a call of desperate importance. I hope that we on this side of the ocean summon the strength to respond.

Peter Beinart

Avraham Burg's Portion

*T*HE WEEKLY PORTION BELONGS TO EVERYONE. In the past, the weekly biblical portion served as a basic arena for Torah learning among ordinary Jews, a way to spend their few weary hours of free time. For scholars the portion offered an expanded, fertile ground for developing ideas and interpretations, for debating and formulating a worldview. The two groups, the scholarly and the plainspoken, met in the synagogue every week and read the week's portion. The weekly portion had the power to connect various opposing social groups. In our time, by contrast, the weekly portion has lost its unifying role. Worshippers in synagogues can hear countless commentaries and insights on the portion, but those who don't attend synagogue are denied the common language, left out of the conversation – the conversation that until recently brought together so many Jews from diverse backgrounds. Even when books about the weekly portion are occasionally released in the secular culture, they are not always books that speak to the heart or the mind of the contemporary secular reader. They speak a language that we find difficult to hear. They frequently address problems that seem divorced from the things that matter in our lives.

In reality, however, these few examples should not be taken as evidence that the portion has no interest or relevance in my life or yours here in twenty-first-century Israel. On the contrary, in my work on the television program *Welcoming Sabbath* I am moved and stunned again and again to discover how much the weekly portion serves as a source of meaning for so many people from every corner of Israeli society, in their here and now, and in ours. I learn every week anew to my delight what a storehouse of questions and answers, of stories and vantage points the weekly portion contains within itself that connect directly to real life in today's Israel.

Why is it, then, that so little is written today that draws on and expands the portions? Because even though there is nothing easier than building on the foundation of the weekly portions, it is also true that nothing is more difficult. There is nothing easier, because the marvelous culture of the Midrash and the tradition of Jewish homily allow the reader to use the scripture for many purposes that can lead in countless directions. And yet, precisely because Jewish tradition is so open to varied possibilities of interpretation and parable, the act of homily and commentary becomes increasingly difficult over time. The moment a person sits down to frame his impressions and ideas about the weekly portion, questions begin to leap out: What is the real meaning of a truth? What is the true interpretation? What is the correct way to understand the text and its characters? Who is the right person to interpret a text for us? Are beauty and richness of thinking a sufficient criterion for judging the validity of a lesson?

The challenge that emerges from these questions is, in my view, considerable: finding criteria that are not based, as they once were, on rabbinic or academic authority, but that also do not simply accept every possible reading as equal to any other, especially those that are spoken in ignorance or thoughtlessness. Many questions of this sort come to mind whenever I study the biblical tales and the commentary that accompanies them, whether traditional or modern, or when I myself try to write an interpretation or exegesis on a biblical story or character. There is no definitive answer to these questions, and there probably never will be. This volume, however, offers a serious reflection.

Avraham Burg's writing about the portion of the week is an authentic continuation of a long Jewish tradition, even in those places where it challenges the tradition or rejects its conventional values. Burg's *drashot* are "authentic" because they stem from a deep reverence and respect for Jewish tradition. And because he loves the tradition, he does not hesitate to criticize it on occasion. Burg moves freely, with ease born of homespun intimacy, between the interpretations and the exegeses of various generations, along the way laying out his own fascinating personal Midrash. This is a Midrash that carries within it both the faithfulness and honesty of a man for whom Jewish tradition is a launching point for the journeys of the past and the hopes of the future.

The readings of the weekly portion that Burg offers in this book are innovative and surprising. At times they can be infuriating, and at other times deeply moving. His commentaries display a side of him that is not familiar to much of the Israeli public. They show the erudition of a religious scholar who was raised in a world of Torah study and observance and remains fluent in the idiom of his upbringing. His command of the traditional sources jumps out from every page, and he does not hesitate to share it with his readers. And yet, Burg insists on reading these sources within the context of his own modern, liberal world, in which the values of life, love, tolerance and concern for the weak are sacred values. In his reading of the sources he brings two additional readings. One reading invites the ancient sources to come and stay among us for a while as members of our twenty-first-century family, in all its diversity. The second reading he addresses to us, the secular readers, as if to say: this Torah lies here forgotten; lift it up and treat it as your own, for it truly is yours.

Dov Alboim

Preface

Before the Beginning

*E*VERYONE HAS A PORTION, a story, a tale that sums up his or her life. We all have stories that we tell over and over until they come to symbolize our lives in our own eyes and the eyes of those who listen to us. The stories of the weekly portions are just such tales – on one hand, legends of the larger-than-life characters in Genesis, and on the other hand stories of people just like us, with all the familiar weaknesses and pains. And just like our own personal stories, they repeat themselves over and over until the narratives become truths of mythic proportions, no longer subject to challenge.

No one can claim a monopoly over the great stories of the Jewish people. They belong to all of us. Every generation has had its own commentators who added their wisdom, their experience, their values and their conclusions. Just like today's blog commenters, they have responded and expressed themselves in the margins of that faraway book and turned the weekly portion into a journey through time without end. This journey began long ago, before all else, and to this very day we are invited to add our own layers to it.

That is what the weekly Torah portion is for me. Like everyone else, I live by the rhythms of at least two clocks: the here-and-now and the eternal. The clock of here-and-now drives me with the merciless beat of immediate events. It is surprising, disturbing, demanding. It is filled with human pain and disappointment, along with hopes and plans for a better future. Eternal time, by contrast, beats slowly within me. Time that once was and refuses to disappear. This is the time that peers out from within the weekly portions and their stories. Every year the same story, at the same time, in exactly the same melody. The same, and yet very different.

Every year I am called on to look again at what is written there, to reconsider it and offer a new understanding of something that has been examined and discussed tens of thousands of times before. Every year I am given an opportunity to redesign my past, to correct the mistakes I have made, to change my way of thinking, to change myself. In the present I often find myself trapped. But the past grants me free range for my thoughts and imagination, for a wealth of ideas and spirituality without limits. Fortunately, I cannot live only in the past, just as I have no desire to live only the present. The synchronizing of my two clocks each weekend paves the winding path on which I move backward and forward simultaneously. This is my identity. This is my culture.

In our generation, there are those who seem to see themselves as custodians of the portions' interpretation, by dint of their own authority and the apathy of others. This book seeks to break the monopoly, to free the Torah from the captivity of that single perspective and return it in all its beauty to the rest of us, its true owners. The Torah "is not in heaven," Moses taught us; "it is very near to you" (Deut. 30:12–13).

It is from this passage, in Moses's final address in the Torah's concluding chapters, that the title of this book is drawn:

> For this commandment which I command thee this day, it is not too hard for thee, neither is it far off. It is not in heaven, that thou shouldest say: "Who shall go up for us to heaven, and bring it unto us, and make us to hear it, that we may do it?" Neither is it beyond the sea, that thou shouldest say: "Who shall go over the sea for us, and bring it unto us, and make us to hear it, that we may do it?" But the word is very near unto thee, in thy mouth, and in thy heart, that thou mayest do it. (Deut. 30:11–14)

"Not in heaven" but "near to you" is not just an observation – it is a commandment. As the sages of the Talmud insisted, it places responsibility for interpretation and identity on each and every one of us. The Torah may have come from heaven, but now it is in our hearts and on our lips – yours and mine – for learning and for action. Nor are we free to turn away from this responsibility.

This volume constitutes a small portion of the responsibility, but does not include the larger part of it. There are many more layers of meaning

Preface

tucked away between the biblical verses and characters; all these await liberation in an interpretation not yet discovered. The portion of the week is an endless quarry of thoughts and approaches, which each generation is invited and obliged to unearth, to excavate its own veins of significance, to extract the radiant gold found within the vast spiritual reserve of the Torah of Moses.

This book was written in a dual language: Hebrew and Jewish. The same can be said of its content; it is both ancient and contemporary. Its viewpoint is neither pious nor secularist. If I could describe an imagined, virtual place where it belongs, it would be midway between those who were reared in the bosom of Torah and those whose spirit finds no connection with traditional sources. To the former I render this plea: if you want to be relevant, come out from behind the high walls that have grown up between us. Let yourselves be heard on the issues of the day – war and peace, humanity and the changing family, love, women's equality, the stranger and the convert, the environment, human rights and civil liberties.

To the latter I appeal: come back and join as full partners in the intellectual task of crafting the modern Jewish identity; this is the language and these are the sorts of resources you will need to participate in the discourse of the soul of Israel. And to both groups I say: please, do not walk away. I hope that the pairing of contemporary content and historic spiritual sources will give birth again and again to commentaries that have meaning for each new generation of seekers.

This invitation is twofold. Anyone who wishes to know the sources of our tradition through contemporary eyes is invited to explore within these pages. At the same time, each reader is invited to add new layers of his or her own commentary and meaning to the timeless fundamentals that have sustained Judaism through the ages: Midrash, Chidush and Talmud Torah – homily, innovation and study. As we say when we begin the Passover Seder, everyone is invited. *Kol dichfin* – let all who are hungry for a new way of understanding their Jewishness come and learn. *Kol ditzrich* – let all who are in need of meaning come and join us.

And there is one more invitation, which I address to readers in Jewish communities around the world. In the years since the founding of the

State of Israel, it must be acknowledged, we have not built enough sturdy bridges between our worlds, the communities of Israel and the Diaspora. I hope this book can help each of us to understand the other.

We have been hiding for many years behind a slogan, "We Are One." Many of us, especially members of the generation that witnessed the Holocaust and the birth of Israel, felt that despite our disagreements, despite the fundamental differences between the daily realities of Israeli and Diaspora Jewish life, there were deep common denominators that united us as one indivisible people. Just as we had suffered as one people, it seemed clear, so we would be reborn as one people.

Few of us questioned it. Relations between Israel and the Diaspora rested on three great pillars: remembrance of the Holocaust, the struggle for Soviet Jewry and the centrality of Israel. With the passage of years, however, these forces have begun to ebb. The Holocaust grows ever more distant; what it will mean to future generations will not be the same as what it means to those who lived through it, nor their children who heard their parents' and grandparents' stories. The Jews of the Soviet Union have come from darkness into the light and from oppression to freedom, and for the first time in our history the overwhelming majority of the Jewish people lives in democratic societies and enjoys freedom and equality. And the weakening of the first two pillars has weakened the third as well. In an age of freedom and security, Israel has lost some of its urgency as a source of identification, inspiration and self-confidence to Jews in other countries. Jews in the Diaspora, especially in America, have created a communal culture centered around values of tolerance and pluralism. The culture of Israelis, forged in an ongoing struggle for survival, is harder, more wary, more combative.

Much of the relationship between the two communities today rests on nostalgia for a past that no longer exists, on feelings of guilt and existential fear, on stereotypes and mutual ignorance. Far too little is based on exchanges of substance, on discussions of meaning in a language of shared values. Moreover, there is a sense that the gap between the values of the Israeli and those of the Western Jew is growing with the passing of generations. What is natural to Israelis is foreign to Diaspora Jews, and vice versa. Peter Beinart described the situation concisely and painfully in his June 2010 essay "The Failure of the American Jewish Establishment" in the *New York Review of Books*: "Saving liberal Zionism in the United States – so that American Jews can help save liberal Zionism in Israel – is the great American Jewish challenge of our age."

Like Beinart, I wonder about these challenges. I am worried by what seems to me to be the question of our generation, one that is no less urgent than Beinart's questions. I wonder whether the Jewish people can survive without an outside enemy. In my previous books I have examined the walls of hostility that surround us. I have wondered again and again whether the old walls are still standing, or whether they are at least partly imagined. I have contemplated the question of whether and when we can cross over from a strategy of victimhood and trauma to a theology of faith and openness. At a certain key point in my thinking I reached the conclusion that much of our people is unable to shake the feeling that anti-Semitism determines who is a Jew. We find it hard to walk abruptly away from everything to which we have grown accustomed over the generations: the subjective self-definition that is determined for us by others, outside ourselves, or by our own ingrained confrontationalism. To that end we need to develop muscles that have long gone slack and unused, to revive the rich, positive understanding of Judaism that comes from within. We need to live a Jewish life that is so self-assured, so content in its lot that it does not need walls separating itself from the outside world, supplying a self-definition the way crutches do for an invalid.

That is how my own children were raised and how they live their lives – as Jews bound to the tradition's ethical values, as non-judgmental lovers of humanity. They are free human beings who are, first and foremost, full and contributing members of the family of humankind; only after that are they Jews, and within Jewry, members of the subcategory of Israelis. And to the extent that they find these identities in conflict with one another, they do all they can to resolve it on the universal, human side of the scale. It is for these children and the children of all those who share my beliefs that I have written this book. Too many of them have no access to the basic materials of Jewish culture. They feel like strangers in their own spiritual home. Judaism, with all its beauty and complexity, has been denied them. The Jewish "establishment" in Israel and around the world needs them to assure its demographic well-being, but it ignores their yearning for spiritual well-being.

How do you read a book like this? Bit by bit. A chapter each week, no longer than the week's portion itself. This is not a narrative, nor a systematic, ideological analysis. Think of it as a string of beads, a chain that each of us is invited to weave for himself. You can read it, argue with it, or turn its words into the beginning of a family chat or a conversation among friends. The portion of the week is like the oxygen in the air we breathe – always present yet rarely noticed. I hope the same will be true of this book. My aim is to let these pages engage the general public in the abundant human, moral, universal, historic, national bounty that fills the Five Books of Moses. My words are not meant to end the debate, but to begin it. Every one of the topics presented here lends itself to many interpretations, and everyone is invited to expand or reduce, agree or reject, or even better, to create their own commentary and take it public. This would be my greatest compensation.

While this book was originally written in Hebrew, I would hope that its spirit is not limited by language. Its voice is, first of all, a human one. The English edition presented here is the fruit of many good people's labors, beginning with my dear friend and soul brother, Clive Lessem. We have traveled together for decades along the byways of Jewish life, finding new partners and trying to cure the ills of the world. We were joined by J.J. Goldberg, whose cultural and technical acuities, deeper than the sea itself, turned this English edition into a work that stands on its own merits.

The moment when a new book of Jewish learning is born is an emotional one, and I am filled with gratitude toward my teachers and guides who taught me the ways of American Judaism. To Jonathan Jacoby, who first opened the door for me to this wonderful world of my brothers and sisters across the ocean; we have never parted since, and we never will. To Marvin and Helaine Lender; if all the world's hearts were as warm, generous and caring as theirs, the world would need no further healing. To Edgar Bronfman Sr., who bravely and tirelessly leads the struggle for

Preface

the future identity of the Jewish people. To Brian Lurie, my brother, friend and partner, a visionary and prophet who always stands on the front lines of the Jewish people and urges me to step forward and join him. And all this could not have come to be were it not for the wind in my sails, the boundless spirit of Sami and Tova Segol, those unique individuals, my wise friends and supporters, whose breadth of vision and commitment to the next generation make so much possible, whose inspiration continually pushes me beyond what I thought possible.

The ideas expressed here are the product of many partnerships, and represent a cooperative effort. They began their journey as family conversations on Sabbath eve, while walking to the synagogue, over the dinner table or by candlelight. They embody the spirit of my mother's values and my father's moral teachings, may their memories be a blessing. Over time they became the material for multi-generational, multi-sided conversations, for weekly messages that I wrote to my children and friends on many Sabbath eves. I sent them out as alternatives to synagogue newsletters with their cramped perspectives. Eventually the circle expanded to include my extended family, friends and even complete strangers. Small portions were published in various media, but most are published here for the first time. When it came time to collect these scattered ideas and bind them between the covers of a book, I sought out a partner and found Hillel Achiani, who became my coworker, editor, dear friend and wise traveling companion. He sees the troubles strewn in my path and clears them away, or turns them into new material to strengthen my case, adding his own context and meaning; my debt to him is limitless.

There are no words to express the happiness I derive from my family – from my beloved wife; from my children, who are my friends and partners; from my dear sister who is as close to me as another person can be; from my parents-in-law, Lucien and Jeanine, the finest of people; from my brothers- and sisters-in-law, my cousins and their loved ones. This book was written for them and with them in loving gratitude.

In the Talmud there is a charming old Jewish tale that attests to the conditions of God's smile: as long as we take responsibility for the world around us, we push God out of the decision-making inner circle and even out of the community hall itself. Such was the case in the bitter debate surrounding the oven of Achnai (*Bava Metzia* 59b), when God sat and watched from on high, smiling to himself and saying, "My children have defeated me." So it is in Jewish lore, and so it is in this book, which is devoted entirely to tipping the burden of interpretive and moral responsibility toward humanity. To defeat God through the words of his own Torah, through human understandings both ancient and modern, and so give him an opportunity again and again to smile that wonderful smile of the divine.

Avraham Burg
Nataf, 5772/2011

בראשית
Genesis

Week 1

Bereshit – In the Beginning

Genesis 1:1–5:8

He Created Man: Male and Female

And so we take it again from the top: "In the beginning…." Bear this in mind: Jewish time is not linear – not in the sad, fatalistic sense of the word. Nor is it circular, coming back around upon itself with depressing regularity. Jewish time is a combination of line and circle. It moves in a spiral fashion, like an unfolding circle, doubling back upon itself and yet advancing, a line and yet a circle, and most of all open-ended. Therefore it is precisely at the beginning of the opening portion of the Bible that we are obliged to point out what is coming around again, and what can and must unfold for the first time. *Parashat Bereshit*, the opening portion of Genesis, is fraught with so many issues that it is difficult to decide where to look for the new in any given year. Given all the possibilities, let us deal first with the creation of Man and Woman, and the status of women as it emerges in this telling.

Parashat Bereshit contains two distinct versions of the creation of Adam and Eve. The most familiar is the chauvinist approach that describes the creation of woman from the rib of man. The second, more egalitarian version (which could be the reason it is treated with less reverence) is the one that says, "male and female he created them" (Gen. 1:27). If the creation was indeed according to this version, then the image of God that is within every human is both male and female. If that is the case, it means that God is not simply a male, not merely a father. He is also a female and a mother. And we who have sanctified God's maleness for so many countless generations have lost sight of the female, womanly, motherly underpinnings of the divine. Perhaps in so doing we have abandoned the gentleness of the original God. What does that say about us, standing here at the current endpoint of the unfolding spiral?

God created all of us. God was there at the moment of conception. The God of those first moments was both father and mother. Only afterwards did we come along, the males of the species, and proceed to hide the mother that is within our creator. In this way, for thousands of years, we lost half of the human race, left it imprisoned behind a wall of stoves and washbasins. Only in the past few generations has the process begun of freeing woman from the chains that circumscribed her existence. This generation's God has to reveal himself once again and show both of his/her aspects. We need to reconnect God-the-mother to this generation's greatest human revolution, the gender equality revolution. A God that isn't ashamed of his/her maternal characteristics can bring much more to the world than a masculine God can bring alone. By the nature of things, the male creates by an act of expelling. The mother, the female, creates by an act of accepting. Our world cannot tolerate more expulsions, cannot bear to have more expelled, pushed out, turned away. We need to transform ourselves into a world of acceptance, of the accepting. Of patience that is as long as the months of gestation, not suddenly expended like the moments of expelling. We speak of God when we say in the New Year's prayer that "this is the day the world was born." It is the day that we remember how God bore us, how God carried the nascent world within Godself.

The beginning of the twenty-first century heralds a great war between God and God's creation, humankind. It is unfolding as a century of confrontation, alas, between the religious and the human. Religious zealots are the children of God-the-male, believers in the act of expelling. The children of God-the-female, the patient, inclusive and accepting, must stand and face them. We must not leave the world only to those who believe in half of God and half of God's commandments. Those who are capable of erasing the feminine half of the creator of the world are just as capable of erasing the *not* in "Thou shalt not murder" (Exod. 20:12). This will be, it seems to me, a century of struggle between the priests of Adam and the humanity of Eve. The endless silence of God will continue, and each side will interpret it as a sign of the creator's implicit endorsement.

The European West, mainly Christian and secular, has embarked on a long journey toward adopting Eve's heritage and principles, in two senses. One is the endless curiosity and ceaseless posing of the questions of the Mother of Mothers: Could it be that all this was incorrect? Both Eve and Newton asked themselves: Is it possible to look at the apple differently? Could it be that everything we have been told up to now means something else? Then it would be up to me individually to find alternate routes and different solutions to the things that seemed right and just until I asked the question. The stories of Eve and of Isaac Newton are both stories of the reinvention of human culture by means of the fruit of the tree of knowledge.

The second sense is far deeper and more important. The West, after years of religious oppression, of fanaticism and witch-hunts, has received the most important revolution of all: equality of women in rights, status and abilities. In the space of a few years the human race has doubled itself. Without bloodshed. A society of men and women together aspiring upward toward a human heaven and downward to the earthly grounding of society. No, not all of the West has reached this stage. Men still abuse women. Churches and synagogues still tolerate structural discrimination against women. But the wall has been breached. In a few more generations the male stronghold will fall before the forces of equality. In a few centuries no one in the West will remember the days when woman was the eternal carrier of snake venom into the midst of a male universe. And Israeli Judaism must choose whether to be part of this wonderful revolution or not.

This is precisely the spirit in which my father, of blessed memory, took his leave from this world. Ever the child of Central Europe, orderly and well mannered, he planned his own funeral down to the last detail. Who would come, which car would carry his single, childless daughter from New York, who would speak and what would be written on his headstone. Beside his grave, as his body was being lowered into the ground, his surprising inner truth rose to heaven. For this is what my beloved sister Ada said when she came to eulogize and weep for our father:

> Father asked at his bedside that I say a few words. He explained to me his view that the most important revolution that took place in the past century, the greatest of revolutions, was the entry of women into the world of deeds and creation. This is a greater revolution than the French or Communist revolutions, because in its wake the world gained women as full members in the life of creative action. In every place where this revolution has been completed, society has gained an additional 100 percent of fellow humans who were made full partners in the life of that society. Father went on to say that he feared not all parts of our society were aware of the importance of this revolution.

Change and Renewal: On the Character of Cain and His God

THE STORIES OF GENESIS are so beautiful, their characters so simple and so human, that these primeval figures have become larger-than-life symbols of life itself. The myths hidden between those lines are so familiar that they have become routine. Man, woman, snake, jealousy, hate, love, despair, destruction and rebuilding. The narrative that usually captures our attention is that of the Garden of Eden. Too little time is spent on the portion's best subplot, the story of Cain. In many respects the story of Cain is the story of all humankind, even more than the story of his parents Adam and Eve, of blessed memory.

It is easy for us to ignore Cain, the wretched murderer, killer of his own brother, destroyer of half the human race alive at that moment in Genesis. He is remembered as the Number One Enemy of Humanity, with little but harsh words and unpleasant associations linked to his name. Criminal docket: *The human race v. Cain, son of Adam and Eve.*

But the close reader might find room for an interesting, surprising, even forgiving attitude toward the founder of homicide. It would have been easy for Cain to hide behind excuses. He could have said to God, I'm sorry, but I didn't know what death was. I'd never seen a corpse. I didn't know there was such a thing in the world. Yes, I hit him, I beat him in the field, but I didn't know he would die. I didn't mean it. I had no criminal intent, no malice aforethought. I plead not guilty. But he does not choose the easy way out. He stands before his Judge and confesses openly, "My sin is too great to bear" (Gen. 4:13; frequently translated, "My punishment is greater than I can bear"). Unlike his father, the first evader, who turned defensive and said, it wasn't me but "the woman whom thou gavest to be with me" (Gen. 3:12); and unlike his smooth-talking mother, who ducked and said, "The serpent beguiled me" (Gen. 3:13), Cain admits his guilt and acknowledges the severity of the act. Even though his sin is theoretically less than that of his parents. They had been told explicitly what was permitted and what was forbidden and they chose the forbidden. Nobody had ever told Cain that it was forbidden to kill, and nonetheless he confesses. Look at it this way: God asks each of them almost the same question. Of the father he asks, "Where art thou?" (Gen. 3:9), and of the son he asks, "Where is Abel thy brother?" (Gen. 4:9). The question of *where* – where did you come from and where are you going – is similar. But the answers differ and testify to the differences between the respondents.

From a narrative point of view, it seems to me that God really invested in Cain's education. He cares about him. Even before the deed, he warns him about his angry, frustrated mood swings: "If thou doest well, shall it not be lifted up? And if thou doest not well, sin coucheth at the door; and unto thee is its desire, but thou mayest rule over it" (Gen. 4:7). After Cain's sin God speaks with him and listens to him. He accepts his reply and grants his request for forgiveness. He protects him from further harm. After Cain says his sin is too great to bear, God says, "Therefore, whosoever slayeth Cain, vengeance shall be taken on him sevenfold" (Gen. 4:15). And in Cain's later years God permits him to settle down, to have a wonderful child named Enoch, even to found a city in the name of his son. Cain is permitted to see how his descendants will create material cultures and technological skills the like of which had not been known since the world's creation: "And Adah bore Jabal; he was the father of such as dwell in tents and have cattle. And his brother's name was Jubal; he was the father of all such as handle the harp and pipe. And Zillah, she also bore Tubal-cain, the forger of every cutting instrument of brass and iron; and the sister of Tubal-cain was Naamah" (Gen. 4:20–22).

Why did God invest so deeply in Cain? It would have been far more fitting to stay angry and erase him from the book – like the generation of the Flood, like the children of Sodom and Gomorrah, like the Egyptians in the sea, like generations from time immemorial. For God knew at the first instant what we hadn't learned until recently. That if Man – that is, not the first man, the primordial ancestor, but all humankind – was created in the image of God, then Cain's character is a reflection, through a distant mirror, of one of God's traits. It is not only the good and virtuous in God that we call "in the image." There is also a dark shadow, depressive and sinful, in that image. It is an inseparable part of the divine. What is more, it is not only the evil in Cain that is a reflection of the creator. The ability to regret the past and to accept responsibility for making a better future is also a part of God. The God of Genesis hints to us through Cain that, yes, there is a basic element of evil in God, but no, we are not permitted to despair and fear it forever. Even God and his decisions can be educated and changed through understanding, through taking the right approach. Just as Cain, God's icon (the classical Greek translation of the original Hebrew *tzelem*, or image) on earth, was educated and changed. And this hints at the existence of the other God. This side of God appears to us at its best in a long chain of biblical events, most of them hinted more than explicit, of harsh decisions that burn with rage but also change and soften and testify to the malleability of the Almighty. The God of this week's portion nurtures Cain and stays with him from beginning to end, because he knows that Cain's successful transformation will in the end be his own success and his hope for self-mastery.

This helps to illuminate two more layers of biblical tradition and Jewish religious heritage. Cain is the only character in the creation saga whose fate is linked to the destiny of the Jewish people and the faith of Abraham. Methuselah and Lamech are all but forgotten, and who even knows who Irad and Mehujael were? All of them disappeared from memory, but Cain regularly reappears. When Balaam was reciting his parables to the people camped below, he looked around him and saw "the Kenite [or Cainite] and took up his parable, and said: Though firm be thy dwelling-place, and though thy nest be set in the rock; nonetheless Cain shall be wasted; How long? Asshur shall carry thee away captive" (Num. 24:21–22). The words are rather obscure, but they testify to the stability and security of the Cainite tribe that lives alongside the tribes of Israel.

Drawing on this understanding, Rabbi Moshe Ben Nachman – the Ramban, or Nachmanides – writing thousands of years later in thirteenth-century Spain, interpreted the shared fate of the Jewish people and the children of Cain in this fashion: "This is to say, do not fear when you come upon Israel…, because the people Israel…will redeem…and will not destroy you as she would destroy Amalek" (Ramban on Num. 24:21ff.; Num. 24:20–24 for context). This astonishing biblical family destiny continues to unfold in the Book of Judges: "And the children of the Kenite, Moses' father-in-law, went up out of the city of palm-trees with the children of Judah into the wilderness of Judah, which is in the south of Arad; and they went and dwelt with the people" (Judg. 1:16). The Kenite – that is, the child of Cain – is Jethro, and our own lawgiver Moses is married to Cain's daughter. Imagine that! And Rashi, citing the Midrash, goes even further in absolving the father of all murderers by interpreting the words "and dwelt with the people" in this manner: "He asked the Holy One, praised be he, to invite righteous students for him, and he gathered these pious ones for him" (Rashi on Judg. 1:15). And then there is the legendary heroine Jael, the wife of Heber the Kenite, who smashed the skull of Sisera and was memorialized for all time: "Blessed above women shall Jael be, the wife of Heber the Kenite" (Judg. 5:24).

After this long chain of absolution, assimilation and acceptance of Cain and his stock into the Jewish people, from the lofty Moses on down to the commentators and the common people, the Cainite dimension in Jewish theology and religious heritage starts to become clear. The Jewish worshipper recites twice daily the Shema Yisrael prayer and immediately afterwards whispers, "And thou shalt love the Lord thy God with all thy heart, and with all thy soul, and with all thy might" (Deut. 6:5). The passage of untold years and countless prayers has made the words a matter of rote, to the point where many know them by heart but only a few understand their real significance.

Few of us know this teaching in the Babylonian Talmud: "One is obliged to bless the bad as he blesses the good, as it is written: 'And thou shalt love the Lord thy God with all thy heart and with all thy soul and with all thy might.' With all thy heart: with both of your inclinations, your inclination for good and your evil inclination" (Mishnah *Brachot* 9:5). Loving God isn't only a feeling of grace and a suffusion of light beaming from the faces of innocent believers. God is served as well by the evil impulses within us. There is a divine foundation in Cain that accounts for the existence of sin – and of our power and our will to acknowledge sin, to correct our ways, to change God's decisions and to be changed ourselves. From now on, when we say that to be a Jew is to be a human being created in the divine image, we should remember that to be created in the divine image means to admit that there is a bit of Cain in each of us. His story is a warning. But like Cain, we have received both warning and a hope for a long life in which to atone.

Week 2

Noach – Noah Was a Righteous Man

Genesis 5:9–11:32

Noah's Flour and Abraham's Torah

For years I was extremely critical of Noah. I didn't like his silent character, his failure to open his mouth, to utter even a single word of protest as God stormed across the world in his murderous, watery rage. Unlike Abraham at Sodom, unlike Moses facing the sin of the Golden Calf. I had always thought that the essence of scripture was in its words; I never noticed that there is a scripture of words and a scripture of deeds, and that they are not necessarily the same thing.

I interpreted Noah's silence as impotence, and when the commentaries and the Midrash derided him and mocked his name, I happily joined in. "These are the generations of Noah. Noah was in his generations a man righteous and wholehearted" (Gen. 6:9). Here's what Rashi has to say: "Some among our rabbis interpret 'righteous in his generations' as praise, and conclude that if he had lived in an age of righteous men, he would have been even more righteous. Others interpret it as criticism, saying that by his own generation's standards he was righteous, but if he had lived during the generation of Abraham he would not have been considered at all." The compliment is not really a compliment, and the criticism is harsh and piercing.

Today I think of Noah altogether differently. These critical positions place Noah on an artificial human plane. This is not where he belongs. They compare him – unflatteringly – to Abraham, Moses, and Samuel. Those figures spoke with God, spoke for God, fought with him, complemented him. They are the heroes of the verbal Bible, partners in conversation with the One who "spoke and the world came into being." Compared to them, Noah would indeed "not have been considered at all." But that is not his place. In the biblical story, Noah is neither a lawgiver nor a prophetic voice. Noah belongs among the people who build and do, not those who think and speak. Noah is a pioneer, not an intellectual, a manual laborer rather than a noted philosopher. When they needed a little ark, a mere shoebox that could float a bit on the Nile, Moses's mother was handy enough to do the job – and what a tale they made of it. But when they needed to save the human race and every species of animal and vegetation, and required practical skills and manual dexterity, they brought Noah into the story and did not begrudge him. He was good at big arks, rescue missions and practical details, not at creating theories and revealing truths. Compared to this side of Noah, "they" wouldn't be considered at all. Whom did they save? Not even a single righteous person in Sodom.

What, then, was Noah's mission? Did he bear up successfully, at least partially? Or was his failure as resounding as those sneering commentators say? Noah was a direct descendant of Adam, his children, and their adventures. Adam was given specific tasks in the Garden of Eden. His tasks were all connected to nature, to creation, to the whole of creation, to the land and its labors. "God said, 'Behold, I have given you every herb yielding seed, which is upon the face of all the earth, and every tree, in which is the fruit of a tree yielding seed – to you it shall be for food'" (Gen. 1:29).

Or:

> The Lord God took the man, and put him into the Garden of Eden to dress it and to keep it. And the Lord God commanded the man, saying, "Of every tree of the garden thou mayest freely eat." (Gen. 2:15–16)

Or:

> And unto Adam he said: "Because thou hast hearkened unto the voice of thy wife, and hast eaten of the tree, of which I commanded thee, saying: thou shalt not eat of it; cursed is the ground for thy sake; in toil shalt thou eat of it all the days of thy life. Thorns also

and thistles shall it bring forth to thee; and thou shalt eat the herb of the field. In the sweat of thy face shalt thou eat bread, till thou return unto the ground; for out of it was thou taken; for dust thou art, and unto dust shalt thou return." (Gen. 3:17–19)

Cain was the paradigmatic heir and successor of Adam, the earth's first farmer. And that is how he is defined: "Cain was a tiller of the ground" (Gen. 4:2). That is how he expressed his devotion and faith: "And in process of time it came to pass, that Cain brought the fruit of the ground an offering unto the Lord" (Gen. 4:3). That is how God relates to him; the context and associations of the conversation about Cain's action play on the etymological connection between the Hebrew words for man (*adam*), blood (*dam*), and ground (*adamah*):

> The voice of thy brother's blood crieth unto me from the ground. And now cursed are thou from the ground, which hath opened her mouth to receive thy brother's blood from thy hand. When thou tillest the ground, it shall not henceforth yield unto thee its strength; a fugitive and a wanderer shalt thou be in the earth. (Gen. 4:10–12)

And the penitent wails:

> Behold, thou has driven me out this day from the face of the land; and from thy face shall I be hid; and I shall be a fugitive and a wanderer in the earth; and it will come to pass, that whosoever findeth me will slay me. (Gen. 4:14)

So much soil and earth that it is impossible to understand the Bible's description of Noah except as a continuation of that same conversation among farmers who love their earth. After he left the ark and was saved, Noah did an interesting thing: "Noah the husbandman began, and planted a vineyard." (Gen. 9:20): This was not Noah the seaman, not the savior of mankind nor the righteous man of earlier in the tale. This was a man of the soil, a husband to the soil as if wedded to the soil. He husbanded the earth and the earth was his bride. Their relationship was intimate to the point of fertilization and pregnancy. Noah the successor to Jubal and Tubal,

Noah the inventor of modern agriculture – until then, man had been a gatherer of fruits and vegetables. But Noah was not satisfied with merely gathering ripe fruit from the tree. Noah was an agronomist. He planted, grew, harvested and preserved. Noah was the first vintner and epicure, the creator of wine from the fruit of the vine.

God cursed Adam, "Cursed is the ground for thy sake" (Gen. 3:17). And hence the expectations of Noah: "This same shall comfort us in our work and in the toil of our hands" (Gen. 5:29). After years of the curse of inefficient and unproductive tilling of the earth, Noah came and was expected to be a man of the soil. And this is what he did. He wedded himself to the soil and from it he birthed the foods that saved the human race. Thus the midrashic tale attests: "The tiller of the soil became husband of the soil" (Midrash Aggadah [Buber], *Genesis* 9:20). Nor was Noah merely a good husband to the earth; he was also a good father to her produce. Noah saved the first creation that came before the Flood by means of the ark, and he developed the new creation that followed the Flood. Therefore it is said of him that he "was in his generations a righteous man and wholehearted" (Gen. 6:9). He was of two generations – one before the Flood and one afterward – and in both he fulfilled a great task. He redeemed the human race from the earth-curse of Adam, and comforted us in the sorrow and grief caused by the actions of those who came before him.

The rabbis of the Mishnah used to say that if there is no flour, there can be no Torah – that is, learning and culture cannot survive without the basic essentials of life. By this measure, Noah was the flour; only in his wake could Abraham come with his Torah, his message of revealed truth.

The Flood and the Holocaust

THE TORAH IS NOT A HISTORY BOOK. Its accounts are not necessarily facts. The Torah is a divine-human book of faith whose stories are parables and symbols representing deep and complex worlds of spirit, just as its commandments are archetypes of a world of practical, everyday necessity. The story of the Flood has no significance from a factual point of view. It doesn't matter whether there was a true flood or just a heavy rain.

It doesn't even matter if we can prove that floods appear in numerous peoples' religious mythologies. The story of the Flood is a metaphor for the relationship between the creator and his creations.

The story is a simple one. In last week's portion the Torah told of the creation of man, of his sin and the sins of his wife and his snake, of the expulsion from the Garden of Eden, the loss of immortality and the birth of death as a part of human life. On the surface, Adam's weakness and Eve's curiosity brought us to this point. But on second glance, this is the critique of God's own childishness. He created man, programmed him and then expected him to behave like a cowed automaton. The moment Adam deviated from his assigned path, God lost his composure, became enraged and banished him. He took the ball back and didn't want to play anymore, so to speak. In this week's portion that process repeats itself on a global scale. The creator rebukes himself, regrets the creation and, saddened to his very core, lashes out murderously: "I will blot out man whom I have created from the face of the earth" (Gen. 6:7). Only much later in the Bible does God mature, change, relax and become the God who is patient with his world and his faithful. At this stage every solution that occurs to him is violent, homicidal and vengeful: the expulsion from the Garden of Eden, the Flood, the destruction of Sodom and Gomorrah, the killing of the firstborn sons in Egypt and so on.

Not surprisingly, more than a few scholars in recent generations have treated the Flood as analogous to the European Holocaust of the last century. But those comparisons are wrong. In the Flood humankind had nothing to say, because God wasn't listening. By contrast, the Holocaust was not an act of God but a destructive act of man, who did not hear a thing. How is the God who once utterly destroyed the world by flood different from the God who didn't intervene in Hitler's flood? Back then, God managed the world down to the last detail. Nowadays, it appears, he doesn't. Back then, God didn't allow his creations any free choice, but rather expected robotic discipline and unstinting obedience. And in the last century it seemed that God was not present at all. What's more, the Holocaust lacked virtually any element of faith, if only because the victims had no choice.

When the Jews went up on the pyres of the Inquisition, they did so largely by choice. They could either convert and live or be burned with the Shema Yisrael on their lips. It was the same through most of the troubles of the Jewish past, from the trials of Abraham and Job onward. Those tested could always choose the other option. To die on the altar of one's truth was a noble religious choice, but Hitler didn't offer the choice. Everyone – believers and skeptics, religious and apostate, keepers of the faith and the offspring of newly converted Christians – was thrown into the showers and then to the pits of death. And of course it goes without saying that a place with no choice cannot know what it means to be tested, to choose between good and evil, to decide out of conviction rather than compulsion, apostasy or denial. And in a place where God cannot be chosen out of conviction, where can God be found?

Belief in God is possible only in a place where God has contracted himself and made it possible for man to choose in a space free of his divinity. Just as the Flood was God's limitless anger, leaving no space for man to choose, the Holocaust was God's absolute contraction in the face of man's limitless evil. It seems that even the biblical narrator does not feel comfortable with God's educational methods. According to the biblical narrative, Noah does not thank God for his amphibious salvation; he builds an altar, plants a vineyard and then gets drunk and digs himself even deeper into his old silence. It is only God who restrains himself a bit, swearing that "the waters shall no more become a flood to destroy all flesh" (Gen. 9:15). That's what God comes to understand as his responsibility for the consequences of his harsh nature. What is more, in light of the terrible destruction he sowed, he obliges his creations, humankind, not to shed blood, not to murder. To be better than God.

And the people of our generation? It's hard to know whether we have improved or not. The Holocaust is too close; its deepest questions have not yet been asked and its answers cannot yet be known. Nonetheless, the direction is clear. The old religions need new theologies – both ours and our sister religions, Christianity and Islam. At this stage, it is clear to me that a theology of revenge is not worthy of being called a true religion. Likewise, the belief that the world always was, is and will be against us is a grave existential error. Similarly, the Holocaust theology that justifies all the wrongs we commit on the grounds that they pale before the wrongs that have been done to us is a fundamental mistake. The individual and the collective are owed a new theology that relinquishes the doctrine of divine providence, of God as babysitter. A God who manages all the details is a God who leaves no breathing space for humanity to build, create, repair and be a partner. That would be a God of robots, the God of the Flood, remade. It would amount to a God who released believer and skeptic alike from any responsibility. A God of fear, prohibitions, limits and restrictions is a God irrelevant to our generations, to us who so desperately need a God of love, a force for permission, initiative and curiosity. Many of us yearn for a God who forgives, a Father of mercy rather than vengeance, for a Lord of peace and not a Master of war.

The new Torahs that emerge from the Holocaust must point the way toward the shaping of a better humanity, toward teachings that do not give rise to victimizers like the Nazis nor permit victims to be destroyed as we were – as the Gypsies and gays who were there with us, as the Armenians before us and the slaughtered of Rwanda and Cambodia after us. The new theology, particularly the Jewish one, must break through the boundaries of the old faith, and turn faith in humanity as the creation of God into the foundation of its tradition and rites, as an obligatory basis for dialogue among the believers of all religions who are prepared to break down their own boundaries and defend us and the world from bloodshed in the name of closed-minded religion or arrogant humanism. The time has come for the faith of Noah and his commitment to repairing the world; the time of beliefs in destruction, whether divine or human, is over.

Week 3

Lech Lecha – Get Thee Out

Genesis 12:1–17:27

Abraham, Defender of the Fledgling Faith

THE CULTURE OF THE CHRISTIAN WEST, the culture of the Muslim world and the culture of the Jewish community are, in the final analysis, the cultures of Abraham. Some call them revealed religions – religions with a central hub that turns on an axis of divine revelation, and an outer rim that awaits a final revelation and redemption in the end of days. That might perhaps explain why revelation and redemption sound and unfold so similarly. We frequently hear that it was Abraham who discovered God and spread his teachings and his faith to the ancient world. It is a view shared by philosophy and legend alike.

This is how Maimonides, the rationalist philosopher, a stranger to mysticism, describes him:

> Because he had been weaned on them, [Abraham] began to find his thoughts wandering. While still young he began to think night and day. He began to wonder how it could be that this wheel was perpetually turning if no one was turning it or driving, since it was impossible that it should turn itself. He had no teacher or instructor. His roots were in Ur in the Chaldees among foolish idol worshippers, and his father and mother and all the people worshipped idols and he worshipped with them. And his heart began to rebel and seek understanding until he found the true path and came to understand the course of justice out of his own native wisdom. And he knew that there is one God, the Driver of the wheel, the creator of all,

and there is no other God but him. And he knew that all the world had erred, and the thing that caused them to err was worshipping idols and artifacts until their knowledge of truth was lost. And when he was forty years old Abraham came to recognize his creator. And because he recognized and knew, he began to answer questions for the people of Ur of the Chaldees and to administer justice among them and to tell them that this path they were following was not the path of truth. And he smashed the idols and began to inform the people that nothing should be worshipped except the God of the world and that it was to him that one should bow and sacrifice and pour libations, that all future creation would recognize him. (Maimonides, *Mishneh Torah*, Hilchot Avodat Kochavim 1:3)

The key words in Maimonides's description are *recognize, understand, know* and *inform*. Maimonides is true to his teaching: just as prophesy is not an automatic divine bounty that flows into the head of the prophet from above, but rather an intense human spiritual effort from below to which humankind must strive all its days (and a chosen few may even achieve it), so it is with belief. It was Abraham who reached God, not God who found his first believer. So it is with prophesy, and so too, it seems, with the understanding of belief.

But this is not how the Bible tells it. The Bible has a very clear story line that typifies relationships of revelation and concealment between God and his creations, and it differs in its essence from Maimonides's way of thinking. Almost never did we or our forebears seek him. It was always he, God, eternally in search of man. "Where art thou?" (Gen. 3:9) is the question of questions in his relations with the ancients. With Cain, he asks, "Where is Abel thy brother?" (Gen. 4:9). Likewise with Noah, and with Abraham: "Now the Lord said unto Abram: 'Get thee out of thy country, and from thy kindred, and from thy father's house, unto the land that I will show thee'" (Gen. 12:1).

In the story of Moses and the bush, it is God who initiates, reaches out, tempts and approaches: "And when the Lord saw that he had turned aside to see, God called unto him out of the midst of the bush, and said: 'Moses, Moses.' And he said: 'Here am I'" (Exod. 3:4).

Beyond the difference in approach between the authentic story of God, who lays his staff upon humankind, and the tradition that departs to have man be the one who lifts himself upward to the spiritual heights and the revelation of belief, it is interesting to try and answer a question on which the Bible is silent: Why Abraham? We don't really know much about the past of Abraham, known in Arabic as *al-Khalil*, the friend (hence the Arabic name for Hebron, the city where Abraham lived and died: *Al-Khalil*; my mother, a Hebron native, was known to her Arab friends as the Khalilit, the Hebronite, the friend). Suddenly, in the autumn of his days, he appears on the stage, his powers at their height, and from that moment on the history of human belief is utterly changed. An uninterrupted reading of the biblical narrative from the chaos of the creation through Haran, Ur of the Chaldees and the tent encampment in Beersheva makes it clear that Abraham was not some coincidental cultural caprice but the logical outcome of an unfolding progress from creation to belief, a consistent human evolution from the bodily to the spiritual.

What happened in the progress of humanity that allowed for the sudden appearance of belief? In my previous book, *God Is Back*, I tried to define belief as I understand it:

> What is knowledge? When I sit in a room with several people, I know that they are people. Because I see them, hear them and occasionally smell and touch them. But I don't know what lies beyond the walls of the room. Everything inside the room is knowledge, and everything outside the room is belief. I believe that beyond those walls there are more people and a world filled with happenings. Believe? Yes. Know? No. But belief has a thorn. At the point at which tangible knowledge ends and belief, as it were, begins, doubt begins as well. Maybe there is no world out there. Maybe it's all emptiness. Maybe the whole universe consists of nothing but the self – me – and there's nothing else out there. Maybe there's another world out there with people just like us, or maybe the world was destroyed in a sudden flood and they forgot to mention it on the news. Maybe, maybe, maybe…
> It turns out that belief and doubt came into the world together, as a package, and everyone has to choose the glasses through which they

will view reality. The doubter knows the room and questions what is outside it. The believer knows the room and believes there are many more rooms beyond. Belief and doubt, spoken as one. (Burg, 33)

Humanity's earthly senses evolved slowly over the course of the generations between Adam and Abraham. When Adam and Eve taste the fruit of the forbidden tree, we understand at once that the sense of taste is working, and from that comes the ability to decide what is tasty and what is not, what is poisonous and what is not, what is permitted and what is forbidden. When God asks Adam and Eve, "Where are you?" the answer is, "I heard thy voice" (Gen. 3:10). Which is to say, the ear is working as well. And when Lamech turns to his wives and pleads, "Give ear to my speech," we understand that this is not just a matter of hearing but of listening and understanding. As to the sense of vision, the text says explicitly, "And the eyes of them both were opened, and they knew that they were naked" (Gen. 3:7). When Abel brings his fragrant sacrifice with its sweet aroma it becomes clear to the reader that the nose its doing its assigned job. Cain and his descendants, and Noah and his issue after them, proved to us in the previous weeks' portions that the human race had refined its biological senses to include touching, stroking, designing and building an entire material culture of metal work, music, construction, agriculture and all the rest. When all the senses were well tuned, the time had come for belief that transcends the physical senses. Abraham was thus the natural successor to Adam, Cain and Noah. Once they had laid the sensory groundwork, he was able to harvest the fruits of transcendent understanding. The time of Abraham's faith arrived when humanity had completed the process of recognizing its senses.

And still the question remains, why is it that in the Torah narrative, God seeks out his believers in each generation, whereas in Maimonides's telling, the believers, successors to Abraham, are the ones who seek, recognize, know and understand God? Perhaps Maimonides didn't want to be so radical, but rather was trying to build a bridge between the biblical narrative with its logic, on one hand, and the subversive Aggadah tales of the Midrash which had advanced so far in his time that Abraham had become the one who revealed belief in God to God himself. Here is how the Aggadah put it:

> To what may Abraham be compared? To one who saw his beloved king wandering in darkened streets. The subject looked out and shone a light on him through a window. The king looked and saw his subject and said to him, now that you have shone light for me through the window, come and light my way. God said to Abraham, now that you have shone light for me from Mesopotamia and its environs, come and shine my way from the land of Israel. (Gen. Rabba 30:4–5)

I find the courage and daring of the Midrash quite wonderful. The King of kings, God himself, has lost his way, lost his faith, and is wandering in darkened streets. God is outside in the alley while his loving subject sits safe in the comfort of a well-lit home. The role reversal leads logically to this role of the worshipper who is also the revealer, Abraham – the man with the flashlight who manages to lead him out to the main street of town and into the warm embrace of his masses of believers. That is, Abraham not only revealed God, he led him back to the ways of the world. The father of believers showed God how to believe in himself again. Maimonides would not and could not have gone that far and yet remained closely tethered to the biblical text, which he found less than compelling, hence his middle path: on the one hand, humankind's responsibility for faith that transcends the immediate senses and can lift him to the highest peaks, and on the other hand, the God of Maimonides who never wandered in dark alleys.

In a later portion we will revisit Abraham to note that he revealed belief, but rid himself of his ability to doubt, and this led him astray.

Of Woman and the Land of Birth (Motherland)

THERE IS PROBABLY A GREAT DEAL of symbolism in the fact that the first portion that is entirely ours, that speaks of the Jewish people and not of all humanity, is the portion known as *Lech Lecha*, or "Get Thee Out." This is the same mythic portion in which the story of creation is reduced from the entire human race – from Adam to Noah – to the receptacle of the Jewish people and the nation of Abraham alone: "Lo, it is a people that shall dwell alone, and shall not be reckoned among the nations" (Num. 23:9). There is hardly a line that lacks that focus in this foundational portion. Therefore I will make do with three brief comments on these themes that so occupy us.

"Get thee out of thy country, and from thy kindred, and from thy father's house" (Gen. 12:1). Thus God commands Abraham, who is still known by his original name, Abram. And the old man gets up and goes. This is the first time that the term *moledet* (motherland or native land) appears in the Hebrew language and in the Bible. Look at how far the term and the language have traveled since then. We use the term *moledet* as a synonym for Israel – the land and the state, geographic and political. The place we fight over and take refuge in, where we kill and are killed but never surrender.

Yet for Abraham, *moledet* was apparently just the place where he was born. It's simply a physical descriptor, identifying the point where his journeys originated. This *moledet*, the native land, is something we leave in order to reach a further shore. I wrote *apparently*, because I think that the use of the term *moledet* for the place where the nation began is not coincidental. Our native land is, in fact, in the place we know as *galut* (exile). That's where Abraham was born and where he discovered the One God. All of our matriarchs came or were brought from that exile: Sarah, Rebecca, Leah, Rachel, Bilhah and Zilpah. In that exile the tribes were born. In the Egyptian exile the tribes became a nation, and outside the Promised Land of Israel – in the Sinai desert – the nation received the Torah. Therefore when we speak in the future of Abraham's going forth from his native land, we should think of it as leaving. That homeland, there in the exile and Diaspora, is a place we should cling to and not give up – just as we cling to the national, political homeland of Israel. Because there is no Jerusalem without Babylon, just as there was no Babylon that did not know the longings of its exiles for Jerusalem.

Afterwards a family dispute broke out between the shepherds of Abraham and the shepherds of Lot – a tribal family conflict over this small stretch of land, because "the land was not able to bear them, that they might dwell together" (Gen. 13:6). And Abraham's solution was the first territorial compromise: the partition of the land between the two peoples living there. The act of partition was done in the very generation that received the promise. Perhaps the act of the fathers will serve one day as an example to the children.

And finally, Hagar. From the text it appears that the biblical God says a great deal, but does not speak or communicate much, particularly with the women who populate his world. He speaks with his intimates and sparring partners. Adam, Noah, Abraham, Moses. In the Garden of Eden he exchanges words briefly with Eve over the fruits of the garden, the snakes and the tempted gentlemen – but that's it. Afterwards the dialogue between God and woman ceases for several generations. Even with Sarah, the mother of the nation, God speaks only indirectly. He speaks with Abraham and "Sarah heard in the tent door" (Gen. 18:10). There is no direct speech between God and a woman of the house of Abraham until Rebecca, suffering through the birth of her twins, initiated a dialogue when she "went to inquire of the Lord" (Gen. 25:22). But there is an important truth hidden between the lines of our text. There is a conversation between Hagar and a messenger of God: "And the angel of God called to Hagar out of heaven" (Gen. 21:17). It is Hagar who renews the dialogue between heaven and the women of the earth.

Week 4

Vayera – He Appeared

Genesis 18:1–22:24

You Shall Hear the Cry of the Oppressed

*T*HE THOUGHT OF COMMENTING on *Parashat Vayera* immediately prompts the desire to write something soothing, to get away from the binding of Isaac, the destruction of Sodom and the strange story of Sarah's strange pregnancy. The portion has other, gentler lessons to teach – for example, about the Torah's approach to hospitality, about models of acceptance and rejection (compare Abraham's warm welcome of the three visitors to his tent in Mamre with the brutal reception they receive in Sodom). But Israeli reality has a way of intervening and pushing off the comfortable choices to some point in the distant future. This is a holy land where blood cries out from every inch. Yes, Israeli blood and Palestinian blood flow more cheaply than ever, but also Ethiopian blood, spilled in fear and shame down the drains of our blood banks, and the blood of gays and lesbians dehumanized on the streets of Jerusalem, uniting rabbis, imams and bishops of every faith in their hate. We are left, then, with no choice but to look at the portion again and try to understand the Torah of the outcry. Who cries out, and when? Which outcries leave their mark and which dissolve into a still, small whimper?

It seems to me that every time God comes down to our level, it ends badly. When he came down to see what was going on in the Tower of Babel, the entire earth fell into a muddle. "And the Lord came down to see the city and tower, which the children of men builded. And the Lord said: 'Behold, they are one people, and they have all one language; and this is what they begin to do; and now nothing will be withholden from them, which they purpose to do. Come, let us go down, and there confound their language, that they may not understand one another's speech'" (Gen. 11:5–7). And again in the case of Sodom, something distracts God's attention and he decides to go down and understand what is going on among the dwellers below: "And the Lord said: 'Verily, the cry of Sodom and Gomorrah is great, and, verily, their sin is exceedingly grievous. I will go down now, and see whether they have done altogether according to the cry of it, which is come unto me; and if not, I will know'" (Gen. 18:20–21).

In each case God consults, but the narrator doesn't say with whom. God turns to those present and says, speaking in plural voice, "Let us, then, go down," and in our story he comes to converse with Abraham, his friend. But these discussions don't produce a positive verdict or lenient sentence. What comes is the scattering of the rebels of the Tower of Babel and the deadly earthquake on the limestone plain of Sodom by the Dead Sea. Something is deeply unsettling. It is not only the eternal "why" of God's absoluteness. Why doesn't he have any shades of gray? Why is he only an open-handed creator or a strong-armed Destroyer? But the most disturbing question is the "technical" one: What catches God's attention and how does it happen? When does he respond to events and when does he ignore them?

In the biblical myth of the Tower of Babel the answer is simple. The tower has reached the outskirts of his heavenly abode. The people of that generation had so vastly improved on the human technology first developed by Cain that they were ready to embark on a scheme the likes of which had never been seen: "And they said one to another…, 'Come, let us build us a city, and a tower, with its top in heaven, and let us make us a name; lest we be scattered abroad upon the face of the whole earth'" (Gen. 11:3–4). With neighbors like these, even the Dweller on High had no choice but to complain to the zoning board.

But what of Sodom? What caught God's attention there? Answer: the outcry – "the cry of Sodom and Gomorrah." But who was crying out? What were they protesting? What alarm finally managed to break through the

Vayera

elaborate defenses of the One who had vowed never to bring another flood to destroy the world? What was the charge that managed to reach the Throne of Glory and goad its occupant to descend to earth once more? The portion doesn't say. This scriptural silence regarding the source and nature of the outcry opens the door to the fantasies of the sages of the Midrash, such as the legend of Lot's daughter: "Once there was a poor man there who was dying of hunger, and the daughter of Lot, whose name was Kallah [Bride], would go to draw water and put a loaf of bread in her bucket to give to the poor man. The people of Sodom wondered what this poor man was living on, and when they checked they found that Lot's daughter was supporting him. And what did they do? They stripped her and smeared her with honey, and the bees and flies ate the honey and stung her until she died. And thus it is said, they made a bride" (Midrash Aggadah [Buber], *Genesis* 18:20).

There are many legends of this sort scattered throughout the various books of Midrash and commentary, and they all have one common denominator: the outcry that burst out from Sodom was not the cry of the oppressed but the cry of the righteous few who lived there and did all they could to preserve their humanity in the face of the brutality of those cities. How many of them there were, we don't know. Nor do we know whether theirs were the lives Abraham was negotiating for. But we do know the mind of the writer of this midrash. He assumes that there is no human evil so deep that it does not have acts of genuine human kindness alongside it.

And so we travel from that place and time to our own and we ask the same question: Are there enough persons of righteousness among us? For the Ethiopians, for the people of Gaza, for the members of the gay community? If Abraham were bargaining for our lives, would he manage to prevent our destruction at the hands of him who "chose the Torah and Moses his servant and Israel his people and the prophets of truth and justice"? And what if this argument has already taken place in some venue that we don't know about? What if the judgment has already been handed down without our knowing, and now we can only watch the painful execution that unfolds, as always, without our ever having noticed the advance warnings?

Because I feel very deeply about the silent, pent-up cries all around us, I'd like to share an impressionistic thought arising from these matters. Homosexual relations are known in many languages, including both English and Hebrew, as sodomy. As such, they are an integral part of our discussion of the portion. Anyone can have their own theories about the origins of the ancient prohibition. What we should note is that a prohibition so sweeping that it's labeled an abomination – "Thou shalt not lie with mankind, as with womankind; it is an abomination" (Lev. 18:22) – hints at a reality sufficiently widespread that a serious prohibition was considered necessary to combat it.

I'd like to assume that the opposition derived at least partly from a worldview that saw life as holy, and its holiness was the holy of holies. Sex without fertility, childbirth and continuity cannot be sanctified in a system that seeks above all to bring life into the world. Does this fundamental still have a place in today's world? It's highly unlikely. Many same-sex couples share a love that is as far from abominable as one can imagine. For many of them, their partners are their family. In addition to that love and commitment, modern legislation and advances in medicine and biotechnology have made it possible for many of them to join the circle of parenthood and fertility and become fine parents in the ever-changing, expanding framework of the modern family.

Under these circumstances, anyone who can accept the value of the changing family should be able to let down their defensive walls and let go of the anti-gay repugnance drilled into us. They could be handled with the same sort of annulment rulings that the Mishnah applied to other biblical commandments when times or sociological circumstances had changed. The sages of the Mishnah boldly annulled the commandment of bitter waters that the scripture prescribed to identify unfaithful wives when adultery was on the increase. They annulled the ceremony of slaughtering the headless calf that was supposed to deter incidents of random murder. From now on, let us say that as same-sex couples and their offspring increase, the abhorrence of lying with male or female is no more.

Abraham's Great Failure

"And it came to pass after these things, that God did prove Abraham" (Gen. 22:1). Generations upon generations of commentators dealt with the question of what were "these things" that were followed by the binding of Isaac. From the preceding portions we learn that "these things" included the tangled web of dreadful familial relationships within Abraham's clan. "These things" included Sarah's jealousy of Hagar, the expulsion of Hagar and Ishmael from the encampment of Abraham the friend of God, Sarah's pregnancy and the birth of Isaac. This web of relationships developed over a long period. At the end the father of the family – the father of the nation – nearly killed his firstborn son, Ishmael.

But Abraham is a Jewish executioner. He tries very hard to kill this gentile, this son of a gentile woman. But he's not really up to the task. What was he thinking when he dismissed Hagar, this woman whom he had bedded, with whom he conceived the first fruit of his loins? He was a veteran wanderer, after all, a man who understood thirst, who knew the caravan routes, who had had his fill of desert craft. He knew enough to know that those two, the woman and the little boy, would not survive the vast, hot desert. It seems he wasn't thinking. In the face of Sarah's anger, he chose to hide behind the divine command, "in all that Sarah saith unto thee, hearken unto her voice" (Gen. 21:12), without thinking, without protest.

At Sodom he had stood and roared at heaven "that be far from thee; shall not the Judge of all the earth do justly?" (Gen. 18:25). And yet in his own home he was like a pussycat – creeping silently on all fours, tamed by the whip and baton of the first lady. True, it is written that "the thing was very grievous in Abraham's sight on account of his son" (Gen. 21:11). Well, it grieves me that people are starving in Calcutta and they're chopping down the rainforests in Brazil, but I don't go and do anything about it. Grieved is a feeling, not an action. Not even a protest. Abraham sinned by very grave omission.

This dysfunctional relationship between father and sons continues in his most famous test, the binding of Isaac. Later writings embellish and glorify Abraham for standing up to the test. So strong was his faith, they taught us to think, that he didn't even hesitate to bind his son, his one chosen son, his beloved Isaac, on the sacrificial altar of his faith. A blind faith, devoid of checks or inhibitions. Does the text really support the theory of his successfully standing up to the test? For years I thought it did. Because for years and years I was trained to divert my eyes from what was written. This portion and its tales are read not just on their assigned Sabbath but also on the two days of Rosh Hashanah, the Jewish new year holiday. This must be a tale of success, no? The binding of Isaac has become such a grand, overarching idea that we often forget there was no actual slaying in the end, only a trussing. To this day Isaac remains firmly bound up within a continuing biblical plot in which children are abused or abandoned before being turned into eternal symbols – think of Ishmael and Isaac and beyond to Joseph and baby Moses.

So what went wrong? Abraham did indeed get up that morning, loaded up his donkey and went with Isaac for an outing of several days' duration. Perhaps they had done this in the past, but this time they didn't bring along their usual lamb for sacrifice and dinner. Isaac wondered about the change in behavior: "Behold the fire and the wood; but where is the lamb for a burnt-offering?" (Gen. 22:7). And the old man answers evasively, "God will provide himself the lamb for a burnt-offering, my son" (Gen. 22:8). Some commentators see this as Isaac's first hint of what is to come: the lamb for the slaughter is you, my son.

The rest is well known. The binding, the wood, the hand raising the knife and suddenly, "the angel of the Lord called unto him out of heaven...."

> "Abraham! Abraham!"
> "Here am I."
> "Lay not thy hand upon the lad, neither do thou any thing unto him; for now I know that thou art a God-fearing man, seeing thou has not withheld thy son, thine only son, from me." (Gen. 22:11–12)

This is the test in a nutshell: "Now I know."

Today I look at this and I'm convinced it can't be right. It can't be that Judaism, which is a religion of humanity as much as it is a faith in God, would hold up Abraham's serial willingness to sacrifice his sons as the truest test of faith. If that is the faith, it isn't my faith. If that is success, permit me to fail. I would never sacrifice you, my children! Your long, healthy lives are the core of my life's faith. It is for you that the world was created, and it's for you that I struggle to change and heal the world.

I'm forced, then, to look between the lines for another interpretation. Perhaps you've noticed that just a few verses earlier, God and Abraham were chatting like two friends. God consults with him about Sodom, and Abraham shares with him his feelings about Sarah and Hagar and the uproar in the harem. Buddy buddy.

And yet, suddenly, at the climactic moment of the sacrifice, who comes to save Isaac? Who stops God's great friend from slaughtering his son and heir? Not God, you'll note, but "the angel of the Lord called unto him" (Gen. 22:11) – that is, a messenger. And from the moment that Isaac is bound there are no more conversations between the two friends. God stops speaking with Abraham, right up to the day he dies. The vessels have been shattered. No more chats.

When I read the story this way, I'm convinced that God was angry with Abraham, so angry that he could no longer speak with him. The truth is that God tested Abraham and Abraham failed the test. The price of failure is heaven turned silent, God turned away. The test proved that Abraham believed too strongly, that he loved God more than he loved those he loved. But God, the object of the greatest faith, knows this is wrong. God doesn't want blind, uncontrolled, uncritical faith. God wants his believers, parents and children, to believe without fear of the knife, without bloodshed, without the tears of the bound.

God wanted to check whether man had achieved independence, whether or not he had self-control, and Abraham proved he did not. Man was not ready for an independent belief capable of thinking critically about the values and commands of God.

Abraham failed this great test. The smaller failure was the expulsion of Hagar and Ishmael. The great failure was his blind willingness to slaughter

Isaac. Is it any wonder that the Midrash and commentary understood this as the obvious connection between this week's portion, the binding of Isaac, and the death of Sarah in next week's portion? Listen to Rashi's critique: "'And Abraham came to mourn for Sarah, and to weep for her' (Gen. 23:2) – and the death of Sarah is appended to the binding of Isaac, because when she learned of the binding, that her son was prepared for slaughtered and was very nearly slaughtered, her soul left her and she died." I imagine a scene like this: Abraham comes back from the sacrifice with Isaac in shock, like a child who has been rescued from the worst sort of abuse. They return together to the encampment, and all it takes is one look to understand everything. Sarah understands and she dies, and Abraham is left to live with his failure until he finds healing.

Week 5

Chayei Sarah – The Life of Sarah

Genesis 23:1–25:18

The Strength to Concede

*C*HAYEI SARAH (THE LIFE OF SARAH) is an interesting portion. It's not unusual to find that a portion of the Scripture dealing with death begins with a word connected to life. Thus "The Life of Sarah" deals with the death of the matriarch at age one hundred twenty-seven; similiarly, the portion that begins, "And Jacob lived," tells the story of the death of the aged, tortured third patriarch. It's tempting to think that one person's death is in essence the beginning of somebody else's independent life. It's only when Abraham and Sarah pass away, for example, that Isaac and Ishmael are able to come together for the funeral. In the same manner, only when Jacob dies can a real dialogue begin between Joseph and his brothers. When the old folks die, the young are free to redesign the world according to the understandings of their generation and the next.

And so, with the death of Sarah, the domineering and rather devious matriarch, a great many things became possible that couldn't have happened when she was alive. Hagar, according to the Aggadah, changed her name and returned to Abraham's tent as Keturah. Ishmael was able, as we noted, to reestablish his connection with his brother and childhood friend, Isaac. But the most important change was that Rebecca was brought from Aram to Canaan to be Isaac's wife. "And Isaac brought her into his mother Sarah's tent, and he took Rebecca, and she became his wife; and he loved her. And Isaac was comforted for [the death of] his mother" (Gen. 24:67).

However, it is not only Sarah from whom we take our leave in this week's portion, but Abraham as well. As such, this is the right moment to take stock of the first patriarch's hidden legacy. The Mishnah tractate known as *Pirkei Avot* (The Ethics of the Fathers) has this to say: "Our father Abraham was tested with ten trials, and he withstood them all, to make known how great was the love of our father Abraham" (Mishnah *Avot* 5:3). The Mishnah doesn't specify what the ten trials were; the text leaves the question open-ended, in effect inviting us to come and explain it ourselves. It's almost certain that the binding of Isaac was one of these tests, since the Scripture says explicitly, "God did prove [that is, test] Abraham" (Gen. 22:1). The seminal command, *Lech Lecha*, "Get thee out of thy country" (Gen. 12:1), was a profound test. So was the command to obey Sarah when she insisted that Abraham go against his nature and feelings and banish Hagar and Ishmael ("In all that Sarah saith unto thee, hearken unto her voice"; Gen. 21:12). There were a few others along these lines. Here I would venture to suggest – and I'm not the first to do so – that burying Sarah was a major test for Abraham. To understand why, let's review some of the previous tests.

What is the thread that connects the leaving of his distant birthplace for a new, unknown homeland, the banishing of Ishmael and the binding of Isaac? All three demand that he give up something basic and precious. In *Lech Lecha*, Abraham was called on to give up his native surroundings, his homeland, and to venture into the unknown. In deciding to gamble on an abstract promise he is giving up the sights, sounds, tastes and smells that constitute his natural setting and trading them all for an unknown land. In banishing Ishmael he is called upon to give up one of his great loves, his firstborn son, because of Sarah's aloofness and hauteur. Finally, in the binding of Isaac, Abraham is called upon to give up his naïve faith in the God who promised him, "in Isaac shall seed be called to thee" (Gen. 21:12). "How can my offspring carry on my name if tomorrow I am to snuff out his life like a candle?" the old man must have wondered, simple believer that he was, as he set out at dawn for the land of Moriah. Giving up one thing after another, after another – this is the common feature in the tests of Father Abraham.

Chayei Sarah

The same feature appears in the burial of Sarah. God had promised him the entire land, every spot where he set his foot from the great River Euphrates to the River of Egypt. But now, when he comes to bury the love of his life, he doesn't listen to the natives who tell him in every possible way that this is his land and he can bury his dead wife any place he wishes. First come the Hittites – "Hear us, my lord: thou art a mighty prince among us; in the choice of our sepulchers bury thy dead; none of us shall withhold from thee his sepulchre" (Gen. 23:6) – offering a choice burial plot absolutely free. Next Abraham receives the same offer from the owner of the site himself, Ephron the Hittite: "Nay, my lord, hear me: the field I give thee, and the cave that is therein, I give it thee; in the presence of the sons of my people I give it thee; bury thy dead" (Gen. 23:11). Again, a gift, free of charge.

But Abraham insists. He wants to pay. This is a strange way for a lord of the land to treat his subjects. When does anyone pay for property that belongs to him? But Abraham digs in his heels, in a sort of backwards bargaining in which the seller doesn't want to take money and the buyer presses the money on him, until finally "Abraham weighed to Ephron the silver, which he had named in the hearing of the children of Heth, four hundred shekels of silver, current money with the merchant. So the field of Ephron, which was in Machpelah, which was before Mamre, the field, and the cave which was therein, and all the trees that were in the field, that were in all the border thereof roundabout, were made sure unto Abraham for a possession" (Gen. 23:16–18).

To understand Abraham's action we need to understand what he was giving up, and what test he was forced to withstand in those difficult days. The easiest thing would have been to accept the forsaken cave at the edge of Ephron's field, to bury Sarah there alongside a few other anonymous graves and be done with it. But Abraham knew even in his moment of grief that he wanted an eternal resting place, and so he gave up the divine promise and chose the alternative. It seems to me to be an improvement on Abraham's territorial approach in his conflict with his nephew Lot. In the dispute between Abraham's shepherds and Lot's shepherds, Abraham suggests dividing the land from left to right, saying, "Let there be no strife,

I pray thee, between me and thee, and between my herdmen and thy herdmen" (Gen. 13:8). In that case he conceded for the sake of a realistic, immediate peace, but here, in the purchase of the Cave of Machpelah, it is a matter of a more sweeping perspective. Abraham gave up what was his and bought part of what had been promised to him as an investment in a better world. No one understood him better than the Netziv, Rabbi Naftali Zvi Yehuda Berlin, the author of the nineteenth-century Torah commentary *Ha'emek Davar*, who wrote this in his remarks on Genesis:

> This was the glory of the patriarchs, that besides being righteous and pious and loving of God as one might be, they were straightforward. That is, they treated the nations of the world, even gentiles who worshipped idols, with love and concern for their welfare, which is the foundation of creation. As we see how our father Abraham prostrated himself to pray for Sodom even though he deeply hated them and their king for their wickedness, as explained in his speech to the king of Sodom (Gen. 14:22–24). In any event, he sought their survival.

So it was in Sodom and likewise in Hebron, the city of our mothers. So it was then, and if only it were so today. If only acquiescence could triumph as the weapon of the brave in the eternal battle with the disastrous aggression of blustering, small-minded cowards.

Everything Stays in the Family

THERE ARE GRAND STORIES AND GREAT CLIMAXES in this week's Torah portion, but it seems to me that the week's most dramatic message can be found in the haftarah, the passage from the Prophets that is read in synagogues together with the portion. Guessing the connection between the haftarah reading and the Torah portion itself was a puzzle that always fascinated me as a child. Sometimes the answer is simple, when the haftarah is a reading from the Prophets that summarizes or hints at the central theme in the portion, like a sort of recap of the portion's top stories for listeners in the

Chayei Sarah

pews. Sometimes, as in the case of this week's portion, the haftarah is more like a subtle afterthought, an editorial in which the the editor tells us what he thinks of the portion itself.

> Now King David was old and stricken in years; and they covered him with clothes, but he could get no heat. Wherefore his servants said unto him: 'Let there be sought for my lord the king a young virgin; and let her stand before the king, and be a companion unto him; and let her lie in thy bosom, and my lord the king may get heat.' So they sought for a fair damsel throughout all the borders of Israel, and found Abishag the Shunnamite, and brought her to the king. And the damsel was very fair, and she became a companion unto the king, and ministered to him; but the king knew her not. (1 Kings 1:1–4)

Why do they compare David with Abraham? Was it perhaps to show the differences between one type of greatness and another, and to mock David for failing in his old age to impregnate the prettiest maid in Israel, whereas the mighty Abraham managed with Keturah to father "Zimran, and Jokshan, and Medan, and Midian, and Ishbak, and Shuah" (Gen. 25:2)?

Perhaps, but it seems to me that the connection between the two stories is a barbed arrow that is meant to skewer both Abraham and David, to highlight the central weaknesses of each and cast each one in the shadow of the other. Let's begin with the matter of women. David's weaknesses in this department are well known: he stole married women, abandoned some of his wives and preferred certain of his children over the others. And Abraham? He can't avoid criticism over the way he raised his two sons, banishing one and nearly slaughtering the other. As for the women themselves, Keturah is Abraham's Abishag. That is, she reflects badly on his relationship with the legendary matriarch Sarah. This same man who did not believe God's promise about the birth of a son at age ninety-nine was able to marry Keturah, get her pregnant with one child after another, shower her and them with gifts and send them on their way – without feuding or banishment, without pain or threat of death in the hot, parched desert. He had learned his lesson and was an outstanding husband and father – the very opposite of his life with Sarah.

And one more common denominator. David lay helpless in his room while in his inner court and throughout the streets of Jerusalem, his capital, the battle for succession was raging. Priests and generals, together with loyalists and toadies, were hanging around the prince Adonijah son of Haggith, who "exalted himself, saying: 'I will be king!'" (1 Kings 1:5), or following Solomon, whose mother Bathsheba was promised, "Solomon thy son shall reign after me" (1 Kings 1:17). All of them were trying their best to manipulate the old king, since a good word from him would legitimize whichever new monarchy arose. These stories contain plots and intrigue, prophets and concubines, princes, heirs and wheeler-dealers. But in addition to being one of the Bible's richest political dramas, this story is also a penetrating criticism of King David and his house. What human depravity this story lays bare in its fearlessly anti-monarchist critique. The narrator almost seems to be asking, "Are these your kings, O Israel?" And the question echoes back to Abraham, since he is the object of the comparison, the aging subject of the portion to which the aging David appears as haftarah. The final chapter of his life is a chapter on fatherhood, and beyond all his well-known failures, including the binding of Isaac, the banishment of Ishmael and more, it turns out that Abraham didn't know how to perform the most sensitive task of any parent: to raise his children as independent, autonomous individuals, capable of living in loving relationships with their brothers and sisters.

The task of raising a family is difficult and often frightening work. It's no wonder that so many of us fail, that so many families are sources of frustration and subjects of psychotherapy. Throughout their lives Isaac and Ishmael were undermined by the parents who should have been raising them together: Sarah against Hagar, and Abraham feebly caught between them. Only after the founding generation had passed on could the two brothers join together and accompany Abraham to the cemetery – separated for one moment from everything that had gone on between them in their lives. It was a rare moment, and one that quickly faded, to our misfortune, from the family of the patriarchs of the nation of Israel; with

Chayei Sarah

Isaac's sons Jacob and Esau, and with his grandsons, conflict and strife continued to set the tone. Yet Ishmael, the Scripture hints, went to his final rest quite differently: "over against all his brethren did he settle" (Gen. 25:18) – which is to say, in plain language, all his children, his comrades, his partners, his kingdom and progeny came to pay him his final honor, appropriately and without resentment. Thus appeared the funeral of a son who was different from the rest of his father's family, a man whose loyalty to his brother was dearer to him than all the jealousies of the houses of Abraham, Isaac and Jacob, each of whom favored one of his children and sowed eternal strife among his descendants.

What a charged haftarah.

And drawing from this charged criticism, Nachmanides, one of the greatest Jewish scholars, has this to say about Sarah and Abraham, the failed parents, taking a judgmental view of those long-gone days that explain so much about relations between Israel and Ishmael right up to our own time:

> "And Sarai dealt harshly with her, and she fled from her face" – Our mother [Sarah] sinned in this mistreatment and so did Abraham in permitting it to happen, and God heard her [Hagar's] suffering and gave her a wild man for a son to mistreat the seed of Abraham and Sarah in all sorts of mistreatment. (Nachmanides on Gen. 16:6)

Week 6

Toledot – These Are the Generations

Genesis 25:19–28:9

Jacob: A Simple Man?

THE FACT IS THAT OUR FATHER JACOB was a liar in his youth. It's also true that by the end of the story, he is the most upright patriarch of them all. As opposed to Abraham and Isaac, he never told anyone that his wife was his sister. He never followed voices that weren't the voices of his heart, the way Abraham did when he banished Hagar and Ishmael, and he never climbed onto an altar in defiance of the most basic instinct of survival. To his misfortune, however, even though he managed to break free of his personal cycle of lies he was never able to escape the culture of lies and deceit into which he was born. Some people are simply unable to change, no matter how hard they try. Look at how many times Jacob changed his surroundings, moved to new places hoping to change his luck, even changed his name and his occupation, and yet he was never able to shake the reputation for dishonesty that he had gotten stuck with early on. From his childhood years right up to his last day on earth he moved from place to place, investing so much energy in wandering, uprooting himself, settling into new places. Perhaps that's why he didn't invest enough of his inner resources in the personal change that might have spared him some of his suffering.

From the moment he entered the world he was stuck with the demeaning name *Ya'acov* (coming up from behind), which became synonymous with slyness and cunning. How did the prophet Jeremiah interpret the name centuries later?

> Oh that I were in the wilderness, in a lodging-place of wayfaring men, that I might leave my people, and go from them! For they are all adulterers, an assembly of treacherous men. And they bend their tongue, their bow of falsehood; and they are grown mighty in the land, but not for truth; for they proceed from evil to evil, and me they know not, saith the Lord. Take ye heed every one of his neighbor, and trust ye not in any brother; for every brother *acteth subtly* [*ya'acov*, the same word as Jacob's name; italics added], and every neighbor goeth about with slanders. And they deceive every one his neighbor, and truth they speak not; they have taught their tongue to speak lies, they weary themselves to commit iniquity. Thy habitation is in the midst of deceit; through deceit they refuse to know me, saith the Lord. (Jer. 9:1–5)

The sad prophet is as much as telling us that our national character during the era of the First Temple derives entirely from the personality of the third patriarch, the father of the tribes, our father *Ya'acov* – Jacob.

A child was born simple and pure, but the name they gave him never left him for a moment. I assume that the marvel of the birth of twins always carries with it the question of why this one was born first and that one second, and vice versa. When Judah and Tamar had their twins Peretz and Zerach (Gen. 38:27–30), the child who broke through first was given a name that was also a trait, *peretz* (breach or breakthrough). That is, the initiator, the first, the competitor. In our story the competitive initiator was in fact the second twin, Jacob. From his birth until his death and even beyond, lies enveloped him like cobwebs and he couldn't rid himself of them.

Let's count the lies in the order that they are recounted in the biblical narrative. The stories of Esau are well known: Jacob grabbed his brother's heel during birth, purchasing his birthright, stealing their father's blessing and more. His relations with Laban were not much better. It's not clear who cheated whom, but the lie shrouded Jacob for twenty-one years living in his father-in-law's home. He wanted Rachel but received Leah. Wanting to be free, he flees by trickery. As they flee, Rachel hides the household idols she stole from her father under her saddle. The women buy and sell Jacob's love and his seed behind his back in exchange for their sons' mandrake flowers. As he enters the land of Canaan, his sons Simeon and Levi deceive him and deceive the men of Shechem: they promise the men of Shechem a marriage agreement that they have no right to offer and never intend to honor. And while the men of Shechem are still weak from the circumcisions they underwent as part of the agreement, Simeon and Levi and their brothers destroy the city.

Later on the sons kidnap Joseph, smear goat's blood on his multicolored cloak and then show it to their father and tell the family's greatest lie of all: "This we have found. Know now whether it is thy son's coat or not?" (Gen. 37:32), leading Jacob to believe that his best-loved son has been killed. Later still, Joseph – who is now viceroy to the king of Egypt – denies his brothers, mocks and hoodwinks them in the finest family tradition. Like father, like son – the master conniver, who knows how to manufacture realities to serve his goals. The brothers return to Jacob with the bad news. In the end, Joseph's strategem brings his father to him in Egypt. But even Jacob's death doesn't end the intrigue. When their father dies, the brothers come to Joseph, the viceroy, and invent a fictitious will that Jacob supposedly left – all so that Joseph won't try to get even with them for their childhood cruelty toward him:

> And when Joseph's brethren saw that their father was dead, they said: "It may be that Joseph will hate us, and will fully requite us all the evil which we did unto him." And they sent a message unto Joseph, saying: "Thy father did command before he died, saying: So shall ye say unto Joseph: 'Forgive, I pray thee now, the transgression of thy brethren, and their sin, for that they did unto thee evil.' And now, we pray thee, forgive the transgression of the servants of the God of thy father." (Gen. 50:15–17)

When Jacob said to Pharaoh, "Few and evil have been the days of the years of my life" (Gen. 47:9), he was essentially saying, I am the most lied-to father in the Bible. Nobody else has been treated the way I have been treated, and I'm not happy about it.

We must ask ourselves: Why? Why did this happen to him? The Midrash sees part of his adventures as tit for tat and tells us about it in sad but marvelous stories. Of Leah, the Aggadah has this to say:

> She would hear people saying, Rebecca has two sons and Laban has two daughters, the elder daughter for the elder son and the younger for the younger. And she would sit at the crossroads and ask people, What does the older son do? He is a bad man, and he robs people. And the small one, what does he do? He is a simple man, a dweller in tents. And she would sit and weep until her eyelashes fell out. (Yalkut Shimoni, *Vayetze* 155)

Leah, the elder daughter, believed she was promised to her elder cousin Esau the bandit, while Rachel, her younger sister, would be happily married to the young, good-hearted Jacob. If we follow this thought just a little further, we can see how the logic of the Aggadah justifies the switching of the brides. Remember, Jacob had bought the birthright of the firstborn by trickery and made himself the legally designated firstborn. It therefore made sense that he should marry the firstborn daughter first. This tit-for-tat storyline continues in other traditional sources right up to the wedding night:

> All night she pretended to be Rachel, until he got up in the morning and "behold, it was Leah" (Gen. 29:25). He said to her: daughter of a swindler! Why did you cheat me? She said to him: And you, why did you cheat your father? When your father said to you, "Art thou my very son Esau?" (Gen. 27:24) you said to him, "I am Esau thy firstborn" (Gen. 27:19). And now you come and say, why did you cheat me?! Didn't your father say of you, "Thy brother came with guile"?! (Gen. 27:35). (Midrash Tanhuma, *Vayetze*)

There is a value in probing deeper than the gloating of the narrator and the Aggadists over the family's miseries. Why did all this happen to our aging ancestor? It could be that everything began with the mother and was passed on directly to the son. Her life's circumstances weren't easy. Certainly she wasn't sheltered like Isaac, who spent his childhood as though swaddled in cotton. He was all but suffocated by his parents' ceaseless efforts to protect him and prevent life from ever touching him. Ishmael was banished, servants were sent abroad to bring him a wife, and his father's fanatical faith nearly cost him his life. Rashi is blunt regarding the joint prayer that the childless Isaac and Rebecca offered up for a child, and the answer God gave to Isaac's prayer but not the prayer of the barren mother: "There is no comparing the prayer of a righteous person, son of a righteous person, and a righteous person with a wicked father; therefore [God answered] him and not her."

Rebecca, according to the later sources, was "the daughter of a wicked man and the sister of a wicked man, and she grew up among the wicked and did not learn from their deeds" (Rashi on Gen. 25:20). Perhaps she didn't learn from them in the sense that she became sly and devious like them, but some of their traits rubbed off on her nonetheless. Look at how skillfully she produced Jacob's disguise and taught him how to deceive his father. And he? Little Jacob, the dweller in tents, was always hanging around the family encampment – probably the worst place to learn honesty and straight shooting. That was where all the rumors ended up, where all the gossip was traded, where all the intrigues were cooked up. To survive there, you had to learn how to cut corners and make compromises with the truth. That was where the worldly-wise mother raised and educated her wise son – and it did not end there.

When the biblical narrator calls Jacob "a quiet man, dwelling in tents" (Gen. 25:27), this is not a redundancy, restating the same quality of mildness. On the contrary, this embodies the very spiritual tension that tore Jacob apart throughout his life: a mild man at heart, but wise in the ways of the encampment. His honesty was inborn, while his campsite survivor's instincts were an acquired trait that helped him succeed in life. The innocent do not necessarily inherit the earth, and whenever his innocence threatened his wellbeing, he was able to fall back on his skills as a camp dweller to survive the complexities of life in our region. Abraham was a one-dimensional believer, and Isaac was his father's follower, largely lacking in character. Only Jacob contained within him all these characteristics. His whole life was an inner struggle in his soul: the straight against the crooked, the simple against the camp dweller, his inner Isaac against his inner Rebecca. And this inner struggle continues right up to our own day.

From Rebecca the Aramean to Ruth the Moabite: On the Path of the Bible

While I was writing, my wife Yael suggested to me that my areas of focus in analyzing the weekly portion are too critical. "You take your personal story and your commentary too far, and I'm not sure that we're ready to absorb such strong criticism." There's no doubt that she's right. As always. But I'm not necessarily wrong. I read the biblical text as it's written, without fabrication. I call things as I see them. But the critical and negative sides of my writing are positive in essence. This is the heart of the Bible as I saw it from the first day I could read it. The Bible I know isn't a parade of perfect, unblemished forefathers. When I read the Talmudic saying, "If the first ones were sons of angels then we are sons of men, and if the first ones were human, then we are as donkeys" (Babylonian Talmud, *Sabbath* 112b), I see a degenerative process that perpetually diminishes any and all current and future human creativity in comparison to a past that was supposedly perfect. The Bible that I love is something different. It tells the story of human frailty. Every character is flawed. Every patriarch and matriarch has shortcomings. It is the very retelling of these weaknesses that spurs us to engage and identify with them. The reader might need to say to himself: if imperfect people like these could do so much for the sake of the world, then I too can improve my own world. What's more, loving the past and its heroes means loving the truth. This is how I understand love: true love is love of the other, with all of his or her flaws, not love of the perfect or the heroic, the stereotypical or cinematic and phony. To love another human is to love despite flaws, indeed to love the flaws themselves, and for that reason I love the heroes of the Bible.

And of all these flawed, compromised characters of the past with all their complexities and guiles, I'd like to single out the story of Rebecca, which begins in this week's portion, *Toledot*. The story of Rebecca is the seed that blossoms into the Book of Ruth. Yes, I know it sounds far-fetched at first, but hear me out.

The Book of Ruth is inarguably the mythic connection point that links the House of David to the national narrative. The narrator who gave us the legend of the beautiful Ruth relied heavily on three foundational biblical tales. All three tales are from Genesis, which is hardly surprising. The earlier and deeper the king's roots can be traced, the greater the legitimacy of his kingship.

The first tale is the story of Tamar, whose two husbands, Er and Onan, both died (Gen. 38:6–10), paralleling the sons of Elimelech and Naomi, Mahlon and Chilion. Their deaths set the stage for the tale of the remarriage and renewed life of Ruth, the matriarch of the royal family of David. Tamar's remarriage was to Judah, the son of Jacob whose name became synonymous with the people of Israel; Ruth's remarriage was to Boaz. Both Judah and Boaz were older men, both were leading figures in their communities and both were successful farmers – Judah a shepherd, Boaz a planter. Both of them had their hearts stolen by trickery: Tamar seduced Judah by disguising herself as a prostitute and waiting by the roadside, while Ruth seduced Boaz by curling up anonymously at his feet during the harvest.

The second story tells the origin of Ruth the Moabite. Who is Moab? He is one of the offspring of Lot. Remember the story of the destruction of Sodom and Gomorrah? Here is Lot, fleeing with his wife and daughters from the burning ruins of the city. The wife looks back and turns to salt, while Lot and his daughters take cover in a desert cave outside Sodom. That night, believing that everything has been destroyed and the world around them has come to an end, the daughters approach their drunken father and trick him into giving them his seed. The children, Ammon and Moab, are bastards. Their father is also their grandfather. And their mothers? Who knows where their consciences led them when they realized what they had done, that the world had not been destroyed and their incest was nothing more than that – incest? They couldn't know that in time they would have a descendant, a child of Moab named Ruth, who would carry on the family tradition of seduction in her own fashion. Ruth approached the head of the clan of Bethlehem in the dead of night. Lot was tired and drunk; Boaz was exhausted after a hard day's work in the field at the height of the harvest season. The rest is our history. The foremother of Ruth the Moabite stole her father's seed and gave birth to an entire kingdom, while her granddaughter stole a clansman's heart and raised the seed of kings.

The last of these stories is the story of Rebecca. The parallels here are numerous. Boaz was old, as was Isaac, at forty years of age. Both men were farmers who planted, plowed, harvested and prospered. Rebecca came to Isaac from far away to the northeast. Ruth too came from far away, on the eastern shore of the Jordan. Both families had influential mothers-in-law: Sarah on the groom Isaac's side and Naomi on the bride Ruth's side. Both farmers met their romantic fates out in the field: Isaac "went out to meditate in the field at the eventide; and he lifted up his eyes, and saw, and behold, there were camels coming" (Gen. 24:63), while Ruth met Boaz on "the portion of the field belonging unto Boaz, who was of the family of Elimelech" (Ruth 2:3).

There are many more points of similarity between the stories. The upshot is that the Bible, as we wrote at the outset, is not merely a collection of mythological anecdotes but a deliberate mesh of interwoven themes, some of them readily apparent, some of them beneath the surface. It's up to us to trace the threads woven through the lace and find their ends so that we can untangle them.

The story of Rebecca is the story of David, and the stories of David are nothing more than pieces of a giant struggle cutting across all the tales of Genesis: the struggle between Reuben, Jacob's firstborn; Joseph, his favorite; and Judah, the ultimate victor. This is the struggle over the treasury of the future kingdom, the storehouse of eternity, over who will be the once and future leader of this eternal people. Rebecca of Genesis is, as such, an inseparable part of the future kingdom. The ancient narrators knew how to weave together symbols and images from the story of Ruth in the original legend of Rebecca, and vice versa. And later readers, like us, get the impression over and over of a naturally unfolding series of stories in which David evolves from an unruly youth to the leader of a desert band of fugitives, and finally to the legitimate king whose earliest roots can be traced to the very earliest days.

Week 7

Vayetze – Jacob Left

Genesis 28:10–32:3

Why Is Jacob, Despite Everything, My Father?

*I*N LAST WEEK'S PORTION WE EXPLORED the web of lies that surrounded Jacob from the moment he was born until he reached his final not-very-restful abode. This week's portion doesn't give Jacob much rest, either. It's not only lies that surround him and his family, but heaps of trouble that pursue them. There are people and families that never in a lifetime experience a fraction of what he went through. But he, Jacob, seems to have been a magnet for all the real and symbolic troubles that can possibly appear in a family, to the point where the reader says to himself, if there was ever a family I would not want my family to resemble, it has to be Jacob's family. There probably wasn't a single piece of it that functioned properly. And so the inevitable question arises: Why was he chosen to be the father of our nation? Why not Joseph, the ruler of Egypt, or Judah, the mighty warrior? For that matter, why him and not Esau? At least Esau isn't known to have accumulated such a burden of shame and infamy.

Generally speaking, I should make it clear that just as I don't consider the Torah a Jewish book of science (as in *How to Create a World in Six Days*), nor do I consider it a history book whose every fact represents actual events. By the same token, I don't think that the patriarchs were necessarily three consecutive generations of father, son and grandson. The *Chumash* tells the stories of three great characters who arose during the course of several generations, each of whom embodied certain character traits and personal, national, moral or religious profiles so worthy of note that they became beacons, symbolic fathers of the entire nation. I think it's even possible that there were no such people at all, and that these characters are archetypes. If that's that case, then why Jacob? What does he represent?

Abraham is the model of the true believer whose faith burns pure right up until his final breath (and even until the final breaths of his loved ones, who pay the price for his passion). Isaac represents an extreme form of the helplessness that strikes us at various times and places. So often in his personal history he was the passive victim of circumstances not of his doing. Like him, we often long for complete, absolute protection from the vicissitudes of life, only to find ourselves surprised each time that life is so much more creative and imaginative than all our careful plans. And Jacob? Jacob symbolizes our national proclivity for disaster. There are some people who simply attract calamity. They're accident prone, constantly tripping over something, never quite managing to come home in one piece from wherever they were going. Jacob was like that and so are we, his children and children's children. The stories are in the past, but their message is eternal because the evil in the universe and in humankind has no expiration date.

We often find ourselves enchanted by stories of runaway children, youngsters forced to leave home to escape family violence. The first of the breed was Jacob, son of Rebecca and Isaac, of the line of Abraham. His older brother, the big, tough hunter, didn't like him or his oh-so-civilized ways, and hated his childish pranks. Things finally reached the point that Jacob was forced to flee for his life from his hot-tempered brother's very specific and concrete threat: "Let the days of mourning for my father be at hand; then I will slay my brother Jacob" (Gen. 27:41). This was a family where every private thought became public knowledge, so someone came along and told Esau's secret to his mother: "And the words of Esau her elder son were told to Rebecca" (Gen 27:42).

And so Jacob sets out on his own, a runaway youth joining the ranks of the fugitives. He goes looking for a family to take him in, in place of his own family, which broke up under circumstances that were partly his own fault. As if it weren't enough that he has to grow up without a father or mother, the same trauma continues to resonate throughout the rest of his adult life. For twenty-one long years he is cut off from his beloved mother. He loses his childhood sweetheart Rachel while she is still young, before they have had a chance to consummate their love or enjoy the freedom they have purchased from her father, thanks to his beliefs and limitations. No loving, supportive mother, no beloved wife, no tenderness.

The family is unquestionably the arena where Jacob's life is pounded out. His wives are switched one after the other: Leah, then Rachel, then the concubines that are deposited between his loins for fruitfulness and multiplication. He lives in constant dread of his father-in-law Laban, fearing that he will steal his daughters and concubines. There's no real trust between him and his wives. Even his beloved Rachel – for whom he labored seven years and then another seven, through summer and winter, in blazing heat and freezing cold – steals her father's idols and hides the truth from Jacob, tries to deny it and finally brings disaster on them both when she turns out to be the address for the death-curse that escaped Jacob's lips in his promise to Laban: "'With whomsoever thou findest thy gods, he shall not live…' For Jacob knew not that Rachel had stolen them" (Gen 31:32).

That was Jacob's relationship with his wives. Things were no better with his children – from Reuben, his firstborn, to Benjamin, his last-born, child of Rachel, his only true love. Besides stealing the blessings and rights of the firstborn from his brother Esau, he essentially usurped his brother's natural role. Perhaps there were customs of this sort in those days, as some ancient archives attest, but the biblical narrator derives no pleasure from these customs. The result is that both of his natural firstborn sons are displaced before his very eyes in the most eternally humiliating fashion. Reuben, his firstborn, exposes the family to the ugliness of incest when he takes his father's concubine Bilhah between the sheets. Reuben violates his father's honor in an act more violent and cruel than Jacob's own act of cheating Isaac and Esau. The result is that Leah's eldest loses his birthright. Likewise Joseph, Rachel's firstborn, is taken from the farm into long years of exile, and Jacob is forced to make do with Judah as his heir and bearer of his line into eternity (for out of the tribe of Judah, *Yehudah*, come the *Yehudim*, the Jews), even though we have no idea how Jacob felt about him.

Sex, forbidden, impure and brutally violent, never ceases to dictate events in Jacob's household. Consider the rape of Dinah in Shechem (Gen. 34:1–31), and its bloody consequences. Consider Judah's involvement with Tamar, his daughter-in-law, lover and whore, who was "with child by harlotry" (Gen. 38:24). Not to mention the business deal Rachel concluded with Leah, trading sex with their husband in exchange for a bunch of mandrake flowers.

And on top of everything else, let's not forget the trade in children that was conducted in Jacob's household. The brothers sold seventeen-year-old Joseph to the Midianites, to the Ishmaelites, to Egypt. Afterward they abandoned Simeon in an Egyptian prison. Then they all banded together against their aged father to trade young Benjamin in exchange for the opportunity to feed their family during the famine that was ravaging the land. Through all these misfortunes that plagued Jacob from his earliest childhood right through his final days in Egyptian exile, his body too was damaged beyond repair, leaving him an invalid. Jacob was a healthy man, a strapping shepherd, familiar with the seasons of the year, the fields and the desert, and knowledgeable in the ways of nature. But after a fierce nighttime struggle with a man whose name remains unknown, he is left with a crippled leg. His hip dislocated, he limps on his perpetually aching leg from that day on (Gen. 32:25–30). And he limps in more ways than one: he doesn't love his first wife, he has grief from his beloved second wife and misery from his concubine and he is forced to witness a bloodbath over the wounded honor of his clan and the rape of his daughter. No wonder he fears the natives, worrying that they might kill him and his household and not be satisfied with merely vilifying his good name, which isn't so good to begin with.

Ladies and gentlemen, this is our father Jacob. A man with a history like this should have given rise to the Tatars, Mongols, Cossacks or some other warlike tribe. And yet, remarkably, this is the man whose troubled life gave birth to the most positive philosophy of life, one of whose finest rules, according to Rabbi Akiba, is: "Thou shalt love thy neighbor as thyself" (Lev.

19:18). The very practical-minded Hillel the Elder rendered the same idea this way: "What is hateful to you, do not unto others" (Mishnah *Avot* 4:5). It's amazing, isn't it? Jacob is the ultimate proof of our claim that the entire Torah is, among other things, the improvement manual for our forefathers' character flaws. It's an improvement process that obligates each and every one of us, all day, every day. As the saying goes: happy is the man who is always improving.

The Genesis Selection Process

THE BOOK OF GENESIS is our national *Origin of the Species*. This is how the process works: The world began as a creation without identifying marks. Adam and Eve were the parents of "all living" (Gen. 3:20). In those first days of history there was no religious-qualitative distinction between Cain and Abel or between Enoch and Methuselah. They were all one great family of the earth. Likewise the generation of Noah was a generation without a defined spiritual or emotional identity that might differentiate among the races of mankind. It was a world of human equality. Only after the Flood did the divisions begin to multiply: "These three were the sons of Noah, and of these was the whole earth overspread" (Gen. 9:19). And later: "These are the families of the sons of Noah, after their generations, in their nations; and of these were the nations divided in the earth after the flood" (Gen. 10:32). This is the first and most basic sort of division: the family unit. Every family in its place, every household in every tribe, and so peoples and nations take shape. Later on a more complex sort of distinction emerges naturally: the division into separate cultures. It was at the Tower of Babel that the first seeds of human cultural diversity took root. Until the Tower of Babel, all the families and all the peoples spoke "one language and of one speech" (Gen. 11:1). Not only did they speak the same language, the phrase "of one speech" suggests that their speech was similar in content. There was a single, worldwide culture (an early form of globalization, if you will). But "the Lord scattered them abroad from thence upon the face of all the earth.... Therefore was the name of it called Babel; because the Lord did there confound [*balal* in biblical Hebrew] the language of all the earth, and from thence did the Lord scatter them abroad upon the face of all the earth" (Gen. 11:8–9).

Until Noah's time, human dispersion was a physical thing, one to the right and one to the left, these to the north and those to the south, west and east. At the Tower of Babel human difference acquired a deeper meaning, first of language and content, and then of recognition and consciousness. Humankind was divided into differing religions, ideologies, schools and bitter existential rivalries. In the midst of this new, shockingly broad human diversity, along comes Abraham to discover the one God and establish his religion. If Noah can be seen as a pole representing the oneness of humankind, Abraham is the opposite pole representing the specific, the exceptional. He is the icon of the partial as a new kind of wholeness. Within his house Abraham establishes the practices of human increase and selection – rules of preference, beginning with his choice of God and continuing on to his choice of heir. He begets Ishmael but banishes him and his descendants to come, "twelve princes according to their nations" (Gen. 25:16). He prefers Isaac, who in turn produces two successors, the earthy culture of Esau and the civilization of Jacob, with all its campsite intrigue. Isaac, like his father and like God, looks at his increase and selects Jacob.

In this week's portion, the story of Jacob's increase begins. Jacob looks around him and selects his preferences, choosing Rachel and Joseph over all the others.

Almost half the Book of Genesis is devoted to Jacob, his annals and his family. The story of the family is spread out across the weekly portions of *Toledot, Vayetze, Vayishlach, Vayeshev, Miketz, Vayigash* and *Vayechi*. The story of Israel's national history is a story of the failure of Jacob and his choices. A failure of selection. Jacob prefers Rachel but gets Leah, Zilpah, Bilhah and all their children. His eyes aren't open until the day he dies. His beloved Rachel has long since been buried somewhere on the road to Bethlehem and he still prefers Joseph over his brothers. He sees greatness where all the brothers see pettiness: "Now Israel loved Joseph more than all his children" (Gen. 37:3). On the surface, the plotline is simply a familiar family chronicle. At a deeper level, it tells the background to the terrible power struggles for leadership of the Jewish people from that time to this. Reuben the firsborn (and what does it get him? Being firstborn never did anyone in that family a bit of good – just ask Ishmael and Esau) against the charismatic Judah against the beloved and talented Joseph. They fight over their father's love. They fight over their maternal status, the tribes of Rachel against the tribes of Leah. They fight over a dry well and keep fighting in the Pharaoh's palace. Their fight continues right on through the rupture in the monarchy. Saul, a descendant of Rachel, is succeeded by David and then Solomon, descendants of Judah and Leah. Then comes the schism of the two kingdoms, the kingdom of Judah and the kingdom of Israel, whose center is on the mount of Ephraim son of Joseph.

Despite all the pain and the criticism, despite the difficulty of identifying with the doings of the patriarchs, it's hard to know who would have been the better choice, Isaac or Ishmael. Both of them are presented in the text as success stories, each one with his own nation and tribes. Nor is the choice between Jacob and Esau entirely clear-cut. The text itself doesn't indicate any moral failing on Esau's part. He is a man of the earth, he honors his father, supports himself and, no less important, he raised up peoples and nations after him. On the other hand, Jacob, whose changed name became the name of the nation Israel, chose poorly.

The entire biblical narrative is a tale of the terrible confrontation between the father's preference for Joseph and history's preference for Judah. One wanted his beloved son, the child of his beloved wife, and the other – history – wanted the son of the despised Leah. The very kingship of David of the line of Leah is a protest against the father's preference. And that, in a way, is the eternal story Israel. Would the soul of our people have been different if the monarchy had not been the royal line of the rejected son, child of the unloved wife? What would have happened if we had been led by a successful and preferred son who didn't need to be forever confronting someone or something to prove himself? Besides, isn't it preferable for a parent to love all his children equally rather than pit one against the other, creating grudges that last into eternity?

While we recount the painful family narrative, we might turn our attention for a moment to the lessons drawn by the Scripture itself. In contrast to the practice of the men of Genesis, who would choose one of their sons above the others, the Book of Deuteronomy has this to say: "If a man have two wives, the one beloved, and the other hated, and they have borne him children, both the beloved and the hated; and if the firstborn son be hers that was hated; then it shall be, in the day that he causeth his sons to inherit that which he hath, that he may not make the son of the beloved firstborn [that is, treat him as though he were older] before the son of the hated, who is the firstborn; but he shall acknowledge the firstborn, the son of the hated, by giving him a double portion of all that he hath; since he is the first-fruits of his strength; the right of the firstborn is his" (Deut. 21:15–17).

The Deuteronomic legislator learned the lesson. If only every father of every family could do the same.

Week 8

Vayishlach – Jacob Sent

Genesis 32:4–36:42

Jacob, and What Isn't Accomplished by Force

As we've noted, more than half the weekly portions in the Book of Genesis deal with Jacob, his personal history and his difficult family. It's no surprise, then, that his character and profile are depicted in much finer detail in the Torah than any of his parents or forebears. Abraham first entered the stage at age seventy-something. Isaac was passive and dependent until his fifties; it was not until then that he began to register as an independent actor, after which we came to know him as an innovative and prosperous farmer – though he remained a weak, ineffectual father. By contrast, we follow Jacob from the moment he is born until he breathes his final breath. We have a front-row seat as he grows and evolves. Let's try to isolate one thread in his story and follow it from beginning to end. By tracing this one thread, we can try to understand some of the dimensions and processes that he carried with him from his earliest days as Jacob, the younger brother, up to his death as Israel, the father of the children of Israel.

Jacob's life story is a long, torturous process of learning the uses and limits of power. Often enough he simply didn't understand the meaning of power. He didn't know that he himself was imbued with great power. He didn't know how to wield it, and many of his mistakes stemmed from his failure to understand it. He was utterly blind to the strength that comes from restraining oneself and refraining from the use of power.

There is a tradition of power and combativeness interwoven through all the stories of the patriarchs. Abraham didn't hesitate to use his strength and the strength of his servants to chase Lot's captors all the way to the outskirts of Damascus (Gen. 14:14), nor did he hesitate to restrain himself and decline a share of the riches of the king of Sodom (Gen. 14:22–23), just as he had conceded to Lot the entire eastern half of the land (Gen. 13:8–12). In the same manner he forcefully scolded God when he famously argued for the people of Sodom: "That be far from thee to do after this manner, to slay the righteous with the wicked" (Gen. 18:25). Isaac, too, after having been bound on the altar as a child, learned the uses of power in adulthood. His newfound skills served him well in his battles over the wells of the Philistines (Gen. 26:18–22) and in his enormous economic success, which brought him his "hundredfold" yield (Gen. 26:12) on his first investment. But Jacob, unlike his father and grandfather, never learned exactly what power was nor how to use it, whether for good or ill. He began his life as a youth with no boundaries, using more force than necessary, and by the end of his life, having learned too many lessons, physically and emotionally scarred, he shunned power to the point of emasculating himself and sabotaging his own essential defenses.

Let's begin our journey by reviewing the banal texture of Jacob's relationship with his brother Esau. At this early stage it's clear that Jacob is using all the combative tricks and stratagems of the campsite. While big, hairy Esau is naively sauntering through the fields, luring animals into his nets, our forefather is casting a net of his own. Jacob's net is woven of intelligence: Where are Esau's clothes? What are Papa Isaac's favorite snacks? Jacob learned to imitate Esau's speech and mannerisms, and to draw on Rebecca's talents and contacts and so much more, all adding up to an ancient version of "knowledge is power." In the next scene, we see Jacob approaching the well at Haran. How they praised his great strength! How, oh how did our hero manage to roll the stone off the mouth of the well (Gen. 29:10)? Every day the shepherds had to wait until they had all assembled, and then together they would roll away the big stone that covered the water of the well, but on this day our hero was so filled with strength at the sight of Rachel, the loveliest of maidens, that with one mighty shove he opened the well and quenched his love and her flock. Great, mighty Jacob.

Still, it might be possible to read the story a bit differently. Perhaps there was an agreement among the local shepherds, any one of whom might have been strong enough to push the stone on his own, that they not touch the stone until they had all gathered and could distribute the water equally. Perhaps the scarcity of water in the region forced them to reach fair-use agreements under which nobody opened the tap until everyone is present, and they avoided the use of force. Toward the beginning of his marvelous book *The Religion of Ethical Nationhood: Judaism's Contribution to World Peace* (Macmillan, 1970), Mordecai M. Kaplan cites Norman Cousins's much-quoted lament that societies continue to pursue ever-greater means of projecting force, despite the fact that "security today depends on the control of force rather than the use of force" ("Special Delivery Systems for War," *Saturday Review*, Sept. 10, 1960).

In the story of the well, Jacob pursued power, perhaps not understanding the agreements that had been reached to prevent its use. It's not surprising that from the moment he set foot in Haran, a dark cloud of hostility gathered over him and remained his constant companion.

Long years of struggle eventually sapped Jacob's strength and brought him at last to the opposite pole. No more tests of strength and power; henceforth, an unending flight from power, authority and displays of force. That might explain his hasty, almost cowardly disengagement from Laban. The biblical narrator is quite correct when describing, as an objective observer, Jacob's departure: "And Jacob outwitted Laban the Aramean, in that he told him not that he fled. So he fled with all that he had" (Gen. 31:20–21). This weakness continues in his meeting with Esau. What is he afraid of? True, his brother has four hundred men, but Jacob has a few bullyboys of his own. He himself had fought all night with that mysterious stranger (Gen. 32:25–30), which ought to show you that it's not so easy to beat an old shepherd like Jacob. He's strong, he's determined, he can take a kick straight to the groin. And his sons are no different, as two of them, Simeon and Levi, will prove in Shechem a biblical moment later. Not to mention Judah, the bold, brave and daring, and even young Joseph, blessed

Vayishlach

with considerable powers of survival – twelve strapping sons, along with men- and maidservants. Perhaps he didn't have the forces to ensure victory on the battlefield, but he certainly could have put up a good fight. But Jacob, once burned by the overuse of force, had now adopted acquiescence as a way of life. He had gone from one extreme to the other. And between the two extremes, our third patriarch lived a life without much balance.

For many years I didn't give much importance to the Aggadic story of Jacob's nighttime struggle at the ford of the Jabbok, the night before he was to meet up with his brother Esau. Just another story, I thought, providing a mythological justification for a strange prohibition in the Jewish laws of kashrut: "Therefore the children of Israel eat not the sinew of the thigh-vein which is upon the hollow of the thigh unto this day; because he touched the hollow of Jacob's thigh, even in the sinew of the thigh-vein" (Gen. 32:33). Today I believe that Jacob's struggle with the mysterious stranger might be the most important turning point in Jacob's life. It was his last physical combat, after which he never again put up a show of force. I'm quite certain that the nighttime struggle left Jacob deeply disheartened. He was accustomed to winning against all comers, whether in a fair fight or by stealth. Suddenly, on the eve of the greatest battle of his life – his rapprochement with Esau – he discovers that he can't win every battle.

But this is not the main lesson. The heart of the matter is that Jacob neither won nor lost, but fought to a draw. His opponent touched his leg and dislocated it. Jacob fought him off until daybreak without a decision. A man who is used to smashing his opponents suddenly finds himself alone in the middle of the night facing someone who is exactly his match. He returns from the fight and decides not to hide what happened. He was the only one there, and if not for his testimony we would never have known about it.

Would it have been so hard for Jacob, the veteran liar, to make up a good cover story for his limp, the delay and his late return from the ford of the Jabbok? Certainly not. He chose to tell the truth because there, that night, he learned that there are things that can't be solved by force, by more force or even by mustering every ounce of strength. There are times when the other side is able to muster the same resources as you. From that time forward Jacob became the father of Jewish nonviolence at its finest.

That night, Jacob was transformed from a disciple of power into the inventor of the theory of strength through submission. He didn't fight Esau for several reasons. It's quite likely that he felt that his brother Esau was basically in the right, and a war without justification is a recipe for disaster and defeat. But the main reason, it seems to me, was that he wanted to break the pathological pattern in his relationship with his surroundings. The force he was accustomed to wielding had turned from an asset into a burden, from a value to a vapidity. What began as a simple desire to change things by fleeing his father-in-law's house became a full-fledged policy after the nighttime encounter that preceded the morning summit.

Nor did his sons Simeon and Levi succeed in their efforts to drag their father back to the place he knew so well, after their slaughter of the men of Shechem. Toward the end of this week's portion he gives them a stiff lecture on the New Jacobism: "Jacob said to Simeon and Levi, 'Ye have troubled me, to make me odious unto the inhabitants of the land, even unto the Canaanites and the Perizzites; and, I being few in number, they will gather themselves together and smite me, and I shall be destroyed, I and my house" (Gen. 34:30). This is the new identity that could not have been articulated in the old words and concepts, which is why his name was changed: "Thy name shall be called no more Jacob, but Israel; for thou hast striven with God and with men, and hast prevailed" (Gen. 32:28). In the last few generations we have learned what *Jacob* means and what is wrong with it, but we haven't yet come to understand fully the meaning of *Israel*, and the concept of power and restraint that is Israelism. But that deserves a portion of its own, and it's not told in the Torah.

The Ethics of War

"JACOB SENT MESSENGERS BEFORE HIM" (Gen. 32:4). The biblical story closes several old circles in order to open a few new ones. Jacob, the exiled fugitive, returns to his own land; Jacob and Esau, brothers separated by enmity, return to each other's embrace. And just as we've put the saga

Vayishlach

of family quarrels behind us, a whole new conflict opens up between the newly arrived shepherd and the local inhabitants, the house of Jacob versus the people of Shechem, herdsmen versus city folk, newcomers versus old-timers. This is one of the most warlike portions in the Torah. It includes a battle between Jacob and Esau that was averted at the last minute; the nighttime struggle between Jacob and the mysterious stranger that lasts until daybreak and leaves our forefather with a permanent limp; and finally, the decisive moment when Simeon and Levi draw sword and dagger and violently snuff out any chance of coexistence with the locals, on account of Dinah, the mother of all rape victims.

In the midst of all these violent stories, a fine line can be discerned that seems to define the difference between just and unjust wars. Even the most peace-loving person knows that there are times when one has no choice but to take up arms to defend oneself. Some situations impose a moral duty of war, even holy war, when the only alternatives are life or death. We give up the idea of pacifism, because we are commanded to "choose life" (Deut. 30:19). War may be necessary to preserve life, on condition that all other options have been exhausted.

The line between just and unjust war is an extremely fine one, and almost always hidden from view. One can take up arms in the most just war imaginable, only to find oneself mired in an utterly squalid and corrupt reality – and vice versa. This week's portion offers initial guidelines for distinguishing permitted and forbidden, right and wrong in the ethic of war.

Let's begin our discussion with a question: Jacob, the simple tent-dweller, was presumably a person of considerable physical strength. Herding sheep for two decades must have hardened him; it certainly toughened him up. We get our first glimpse of his physical prowess at the well in Haran. Undaunted by the other shepherds' hostility, he flexes his muscles and rolls the stone off the mouth of the well, unassisted. Some time later, still at the height of his powers, he wrestles all night with the mysterious stranger, and even against this anonymous, nameless foe he emerges undefeated. Why, then, is such a man so afraid of a war with his brother Esau? Shepherds and angels yes, redheaded brother no?

Apparently Jacob knew that in the approaching war with Esau, justice was not on his side. For twenty years he had been carrying bottled-up feelings of guilt over his theft of his brother's birthright and blessing. Jacob knew that if they came to blows, Esau would be fighting a just war and he, Jacob, even in defending himself, would be fighting on the side of injustice. The late Yeshayahu Leibowitz sensitively shed light on this when he pointed out how carefully Jacob prepared his retinue. He instructed each of his followers as to their place, what to say and what not to say. Jacob's messengers are under orders to give Esau "a present sent unto my lord, even unto Esau" (Gen. 32:19). The word "present," *minchah* in Hebrew, appears five times. And yet, even though everyone else has been thoroughly instructed and prepared, Jacob himself is utterly unprepared.

At the dramatic climax of the meeting itself, amidst the hugs and the tears, kisses, caresses and pats on the shoulder, he blurts out the inner truth that has been weighing on his conscience: "Take, I pray thee, my blessing" (Gen. 33:11). Although this exchange is commonly rendered in English as "my present" or "gift," the Hebrew word that appears is not *minchah*, which has appeared five times already, but *brachah*, the word for blessing – precisely the thing that Jacob stole from Esau so many years before (Gen. 27:35). At this moment of truth, it is the inner truth that comes out, not the spin Jacob has hidden behind for so long. He is returning the stolen blessing. And with a slight rearranging of letters in Hebrew, he might be returning not just the *brachah*, the blessing, but also the *bechorah*, the birthright.

And wonder of wonders, from the moment the theft is made right there is no more need for war. From here on, we are no longer the children of the firstborn, and the stolen blessing is not on our heads. Esau is left with two blessings, the one he received from his father, Isaac (Gen. 27:39–40), and the one returned to him by his brother, Jacob. And we, the descendants, are left with nothing. The conclusion is clear: the aggressor-provocateur, thief of birthrights and blessings, knows deep inside when he is wrong and should not go to war, lest all his strength leave him and his knees buckle under him. As in Jacob's meeting with Esau, so in every unjust war that ever was: injustice cannot triumph.

Vayishlach

Let's return to the preparations for war. The text states that "Jacob was greatly afraid and was distressed" (Gen. 32:8). The Midrash and commentaries all seize on the redundancy – "greatly afraid" and "distressed" – as an open invitation to creative speculation. Rashi offers this: "'He was greatly afraid' that he himself might be killed." But he "'was distressed' that he might kill others." In Jewish understanding, the decision to go to war must be based on two conditions: hatred of killing and fear of death. Soldiers who go joyfully into battle, prepared for a hero's death – perhaps with a noble whisper such as the iconic Israeli war hero Joseph Trumpeldor is said to have uttered, "It is good to die for one's country" – are flawed soldiers in the eyes of Judaism. Judaism doesn't want soldiers who want to die. Judaism wants soldiers who want to live and return home safely from battle. It wants soldiers who fear death because life is holier than any holy martyrdom on the battlefield. By the same token, a Jewish soldier who thirsts for his enemy's blood and isn't distressed at the prospect of taking another's life is not a good soldier. The bloodthirsty soldier goes looking for fights, even pointless ones, and the martyr or *shahid* who goes looking for death will find it, needlessly. Both of them, the eager killer and willing martyr, are unnecessary and harmful.

The best example of a bad and unjust war in all its ugliness is offered at the end of this week's portion, in the war of Jacob's sons Simeon and Levi against Shechem. Simeon and Levi are bloodthirsty brothers who aren't afraid to be killed and aren't distressed at the thought of killing others. It's no accident that Jacob left them with a curse when he died. Shortly after the rape of Dinah and the massacre of the men of Shechem, he scolds them: "Ye have troubled me, to make me odious unto the inhabitants of the land" (Gen. 34:30). The original Hebrew is more graphic; what Jacob told them, literally, was: "You have made me filthy and vile-smelling to the neighbors." This helps explain the curse that Simeon and Levi received as their share of Jacob's deathbed blessing to his sons in the final chapter of Genesis. The common English rendering is "For in their anger they slew men" (Gen. 49:6), but the Hebrew word for "their anger," *apam*, is an often-used metonymy that literally means "their nose." The nose, of course, is the organ of smell. The stink of death from the battlefield stuck to Simeon and Levi just as it has stuck to all soldiers in all unjust wars throughout history. They and their violent offspring are cursed from that day to this, from Simeon and Levi right up to Meir Kahane Hacohen Ben-Levi and his vile followers.

Week 9

Vayeshev – And Jacob Dwelt

Genesis 37:1–40:23

Jacob and His Two Firstborns, Judah and Joseph

THERE IS SOMETHING REASSURINGLY STABLE and secure in the notion of "dwelling," the verb that gives this week's portion its name. It has an air of permanence, of rootedness, unlike more tentative concepts such as sojourning or abiding. The same is true of the Hebrew original, *yeshev*; in various permutations it means to sit, settle down or inhabit. Its root letters, *y-sh-v*, lend their meaning to such essential values as the *yeshiva*, the place where scholars sit together to study Torah (and where, if you will, the spirit of God dwells among them), and the *yishuv*, the permanent Jewish community in the land of Israel. Jacob was surely seeking that sort of permanence and stability in his life when he decided to settle down at last after years of impermanence, instability and upset. But wishing doesn't make it so: "Jacob sought to dwell in tranquility, but the anger of Joseph sprang upon him" (Rashi on Gen. 37:2). Rashi argues that Jacob's hopes to settle down to a quiet farmer's life were upset by the feuding between Joseph and his brothers, which ended up wreaking disaster in the family. Rashi adds, "The righteous sought to dwell in tranquility; but the Holy One, praised be he, said: the righteous are not satisfied with what is arranged for them in the world to come, but want to dwell in tranquility in this world?" And thus begins the final chapter in the most un-tranquil life of Jacob.

At the core of the story is the unavoidable comparison between Joseph and Jacob. Comparisons between generations are not unusual in this family. Thus, for example, Rashi begins his commentary on *Parashat Toledot*:

> These are the generations of Isaac. Abraham begot Isaac…. The jokers of that generation used to say that Sarah was made pregnant by Abimelech [the king of Gerar, who "took Sarah" thinking she was Abraham's sister, Gen. 20:2] since she had lived with Abraham for so many years and not gotten pregnant by him. What did the Holy One, praised be he, do? He made the features of Isaac's face resemble Abraham's to attest to all that Abraham begot Isaac. (Rashi on Gen. 25:19)

As opposed to the physical similarity between Abraham and Isaac, the similarity between Jacob and Joseph is drawn from the arena of shared personal destiny:

> Three times the text begins "the generations of Jacob" with Joseph, for several reasons: one, that Jacob did not work for Laban for his own sake but for Rachel; and the splendor of Joseph's appearance resembled him; and everything that happened to Jacob happened to Joseph – both were hated, both had brothers who sought to kill them and much more. (Rashi on Gen. 37:2)

Their mothers, Rebecca and Rachel, were both childless in their early years of marriage. Rebecca gave birth to two boys, Jacob and Esau, and Rachel gave birth to two boys, Joseph and Benjamin. Both had difficult, painful pregnancies. Both Jacob and Joseph grew up in hostile environments, with brothers who hated them. Both had dreams filled with promise of greatness. Both took birthrights that were not theirs by natural right. In both stories, their hard work paid off well economically for their fathers-in-law, Laban and Potiphar. Both died in Egypt, both were embalmed and both were returned after death to the land of Canaan by their families in elaborate royal funeral processions. And above all, they share the similarity of their long, forced separations from their parents' homes.

Within this remarkable family drama lurks the seed of another story that has yet to germinate, grow and make its presence felt. If you were to stop reading this week's portion at chapter 38, after the third *aliyah* (summons to the Torah) of seven, the logical continuity of the Jewish people's annals would seem clear-cut. Abraham was the preferred son of Terah. Isaac inherited the patriarch's mantle instead of his brother. Jacob, with all his agonizing, continues the tradition this week and chooses Joseph as his heir, even though he isn't the firstborn. But you already know my view: no biblical story is simple. There's almost always a far-reaching historical dimension, laden with no small measure of uplifting, didactic critique for the benefit of readers and believers. This week, the twist is the story of Judah, folded in among the annals of Joseph in a manner that is not the least bit coincidental.

Chapter 38 begins this way: "And it came to pass at that time, that Judah went down from his brethren, and turned in to a certain Adullamite, whose name was Hirah. And Judah saw there a daughter of a certain Canaanite whose name was Shua; and he took her, and went in unto her" (Gen. 38:1–2). The descent, as I understand it, was geographical: from the high Samarian hill country, along the main highway that winds southward through the Jebusite hills and the city of Salem (later Jerusalem), via Hebron and down into the valley of Beersheba. Eventually Judah went from the Judean hills, which weren't yet named for him, to the lowlands of Adullam, the Valley of Elah and the Canaanite cities of the Shephelah lowlands approaching the coastal plain.

The rest of the story is familiar. Judah and the Canaanite woman have three sons: Er, Onan and Shelah. The eldest marries Tamar and then dies. His brother marries her, and then he too dies. Judah, kindly and loving father that he is, refuses to marry his third son to the black widow. At this point Tamar deceives her father-in-law. She dons a galabia and veil and lures Judah, disguised as a highway prostitute. When the honorable father-in-law learns of her pregnancy he decides to have her killed. "Bring her forth, and let her be burnt" (Gen. 38:24), he orders, but she produces the personal effects that he had given her as payment for his roadside romp. Being an old-school gentleman, he offers public acknowledgement: "She is more righteous than I" (Gen. 38:26). Twins are born to them, Zerah and Peretz. The latter fathers a line of progeny that produces King David. There are so many components in this human tale that shed light on the customs and norms of the era: the place of the prostitute in society, the traditions of levirate marriage and of redeeming a brother's widow, the laws of execution by burning of an adulterously pregnant woman, and even the price of a night of pleasure among the high and mighty.

Judah's break with family tradition demands examination. Abraham sent his servant Eliezer to bring back a bride for Isaac from his clan in Haran. Jacob marries a relative, too. Reuben, Jacob's firstborn, sleeps with his father's concubine. Only Judah breaks the mold and marries one of the local women, against whom his great-grandfather Abraham had pleaded: "Thou shalt not take a wife for my son of the daughters of the Canaanites, among whom I dwell. But thou shalt go unto my country, and to my kindred, and take a wife for my son, even for Isaac" (Gen. 24:3–4). And his grandmother Rebecca had spoken of them, too: "If Jacob take a wife of the daughters of Heth, such as these, of the daughters of the land, what good shall my life do me?" (Gen. 27:46). But Judah strikes out on a new path, which characterizes all his great descendants after him. He deliberately marries one of the daughters of the land, and chooses another one for his sons to marry. Boaz, his grandson's grandson, marries Ruth the Moabite, and a list of the intermarriages of David and Solomon and their children would require more than the few pages of a weekly portion.

For years I have been asking myself why David succeeded in his young kingship when the much-admired Saul had failed before him? Why is the kingdom of Judah immortal in memory, while the kingdom of Benjamin, the brother of Joseph, nearly forgotten? There is no shortage of commentaries on the question. The tempestuous personality of the red-haired David was stronger than Saul's manic-depression. Geopolitical circumstances and canny alliances favored David. Politics and statecraft explain a great deal, but it seems to me that more attention should be paid to the marital policies of the house of Judah. While Saul was destroying his sophisticated and experienced allies, the Gibeonites, King David, like Boaz and Judah, was marrying local folk and marrying his sons and daughters to the princes and kings of the region.

From a historical standpoint, the land of Canaan had developed a tradition of monarchic politics that predated by at last five hundred years the conquest of the land by the Israelite desert nomads. A stable economy, trained armies, military technologies, traditions of governance and royal houses had been developed while our ancestors were still wandering around thirsty and hungry in the desert. The children of Judah assimilated this accumulated experience and built on it. Like a choice fruit tree grown from botanical grafting, a well-rooted stock from one strain topped by fruit-bearing foliage from another. The house of Judah was the foliage and fruit, and the daughters of the land with their traditions were the deep roots. Out of this grows the healthy tree about which we still sing, "*chai vekayam*" – it lives on.

And so the biblical narrator stealthily tucks away the seeds of Judah's future greatness in the midst of the story of Joseph's rise to the top. He seems to be telling us that this time, the father's choice won't be upheld. Abraham preferred Isaac. Isaac blessed Jacob – unwillingly, perhaps, but he did it. Jacob continued his fathers' practice and publicly chose Joseph, but the narrator has already let us know his own choice: Judah.

A Sack of Vermin

IF ONE HAD TO DEFINE the Bible's understanding of the roots of monarchy or of government and power, one could probably say that the basic requirements of royalty in Israel include a queen mother who is a woman of dubious background and whose royal offspring may be called first-class sons of whores. Indeed Judaism, which currently attaches such great importance to the mother's lineage, took pains in its earliest narratives to cast every possible aspersion on the mothers of the nation and monarchy and their strange liaisons with the founding fathers.

First there was Abraham, who schemed with his wife Sarah when they went down to Egypt: "Say, I pray thee, thou are my sister; that it may be well with me for thy sake, and that my soul may live because of thee...."

And the woman was taken into Pharaoh's house. And he dealt well with Abram for her sake; and he had sheep, and oxen, and he-asses, and menservants, and maid-servants, and she-asses, and camels" (Gen. 12:13–16). We hardly need to comment on trading a wife for wealth and property, do we?

Isaac, the son who was "like an extension of his father," as alike as two peas in a pod, repeats the exact same trick, albeit without the sexual consummation: "And Isaac dwelt in Gerar. And the men of the place asked him of his wife; and he said: 'She is my sister'; for he feared to say: 'My wife'; lest the men of the place should kill me for Rebecca, because she is fair to look upon.' And it came to pass that when he had been there a long time, that Abimelech king of the Philistines looked out at a window, and saw, and behold, Isaac was sporting with Rebecca his wife. And Abimelech called Isaac, and said: 'Behold, of a surety she is thy wife; and how saidst thou: She is my sister?' And Isaac said unto him: 'Because I said: Lest I die because of her.' And Abimelech said: 'What is this thou hast done unto us? One of the people might easily have lain with thy wife, and thou wouldst have brought guiltiness upon us'" (Gen. 26:6–10).

In Jacob's family the muddle is even more pronounced. Reuben slept with Bilhah in last week's portion, defiling his father's bed. In this week's portion Judah approaches an Adullamite man and marries one of the local Canaanite girls, in direct violation of the prohibition laid down first by Abraham and then by Rebecca against their sons marrying "the daughters of the land." Judah rebels, defiantly planting his roots and assimilating into the local landscape. But he doesn't stop there. He gives his sons to Tamar, another local girl, and in the end sleeps with her himself after she dresses up as a prostitute waiting by the roadside to ambush him and steal his seed. From this union of Judah and the Canaanite courtesan comes the line that leads to our greatest bastard king, David. As for Joseph, he also has his affairs with women this week, or at least affairs with a woman. The wife of Potiphar, the captain of Pharaoh's palace guard, tries to seduce him and ends up having him thrown in prison.

Traditional commentators, following Aggadic Midrash, highlight the juxtaposition of the Judah and Joseph stories. Rashi, for example, notes the quick succession of "the story of Potiphar's wife after the story of Tamar, which teaches that one was for the sake of heaven but one was not for the sake of heaven, because she had seen in her horoscope that she was fated to give him sons but she didn't know if they would be hers or her daughter's" (Rashi on Gen. 39:1).

It's possible that there is historical truth passed on to us through the folk tales and Aggadic legends. It's also possible that the narrative represents a deliberate effort to discredit our founders and kings, so that they and we would know that they were only human, very far from perfection. That is, there seems to be a sort of ongoing system of criticism set up to prevent the endemic arrogance of kings and the despotic tendencies that typically result. The sages of the Talmud looked for the keys to the selection of kings and rulers and asked themselves, as we did in last week's portion, why the reign of King Saul was so brief while the reign of King David, whose character and behavior were so much more questionable, was so enduring. The sages reached this conclusion: "Rabbi Judah said, quoting Samuel: Why did the kingdom of the house of Saul not last? Because he had no flaws" (Babylonian Talmud, *Yoma* 22b). Contrast that with their conclusion about David: "As Rabbi Yohanan said in the name of Rabbi Shimon Ben Yehozedek: A leader is not to be appointed for the community unless he has a sack of vermin tied to his back" – that is, a collection of skeletons in his closet – "so that if his pride runs away with him, others may say to him: take a step backward" (Babylonian Talmud, *Yoma* 22b).

The most interesting commentary on this strange remark, comparing the good Saul to the dubious David, comes from Rashi, the greatest of the Talmud's commentators, who explained it this way: Saul "had no flaws [in his] family," by which Rashi meant that his family was spotless, which is dangerous because "kings who descended from his line to rule Israel might boast" (Rashi on *Yoma* 122b). David, by contrast, had no lack of flaws, and his family background offered a sackful of vermin. What were David's vermin? "Flaws in the family," because "he came from Ruth the Moabite" and before her from Tamar, the matriarch of the royal line, who was, at least at the moment of intimacy and conception in this week's portion, a common roadside prostitute.

In other words, there is an explicit ideology of seeking rulers and leaders of flawed character and flawed lineage so as to give a king's subjects some leverage to balance and offset his kingly mystique in the event that he oversteps his bounds. Outside criticism of the monarchy and limited power are essential elements in the Jewish political tradition. Because we're looking at these concepts at their earliest stages in the Book of Genesis, the ideas have not fully matured. At first glance, these stories seem to be the personal lives of our great national personalities. But that's not the case. The biblical narrator took care to burden three of Jacob's twelve sons with personal and family flaws. Not the others. We know nothing about the sex life of Naphtali, nor the appetites or kinky preferences of Issachar. We haven't a clue whether or not Zebulon was unfaithful. The scripture aims its poison arrows only at Reuben, Judah and Joseph. Why?

Because the second half of the Book of Genesis is the arena where the retroactive struggle over the legitimacy of the kings of Israel is played out. The historic struggle between monarchs of the southern kingdom of Judah and the northern kingdom of Israel reaches deep into the tales of the patriarchs: whom did father love more, who was the beneficiary of the original will, who was blessed and who wasn't, who is destined to the be the anointed messiah of Israel. Judah seeks legitimacy. So does Saul, of the tribe of Benjamin, the leading ally in the coalition of the tribes of Joseph (Benjamin, Ephraim and Manasseh). Likewise the sons of Reuben, who tried to achieve autonomy on the eastern bank of the Jordan, laid claim to national primacy, on the strength of Reuben's biological primacy in the birth order. It was a never-ending struggle during the period of the First Temple, with everyone claiming to be the true heir and every tribe claiming to be the most worthy. And the louder the succession struggles grew, the more the sages who shaped the tradition and redacted the Torah's stories tried to belittle all the contenders alike.

And who won? Obviously, the one who had the most vermin in his sack. Joseph had only the wife Potiphar, from whom he fled as fast as he could. Reuben sinned his one great sin and left the stage. But Judah found the winning formula. He married a Canaanite woman, then married his sons to another one. He then slept with her himself and begot Peretz and

Zerah. Boaz eventually descended from them and then went ahead and married someone who was "not one of us," namely Ruth the Moabite. From that union came David, whose conquests on the battlefield were matched by his conquests among the rooftops and bathing pools of Jerusalem. But Solomon, David's son and heir, set the family record in collecting vermin. He, the son of the Hittite woman, offspring of sin and lust, builder of the greatest palace in all the Bible, was chosen to continue the eternal line of the house of Judah and the children of David. It turns out that the bigger your family sack of vermin, the better your chances for a long reign – and the more embarrassing personal scandals your critics can summon to clip your wings and tell you, when the need arises, to take a step backward.

Week 10

Miketz – At the End of Two Years

Genesis 41:1–44:17

Because We Were Strangers

JOSEPH IS THE ARCHETYPE of the Diaspora Jewish success story. He is the first ever to make it big in the royal court. He is the first to understand what it means to live outside Israel, initially under duress but later by choice. His story raises thoughts of the smallness of Jewish life in a Jewish land, and of the greatness of the Diaspora Jew as Other, forced to compete, to excel and to stand out. In a sense Joseph is the first Einstein – that is, he is essentially a Zionist, but from afar. Jewish, but mostly in relation to gentiles. What's more, Joseph is the first of us who was born outside Israel and made his mark outside Israel. That is, Abraham was born outside Israel and found success in Israel; Isaac was born in Israel and succeeded in Israel; and Jacob was born in Israel and found success abroad, while working for Laban in Haran. Joseph came from outside and succeeded outside. He brief stay in Israel was not of great importance to his future or his greatness. Accordingly, Joseph's story presents us with a difficult choice of themes. Do we use Joseph to shed light on the complicated relationship between Israel and the Diaspora, or do we focus this week on the place of the outsider in society? As usual, we will allow the urgent to displace the substantive, and put off Israel-Diaspora relations for now.

One could read the entire Book of Genesis as a discussion, via personal stories and anecdotes, of the place of the outsider and the Other in human society. Cain, the driven wanderer, is the embodiment of the perpetual outsider who carries his otherness with him from place to place. The story of Abraham's otherness is far more surprising, almost shocking. He discovers his faith in the sublime and ineffable somewhere near the rivers of Babylon, and the first command he receives from his new God is to go and become a stranger elsewhere. God doesn't tell him to deepen his faith in him or to expand his community to include his family or clan. God tells him: go out on a mission. He sends him to be a stranger, a lonely missionary among people who have no common denominator with him. Go be an Other, he tells him, because that, it seems, is the nature of your new faith. The same goes for Isaac, alone in the land of Gerar, for Jacob in all his wanderings and with Joseph, who was the prince of them all. The new faith of the patriarchs is a perpetual protest against normality, a posing of foreignness as an alternative, challenging everyone, everywhere, throughout history.

What, then, is the Bible's policy toward relations with the stranger? At first glance, the welter of principled and normative references to the issue might seem to suggest a particularly lofty moral universe. The Bible loves the outsider and the stranger. On the other hand, sometimes a multiplicity of rules and commandments points toward a debased reality that needs rules spelled out precisely because it hasn't yet internalized them. For example, when we encounter large numbers of rules setting out limits on our sexual behavior, it's a safe guess that conditions during the lawmaker's own time were rather dissolute. Much like our own time: the thicker the controller-general's report on state misconduct, the more official misconduct there must have been. In the same way, when the Torah takes the trouble to warn so many times about our treatment of the stranger, it probably means the reality of life for strangers was hard indeed. The meanness of society's attitude toward them was probably in reverse proportion to the moralizing of the scripture. The loftiness of the biblical language was matched by the depth of human degradation that the Torah was trying to reform. As it was then, the human heart today is still torn between openness to the foreigner and an instinctive rejection.

The Hebrew and English Wikipedia entries on *xenophobia* are as different as the languages, cultures and nations they serve. The English Wikipedia defines it as fear of foreigners or strangers, and describes it as a psychological condition induced in individuals by particular circumstances, notably post-traumatic stress syndrome such as soldiers experience after a war against a different culture. It emphasizes that the xenophobe's fear is inherently irrational and can be projected onto nearly any outside group, "not only people from other countries, but other cultures, subcultures and subsets of belief systems; in short, anyone who meets any list of criteria about their origin, religion, personal beliefs, habits, language, orientations, or any other criteria. While some will state that the 'target' group is a set of persons not accepted by the society, in reality only the phobic person need hold the belief that the target group is not (or should not be) accepted by society."

Hebrew Wikipedia defines xenophobia not as fear but as a feeling of hatred or revulsion toward foreigners. Instead of a psychological explanation focusing on the individual, the Hebrew quotes sociology: "The sociological explanation for hatred of foreigners grows out of the assumption that it is rooted in group norms. The group's norms define how to relate to the foreigner, a member of another group, and there are more than a few societies that narrow the definition of 'human being' to their own members." Much of the article addresses the danger of xenophobia to democracy, "because the commitment of citizens to democratic values, including equality among individuals, is not compatible with the tendency to discriminate and denigrate minorities."

The two views of xenophobia reflect the differing experiences of the two cultures with the phenomenon. Mainstream Americans – that is, white Americans – experience xenophobia as a flaw carried by certain of their compatriots that has an unfortunate effect on other, weaker groups such minorities and foreigners. To Israeli Jews, xenophobia is a force in the world by which other, stronger groups victimize the Jews.

That makes the challenge of combating xenophobia among Jews and Israelis all the more difficult. Before discussing how to fight it, Jews must first recognize that the tables have been turned, at least partly, and that the evil that others inflicted on us for so long, we now have the power to inflict on others.

Let's look at a passage from a lesser known rabbinic text: "Foreigners and masturbators delay the Messiah.... Foreigners are as troublesome to the Jewish people as a skin disease, as it is written, 'And they attached themselves to the house of Jacob'" (Minor Tractates, *Kallah Rabbati* 2:5). Prejudices and generalizations undoubtedly exist in the Bible and traditional texts, because they are human and we aren't unique. The biblical laws and testimonies don't show evidence of genuinely positive attitudes toward foreigners. On the contrary, their standard inclusion in lists of the helpless – "the poor, the orphan, the stranger and the widow" – is evidence of ongoing discrimination. Poverty can be temporary, widowhood is accidental and orphanhood is limited by age, but foreignness is forever.

It's true that memory fades with the passing of years and generations, but there doesn't seem to be a statute of limitations on reminding the descendants of immigrants where they came from. That's why the tradition needs to bring an opposing norm, drawn from the Torah's numerous references to strangers: "Rabbi Eliezer said: Why did the Torah warn in thirty-six places, and some say forty-six places, about the stranger? Because of the biblical verse, 'You shall not afflict or oppress the stranger, for you were strangers in the land of Egypt'? Rabbi Natan said: If you have a flaw, do not tell your fellow, as the rabbis said: One whose relative was hanged should not say to a servant or one of the household, go and string me up a fish, because the very idea of cord is now a sensitive topic" (Babylonian Talmud, *Bava Metzia* 59b). That is, don't bring up rope in the home of a hanged person. There are Jewish minorities living in tense places. Therefore, don't go running off to hang a foreigner, lest they hang our fellow Jews living as minorities. If it weren't for the Egyptian Pharaoh's respect for the foreigner, Joseph would not have become what he became and we would not have been saved the way we were, either individually or collectively.

Over the years the notion of the *ger*, the biblical word for foreigner, has evolved. Once it meant a stranger who came to live in foreign surroundings. Today it refers to a person who has changed his religion. The change is related in part to the deep change in the self-definition of the Jewish people, from a nation bound by territory to a people bound by faith and identity. But despite this most fundamental change, there has been no change, unfortunately, in our attitude toward others who join us. Not everyone understood back then – nor does everyone understand today, for that matter – the danger of interpreting the concept of "chosen people" as a genetic notion. Over the generations, some of our lesser Jewish minds have lost sight of the radically daring idea that ethnic racism could be averted by the easily available tools of conversion and affiliation. Some of our number still believe that we are commanded to fear gentiles, to resist the conversion of loving wives, to relate to the convert as a blemish and to conversion as though it were a treatment for some sort of leprous blister. The convert is essentially a leper in their eyes.

We offer them another traditional text that was written in the distant past but still holds quite true: "The rabbis ruled that when a stranger comes to be converted in our time, he should be addressed in this manner: What did you see that brought you to convert? Do you know that the Jewish people is afflicted, oppressed, torn apart and filled with suffering? If he says: I know, and I am not worthy, he is to be accepted at once" (Babylonian Talmud, *Yevamot* 47a).

The foreigner and immigrant can be a source of enrichment, stimulation and motivation to the society that receives him, as long as he is fully prepared to share the destiny of his adopted home. Ruth the Moabite framed the obligations of the newcomer in just the right order when she made her pledge to her mother-in-law Naomi: first of all, "where thou lodgest, I will lodge"; after that, "thy people shall be my people," and only after that, if at all, "thy God, my God" (Ruth 1:16). That's how Egypt behaved when it took Joseph in, thousands of years ago this week, and in so doing saved itself from famine. That was the trade-off for the ancient tribe of Judah when it accepted Ruth the Moabite, and received David and his line in return. Could the same be said of us today?

Foreign Regimes and Political Prisoners

THIS WEEK'S PORTION, *Miketz*, is a portion of dreams: two dreams of Pharaoh, the effective fulfillment of the chief butler's dream (Gen. 39:9–11) and of course the fulfillment of Joseph's dreams. His brothers bow down before him, just as he had predicted years earlier, and his sheaf stands tall in Pharaoh's palace (Gen. 37:6). Perhaps it is from here, at the end of the story, that the sameness of his dreams is derived. The dream of the sheaves hints at his future economic success, while the dream of the sun, moon and stars (Gen. 37:9) foreshadows his role in the saving of this planet known as earth. But the dreams are a colorful background to other matters. The real story hidden within these family anecdotes, in my opinion, is the place of Egypt in the Hebrew national consciousness. Despite our prayerbook's incessant indictment of Egypt, "the house of bondage," there is a fascination with Egypt, deep in our collective consciousness, that never goes away. Egypt is more than just a neighbor of Israel, a turbulent Middle Eastern state whose best days are behind it. Egypt is place both geographical and conceptual, located both southwest of Israel and deep within the Jewish soul. We'll try to visit that place by exploring this week's portion.

The tales of Joseph close the circle of the Book of Genesis. In just a few pages the family saga ends and the Book of Exodus begins. From then on, almost every story in the Torah takes place on the grand stage of collective Jewish memory. As such, the Joseph cycle is a good transition from the personal and intimate to the august and historical. What's more, Joseph nicely rounds out the origin tales of Genesis. The Book of Genesis began in the majestic kingdom of God and moved quickly to the Garden of Eden, the initial home of the designated master of creation. From there things run rapidly downhill. We encounter small stories, sometimes even petty ones, like that of Sarah and Hagar, the daughters of Lot, with their nighttime indecencies, that of the feuding between Jacob and his father-in-law Lot and so on. Gradually, however, amidst the fragments of personal tragedy, the story rises up again and enters another august kingdom, Egypt. The book opens with God, the king of the universe, and ends with the king of Egypt, who thinks he is a god. The contours are similar, but they're worth a brief review. The divine landscape of the Garden Eden is a scene of rivers flowing out of Eden, while the Egyptian landscape features one great river, the Nile. The snake is the most visible house pet in the opening story, while the Egyptian episode ends with Moses's staff, a simple shepherd's pole that he "cast…on the ground, and it became a serpent" (Exod. 4:3). There are many more parallels, but these are enough for now.

At this point we can just as easily refer to the Joseph stories as the Egypt stories. Here again I return to my political commentary, because all of the mythologies mentioned in Genesis are an echo – sometimes thundering, at other times faint – of the struggles among the tribes over the kingship of Israel in later years. Likewise the story of the fugitive Joseph, the dreamer who became a visionary, who saved the civilized world of his day, is an indirect claim to the northern kingdom of Israel that relies heavily on his legacy. But the Joseph stories are much more than simply Israelite politics. They are the annals of the emergence of the Bible's concept of the state.

The land of Israel was always a bridge, a corridor between two landmasses and two civilizations. This is what gave it its importance throughout history. Its status is apparent in its unique ecology, its collection of plants, birds and land animals, a coming together of Asia, Africa and, to a lesser degree, Europe. Birds pass through Israel on their way from there to yonder. The armies of the great northern empires marched through Israel on their way to conquer Egypt, and the great battles where the pharaonic empire fought off invaders took place on the soil of Israel. Throughout history, whenever nations and empires fought for advantage, the decisive stronghold was always the crossroads. The political orientation of the ancient Israelites was torn throughout the generations between north and south. The tension was not unlike the debate in modern Israel in the early 1950s between advocates of a Soviet versus an American orientation. It was a bitter debate that tore families, movements and parties apart. The prophet Jeremiah, preaching in the sixth century before the current era, asked bluntly, "What hast thou to do in the way to Egypt, to drink the waters of Shihor? Or what has thou to do in the way to Assyria, to drink the waters of the River? (Jer. 2:18). Jeremiah argued for neutrality in the conflict between Assyria to the north and Egypt to the south, because taking either side would bring deadly enmity from the other.

In the end, the traditional sources saw Egypt as less dangerous than the powers to the north. The destroyers of both the southern kingdom of Judah and the northern kingdom of Israel came down from the north. It was from there and from them, the powers of the north, that evil always descended. And yet, somehow, we don't remember them for eternal ignominy in our prayers and holiday rituals. Unlike the empires of the north, Egypt repeatedly served as place of refuge for Israelite political fugitives. It was to Egypt that Abraham went to escape famine, and his life was saved. Jacob and his sons went to Egypt fleeing calamity, and they survived. Joseph was brought down to Egypt and rose to greatness. Jeroboam fled to Egypt and received political asylum from his persecutors, the kings of the house of David, and Solomon married the daughter of Pharaoh in order to stabilize his regional alliances. Why, we must ask, did our ancestors return again and again to the same Egypt from which they had fled after centuries of bitter slavery?

This week's portion, *Miketz*, offers some answers. Egypt was one of the cradles of ancient civilization. Egypt was a classic water culture. One of the traditional rabbinic interpretations of Egypt's Hebrew name, *Mitzrayim*, comes from the map: the broad expanses of desert to the east and west, and between them the narrow straits – *metzarim* – through which the Nile flows, watering the fertile strip called *Mitzrayim*. *Mitzrayim* for the slender *metzarim* hemmed in and protected by the vast, barren wilderness. The kingdoms of the north sat on wide open plains on which enemies were forever clashing as rivals, and kingdoms rose and fell, one after the other. The Assyrians, the Chaldeans, the Babylonians, the Persians, the Arameans and all the rest.

Egypt, by contrast, was the very model of stability. It was difficult to penetrate its desert defenses and nearly impossible to escape. Out of this splendid isolation an independent civilization arose, relying mainly on itself and its capabilities to supply all its needs. Everyone came to live along the waters of the Nile, "for they are our life and the length of our days," as the poet wrote. But how to prevent those living upstream from blocking or diverting the water, thereby imposing drought on the people living downstream, near the river delta and the seashore? Answer: create an organization and regulate the water. This was the birth of centralized government. Moreover, how do you transport the crops of Upper Egypt, near the river's headwaters in the south, down to Lower Egypt along the Mediterranean coast? Answer: on river barges.

Suddenly you have a state with a transportation system, docks, warehouses, passengers and traders moving up and down the length of the state and a technology sector developing new means of sailing. But the needs don't end there. The size of the fields needs to be surveyed, and so geometry and algebra are developed. Volume needs to be calculated for purposes of warehousing and shipping crops, and so the third dimension is introduced into our lives, along with means of measuring it. And if that isn't enough, there is still the law of interlocking canals by which irrigation water is brought from the river down below to the fields up above.

For many years Egypt was characterized not only by daring technological innovation and centralized government, but also by a highly developed economy. The Egyptian economy had economic institutions, a form of banking and other means of exchange alongside a royal monopoly on the central means of production, namely the land. In the words of the Book of Genesis: "And Joseph gathered up all the money that was found in the land of Egypt, and in the land of Canaan, for the corn which they had bought…and Joseph brought the money into Pharaoh's house…so Joseph bought all the land of Egypt for Pharaoh" (Gen. 47:14–20), along with the cattle, sheep and the rest of the assets.

The centralized kingdom on earth had its reflection in the upper kingdom where Egyptians pictured their gallery of gods. It shouldn't come as a surprise that the roles of the gods sound familiar to us. For instance, the sun god Aton, revered as the creator of all and father of the king, was elevated by Amenhotep IV to the status of sole deity, eliminating all the competing gods. Thus Aton became, in effect, the first monotheistic deity, "alone and unique in his oneness" (from the Yigdal hymn, by Rabbi Daniel Ben Yehuda). The victory of Aton is reminiscent of the battle of our one God over the gods of Egypt, as described in the Exodus story: "And against all the gods of Egypt I will execute judgments: I am the Lord" (Exod. 12:12, recited in the Passover Haggadah). Or as in the story of the miracle of the parting of the Red Sea: "Who is like unto thee, O Lord, among the mighty?" (Exod. 15:9, recited in daily prayers – the Hebrew text literally reads, "Who is like unto thee, O Lord, among the gods?") There was a contest, and our good and able God defeated the other gods. Moses, the prince of Egypt, might have been the religious importer who brought the Egyptian theologies he had learned in the Pharaoh's palace into Israelite law and the Torah of Sinai, thus cementing an eternal bond between Egypt and Israel as a bond between a surrogate mother to the child of her womb who is not really her child.

Our ancient weakness for Egypt stems also from the deep connections between our traditions, beliefs and rituals and their Egyptian source. It was not only the belief in the One that began to germinate in Egypt and was spread throughout the world by those departing Egypt, our ancestors. The golden calf, too, is an Egyptian god image. The Ark of the Covenant and the various vessels of the Tabernacle show considerable Egyptian influence. Even the faces of the cherubs on the front of the Ark, according to the testimony of the prophet Ezekiel, are those of an ox, lion and eagle, gods of Egypt. Scholars familiar with the structure of the ancient Egyptian priesthood and religious service say the roles of the Israelite high priest as well as the Temple priests and Levites can be traced to Egyptian precedents.

All these and more are folded into our portion. The content of this portion has to do with statecraft, but its character testifies to the deep cultural affinity binding ancient Israel and the patriarchs to Egypt. True, our ancestors were born in the north and married women from Haran and later local Canaanite women, but their minds were never far from the most important, interesting and influential power of its time, Egypt.

Is it any wonder that classic tales of so many liberation movements begin in distant prisons or detention camps, just like the story of Joseph in the Egyptian prison? Those who are low dream high; the immigrant succeeds by strength of will; the new can influence and change the old. They could dream, our ancient forefathers. Where would we be without their dreams? The prisoners are often the bridge between the oppressor nation and its oppressed subjects. In prison the captive learns the characteristics and weaknesses of his captor, gets to know him from the inside and internalizes all of his advantages. Afterwards all these experiences are melded into the dreams of freedom that are so natural to every prisoner, and you have the recipe for a Nelson Mandela or Andrei Sakharov, Feisal Husseini or Marwan Barghouti – prisoners who emerge from the pit and rise to the greatness of leadership, like Joseph.

Week 11

Vayigash – Then He Came Near

Genesis 44:18–47:27

Egyptian Priest and Hebrew Levite: Two Models of a Man of God

LADIES AND GENTLEMEN, the drama is at its peak. Joseph has been revealed to his brothers. This week's portion offers the reader new tears, old fears, suppressed anger and outbursts of emotion. This play has everything. Years of estrangement end in one moment of recognition. Just a closed room, no one there but him and his brothers: "And there stood no man with him, while Joseph made himself known unto his brethren" (Gen. 45:1). In the aftermath, when the hugs and kisses are barely done, Joseph mobilizes the Egyptian communication network at his disposal and in the first biblical publicity spin he leaks word of the historic meeting, "and the Egyptians heard, and the house of Pharaoh heard" (Gen. 45:2).

The great dramatic tearjerker largely distracts attention from the astounding economic process that Joseph has set in motion in Egypt. The Torah describes stage by stage how the pharaonic regime became centralized and absolutist. Joseph "gathered up all the money that was found in the land of Egypt, and in the land of Canaan" (Gen. 47:14). He collected all the livestock of Egypt in the king's stables, sheepsheds and cow barns; he established a state lands authority and "bought all the land of Egypt for Pharaoh" (Gen. 47:20). In the end the people themselves became his slaves in return for their rescue from the famine. Maybe it happened precisely the way it's told, and maybe not. But it certainly testifies to the deep connections between the history of capital and the development of government in the ancient world, as we discussed in last week's portion. The dependence on the river created a need for a strong, centralized government. This is one of the reasons why Egypt has been characterized for long periods of its history by governmental stability in a unitary state along the length of the fruitful, life-giving Nile.

In the midst of the Bible's fascinating documentation of the emergence of ancient Egypt and the secret of its centralized power is the following, almost incidental verse: "Only the land of the priests bought he not, for the priests had a portion from Pharaoh, and did eat their portion which Pharaoh gave them; wherefore they sold not their land" (Gen. 47:22). The precise political reasons for the preservation of the priests' land and property are not important here. The point is that it is natural that a king would seek God's support and blessing for his aggressive actions; from that day to this it has been accepted as common knowledge that there is no quick way to God's heart that doesn't pass through the pockets of his priests. So it was then and so it is today. But the implications of this verse for us are extremely interesting.

In many senses, Moses founded the religion of Moses and Israel as an alternative to the teachings and beliefs of Egypt. In Egypt our God fought against the gods of Egypt, overcame them and brought his people out of the house of bondage in the narrow space, the *metzarim* between the deserts. But on his way out, Moses had to make a few deals. He gave Aaron the priesthood, meaning responsibility for the rituals and the income from the sacrifices. And Aaron, who had grown up as a slave in Egypt, had never fully internalized the power of the idea of the Exodus from Egypt. His body left Egypt, but Egypt never left his soul and his imagination. He, like the people, never stopped thinking about the place of origin. The people remembered the Egyptian fleshpot. Aaron, too, retained a few memories from there.

It's not surprising that at the moment of truth, when it seemed as though Moses's oversight had been removed and the people, homesick for Egypt, demanded of him, "Up, make us a god" (Exod. 32:1), he would proceed to make them a calf – that is, an image from the Egyptian pantheon. It seems likely that this was the priesthood for which he truly yearned. The calf was probably a concrete expression of Aaron's hidden longings for a priesthood of splendor, status, grandeur, political influence and property, like the priests of Egypt whom he might well have known up close. This is one of the earliest traces of evidence of what is known as the Stockholm syndrome, in which people held captive by strangers develop an empathy and emotional identification with the narrative and behavior of their captors. This syndrome arises from the desire to identify with the powerful.

In contrast to the others, Moses tries to present a model of a different life: the Levite who is not a priest. The Bible is filled with internal contradictions on the question of who is a Levite. Is the Levite a priest, or a separate, independent identity? Today it's sufficient to note that at this early stage in the biblical narrative, there is not yet a decision. It took a process of many years' duration for the separate identities and duties of the Cohen, Levi and common Israel to coalesce. There is no final decision, but there are certain broad guidelines. It emerges, so it seems to me, that there were priests who descended from Aaron and tried their best to resemble the priesthood with which they were familiar. Just as our ancestors took the monarchy from the nations around them, so the models of ritual and priesthood were adopted from neighboring peoples and sanctuaries.

In contrast to the Egyptian priesthood, which stood above the Egyptian people in property and estrangement and didn't share the people's enslavement and daily hardships, and in contrast to the priesthood of Aaron barricaded in its desert Tabernacle and its walled-off sanctuaries in Jerusalem, Moses put forth the model of the Levite. Moses tried to preserve the people's original spirit, the one that hadn't been crushed during the centuries of Egyptian slavery. This was a spirit that had not assimilated or conformed, but stayed true to its roots while waiting for the redemption that would allow it to reawaken and return to center stage. It is the spirit of the eternal wanderer, the stranger, the Other, the challenger, always fertilizing and enriching its environment. It is the Levite who does not share an estate or patrimony like the other tribes of Israel, but remains untethered, symbolizing the perpetually restless Jewish spirit that moves from Egypt to Israel and beyond.

When I consider the countless recollections of Egypt in the Jewish consciousness, I often think about the fact that Moses wanted us to remember the independence of spirit and identity that we maintained there, not just the brutality of our Egyptian slave-masters. Aaron wanted to be a Hebrew-speaking Egyptian priest, propertied and land owning. There was a danger hovering above Aaron and his Tabernacle priests of turning into an entrenched religious establishment, rigid and hidebound. That was how it had been in Egypt, and that was how it was to be in the Promised Land. Moses rebelled against the priests of his adopted father, Pharaoh, and no less against those of his spineless elder brother. Moses was a wilderness leader. That was his faith. And the model of the Levite as a man of God that he crafted was a reflection of his character.

When Moses inserted the verse about the priests' land holdings (Gen. 47:22) into this week's portion about Joseph, he was essentially saying, I don't want to be like this. These are priests of enslavement and oppression. I am interested in Levites of empathy and solidarity. Moses was looking to create religious leaders whose natural surroundings were in the company of those who needed them most, with the orphan and widow, the stranger and outsider, among the homeless and landless like the Levites themselves. Hence the verse in the Book of Deuteronomy, Moses's own book, that captures more than any other the inner core of the Levite type: "And thou shalt rejoice before the Lord thy God, thou, and thy son, and thy daughter, and thy man-servant, and thy maid-servant, and the Levite that is within thy gates, and the stranger, and the fatherless, and the widow, that are in the midst of thee, in the place which the Lord thy God shall choose to cause his name to dwell there" (Deut. 16:11).

This is the spirit toward which Judaism is meant to aspire. Over the generations the tribe of Levi became the teacher of Torah and imparter of the law. These two are the most dynamic pillars in the evolution of Jewish culture: constant educational reform and ongoing judicial activism. Throughout the long generations of the Jewish dynamic, most generations belonged to Moses; only a few were periods of Aaron. You can judge for yourselves which type defines our time. Are we a generation of Moses and the Levites, identifying with the hardships of the weak who are within our gates and in our midst, or closed off and denying like the priests of Aaron – and of Pharaoh?

Rachel and Leah, Joseph and Judah

THERE ARE STORIES OF THE ORDINARY and there are tales of peak intensity. The latter capture a decisive moment and present the hidden that encapsulates everything. "Then Judah came near unto him" (Gen. 44:18) is one of those moments. The biblical story wanders along to its own beat, sometimes slowly, sometimes quickly. The biblical language matches the rhythm, a language of verbs rather than adjectives or names. Sometimes nine months can be packed into a single phrase, "And she conceived, and bore..." (Gen. 4:17; 21:2; 38:3), and at other times an entire human history is hidden within a few words: "These twenty years have I been in thy house: I served thee fourteen years for thy two daughters, and six years for thy flock..." (Gen. 31:41). This week's portion travels in the fast lane, the more so since it is devoted to a description of a specific event. And we? Our job is to wipe away the tears, to peel away the layers and find the deeper story hiding beneath the brief description of that moment in the palace: "Then Judah came near unto him."

In my mind's eye I can see the reception chamber of the king's viceroy. He stands over here, tall and majestic, dressed in royal garments, surrounded by his servants, officers and courtiers. And they stand over there, perhaps still bedraggled from their trip, dusty and smelling of sweat. And then in one instant, driven by pure instinct, Judah breaks away from his brothers and steps forward. He did not rush; he "came near," stepping firmly but not heavily, so as not to seem threatening to the kingdom and its lofty official. Before this significant step there was a sharp-edged conversation between Joseph and his brothers, and before the conversation came Joseph's crafty manipulation. The brothers had come back to Egypt for food. Joseph gave them what they came for, but also hid a silver goblet in Benjamin's saddlebag.

The brothers set out contented, satisfied with the bread in their basket. But alas, at an inn along the highway a rider catches up with them, a messenger sent by Joseph, and he discovers the "theft" and brings them back in humiliation as escaped prisoners to the house of the viceroy. There Joseph, still hiding his true identity, lashes out at them: "And Joseph said unto them: 'What deed is this that ye have done? Know ye not that such a man as I will indeed divine?'" (Gen. 44:15). When Joseph says "such a man as I" he means one thing but they hear something else entirely. They naturally hear what all Egypt knows, that "such a man as I" means the sort of man who understands the secrets of the occult, interprets dreams and understands human nature – a leader who rose to greatness by dint of his command of supernatural forces. A man who has powers at his command that are not available to an ordinary human. Joseph, on the other hand, means something utterly different. When Joseph says "such a man as I" he is thinking of himself and his mother's legacy. Remember several portions back how Laban chased after Jacob and his retinue? Remember how he rummaged through their tents (Gen. 31:33) searching for his stolen household gods? Who was it that stole the gods and kept them from being found? Why, Rachel, of course. Rachel, the mother of the annoying Joseph and of Benjamin, the accused thief. Joseph is really speaking in the language of his parents: Jacob, who stole his brother's birthright, and Rachel, who stole her father's gods. He himself has defined his own personal history in terms of theft, "For indeed I was stolen away out of the land of the Hebrews" (Gen. 40:15), and he is speaking that same private language with Benjamin, his one full brother.

And just as Joseph is carrying on his mother Rachel's dialogue with his brother Benjamin, half-brother Judah is replying in the practical, down-to-earth language of his mother Leah. His mother is the one who traded conjugal rights with Jacob in return for the mandrake flowers that Reuben had gathered in the field. Her son Judah is no less practical than she: he's looking for a deal to get out of a sticky situation.

What, then, is the legacy of Rachel, she who died in childbirth? The Midrash, as we have discussed, doesn't really forgive her for her deviousness. A plain reading of the text presents her as history's third thief (together with the daughters of Lot). Still, there is more to Rachel than that. The legacy of Joseph and Rachel is the ancient embodiment of our people's split personality. Many years after her time, when the columns of exiles and captives march in chains out of the northern kingdom into captivity and exile at the time of the fall of the First Temple, there will be a woman who will stand by the side of the road and weep for them. Someone will mourn inconsolably. "A voice is heard in Ramah, lamentation and bitter weeping, Rachel weeping for her children; she refuseth to be comforted for her children, because they are not" (Jer. 31:15). Who are these children of hers? Rachel bore two children, Joseph and Benjamin, and then died (Gen. 35:19). As history tells it, ancient Israel was destroyed in two stages. First to fall was the kingdom of Israel, with its capital in Samaria, in the year 722 BCE. The second was the kingdom of Judah in 586 BCE. That is, first the kingdom of her son Joseph fell, and then her son Benjamin too was taken into exile with the fall of the kingdom of Judah, of which the tribe of Benjamin was a part

When the prophet spoke of the "voice…heard in Ramah," one could obviously interpret it as an actual voice crying out, loud and bitter. It's better, though, to look first at the facts to see what Jeremiah had in mind. Jeremiah knew the country and its topography very well, and when he spoke he was thinking of a place known as Ramah, or "high place." (This might be the modern Palestinian village of Al-Ram, north of Jerusalem on the main road that winds north from Hebron to Bethlehem, to Jerusalem and then on to Ramah. Or perhaps it refers to Ramallah, "God's high place," referring to the hilly plateau surrounding it.) But how do we know that the prophet is speaking of a high place and not a high sound? Because it says so several chapters later in the same Book of Jeremiah: "The word which came to Jeremiah from the Lord, after that Nebuzaradan, the captain of the guard, had let him go from Ramah, when he had taken him being bound in chains among all the captives of Jerusalem and Judah, that were carried away captive unto Babylon" (Jer. 40:1). Here it is, spelled out: Ramah was a prison camp, a concentration camp, out of which the convoys of prisoners were sent into exile, with Jeremiah among them.

The inner connection between the cry of the bereft mother standing alongside her descendants watching them depart into exile and the Joseph stories in the Book of Genesis finds expression in the words used to tell the two stories. Jeremiah was sent from Ramah, which is on the main road that runs through Jerusalem, Bethlehem and Hebron. Joseph began his long journey south to Egypt with a brief trip northward along that same road, sent from Hebron by his father to find his brothers with their flocks near Shechem (Gen. 37:14). That road runs along the ridge, connecting the Judean Hills to the Hills of Samaria; it is the road of exiles, connecting Joseph, the first exile, to Jeremiah, the final exile. Afterwards, of course, Joseph's brothers abuse him and sell him into slavery, then dip his coat of many colors in the blood of a slaughtered goat and bring it to their father to convince him that Joseph is "without doubt torn into many pieces" (Gen. 37:33). What did Jacob do then? He "mourned for his son many days" and "refused to be comforted" (Gen. 37:34–35).

Jacob refuses to be comforted over his son; Rachel, weeping at Jeremiah's prophesy, likewise refuses to be comforted. This is truly a conversation between spouses, Jacob and Rachel, who use the same language across the abyss of time that separates the era of the patriarchs from the prophesy of exile.

The ending is all tears of joy: "Then Joseph could not restrain himself before all them that stood by him.... And he wept aloud; and the Egyptians heard, and the house of Pharaoh heard" (Gen. 45:1–2). Rachel, standing alongside the highway, is comforted from her weeping by God, speaking through the prophet: "Refrain thy voice from weeping, and thine eyes from tears" (Jer. 31:16). Such a weepy family. The cries of Rachel and Joseph are well connected, tears diluted with more tears: the tears of Joseph's exile in Egypt and the tears of the people leaving their ravaged land for a hard, cruel exile; the tears of relief when Joseph reveals himself to his brothers and the tears of the mother's comfort at the greatness promised for them and us when they return from exile – "There is hope for thy future, saith the Lord; and thy children shall return to their own border" (Jer. 31:17).

Week 12

Vayechi – And He Lived

Genesis 47:28–50:26

The End of the Story

I LOVE THE HUMOR THAT SOMETIMES TWINKLES in the names we give the weekly portions. For example, I find it delightful that the portion in which the Ten Commandments appear, establishing the basic law of the Jewish people, is named after the high priest of Midian, Jethro. Another example is the portion in which Abraham arrives in the Promised Land, which is known by a phrase that means the very opposite of arrival: *Lech Lecha* (Get Thee Out). This week's portion, *Vayechi* (And He Lived), deserves a place of honor in this category of biblical irony. On this Sabbath Jacob dies. He returns his soul to his creator and is gathered to his fathers. Jacob's death is quite final, unlike King David or the Lubavitcher Rebbe. What else could a portion dealing with such an illustrious death be called but "And He Lived"?

Jacob's departure from this world and return to the dust of the earth is particularly impressive. It raises many thoughts about death and separation and the proper, honorable way to go about achieving them. Jacob calls Joseph, his leading and best-loved son, and makes him swear that he won't bury him in Egypt. Apparently he has had his fill of exiles and wanderings between the kingdoms of the north and the kingdom of Egypt. He wants his eternal resting place to be where his forefathers lay. He blesses Joseph and his other sons, using the emotional moment as an opportunity to offer a last-minute explanation for the rushed and undignified burial of Rachel along the highway. After blessing his grandchildren he gathers his sons, blesses most of them and curses Reuben, Simeon and Levi. After assigning the blessings Jacob dies, is embalmed and is dispatched with a royal funeral, which ends in a kingly procession from Egypt to the family burial place in Hebron. In this portion, however, what's left unsaid is much more interesting than what is said. The following paragraphs are directed toward that mystery.

Two questions linger in the background of the story – one immediately evident, the other less obvious. The first question concerns Joseph. The adult Joseph, in his later years of power and authority, is portrayed as good, forgiving and merciful. If that were the case, if he were so kind-hearted and forgiving, why didn't Joseph bring his father and brothers to Egypt as soon as he had left prison and risen to power? Why didn't he at least send a sign of life to his worried father? The second question that bothers me is what happened in that emotional reunion between Joseph and his father Jacob? Who spoke and who was silent? What was said and what was left unsaid?

To answer these two questions, which are not raised explicitly in the text, much less answered, we need to ask one more question. Everyone in the house of Jacob went down to Egypt: Reuben and Simeon and all the rest, even little Benjamin. Everyone died in Egypt. That much is spelled out explicitly: "And Joseph died, all his brethren, and all that generation" (Exod. 1:6). If so, why did all of them remain buried in Egypt except for Joseph? In a few more weeks, in the portion known as *Parashat Beshalach*, we will read the following: "And Moses took the bones of Joseph with him; for he had straitly sworn the children of Israel, saying: 'God will surely remember you; and ye shall carry up my bones away hence with you'" (Exod. 13:19).

Two hundred ten years after the oath that closes this week's portion – "And Joseph took an oath of the children of Israel…'and ye shall carry up my bones from hence'" (Gen. 50:25) – Moses executes that final testament. Here we have the children of Israel leaving Egypt in haste on Passover night with a heavy Egyptian sarcophagus in tow, bearing the mummified body of Joseph. They wander in the desert for forty years, carrying the sarcophagus every step of the way. In effect, the desert wanderings of the children of

Israel bear the weight of two burdensome crates: one containing Joseph's bones and the other containing the tablets of the law, as well as the shards of the first, broken tablets. They are wandering between the broken tablets and the dry bones.

Why only Joseph? Did the other brothers not charge their children to gather their bones? Why not? Why isn't this so much as hinted at in the scripture? And if the brothers did leave such a charge, why weren't their bones taken along? In other words, why was Joseph carried up out of Egypt after his death while his brothers remained below, buried in Egypt?

Now let's return to the earlier questions. I think Joseph never told Jacob anything about what happened in that pit in Dothan on the day he was sold. He had managed to turn that enormous trauma into a divine blessing. True, it took him years to overcome his anger, shock and hatred. It took him long years to cleanse his system of the lingering resentment and rejection. He managed to create a new dynamic of reunion only once he felt himself truly able to say to them, "Be not grieved, nor angry with yourselves, that ye sold me hither; for God did send me before you to preserve life…to give you a remnant on the earth, and to save you alive…. So now it was not you that sent me hither, but God" (Gen. 45:5–8). If Joseph and his brothers had met earlier, when he was still consumed with anger, we all would have suffered the curse of the prophet Obadiah: "And the house of Jacob shall be a fire, and the house of Joseph a flame…and they shall kindle in them, and devour them" (Obad. 1:18). Only once he has rediscovered his faith in the good can he return home, or, more precisely, bring his home back to him. I see Joseph as the ultimate believer in the faith of Genesis. Of all the characters in the tales of Genesis, he is the one who learns to believe in forgiveness, the son of the Father of Mercy and not a fanatic follower of the God of Vengeance. Only then, as a new man, could he return to his family and his roots.

The conversations between father and son are all filled with personal details. Jacob is ready to die of sheer happiness. He apologizes for the hasty burial of Rachel. They speak about the future of the grandchildren and arrangements for the funeral: "Bury me not, I pray thee, in Egypt" (Gen. 47:29). Jacob does most of the talking, while Joseph says hardly a word.

He simply doesn't reveal anything. It's hard for anyone reading this today to believe such a thing would be possible, and apparently it was hard for his brothers, too. They don't know what was said and what was left out in all those conversations, and once Jacob is dead, they're afraid they're about to face Joseph's revenge: "It may be that Joseph will hate us, and will fully requite us all the evil which we did unto him" (Gen. 50:15). And so they come up with another cover story, telling Joseph that Jacob had left word to forgive "the transgression of thy brethren" (Gen. 50:17). Once they had lied to Jacob about Joseph; now they are lying to Joseph about Jacob. But Joseph has already moved on. He's found wholeness and serenity, and so he reassures them, "Fear not, for am I in the place of God? And as for you, ye meant evil against me; but God meant it for good, to bring to pass, as it is this day, to save much people alive" (Gen. 50:19–20).

Along with anger, Joseph has learned to conquer a few other negative and childish character traits. His brothers had betrayed him because he had betrayed them, "and Joseph brought evil report of them unto their father" (Gen. 37:2). As a youngster he was a tattletale. They couldn't even speak to him calmly, and so they rid themselves of him in a shocking act of domestic abuse. When Joseph grew up, he came to understand his own role, his share of responsibility for his misfortune, and he did everything he could to change. Interestingly, the process of taking his own measure and recalibrating his instincts has a numerical quality: the text speaks of Joseph "being seventeen years old" (Gen. 37:2) at the beginning of this cycle, when he had his fateful clash with his brothers, and ends by telling us that "Jacob lived in the land of Egypt seventeen years" (Gen. 47:28). So it is, measure for measure: it took Joseph seventeen years to become the damaged person his brothers sent to Egypt, and seventeen years to measure up at last in his father's eyes and prove that he had changed.

He fought against that malicious instinct, and when he had won that inner battle with himself he came into his own. Despite his emotional struggles he did not tell his father the real tale he could have told about his brothers and what happened by the pit. He had become an adult devoid of malice, no longer spreading rumors or lashing out at others. Compare this to Abraham, who banished one son and bound the other to an altar;

to Isaac, who hurt both his sons by confusing their blessings; or to Jacob, who remained at odds with Levi, Simeon, Reuben and the others until the day he died. Joseph had become, almost as God is described in the Yom Kippur prayer, a pardoner in Israel and forgiver among the tribes of Jeshurun.

This week's portion closes another linguistic-literary cycle. When Joseph's brothers "took him, and cast him into the pit" (Gen. 37:24), they were literally executing a downward motion. Then they sold him to a passing caravan of merchants, and "Joseph was brought down to Egypt" (Gen. 39:1). His entire journey from his father's house to Pharaoh's palace was a process of descent, lower and lower. But once he overcame his inner demons he could begin an upward journey, until he could finally tell the children of Israel to "carry up my bones" to his final resting place in the land of Israel, a place always seen as a height to ascend, regardless of the physical altitude where the journey began. The brothers, by contrast, never managed to conquer their compulsions, their instincts for lying and quarreling. They went down to Egypt and stayed down. They couldn't extricate themselves from their black hole, and so they were buried in it, in the empty pit within themselves. They had tried to lower him into oblivion, but he raised himself back up and so he lives on. They, on the other hand, kept themselves momentarily aboveground at the mouth of the pit in Dothan, but in the end they disappeared into the oblivion of their Egyptian graves and the pit they had dug in their own souls. The pit is always within us; it's up to us to decide whether to stay down there or lift ourselves up.

Freedom and Slavery – Introduction

*P*ARASHAT *V*AYECHI ENDS the first of the five books of the Torah. It's a book filled with personal anecdotes, quite a few human oddities and a great many human flaws. There are many lines crisscrossing the book's surface, including sagas of dysfunctional family, rulers and ruled, heroines and concubines, banishments and reconciliations. Another fundamental theme constantly present in the book is the birth of the most chronic of all Jewish characteristics: otherness. The very first command the newly revealed God gives to Abraham, the prince of faith, was to get out of "there." The place where God is revealed cannot be the place where God's word is spread, and so God decides to remove Abraham from the place he grew up: "Get thee out." Like father, like son: Isaac was a stranger to the people of Gerar, as was Jacob in Haran and Joseph through all his adventures in Egypt.

The lesson is clear: always go beyond the existing and the known. Never stay put and rest on what has already been achieved. Push the envelope, spread the faith far and wide, and when you come to a new place, shake things up until they change, and then move on. In the next book, the Book of Exodus, Moses will try to continue the magic. Until his last moment he will try to stretch the personal capacities of the leaders and founders of the Jewish nation and turn them into the characteristics of a fully-fledged people – a people that feels it belongs only when it is a stranger.

Beyond the general themes of the book that come together in this final portion, there is also the personal story of Jacob and his family. Jacob leaves the stage of history, accompanied by all his sons. The character portraits of each tribe sketched out by their father Jacob on his deathbed add up to a multifaceted, large-scale family and national collective. But all this was preceded by the dying Jacob's private, one-on-one conversation with his best-loved son, the firstborn of his beloved Rachel, Joseph. At the end of their final private moment together, after Jacob has enjoined Joseph that he "bury me not, I pray thee, in Egypt" (Gen. 47:29), he bows to his son: "Israel bowed down upon the bed's head" (Gen. 47:31). Strange, isn't it? We would expect Joseph to bow his head in respect to his father one last time. We might also guess that Joseph would fall on his father's shoulder and weep the way he wept when he revealed himself to his brothers and when he had his first, emotional reunion with his aged father who had come down to Egypt. But somehow, on this final day, Joseph's tears had dried up.

This role reversal at the moment of farewell is a mystery that calls for an explanation. Looking at this final homage paid by the dying father to the king's viceroy, the Babylonian Talmud says this: "When you meet a fox in his prime, bow down to him" (Babylonian Talmud, *Megillah* 16b). This

Vayechi

is biblical politics at its finest. The first rule of survival is to bow the head before the current ruler. And if a new ruler takes his place? We'll bow to him. That's how to survive.

Is the idea of the "fox in his prime" stabilizing or subversive? Does it mean deference to every sovereign, following the Talmudic dictum, "the law of the kingdom is the law," or does it imply a constant ferment that doesn't genuinely respect the authority of the regime and is merely waiting out the storm? In my opinion, it's both. The idea of showing deference to the ruling authorities has deep roots in Jewish ethical and political thinking. The sages of the Mishnah, writing in *Pirkei Avot* (Ethics of the Fathers), were clear that human society cannot survive without a central governing authority to organize and enable. Emblematic of that view is the saying of Rabbi Hanina, quoted in the Vatican manuscript of the thirteenth-century scholar Rabbi Yonah of Girona as saying, "Pray for the peace of the government, for were it not for the fear of it, we should have swallowed each other alive" (Mishnah *Avot* 3:2). Man by himself is an egotistical creature, and only government can bring order to the relations between one selfish person and another. Under this approach, government is a social necessity of the highest order. No one expressed this view more memorably than Thomas Hobbes in the dedication of his 1651 work, *De Cive* (Regarding the polity): "Man to Man is an arrant Wolfe," or as modern commentators put it, "Man is a wolf to man."

The opposite view – that one must bow one's head to the ruling authority, but not take it too seriously – has equally deep roots. The current ruler may be a fox, but only a temporary one. Humankind is born in freedom and should never give up its independence except in pursuit of some temporary, tactical end. Lowering the head can be a practical measure, a display of flexibility like the bulrushes show beside a riverbank when they bow in the face of a passing wind and then straighten up again.

The relationship between Jacob and Joseph in Egypt at that particular moment is not merely a human encounter, unusual and touching as it may be. It goes to the heart of our own relationship with government – any government. On the one hand, it reveals absolute lack of faith in the sovereign dominion of one person over another, since "you are servants to me, not servants to other servants" (Babylonian Talmud, *Kiddushin* 22b). On the other hand, it shows the understanding that limits are needed to the anarchistic impulse to rebel against all human authority. It could be that Jacob bowed his head before Joseph in sincere acceptance of royal authority. It could also be that Jacob lowered his head nonchalantly, while his true feelings were closer to those of Mordecai of Shushan, who would not bow to Haman or any man (Esth. 3:2). Judaism is in constant tension between these two poles. At one pole is a constant desire to challenge fixed authority, because unmoving authority means slow decay of the spirit. At the opposite pole is a never-ending dream of a kingdom that will finally give solid ground to a people as impermanent as a sand dune, as footloose as Abraham, shaped and reshaped like Jacob by every passing breeze – the Jewish people that dreams of dwelling in peace like our aged father Jacob, who passes from the world in this week's portion.

Encore

Genesis

THE BOOK OF GENESIS begins with vast, mythic stories of creation and concludes with simple, inward-looking human stories about families and individuals, and their lives, loves and hatreds. The unsophisticated reader finds pleasure reading the book, then returning to it again and again. For countless generations, readers have looked to Genesis as a chronological narrative of factual events, stories of actual, historical fathers and sons. Abraham begat Isaac, who begat Jacob. Jacob had twelve sons, the fathers of the tribes of Israel, and their sister Dinah, all of them the offspring of the one father and his four wives and concubines. The more sophisticated reader accepts these stories, but not at face value. For him, the characters in the drama of Genesis are archetypes representing various strains of humanity – good and bad, honest and malevolent, devious and straightforward. They are intimately mingled together in a human tapestry within which each of us in every generation can find ourselves portrayed.

Still, how might we trace the contours of this book and its tales? The simple thread is the family saga. Here we find a very human, everyday portrayal of a large patriarchal clan. The narrator seems to be telling us through these stories to look past their pettiness to see their greatness, to learn as they did to overcome daily trivialities. Others will prefer to read between the lines to find the biblical narrators' unceasing criticism of personality cults of any sort. There is no person or creature of nature to whom we may attribute godlike qualities or shackle our spirits. This piercing, unending criticism of the nation's leaders and founders is a part of our national vision of freedom, whose foundations rest on the soil of our lives in the Book of Genesis.

Another theme running through the stories of Genesis is the repeated echo of later Israelite politics and palace intrigue. The story of Judah and

Joseph foreshadows the confrontation between the kingdoms of Judah and Israel that would erupt centuries later on Mount Ephraim. Reuben's argument with the other brothers after the sale of Joseph is the first crack in the later rift between the tribes living west of the Jordan and the two and half tribes on the eastern bank. It's also possible to broaden this reading and turn the household disputes between two sons of Abraham, Isaac and Ishmael, into harbingers of the historic confrontation that continues to shed blood to this very day.

But because our concern is with human beings, in all their shame and glory, I think it's possible to identify character types by which to catalogue the heroes of Genesis. We can divide the characters of Genesis into archetypes, which we might term the Children of Abraham and the Children of Isaac. On the surface, we have before us a family whose children resemble each other and stand apart from the other residents of the land of Canaan. The Midrash and commentators emphasize the continuity of the family line, recalling the strikingly advanced ages of its centenarian progenitors and underscoring the strong physical resemblance of Isaac to Abraham (recall Rashi's comment on Gen. 25:19, cited in our chapter on *Vayeshev*, in which he cited the presumably facetious Midrash that God made Isaac's face resemble Abraham's to cover up the fact that Sarah had been impregnated by Abimelech). So if the son resembles the father and the elderly mother's pregnancy was apparent to all, the problem is presumably resolved. Nonetheless, the deeper character types, some of them visible only from a distance and with the passage of time, show us two essential human foundations underpinning the Genesis tales: the Abraham foundation and the Isaac foundation.

Who is Abraham? We looked at the person in *Parashat Lech Lecha* and explored his energetic personality. In his eighth decade he revealed God. He and his wife converted some associates to the new faith, smashed his father's idols, rebelled against the authority of King Nimrod and spread the message of monotheism. It's quite a list of accomplishments. Anybody else would have retired at this point, sat at home to savor his achievements, watched the results and enjoyed the honors due to people of such distinction. Anybody else, but not Abraham. No, he was the founder of the "get thee out" school, which teaches a philosophy of never-ending restlessness.

The Abrahamite never rests on his laurels. The moment he reaches his goal, his sights are set on the next mountain to conquer and the new challenges waiting on the other side. The Abrahamite is a radical, a revolutionary and a wanderer. He casts the seeds of his ideas wherever the wind will carry them. Eve, the first woman, was an Abrahamite by nature. She too was endlessly curious, forever daring, unable to stay inside the box. Eve could never take "no" as the final answer. It's possible that Abel was an innovator and explorer as he grazed flocks far over the fields. Nor should we forget our restless father Jacob. True, he couldn't stop complaining about what he described to Pharaoh as the "few and evil…days of the years of my life" (Gen. 47:9). And yet one cannot but be impressed at his travels, his discoveries and innovations, the worlds he saw and saw through. Likewise his son Joseph, who wandered in his imagination, stifled by the narrow world of his family encampment, somehow ended up as deputy to the king with the whole ancient world as his field of dreams.

The opposite of the Abrahamic model is the still, passive type that we might call Isaacate. The peak moment in Isaac's recorded career is his binding on the altar. We can never know exactly what happened there and why. We're left with nothing but dim memories and circumstantial evidence. The serving boys and the donkey were not present at the altar. Angels and divine voices don't visit us anymore. As such, we are left with those two, father and son, who swore themselves to silence. All we know of those terrible minutes is the binding itself. In a literal sense, we are told that Abraham tied his son physically to an altar.

Symbolically, however, Isaac remained bound for a long time afterward. He worked the land, planted and harvested, dug wells and tried to sink his roots ever deeper in the land that his father loved. Isaac was the only one of the patriarchs who never left the land of Israel. The Isaacate type sits at home, permanently fixed in place. The other type was free, without boundaries, but this type is bound, tied down, denied options. Cain the farmer was like Isaac before he was condemned to wander, and the freedom of his brother Abel, roaming over the fields with his flocks, appeared to him as a serious threat. Noah was another passive type, lacking initiative. Even Esau, for all his hunting, could not get beyond his home territory, unlike Jacob, who managed to flee, emigrate and wander. Likewise, Joseph's brothers were, in the final analysis, the stationary sort. They began by banishing the brother who looked too far afield and ended up buried somewhere in Egypt, in the land of Goshen. Joseph didn't stay with them; hundreds of years after his death he was still able to ensure that the children of Israel departing Egypt would take his bones with them. The Abrahamic has Abraham's energy even in death.

These basic character types in the Book of Genesis offer models on a much larger scale, for nations and kingdoms, cultures, histories and destinies. And with this we can leave the Book of Genesis, a book of individuals, and begin the book of nations, the Book of Exodus.

שמות
Exodus

Week 13

Shemot – Names

Exodus 1:1–6:1

The Creation of Man

THERE ARE CERTAIN RULES that I honestly don't understand in the way the Bible tells its stories. Every tale feels as though it has been told before, in a slightly different manner. Consider this story: in *Parashat Ki Tissa*, which will be read eight weeks after our current portion, Moses will come down from Mount Sinai radiant with joy. Something had stayed with him from all the thunder and lightning that surrounded him when he was atop Mount Sinai receiving the Law. "And he was there with the Lord forty days and forty nights…. And it came to pass, when Moses came down from Mount Sinai…that Moses knew not that the skin of his face sent forth beams while he talked with him…. And when Aaron and all the children of Israel saw Moses, behold, the skin of his face sent forth beams; and they were afraid to come nigh him" (Exod. 34:28–30). In order to avoid being completely cut off from the frightened people around him, he wrapped his head in a veil. He hid behind a mask that he removed only when he was in conversation with God.

There is indeed an original story about a shining apparition that frightens anyone who is not familiar with it. But the one we have just told is not it. In the remarkable story we just told, the voices are familiar from this week's portion, *Shemot*. True, there is a role reversal in *Shemot*. On Mount Sinai God will appear wrapped in fire and his words will come forth from the flames. But in the original version, in *Shemot*, when Moses first meets God in a bush, it is the fire that is radiating and Moses who is afraid. "Now Moses was keeping the flock of Jethro his father-in-law… and he came to the mountain of God, unto Horeb. And the angel of the Lord appeared unto him in a flame of fire out of the midst of a bush; and he looked, and, behold, the bush burned with fire, and the bush was not consumed.… And Moses hid his face, for he was afraid to look upon God" (Exod. 3:1–6). Moses, God, fire and the hiding of a face.

Similarly, the story of the sea that is parted by Moses during the Exodus from Egypt turns later on into the parting of the Jordan by Joshua (Josh. 3:15) and later still into the parting of the Jordan by the prophet Elijah (2 Kings 2:8) when he travels with Elisha to take his fateful ride to heaven in the fiery chariot, and once more by Elisha (2 Kings 2:14) when he returns without his master. Or perhaps it is a paradigm that reappears not just in biblical tales but throughout the historical narrative of the Jewish people to describe the parade of oppressors who rise up against us to kill us. To paraphrase the Passover Haggadah, in every generation one is required to see himself as if he himself had faced some oppressor who rose up against him to kill him. And each of these is a manifestation of Pharaoh in his various incarnations: Pharaoh himself, Amalek, Nebuchadnezzar, Sennacherib, Haman, Antiochus and all the rest that followed. In short, the tales of the Bible have a format of eternal return and borrowed motifs, recurring and moving forward at the same time with repetition and elaboration inextricably woven together. It's worth taking a moment to look at our portion through this prism to see what previous generations might have missed.

We have been taught from childhood to believe in the evolving human story: Adam, Noah, Abraham and his children, the tribes, Moses and so on down through history. And yet the reader's attention is almost never directed toward the structure of this week's portion, *Shemot*, which looks like a mirror image of *Parashat Bereshit*, the opening portion of Genesis. The line is not direct but subtle. In both of them, the same human and structural elements are at play. There is only one difference: if what happens in *Bereshit* is final, the events in *Shemot* are only the beginning. What do I mean?

The Book of Genesis begins with a mighty effort by the creator of the universe to bring a new order to the world. The previous world order doesn't appeal to him. And the king of the universe rose up and reorganized the unformed void that had characterized it until that moment of beginning. The Book of Exodus begins the same way. Thus spake the god of Egypt, who went by the name of Pharaoh: come, let us reorganize the social structure of our world and bring order to the unformed demographic void of Egypt. And the new Pharaoh, who saw himself and was seen by his people as both king and god, began to impose harsh decrees on the tribes of Israel, who "were fruitful, and increased abundantly, and multiplied, and waxed exceeding mighty; and the land was filled with them" (Exod. 1:7). So, too, both stories have rivers at their center: four rivers in the first story – the Pishon, Gihon, Tigris and Euphrates (Gen. 2:10–14) – and a single river, the Nile, in the second story. In both stories there is a great expulsion. Adam and the human race are expelled from the Garden of Eden, and Moses and the Hebrews are expelled from Egypt. In both stories there are pivotal murders that change the course of destiny: the murder of Abel by Cain, the murder of the infant boys by Pharaoh's henchmen (Exod. 1:22) and the murder of the Egyptian by Moses, the prince of Egypt (Exod. 2:12). In both places the killers, Cain and Moses, had the privilege of establishing the human civilization of the succeeding generations.

Looming over all these things is the most important element of all – the woman. In the Book of Genesis it is our mother Eve who violates the divine command, pushing past the boundaries of the permitted to engage the forbidden, and so invents curiosity and free choice. In the Book of Exodus the five women in Moses's life – his mother Jochebed, his midwives Shiphrah and Puah, his sister Miriam and Pharaoh's daughter, who rescues him from the water – all conspire to frustrate the will of the Egyptian tyrant. They dare to take a stand on the side of life and not carry out the sentence of death by drowning in the Nile decreed on "every son that is born" (Exod. 1:22). From the conduct of these ancient heroines, a cry of freedom was heard that continues to echo today.

Why were these stories constructed in this fashion? Perhaps it was coincidental, but more likely by intention. And if we're dealing with intentions, did the author mean to imply that the creation of the people and nation of Israel in Exodus was a miniature replica of the creation of the world in Genesis? Perhaps it was a scaled down system that was meant to offer a correction and improvement of the first creation. The first creation left behind the sour taste of accumulating human failures, of Cain, Lemach, Noah, Sodom and Shechem. But in the Exodus from Egypt, which was itself a creation – the creation of the nation Israel – a process was begun that, though difficult, was without doubt fundamentally different.

The Book of Genesis taught us that God's first creation did not include the necessary tools or skills to accommodate frustration, miscalculation or failure. The creation of Egypt, on the other hand, which was created by humans "from Egypt, even until now" (Numb. 14:19), assumes in advance that every physical step forward toward a given promised land will be accompanied by a psychological step backward toward a starting point in the fleshpot of captivity. There seems to be some sort of flaw in divine perfection. As long as it can't make accommodations for imperfection, it leads again and again to outbursts of menacing, homicidal rage from an all-conquering God who can't conquer his own temper. The human drama is the complete opposite of supreme perfectionism – it's all full of cracks, crisscrossed with splits, dents and scratches. That's why God is constantly disappointed in Genesis. That's why he is constantly starting over from the beginning, regretting the mistakes he's made and trying out the next perfect idea. Human beings are not at all like that. They – that is, we – are capable of reaching an elevation that repeatedly starts from the bottom and reaches some surprising new height. Humankind has the capacity to know the frustration of failure and yet not hesitate to try again and again to fix what's broken. I have to assume that if they had asked Moses at some point near the beginning, at the burning bush, whether he thought that one day in the twenty-first century they'd be sending e-mails about him, writing deep commentaries and sermonizing about him in synagogues and study groups, I think he would have laughed like a grizzled old shepherd and dismissed us with a wave of his calloused hand – and not only because he couldn't have had the faintest idea what electronic mail is. And still, Moses's creation has stood up longer and weathered more challenges than God's, with his chronic impatience and recurrent outbursts of disappointment in his own creations. This tells us something about the Book of Exodus, in which God's creation is completed and humankind's creation begins.

Let My People Go

THIS WEEK'S PORTION, *Parashat Shemot*, is not just a story, nor a mere collection of memories of our ancestors in the days of slavery. *Parashat Shemot* is a foundational story. True, it is full of intriguing anecdotes: the conversation at the burning bush; the rod that slithers like a snake; the prince who is rescued from a watery doom only to kill a man, flee into the desert and meet his wife by a well; a God who chats with a stuttering mortal; a prince of Egypt who weds the daughter of a Midianite high priest – all this and more. But the sum total of the portion is not the marvelous memories of a dim past, but the eternal truth that forms the background. The inscription on the Liberty Bell in Philadelphia reads, "Proclaim liberty throughout all the land unto all the inhabitants thereof" (Lev. 25:10). The quote comes from the elaboration of the laws of the jubilee year at the end of the Book of Leviticus. We will get to the idea of freedom when we reach that week's portion, but for now it's enough to note the biblical underpinnings of the sweeping human dictate: "For unto me the children of Israel are servants; they are my servants whom I brought forth out of the land of Egypt" (Lev. 25:55). For me, this verse is the irreducible essence of the Jewish spirit. To loosen the chains of the oppressor, to be free of human bondage, we need to look up through the eyes of the spirit to the ideas of the sublime that lie beyond human malice. Freedom begins within, deep in the soul, and only afterwards does it find expression in the world of the physical and the political.

There are many believers, and even more who call themselves religious, who know their religion and their Judaism through the narrow prism of the mitzvot, the rabbinic laws. On the eve of the festival of Sukkot they descend on the markets with a magnifying glass to make sure the leaves haven't become separated, heaven forbid, at the tip of the *lulav*, the ceremonial palm frond, even though when they venture out into creation itself, into nature, they can't tell a palm from an olive tree. On Yom Kippur, the Day of Atonement, they carefully dry their tongue and savor their temporary hunger, but as they stroll home during the midday break in the service they cheerfully trade the lowest sort of gossip. They know the details of the commandment but not its spirit.

I see *Parashat Shemot* as the big picture that rises above the anecdotal details. This is the portion of the Torah of Jewish freedom, the living spirit of the Jewish people. This spirit has, sadly, turned hard and grim in recent years. It's time to revive it and bring it back into the center of our lives. Portions of the following words are taken from the introduction to my book *God Is Back*: Where in all the imperial expanses of the Jewish spirit can we find the seeds of the liberal mythos, the mythos of freedom? As with all Jewish beginnings, it seems that everything began with the Exodus from Egypt. The Exodus was the great saga of the Jewish people that became the foundational narrative of all notions of freedom. More broadly, the original Exodus is the groundwork for many of the ideas of freedom and liberty throughout the world since time immemorial.

It's hard to imagine today, in an era of open communication, of the United Nations Declaration of Human Rights, of constitutions, independence and armies to protect them, what slavery meant in ancient Egypt. The times, the rhythms and sensibilities then were completely different. For hundreds of years, the children of the tribes of Israel were born into a slave's consciousness. God had chosen us for servitude. Daddy was a slave, mommy was a serving girl and everything you knew was in thrall to the tyranny of King Pharaoh and the whims of his soldiers, priests and Egyptian subjects. It's hard to imagine that anyone could have conceived of lifting their heads, looking around and imaging something different. There was no example of another society to imitate, no television news, no protest movement, no armies of lawyers or civil rights organizations. But suddenly, centuries of waiting exploded like a geyser, like boiling lava, and transformed the face of the whole monotheistic world beyond recognition. Freedom was born.

Pharaoh had decreed: "Every son that is born ye shall cast into the river" (Exod. 1:22). I don't fully understand the pharaonic decree. Why would a powerful king like Pharaoh, knowing that Egypt's economy was dependent on the cheap labor of his Israelite slaves, be prepared to kill his own workers and damage his economy? Especially in an era when labor meant muscle, and men's muscles were obviously stronger than women's? Did he know by some royal intuition or the readings of his stargazers and astrologers that an heir and challenger was about to be born? Did he want to kill him the way that Herod, hundreds of years later, would chase after the star of Jesus into the mangers of Bethlehem to kill him? Who knows?

In any event, the revolt was begun by two Hebrew midwives who simply violated Pharaoh's edict and didn't kill the children. When Moses was born, his mother Jochebed joined the movement. She didn't kill her newborn son. She didn't abandon him or drown him. She didn't hand him over to the authorities for elimination as Pharaoh had ordered. For three months she hid him from the watchful eyes of the Egyptian police, and when she couldn't hide him any longer she put him in a basket and set him afloat on the Nile. Was Jochebed the only one to think of this, or was it a common practice? We don't know. But now a fourth woman joined the movement. Jochebed sent her daughter Miriam down to the Nile to keep an eye on the basket. Not Aaron, Moses's older brother, nor her husband Amram, who hardly plays a role in the story other than as sperm donor. It was a woman who was chosen to continue the quiet uprising of the midwives and mothers. And then an amazing thing happened: a fifth woman came down to the Nile, the daughter of Pharaoh, and fished out the basket and the baby inside. She saved him, raised him, taught him the ways of the palace and prepared him to be the redeemer from outside, the dreamer and visionary who would save his oppressed people from her father and the whips of his henchmen.

These five women changed the face of history. Thanks to them the assembled tribes of the sons of Jacob the Israelite rebelled, fled and united into a people whose eternal constitution begins with the recognition of God – not the God of Genesis, the God who created the world, but the God "who brought thee out of the land of Egypt, out of the house of bondage" (Exod. 20:2). This marvelous story and the immortal words of Moses to Pharaoh, his onetime benefactor and current enemy, still echo through the arenas of every fight for freedom: "Let my people go." That was what the Jews of the Soviet Union called their struggle for freedom from the claws of the KGB and the communist regime. That was how the black slaves sang of their cry for freedom in the sweltering cotton fields of the American South. "Let my people go" is the battle cry of all freedom-loving people: South Sudanese fighting the oppressive regime of the fundamentalist Muslim north, feminists resisting the yoke of patriarchy, gays battling the prejudices of a conservative society. Five women and a prince, born Israelite and raised Egyptian, gave the world the unique gifts of freedom, solidarity and human dignity.

Much has been made of the fact that the Jews were the first to discover the monotheistic idea of the oneness of God. To my mind, the gift of freedom that the ancient Hebrews gave themselves and humankind is at least as great as the idea of monotheism, if not greater.

The Torah commands us many more times to remember the Exodus from Egypt than the creation of the world. The creation was a top-down action, untouched by human hands. The Exodus and its attendant freedoms, by contrast, entailed a great deal of human involvement. The Exodus teaches us that creation and renewal do not come only from God above. Humanity down below bears considerable responsibility as his partner. For that reason, the redemption from Egyptian bondage has become the underpinning of all standard approaches – the orthodoxy – of Jewish thought. As the scripture puts it:

> It is not in heaven, that thou shouldest say: "Who shall go up for us to heaven, and bring it unto us, and make us to hear it, that we may do it?" Neither is it beyond the sea, that thou shouldest say: "Who shall go over the sea for us, and bring it unto us, and make us to hear it, that we may do it?" But the word is very nigh unto thee, in thy mouth, and in thy heart, that thou mayest do it." (Deut. 30:12–14)

Judaism means responsibility among human beings here and now; as for the rest of it – go and learn.

No one ever expressed the Jewish spirit of universal freedom better than the great Hebrew poet Shaul Tchernichovsky in the poem "Credo," written in 1892 while he was a seventeen-year-old youth in Russia, which in my mind could have been the anthem of the state of Israel and of all free people:

Laugh, laugh at all my dreams, my dearest;
Laugh, and I repeat anew
That I still believe in man –
As I still believe in you.
For my soul is not yet unsold
To the golden calf of scorn
And I still believe in man
And the spirit in him born.
By the passion of his spirit,
Shall the ancient bonds be shed.
Let the soul be given freedom,
Let the body have its bread!
Laugh, for I believe in friendship,
And in one I still believe,
One whose heart shall beat with my heart
And with mine rejoice and grieve.
Let the time be dark with hatred,
I believe in years beyond,
Love at last shall bind the peoples
In an everlasting bond.
In that day shall my own people
Rooted in its soil arise,
Shake the yoke from off its shoulders
And the darkness from its eyes.
Life and love and strength and action
In their heart and blood shall beat,
And their hopes shall be both heaven
And the earth beneath their feet.
Then a new song shall be lifted
To the young, the free, the brave,
And the wreath to crown the singer
Shall be gathered from my grave.

(Translated from the Hebrew by Maurice Samuel)

Week 14

Va'era – And I Appeared

Exodus 6:2–9:35

Righteous Gentiles

NOT LONG AGO my niece Shira sent me some comments on the weekly portion in which Moses was saved by Pharaoh's daughter. She compared the historical events with the life stories of her two grandmothers, who had died at the end of a long, full life after first experiencing a childhood of terror and persecution, from which they were saved by non-Jewish neighbors. Here is what she wrote: "I choose to be an optimist, and following the life experiences of my two grandmothers, to believe in people like Olga and Mikolai, like Umm and Abu Shaker, like Pharaoh's daughter, who made the right choice. Because of them I stand here today. Because of people like them, because of personal friendships that break down walls, life has a chance, and maybe even coexistence."

Here is how my beloved father-in-law Lucien answered her: "Rabbi Samson Raphael Hirsch made a contribution to our Shira's method of commentary.... 'Pharaoh's daughter called her foster son *Moshe*, one who *draws* out of the water, and not *Mashui*, one who is *drawn* from the water. Perhaps this gives us an indication of the whole tendency of the education which the princess gave her foster son...that all his life is he to have a tender heart for other people's troubles and always be on the alert to be a *moshi'a*, a deliverer in times of distress. His Hebrew name always kept the consciousness of his origin awake within him. The princess surely inquired of the mother the Hebrew term for expressing this thought, otherwise she would have given him an Egyptian name. In all this we can see the noble humane character of Moses's savior" (Samson Raphael Hirsch on Exod. 2:10).

Not long ago the entire government of France cited an initiative begun by my father-in-law. At the Pantheon, the most important memorial site in Paris, a grave was dedicated for the "unknown righteous gentile." (You may not know, by the way, that Israel has recognized more than twenty-one thousand righteous gentiles to date, among whom the entire Danish underground is counted as one person, and the entire Danish people as a subset of this.) Both their comments, my father-in-law's and my niece's, open a window for us to discuss the very fine but clear line threading through the story of the Exodus, namely the story of the righteous gentiles.

The first to follow this path were the midwives. True, the scripture explicitly calls them "Hebrew midwives" (Exod. 1:15). But the traditional commentaries on the words "Hebrew midwives" question whether they were indeed "Hebrews" of the seed of Israel or Egyptian midwives whose occupation was helping to deliver the children of Hebrew women. The nineteenth century Italian Jewish scholar Samuel David Luzzatto summed up the dilemma as follows: "It was the opinion of the sages of the Talmud that these midwives were from the seed of Israel. And [other] opinions held that they were Egyptians who delivered Hebrew children, which seems likely. For how could he have ordered the daughters of Israel to destroy their own people and believe they would obey?" (Samuel David Luzzatto on Exod. 1). Let's go with Luzzatto's argument. If that is the case, then Shiphrah and Puah were the first righteous gentiles, Egyptian women who dared to defy the tyrant and remain in memory for all time.

Pharaoh's daughter is unquestionably another righteous soul of humanity. We have no reason to doubt her origins and background. She is the daughter of Pharaoh. And out of the midst of Pharaoh's house she brings her kindness to Moses, child of the Nile. This narrative idea of a sensitive human king or prince who goes out to the people and their suffering reappears in various forms in the Bible, as it does in the literatures of all peoples. This is precisely the role of Esther in the house of King Ahasuerus. Much the same could be said of the efforts of King David's son Absalom to capture the hearts and minds of the people (2 Sam. 15:6) as a popular, populist prince from the heart of the royal establishment.

Thank God the Egypt of our story is more than these three heroic women. That narrow thread of righteousness and human justice stretched across the whole of Egyptian society, even though the stories of these heroes remain mostly hidden. When Israel leaves Egypt in the portion we will read two weeks from now, there will be a mass parting of nation from nation and people from people. Some of these farewells will be harsh. Worker will take revenge on taskmaster, slave on oppressor, serving girl on mistress. But some of the farewells inevitably were emotional. Not for nothing was the day of parting described this way: "'Speak now in the ears of the people, and let them ask every man of his neighbor, and every woman of her neighbor, jewels of silver, and jewels of gold.' And the Lord gave the people favor in the sight of the Egyptians" (Exod. 11:2–3). There were friendships between Egyptians and Israelites. The Egyptians felt a need to compensate their departing neighbors, or perhaps simply to outfit them for their journey out of Egypt. (Later on, in the next chapter, it turns out that some Israelites exploited the opportunity, overreached and abused the Egyptians' good will: "And the Lord gave the people favor in the sight of the Egyptians, so that they let them have what they asked. And they despoiled the Egyptians" [Exod. 12:36].)

Even before the great Exodus, however, came the lesser exodus. Moses left Egypt, fleeing Pharaoh's anger after beating an Egyptian man to death and nearly doing the same to a Hebrew man (Exod. 2:14). He arrived as a stranger at the well in Midian and found refuge in the home of the high priest Jethro, who gave Moses his daughter Zipporah as a wife. This is the same Jethro who came into the desert to unite the families and showed kindness to Israel, his kinsman's people. He too is a righteous gentile who crowned our earliest mythology with his daughter Zipporah, the wife of Moses and mother of his children.

My late mother's Bible teacher, the commentator Nechama Leibowitz, called our attention to the fact that wherever the concept of "fear of God" is mentioned, it has to do with non-Jews: "But the midwives feared God" (Exod. 1:17); Amalek "feared not God" (Deut. 25:18) and elsewhere. The practical expression of fear (or lack thereof) of God is always in treatment of the stranger, the Other, the weak and helpless. "The fear of God in the Bible is a demand required of every human created in the divine image…

and if there is no fear of God in his heart, in the heart of the gentile, he is considered as though he had betrayed all of his obligations.... In all those places 'fear of God' is expressed in one's behavior toward a member of another people, toward a member of a minority. For this treatment of the stranger, the powerless and the unprotected is the acid test – whether there is fear of God in the heart or not" (Nechama Leibowitz, *New Studies in Shemot*, 33). The biblical God-fearer is the ancient brother of the modern righteous gentile, and those who do not fear God will often turn out to be perpetrators of crimes against humanity in general and against our people's humanity in particular.

Thus, for example, when Abraham deceives Abimelech, king of Gerar, and presents his wife Sarah as his sister, Abimelech rebukes him: "What sawest thou, that thou hast done this thing?" (Gen. 20:10). And Abraham responds defensively, "Because I thought: Surely the fear of God is not in his place; and they will slay me for my wife's sake" (Gen. 20:11). To which Rashi, imaginative as always, offers the following Midrash: "Will a guest who comes to town be asked about food and drink or will he be asked about his wife? Is she your wife or your sister?" In other words, Abraham doesn't know whether the local people are kind, hospitable people who will accept him and his family as they are. Or are they not righteous gentiles, God forbid, and will they ask him about his wife and molest her and him? Or will they perhaps even try to borrow her for a night or two? And so he lies, showing the stranger's fear of local bullies and bosses. He actually abandons his wife to their devices and proves to us in yet another way that fear of God and treatment of the stranger are inextricably bound together in the ancient biblical world.

It's said that medals are handed out only in places where the system has broken down, stopped functioning and no longer does what it is supposed to do. By that logic, righteous gentiles are the alternative to human evil, winners of the medal of hope for a better world that may yet learn to conquer humanity's worst instincts. Everywhere that the rule of law, order, fairness and the sanctity of human life collapse, a struggle must break out between the spreading evil and the human goodness that rescues children and risks its life for the persecuted, the raped and the helpless. The torch of darkness is fated to flicker and die, but if there is not even a small human light there, how can the flame of humanity burn again?

The lessons of human tragedy, whether great or small, cannot be reduced to a mere cry for more power, so as not to encounter another Amalek, Sennacherib or Hitler. There must also be a search for the good Amalek, the good Samarian, and the good German; with them we can repair the world again and make it even better. Too many have taken the oath of "never again," intending that this should never happen to us again. They are so focused on themselves, on the Jewish people and Jewish history, that they have never noticed the lessons of the biblical stories of Egyptian bondage and liberation: that it should never again happen to anyone. This is the legacy of the Egyptian midwives. This is the teaching of Pharaoh's daughter. These are our orders from the God-fearers, rebels against the kingdom and the lovers of mankind from among Pharaoh's slaves. And let's spell it out again: fear of God was not intended as religious extremism, but as a balance and restraint against unbounded human tyranny.

There is one more benefit to the unending search for the righteous gentiles who save the light of the world. They always ask us by their very existence: Are there enough righteous persons among you who preserve the flame of goodness and humanity by your treatment of the stranger and the Other? They oblige us to confront ourselves honestly and answer the question of whether our enemies can look at us and tell themselves that we are not all alike, that we are not pure evil. Who is the Israeli Schindler or the Jewish Wallenberg of our generation? Who is the daughter of Pharaoh who will draw an enemy from the water and make him into a prince of his people's freedom and the world's?

The Government and the People; The People and the Government

THIS WAS MY BAR MITZVAH PORTION. Every year when it comes around again I remember the anxiety I felt as I stood there on the *bimah*. How did it happen, I asked myself between one Torah blessing and the next, that I have to chant a portion with so many plagues? There are ten plagues in the Torah, and 70 percent of them are in my portion. Drawing on my private feelings about my portion, I would like to suggest a different reading of the plagues and their lessons.

The narrative framework that describes plagues is generally consistent: a warning is passed from God to Moses, from Moses to Pharaoh, from Pharaoh to his own hard heart. Then comes the plague and a bit of pharaonic regret, and we return to the beginning of the cycle. Sometimes the king's magicians manage to produce the same effect with their own magic, diminishing its supernatural impact and reducing Moses to some sort of a cross between Houdini and David Copperfield, as if to tell Pharaoh, and us, that it's just another stunt. Each time, God somehow rescinds the plague and allows Pharaoh to escape again and again. The story leaves a feeling of unfairness, of overkill. It would have been possible to break Pharaoh and his minions the first time around, to start out with, say, the slaying of the firstborn sons. If that didn't convince him, slay the firstborn daughters, and if that didn't do the trick, move on to child number two, then three. Or, if you will, start with the plague of blood. No problem – if necessary, add more blood and then even more blood. That's how it's done in the Middle East.

Perhaps the biblical drama was meant to show us the vast arsenal of divine creativity. In modern terms, we could characterize the first nine plagues, from blood through darkness, excluding only the slaying of the firstborn, as non-lethal weaponry aimed at deterrence and global policing without the devastating finality of the Flood, Sodom and Gomorrah, etc. At every turn, however, the all-powerful God of the Hebrews ran up against the petty stubbornness of Pharaoh – sometimes hard-hearted and thickheaded, sometimes sycophantic and petulant, sometimes even momentarily regretful, until he suddenly regrets his regretfulness and reverts to type. Countless generations have tried to explain the plagues in various ways, from rationalist theories about acts of nature to simple faith in divine miracles, to the cynically dismissive contention that the whole story is just primitive mythology of no importance whatever.

What's lost in all these narratives, it seems to me, is the plain reading that tries to unravel what it was that finally made Pharaoh break. What was the internal process within Pharaoh and within Egypt that led to the great change? What wisdom can we gain from this?

Above and beyond the details, the story of the plagues deals with the education of Pharaoh, the broadening of the horizons of his awareness. At the first summit meeting between the Hebrew brothers Moses and Aaron and the king of Egypt, Pharaoh gives them the brush-off: "Who is the Lord, that I should hearken unto his voice to let Israel go? I know not the Lord, and moreover I will not let Israel go" (Exod. 5:2). This lack of knowledge will come back ten times to plague him, so to speak. Each new plague will teach another lesson to Pharaoh and all Egypt, to augment their deficient knowledge base:

> And the Egyptians shall know that I am the Lord (Exod. 7:5).... In this thou shalt know that I am the Lord (Exod. 7:17)...that thou mayest know that there is none like unto the Lord our God (Exod. 8:6).... To the end that thou mayest know that I am the Lord in the midst of the earth (Exod. 8:18)...that thou mayest know that there is none like me in all the earth (Exod. 9:14)...that thou mayest know that the earth is the Lord's (Exod. 9:29)...that ye may know that I am the Lord (Exod. 10:2).... Knowest thou not yet? (Exod. 10:7).... That ye may know (Exod. 11:7)...and the Egyptians shall know (Exod. 14:18).

Ten lessons for one missing piece of knowledge. A lesson and a plague, a plague and a lesson. Sometimes Moses gives advance warning, sometimes not. Sometimes he comes to Pharaoh and sometimes not. In the Book of Psalms it is said that the plagues came directly from God, but here in the Book of Exodus, Moses is the author. Either way, the confused reader might well come to feel that it's not just Pharaoh who doesn't know God – God doesn't really know Pharaoh, and the result is a rather violent dialogue of the deaf.

Throughout all my years of revisiting these plagues, once a year on the Sabbath of my bar mitzvah portion and once a year at the Passover Seder,

Va'era

I always had the sense that the real secret to the liberation from Egypt was the plague of hail. There's something about it that sets it apart from the other plagues. On the one hand, it's supposed to be the plague of all plagues, the final arrow in the quiver of the Almighty: "For I will this time send all my plagues upon thy person, and upon thy servants, and upon thy people; that thou mayest know that there is none like me in all the earth" (Exod. 9:14). Does the word *all*, as in "all my plagues," mean that this plague is many plagues rolled up in one, or that this one is harder than all the previous ones? It doesn't really matter, because the difference in this plague is a matter of substance, not style. For the first and only time, a warning is sent out to the general public, giving people – not just Pharaoh and his house, but the population at large – a chance to save themselves from the worst of it. "Now therefore send, hasten in thy cattle and all that thou hast in the field; for every man and beast that shall be found in the field, and shall not be brought home, the hail shall come down upon them, and they shall die" (Exod. 9:19).

No warning was given before any of the other plagues, except to Pharaoh and his circle, of course. It appears that Egypt's governing authorities never bothered to warn the general public about the approaching plagues. No one told them to store up water before the river turns to blood, to lock away their livestock before the cattle plague, send out hunters to stop the swarming beasts, set out nets for the frogs, scrub their hair for lice and for heaven's sake don't scratch the boils. Nothing. Pharaoh knew what was coming, but his battered subjects were kept in the dark to be ambushed, barraged and left to pay the price for his callousness and obstinacy. The Egyptians in the story are always passive victims, whether of God or Pharaoh. But this time, in the plague of hail, things are different. It seems that God and his servant Moses had figured out that plagues without explanation, violence without an alternative, are not an effective educational tool. It simply wasn't working.

The Egyptian campaign was fundamentally different from the Israelite campaign. When Moses was sent to Israel, God sent him out to the people. "And God said moreover unto Moses: 'Thus shalt thou say unto the children of Israel: The Lord, the God of your fathers…hath sent me unto you.... Go, and gather the elders of Israel together'" (Exod. 3:15–16). The Israelite campaign began from below, from the people. The plagues of Egypt, up to the plague of hail, were aimed at persuading the leader, at achieving change from above. But the moment that the masses were given the option to choose – to stay in the field and die or run home and live – the inner persuasion had begun, leading the people to disengage from one another, and so leading to the redemption from Egyptian bondage. Some of Pharaoh's servants rushed their slaves and livestock indoors and were saved. But "he that regarded not the word of the Lord left his servants and his cattle in the field" (Exod. 9:21) – and died. Persuasion was quick. Right at the beginning of next week's portion, *Parashat Bo*, we can see the results, when "Pharaoh's servants said unto him: 'How long shall this man be a snare unto us? Let the men go, that they may serve the Lord their God; knowest thou not yet that Egypt is destroyed?'" (Exod. 10:7). Until now, no one had spoken that way to the dictator. Only from the moment that God and Moses appealed to Egyptian public opinion, as they had done with the Israelites at the beginning of the Book of Exodus, and offered an option different the Pharaoh's, did the tyrant's hard-line policy begin to unravel.

Put differently: when people are given a choice, they will ultimately make the decision that is right for them. And the people, any people, know better than their rulers and leaders what will serve them best. It's true of flesh-and-blood kings, and in my opinion it's also true of faith in God. Let people choose and you will find a strong society and a durable tradition. Impose their religion, or their politics or government, and you'll lose them for generations to come.

Week 15

Bo – Go In

Exodus 10:1–13:16

Slaves of Time

THIS WEEK THE STORY OF THE EXODUS reaches its climax. The last plagues come down on Pharaoh and his house. The gates of Egypt are thrown open wide and "my people go." Thus the Middle Eastern drama of days gone by, whose echoes still spark the imaginations and shape the values of the three great monotheistic faiths. Such myths often fired the imagination of the ancient world, and a few have survived to our time. For example, the Roman gladiator Spartacus led a slave revolt against the Roman republic in 73 BCE. Leading an army of gladiators and runaway slaves, he fought off the trained legions of Rome for nearly three years in what historians call the Third Servile War, before being defeated. His story happened in the far distant past, but it continues to resonate. Numerous modern revolutionary movements drew their inspiration from Spartacus, including the most famous: the Spartacus League, led by Rosa Luxemburg and Karl Liebknecht during the Weimar Republic in Germany. Fictional versions of his story continue to grow in number. Arthur Koestler's first novel, *The Gladiators*, published in 1939, was based on the Spartacus story.

Howard Fast wrote a novel titled *Spartacus* in 1951 that was made into an Academy Award-winning movie in 1960, starring Kirk Douglas and directed by Stanley Kubrick. In Fast's telling, Spartacus was a sort of ancient communist fighting the Roman establishment to liberate the slaves. Perhaps not coincidentally, the screenplay was written by Dalton Trumbo, one of the blacklisted Hollywood Ten, and his on-screen credit in

Spartacus is said to have ended the Hollywood blacklist. The Kubrick film was re-released in 1967 and again in 1991. Fast's novel was adapted again in 2004 as a made-for-television movie. Yet another version was launched in 2010 as a Starz Network cable television series, *Spartacus: Blood and Sand*; the series is entering its third season at this writing, and is focused more on action and sex than politics. Aram Khachaturian composed a ballet on Spartacus in 1954, considered one of his greatest works, and later adapted the music into a series of orchestral suites that continue to be popular as theme music on British television. The Soviet Union sponsored its own international sports competition, the Spartakiad, for decades until the collapse of Communism. Spartak is still the name of Moscow's most successful football and hockey clubs. Finally, Spartacus is also the name of the newsletter of the Communist youth league of Israel. Perhaps that's why Moshe, or Moses, is the most popular name in Israel.

What is it about the never-ending battle between slave and slave-master that so fascinates us? It might be the undying human hope to rise above our condition and better our lives. We seem to tell ourselves that if an enslaved people can defeat a brutal despot like Pharaoh, then maybe I can do something about my abusive boss or my violent husband. Because human society will always be plagued by cruelty, mean-spiritedness and oppression, the spirit of freedom will never cease pulsing within us.

The stories that open the Book of Exodus recount a clash of civilizations. It is not merely a confrontation between Hebrew society and its Egyptian sister-society, but a clash between two basic visions of the human spirit: oppression versus freedom. There will always be people who want to dominate others. There will always be people who want to be dominated by others, who will willingly bow their heads in submission before the peremptory power of their overlords. Like that solitary slave who says: "'I love my master…; I will not go out free….' Then his master shall bring him…to the door, or unto the door-post; and his master shall bore his ear through with an awl; and he shall serve him forever" (Exod. 21:5–6). So it is with people and nations whose souls have been beaten down and conquered. Hebrew civilization rose against them like a storm, fixing its sights on the eternal struggle of free people against oppressors.

Bo

Where is the center of the struggle? What is its focus?

The point where slave and master collide, the axis along which worker and boss confront each other, is time. Every struggle for freedom is a struggle to seize the mastery of time. The oppressor says: I will! I will determine when and how hard to work. The freedom fighter says: when my time is under my control, I will be the master of my fate. Fate and time are one and the same. We often speak of being "master of one's fate" or "a slave to the clock," rarely noticing that they are two sides of the same coin. Because time is the point where slavery and redemption collide, it can help us shed light on Rashi's first and most famous biblical exegesis, from the very beginning of Genesis: "'In the Beginning' – Rabbi Yitzhak taught that the Torah need not have begun anywhere but at 'This month will be for you'" (Rashi on Gen. 1:1). According to this otherwise unknown Rabbi Yitzhak (who might be Rashi's father or teacher), the true beginning of the Torah and of Jewish culture is not at the mythic story of creation but at one cardinal moment in the life of Jewish people described in this week's portion, the moment of departure from Egypt, about which God says to Moses, "And the Lord spoke unto Moses and Aaron in the land of Egypt, saying: 'This month shall be unto you the beginning of months; it shall be the first month of the year to you'" (Exod. 12:1–2). Why is this commandment so important? Why, for that matter, does God present himself in the Ten Commandments as the "God, who brought thee out of the land of Egypt, out of the house of bondage" (Exod. 20:2), and not as the God of Genesis, creator of heaven and earth?

Because the essence of the Torah, the covenant between God and his people, is freedom and the mastery of time. The Exodus is not a mere slave rebellion, an achievement of personal liberty for each of the rebels to the point of anarchy, but an act of taking responsibility for time. When God issues a command that "this month will be for you," he is saying: you are masters of time, and not its slaves. When you were slaves, anyone could tell you when to get up, when to go to work and when you could rest, if at all. Your time was not your own. Now the responsibility is back in your hands. You fix time for yourselves. And not just the clock, but the calendar.

Here is how Rabbi Ovadia Sforno, a fascinating sixteenth-century Italian scholar, explains the verse: "This month shall be unto you the beginning of months. From now on the months will be yours to do with as you wish. In the time of slavery the days were not yours but were for the service of others and their will. Therefore, 'it shall be the first month of the year to you,' because this was the beginning of your choosing reality" (Sforno on Exod. 12:2). "Choosing reality" is an ancient Hebrew expression that simply means freedom of choice. And this is the sum of Jewish civilization: a culture of freedom of choice; a special calendar and a Sabbath at the end of the week that are the expressions of Jewish freedom, the freedom of a free people in time.

Before leaving this theme a cautionary note is in order. The Israel and Egypt of the Exodus are not necessarily nations as defined by demography or genetics. Above all they are symbols. In different circumstances the roles can just as easily be reversed, whether by inattention or malice. The oppressed can become the oppressor, and a past history of victimhood will be no excuse. Even Israel can become an Egyptian taskmaster. The classic Israeli poet Natan Alterman summarized the plagues in this manner in his poem "On the Road to No-Amon [the Egyptian city better known as Thebes]," the opening of his astonishing epic, *Songs of the Plagues of Egypt*, written as the first reports of the Nazi genocide were emerging and published in 1944:

> No-Amon, with your axes of iron
> Your gates, uprooted by night
> They will come, plagues of Egypt, upon you
> To mete out to you justice by night.
> No-Amon, then it rose to the moon
> The first cry, with no one to hear,
> And the strong man who ran to the gateway
> Collapsed, while still running, from fear.
> Shrouded in cries, the king's city
> Tossed forth in a wondrous hurl.
> From chambers of grandeur to salt grains
> From crown down to rags cast aswirl.
>
> . . . .

> And your night with its pride, now forgotten
> And time like a vault cracked asunder
> And your dust carried off in the wind with the dust
> Of great cities the sands have swept under.

Every generation has its Egypt, its great cities of despots who met their ends in dust carried off in the wind. And over against the symbolic No-Amon there always stands the spirit of freedom – the plagues of Egypt against the Exodus from Egypt. So it was with the first great human act of redemption and so it was in the vision of Maimonides, who saw the final redemption in the end of days this way: "There is no difference between this world and the messianic era except the oppression of kingdoms" (Maimonides, "The Laws of Kings," 12:2). That is, in the longed-for days to come the world will behave just as it does now. The sun will rise in the morning and winter will be cold. The only difference will be that nations will not oppress one another, peoples will not seek domination and no one will be a slave or prisoner of his neighbor. In those future messianic days there will be no more Egyptianism. The language of human values will be freedom of choice, time, liberty and self-determination. Perhaps that is why we end the blessings of the Jewish festival holidays with the phrase, "who sanctifies Israel and the seasons of time," as if to remind ourselves that the passage of holiday seasons embodies our command over time, and command of time is the essence of freedom.

The Ethics of Slaves

TONIGHT IS THE NIGHT! This portion is the nation's founding moment. The Exodus from Egypt is underway. Egypt is in turmoil, parents are burying their firstborn sons, the king's messengers are searching for Moses by candlelight. There is a feeling of darkness in the air, as though the plague of darkness had not yet ended and the losses in each family were part of Egypt's larger gloom. And so it came to pass at midnight that the Israelites of the land of Goshen went knocking on their Egyptian neighbors' doors "asking" for objects of silver and gold. In so doing they were obeying the command that had come down from God to the people through Moses: "Speak now into the ears of the people, and let them ask every man of his neighbor, and every woman of her neighbor, jewels of silver, and jewels of gold" (Exod. 11:2). This action has always struck me as a sort of euphemism. Let's admit the truth: they weren't asking. Their neighbors' world was crashing down on their heads, their share of divine retribution by the God of the Hebrews for their nation's four-century mistreatment of his people, who were headed for the door. The wording may have been a request, but the facts were a last chance to buy their way out of celestial doom. That's why the scripture's description of the actual event seems more accurate: "And they despoiled the Egyptians." It might well have been a justified despoliation. But it was hardly a request.

Why was this permitted? It was a night meant for affirming the highest values of the departing nation, without revenge or retaliation, murder or last-minute vandalism. It was a night of extraordinary national discipline, the sort that few peoples ever demonstrate and might never come again. Only one deviation was permitted – the taking of silver and gold objects and items of clothing. Looking forward, we can see these requests as laying the groundwork for the wealth of the new nation and the individual capital of its citizens. They created the assets that would later enable the offerings and gifts that built the tabernacle. If not for this, where would the fleeing slaves ever find any property to offer up, as they were commanded, "And this is the offering which ye shall take of them: gold, and silver, and brass; and blue, and purple, and scarlet, and fine linen, and goats' hair; and rams' skins dyed red, and sealskins, and acacia-wood; oil for the light, spices for the anointing oil, and for the sweet incense; onyx stones, and stones to be set, for the ephod, and for the breast-plate" (Exod. 25:3-7)?

But the biblical narrative never looks only forward; it is always interwoven in some way with threads of the past as well. When Joseph rose to power he initiated an economic process of enormous proportions. He bought up the lands, the cattle, the sheep and the livestock. He bought up nearly everything, leaving almost nothing in the private hands of the individual citizen and his household. As the newly purchased Egyptians say to him at the end of the second year of famine, "We will not hide from my lord, now that our money is all spent; and the herds of cattle are my lord's; there is nought left in the sight of my lord, but our bodies, and our lands" (Gen. 47:18). If this was the condition of the Egyptians, the lords of the land, it's hard to imagine the poverty and disgrace of the slaves of slaves, the Hebrews who were slaves of Pharaoh and his Egyptian servants.

With the ironic smile of the lord of history, Joseph's brothers and their descendants became the ultimate victims of the economic centralism at the beginning of the story – and the beneficiaries of the privatization at the end. Joseph was the one who created the system that placed the king and priests at the top and the people and slaves at the bottom. On the day that Egypt's economic structure collapsed, when the slaves, the producers of the nation's wealth, took away the productive power of the economy – themselves – on that day the privatization of nationalized property got underway. For if all the assets of Egypt since the days of Joseph were the property of the pharaonic dynasty, including the silver and gold, then the "despoliation" we have spoken of would have amounted in essence to robbing the state treasury and liberating part of the assets locked up in its vaults. The descendants of the tribes broke up the system of Joseph their ancestor into its component parts. What was expropriated from the masses for the benefit of the upper classes essentially returned to its owners. Perhaps it wasn't a perfect bank transfer. Not every pot was returned to its previous owner, nor did every gown end up in the wardrobe of the precise freed slave to whom it belonged. But somehow, compensation for the labor of Pharaoh's worker ants found its way into the right and proper hands – the hands of the workers who had created Egypt's capital.

This also helps explain the connection between the memory of the Exodus, the memory of the dramatic evening described in this week's portion, and the commandment of the Jubilee year in which we are obligated to free all slaves and return all property to its original owners. The commandment of the Jubilee, in which capital and assets return to their original owners, rests squarely on the memory of Egypt. At the end of the Book of Leviticus, after the elaborate listing of the rules of freedom and liberty accompanying the Jubilee, God speaks out in his own voice: "I am the Lord your God, who brought you forth out of the land of Egypt, to give you the land of Canaan, to be your God" (Lev. 25:38). The Exodus from Egypt is not merely the longed-for liberation but also, and perhaps mainly, the memory of the social and economic reform required of a state and society any time its institutions calcify to the point of corruption, exploitation and oppression. The Jubilee is the pinnacle of the process of human equality, and for that reason the verse was explicit: the children of Israel did not exploit Pharaoh and his palace nor invade the houses of the wealthy and powerful. They did not loot the palaces like the rebels of the French or Russian or Iraqi revolutions. They approached their Egyptian neighbors personally, one to one. It was for their sake and the sake of their generosity that the blessed law of the Jubilee was enacted.

The ancient texts probably reflect a complex reality. Some of the people, both Israelite and Egyptian, had their place at the righteous end of the spectrum: "'And let them ask every man of his neighbor, and every woman of her neighbor, jewels of silver, and jewels of gold.' And the Lord gave the people favor in the sight of the Egyptians" (Exod. 11:2–3); others, Israelite as well as Egyptian, were part of the misbehavior that appears in next week's portion, the despoliation. There were Egyptians who acted with good will, but there were also Israelites who were intent on stealing towels, soap and plumbing fixtures: "And the Lord gave the people favor in the sight of the Egyptians, so that they let them have what they asked. And they despoiled the Egyptians" (Exod. 12:36). The Egyptians were offering willingly, but these Israelites simply took.

That's one of two subtexts to the story, a social and economic message that shouldn't be ignored. The other subtext is its character testimony regarding the nation leaving Egypt. It isn't an indictment, but a psychological profile of someone coming suddenly out of darkness into the light, almost without preparation. The narrative has tried for years to instill in us the sense that God was at his best in Egypt, in top form. Our ancestors were ordered to paint their doorposts and entryways with blood from the Passover sacrifice. We've always understood the marking on the doors to carry two messages. First, it was a mark of defiance to the Egyptians: "Here dwells a Hebrew rebel, and I no longer fear you." Second, it was a sign to God, indicating which house may be entered to do the bloody deed and which house to pass over so its inhabitants can celebrate the Passover: "And the blood shall be to you for a token upon the houses where ye are; and when I see the blood, I will pass over you, and there shall no plague be upon you to destroy you, when I smite the land of Egypt" (Exod. 12:13).

Isn't this a bit odd? God, who knows when to kill a son but not a daughter, who can distinguish a firstborn son from a second, can't tell a Hebrew from an Egyptian? He needs marking tape to figure it out? The commentary and Midrash are hard-pressed at this oddity and offer some evidence as to the Almighty's inability to control his own creatures: "Once the destroyer is let loose it does not distinguish between the righteous and the wicked, as it is said (Exod. 12:22), 'and none of you shall go out of the door of his house until the morning'" (Yalkut Shimoni on Isaiah 26, 432). That is, we are saved, but God, sorry to say, lost a bit of control over the goings-on. They are forewarned: don't go outside and don't run into him or his messenger, the destroying angel, or it will cost you dearly, because he's blinded with blood and can't tell who's who. So we've been taught all through the years.

Today it's possible to suggest a different reading of the events of that night. The hidden message, it seems to me, is something else entirely: it's not that God didn't trust himself and was afraid that he might lose control and hurt the innocent. This fear never characterized our God and his sensibility. He liked to lose control now and then, as the firstborn of Egypt and the drowned of the Red Sea could testify. On the contrary: Abraham, who knew him better than anyone, was suspicious enough at Sodom to demand, "Wilt thou indeed sweep away the righteous with the wicked?" (Gen. 18:23); yet here in Egypt we find God meting out collective punishment, and not a single voice, neither among us nor among the Egyptians, stands up and objects. Only later, much later, at the sea, do the Midrash and Aggadah look back and observe in the name of God the destruction and loss, the lack of distinction between the day-old firstborn who has not yet sinned and the adult who has sinned, and the accumulation of victims of the plagues in the fields of Egypt and on the banks of the Nile. Only then do they understand that to drown "six hundred chosen chariots, and all the chariots of Egypt, and captains over all of them" (Exod. 14:7), was simply too much killing. One mustn't overdo things. And so in the name of the creator of the universe they issue a retroactive and undying correction: "At that time the ministering angels sought to utter songs before the Holy One, praised be he, and the Holy One said to them: My creatures are drowning in the sea and you utter songs before Me?" (Yalkut Shimoni on Deut. 28, 940).

Where did the sages of the Midrash find the courage to speak that way, after the fact, in the name of God who had destroyed Egypt without mercy? From the verse, "And none of you shall go out of the door of his house until the morning." God knows exactly what's going through the mind of the slave. Every day, day after day, he and his father and grandfather and their fathers before them had gotten up and gone out to work, to bricks and mortar and whips and the abuse of their overseers. Suddenly comes the long night, the night of the smiting of the firstborn, and the rumor spreads through the encampment: no work tomorrow. Centuries of habit are about to be broken. And the rumor goes even further: not only aren't we getting up for work, but there's no one to work for because all the firstborn of Egypt will be dead.

Here I'd like to suggest a detail in God's defense. With the slightest change of a single Hebrew letter, shortening a *vav* to a *yod*, the *bechorim*, firstborn sons, become *bechirim*, the elite, the high-born. Not the firstborn of each family in Egypt, but the first families of Egypt. It seems to me that the elite, those who held positions of influence and were directly involved in the oppression of the Hebrews, were smitten and punished. One can find a hint hidden in the verse that describes the trail of victims, "from the firstborn of Pharaoh that sat on his throne, unto the firstborn of the captive that was in the dungeon; and all the firstborn of cattle" (Exod. 12:29). We know from Joseph's story about the Egyptian prisons where Hebrew men were tortured for no reason. It could be that the plague of death was directed at the captains of the dungeon and the rest of the prison system, including the "trusted" prisoners who were put in charge of the worst abuse in prisons all over the world, and all the rest of the abusers within the system. As for "the firstborn of the cattle," that seems clear: cattle were a symbol of an Egyptian deity, and the elimination of a local deity is hardly mere symbolism. The three target populations of the plague of death were the three key symbols of the regime: monarchy, law enforcement and the intimidating religious establishment. On that night, at midnight, a clear distinction was made between the responsible elite, who were targeted for elimination, and the decent people, the righteous gentiles, who were ready the next day to greet their Hebrew neighbors with good will and send them on their way with the best that Egypt had to offer of provisions and ready cash.

Under these circumstances, when God and his messengers were making their way through the streets and closing accounts with those who had wronged us for so many centuries of bondage, he didn't want the suddenly freed and bewildered slaves wandering the streets looking for revenge. He didn't trust our forebears. He knew that a slave who breaks free can at first be a destructive force, unable to tell right from wrong. The newly freed slave can kill those who had no part in his suffering. So God commanded them to stay at home. "Don't go out in the street," he ordered. "Don't turn the process of divine justice into a human bloodbath." Understood this way, the revolt of the Hebrew slaves in Egypt is one of the only revolutions in history in which freed slaves did not slaughter their slavemasters. Not only was it a revolution in values, it also had hidden within it a message about the proper path from slavery to freedom: the path of ceaseless caution, of careful distinction between guilty and innocent, between right and wrong, between the righteous and the oppressor and between those who deserve divine retribution and those who don't. People should not rush into the streets in the heat of passion seeking revenge, simply because they want to. The Exodus from Egypt is a warning sign: freedom without revenge, liberation without bloodshed, redemption and independence without paranoia. This is the Jewish path. This is the Exodus that we recall so often in our text and in our prayers.

Week 16

Beshalach – When He Had Let the People Go

Exodus 13:17–17:16

The Weakness of God

AT THE SEA, AFTER THE DANGER of drowning has passed, after Israel has been saved and six hundred of Pharaoh's elite charioteers have drowned in the sea, the scripture sums up the essence of the ancient faith in this fashion: "And the people feared the Lord; and they believed in the Lord, and in his servant Moses" (Exod. 14:31). There is a direct, intimate connection between what the people see and their belief in God, as though our text were quoting some sort of Israelite tag line that said, "See it, believe it; don't see it, don't believe it." God has been through a great deal since then. He's gone from babysitting and sewing underwear for his creatures in the Garden of Eden, intimate chats with his believers by the terebinths of Mamre (Gen. 18:1–15) and drowning their enemies in the sea, to the point where he has disappeared from human events and left us more mature and much more alone in our own time. I once wrote myself a note that I've saved:

> How is it possible to understand God's words and intentions when human beings created in his image could dress up in storm troopers' uniforms, pin the swastika on their shirts and do the things they did? Are they part of his "likeness," too? Right there and then God stopped being comprehensible, because those are things that can't be understood in any human logic. His Almightiness was put to a

serious test, and even his eternal goodness is in real doubt. To frame the theological dilemma of the Holocaust accurately, I need to turn to the wisdom of one of the great Jewish thinkers of the twentieth century, Hans Jonas, who was born in Germany, went to Palestine as a young Zionist and spent most of his career teaching in New York. One of his most important works for our purposes was a lecture on the significance of the idea of God after the Holocaust. Jonas frames his remarks around the classical problem of evil in the world: If there is an almighty creator who embodies absolute good, how can evil exist in the world? On this question he says:

"Only a completely unintelligible God can be said to be absolutely good and absolutely powerful, yet tolerate the world as it is. Put more generally, the three attributes at stake – absolute good, absolute power and intelligibility – stand in such a logical relation to one another that the conjunction of any two of them excludes the third…. But if God is to be intelligible in some manner and to some extent (and to this we must hold), then his goodness must be compatible with the existence of evil, and this it is only if he is not *all* powerful. Only then can we uphold that he is intelligible and good, and there is yet evil in the world" (Hans Jonas, "The Concept of God after Auschwitz: A Jewish Voice," *The Journal of Religion* 67, no. 1 [January 1987]: 9–10).

Jonas was raised in a liberal Jewish home in Germany at the beginning of the twentieth century, and continued throughout his long life to consider himself a religious Jew, though not traditionally observant. His early passion for philosophy met a shattering challenge in 1933, when his teacher Martin Heidegger joined the Nazi Party. He moved to Palestine shortly afterward, fought the Nazis in the British army's Jewish Brigade, and then returned to Palestine only to learn that his mother had died in Auschwitz. After fighting in Israel's War of Independence he settled in New York and spent his life teaching and exploring, seeking to reconcile the ideals of philosophy and the darker realities of life. The result was one of the intellectual cornerstones of post-Holocaust theology.

In "God after Auschwitz" Jonas didn't seek to explain God's flawed behavior in the Holocaust. He accepted that as fact, and tried to understand the nature of a God who would allow it to happen under his watchful – or sleeping – eye. He was one of the first to read the new religious map and see the need for Jewish believers to discard the traditional way of believing in God and adopt new models of faith.

Considering how precisely Jonas's teachings describe my feelings, I can't escape the conclusion that God – who was so intelligible and present for my parents and teachers – has withdrawn from the world that I and my generation inhabit. As a result, the structures of religion are undergoing profound change. They will have to provide new definitions of human responsibility. The old relationship between the believer and God was like the relationship between the witness and the criminal justice system. We're called again and again to give testimony or sit on a jury that has decided there is a God and we must serve him. Since the time of the Exodus a religion of witnesses has taken shape, seeking proof in history even as they conserve it, as the text says: "And Israel saw the great work which the Lord did upon the Egyptians, and the people feared the Lord; and they believed in the Lord, and in his servant Moses" (Exod. 14:31). That God operated in history, and his handiwork and its outcome were visible and tangible.

It's easy to understand why an eyewitness would become a believer and willingly testify to the greatness of the divine. When the Midianite priest Jethro, Moses's father-in-law, hurried off to a family visit with his daughter and grandchildren at his son-in-law's camp, the text explains quite simply that he came because he "heard of all that God had done for Moses, and for Israel his people, how that the Lord had brought Israel out of Egypt" (Exod. 18:1). The commentators turn this grapevine communication into a victory for the Israelite prophecy of Moses over the Midianite faith of Jethro. "What did he hear that made him come?" Rashi asks, and answers, "The parting of the Red Sea and the war against Amalek." The historical occurrences of "all that God had done" brought the high priest of the Midianite religion down here to the desert.

In the same spirit, Moses convinces God to reverse the death sentence he has decreed against the Israelites after the sin of the Golden Calf:

Beshalach

"Wherefore should the Egyptians speak, saying: For evil did he bring them forth, to slay them in the mountains, and to consume them from the face of the earth? Turn from thy fierce wrath, and repent of this evil against thy people" (Exod. 32:12). He's worried about international public opinion, about God's place in the history books and about the negative character testimony that the Egyptians will offer, heaven forbid, if the sentence is carried out. This is the God of history.

This logic was adopted by the Christian church that emerged from the Judaism of the Second Temple era. Christianity saw the Jewish mother-faith as *Judaea Capta*, the defeated Jewish commonwealth. The real-world defeat and humiliation of the "old church," meaning us, was taken as eternal proof of God's new priorities. If the new church was flourishing and prosperous while the old Jewish one was withering in scorn, it was a sign that the God of history had spoken his peace, and the Jew was the disgraced witness to God's preferences. We could offer countless examples to show that the religion up to the time of the Holocaust was structured as a summary of God's appearances in history, or at least as a collection of eyewitness accounts by his believers. Their vision was proof in their eyes, and believing meant being ready to stake one's life against the myopia and blindness of those around.

This is the origin of the mountains of rulebooks that all presume to represent the revealed will of God. As religion evolved, it taught that correctly following the rules would bring heavenly approval, which in turn would bring earthly compensation to the believer or believers. The Bible itself shows occasional glimmers of this doctrine of reward and punishment. We are commanded, for example, to "honor thy father and thy mother" (Exod. 20:12) and are immediately offered the concrete incentive, "that thy days may be long." In time the doctrine of reward and punishment developed into a virtual barter system, a direct transaction of reward in exchange for commandment, misfortune in return for misstep. But this simplistic doctrine of God as vendor and believer as customer finds its antithesis in the model of Job.

Carl Gustav Jung, scholar of religion and disciple and opponent of Freud, wrote a marvelous monograph, *Answer to Job*, in which he claimed among other things that "the Book of Job serves as a paradigm for a certain experience of God which has a special significance for us today" (*The Portable Jung*, ed. Joseph Campbell, trans. R.F.C. Hull [New York: Penguin, 1971], 526). He tried – and partly succeeded – in his goal of understanding "why and to what purpose Job was wounded, and what consequences have grown out of this for Yahweh as well as for man." In the midst of Job's terrible sufferings we find the difficult conversations between Job and his wife and companions. They beg him to rebel against the divine decree. His wife and companions share an attitude common to most of humanity, whereby the believer expects a reward: I believe and God compensates me, I ask and he gives, I pray and he answers. But Job has moved far beyond that approach. He draws a complete separation between the historical reality of his physical life and the spiritual condition of his soul. He believes in God with no expectation of reward. He knows there is no connection between the righteous and the experience of good, nor between the wicked and the experience of evil. Like us, he has encountered situations in which "the way of the wicked" (Prov. 4:19) is well paved. Job is one of the first and only figures who learns to separate faith from history. In many senses Job is the model on which a new theology must be based.

I am well aware, both from first-hand experience and from conversations with friends and ideological opponents, how hard it is for religious traditionalists to accept the reality of a God who is not all good or all-powerful, or is so incomprehensible to us that observance of commandments might be beside the point, either because he meant something entirely different or we simply don't understand. Precisely because it is so difficult to connect the points of the triangle of faith – Jonas's God of goodness, power and accessibility – a new bridge between God and man is needed, one that will allow us to act in the world as though we understand the intention of creation. Instead focusing on God's failure at Auschwitz, Birkenau, Majdanek and Dachau, I want to place the responsibility on myself, on all of us, on humanity, and remove God from the flow of daily life and human events. I have no control over God, nor can I say for certain precisely what sort of control he has over me. But the reins of human life are in my hands. They are here and now, and I can speak, agree, accept, reject, struggle, understand or contradict whatever they do. Accordingly, I would like to build a world that rests on faith in humankind and its communities and ignore God and the things he is reported – by hearsay – to have said.

The religion of responsibility suggested here gives the believer a different status. I refrain from bearing witness to the greatness of God on earth – I myself am the testimony. If my individual conduct is proper and befitting of my humanity, then the greater humanity of which I am a part will function that much better. I am the best testimony to the condition of the world, its creator and its creatures. On the other hand, if I adopt the opposite stance – if I become malicious, indifferent, greedy and violent – then I amount to hostile testimony. From now on we need to say: Man is not witness to the greatness of God, but rather, the greatness of Man is testimony to the greatness of creation. God's fingerprints are stamped on each one of us – his image and the shadows of his memory. If our behavior is fitting and upright, then the image that we reflect is lifted up along with us. And if not, then the image of God descends into something dark and threatening. It is as Tchernichovsky wrote in the poem quoted in our commentary on *Parashat Shemot*: "That I still believe in Man – As I still believe in you."

The Reeducation of God

THIS WEEK'S PORTION BEGINS by revisiting an issue we examined last week: the slave's relationship with power. As we saw, God ordered the Israelites to stay indoors on the Passover night of redemption, fearing that the pent-up anger after years of slavery might turn us into an angry, revenge-seeking mob. This week's portion, *Parashat Beshalach*, opens by presenting the other side of that relationship between power and the weak.

He understood us well, the almighty creator who chose our forefathers. Hooligans, bullies, frustrated workers, hot-headed youth and even ordinary, hard-luck drifters are capable of venting their anger on the first target that crosses their path. It damages the victim, to be sure. But this doesn't constitute genuine power. The physical strength of individual members of a group isn't the same as group power. In fact, this is weakness. There are many examples in history and modern life of this mysterious link between street violence and national weakness. We might even take it one step further: the greater the violence on the street, the more the strength of the group or nation is drained away, even to the point of helplessness.

God feared last week that an explosion of street violence would undermine the Israelite nation's newly acquired power. The same fear drives him this week as well. Headed into the desert, "God led them not by the way of the land of the Philistines, although that was near; for God said: 'Lest peradventure the people repent when they see war, and they return to Egypt'" (Exod. 13:17). He fears that when they come face to face with the harsh reality of war, everything will collapse in an instant.

On the level of history, the military realities of that period can be seen in God's concern as he leads the people. The land of Israel, geographical Palestine, was the land bridge between the Mesopotamian kingdoms to the north and the Egyptian empire to the south. In that period, Canaan was an Egyptian province. Three main overland north-south routes traversed the country, as they do today: the road that passes through the low-lying Jordan Valley; the path of the patriarchs along the central mountain ridge (from Beersheba north through Hebron, Bethlehem, Shechem and modern Jenin into the Jezreel Valley en route to Damascus); and most important, the sea coast highway, Via Maris of Roman times, which our text calls "the way of the land of the Philistines." This last route followed the Mediterranean coast and passed through the Philistine cities of Ashkelon and Gaza. The section that crossed the northern Sinai into the Nile Delta was dotted with military fortifications, meant to defend against invaders from the north and east and to protect caravans carrying trade. From the point of view of the fleeing Israelites this route made no strategic sense, since it would have led them from the house of bondage straight into the Egyptian army's strongholds. Therefore God led them south, bypassing the army by crossing the Red Sea and heading into the desert.

The whole of *Parashat Beshalach* is marked by a tension between two stories that serve as fundamental narratives: at the beginning of the portion, the war with the Egyptians at the Red Sea that was averted by miracle, and at the end, the war with Amalek. "Then came Amalek, and fought with Israel in Rephidim" (Exod. 17:8). The first war, in which we never took up arms, ended when God delivered a knockout blow on our behalf. "Pharaoh's chariots and his host hath he cast into the sea, and his chosen captains are sunk in the Red Sea" (Exod. 15:4). And from that day to this, twice every day in the morning and evening, we drown them again in our prayers. The second war was an entirely human war, us against them. Here too we won a clear, unambiguous victory. "And it came to pass, when Moses held up his hand, that Israel prevailed; and when he let down his hand, Amalek prevailed" (Exod. 17:11). That was a hard day, the day of the first battle in our history. Of course there were dead and wounded, but the end was decisive: "And Joshua discomfited Amalek and his people with the edge of the sword" (Exod. 17:13).

Why then has our people's memory failed to record the defeat of Amalek as a victory, turning it instead into a never-ending war that has never been decided? And to sharpen the question, let's take particular note of two verses. One places us on the Red Sea shore, when the people are on the verge of despair. As Pharaoh approaches and we are minutes away from becoming his victims, Moses calms the people: "Fear ye not, stand still, and see the salvation of the Lord, which he will work for you to-day; for whereas ye have seen the Egyptians to-day, ye shall see them again no more forever. The Lord will fight for you, and ye shall hold your peace" (Exod. 14:13–14). And at the end of the war with Amalek, Moses obliges God to triumph, and one of them – either God dictating or Moses writing – takes this vow: "The hand upon the throne of the Lord: the Lord will have war with Amalek from generation to generation" (Exod. 17:16). At that moment, both military victories were clear-cut. And yet, God commanded us to remember things differently: "And the Lord said unto Moses: 'Write this for a memorial in the book, and rehearse it in the ears of Joshua: for I will utterly blot out the remembrance of Amalek from under heaven'" (Exod. 17:14). Why?

In order to give a partial answer to the difference between the legacies of two wars whose outcomes were equal – unambiguous victory – but whose memories are different, we need to look at the biblical context in which the two war stories are told. Professor Yeshayahu Leibowitz counted the number of verses in the portion, and found they fell into two equal groups. The first fifty-eight verses tell of euphoria. Masses of people march out of the Egyptian prison. Pharaoh and his chariots chase after them. God splits the sea. Moses leads the procession while Miriam regales the people with dance. In this miraculous chapter, even war is resolved by miracle. Miracle is the name of the game in the first half of the portion.

In the middle of the portion and through the next fifty-eight verses, the God of miracles comes face to face with human reality, specifically Israelite reality. This half brings a stream of complaints, whining, despair, insolence and rebellion. There is not enough food, not enough water, and people begin to protest that they were better off in Egypt; finally, the Israelites are attacked by Amalek. The transition from euphoria to funk is instantaneous. As sublime and effortless as God's war by the sea had been from Israel's point of view, the war with Amalek was mundane, bloody and exhausting. This is a portion in which the miraculous gives way to a national discontent that has never truly dissipated.

The difference between the two halves of the portion seems obvious: God's war by the sea is a miraculous, one-time event that began and ended on the seashore. Joshua's war against Amalek is on a human scale, part of a process of sweat and endurance that marks human endeavor ever since. In a larger sense, leaving Egypt is part of an overarching process in which God effectively takes his leave from the human arena.

Look at the sequence of events: up to the revelation at Mount Sinai, God appears in a riveting cycle of amazing, one-time spectacles, including the expulsion from the Garden of Eden, the Flood, Sodom and Gomorrah, the Exodus from Egypt and the giving of the Torah. Remarkably, almost every one of these appearances is followed by a fall. Adam was expelled from the Garden of Eden, but the lesson seems not to have had much impact, and the next generation moved from disobedience to murder. There was a great Flood, but violence and thievery did not cease. Sodom and Gomorrah were destroyed, but wickedness and depravity did not vanish from the world. The sea was split, but three days later the complaints and insubordination

Beshalach

had begun. The Torah was handed down amid thunder and lightning, but within forty days the Golden Calf had been forged amid sin and sinners.

This week's two-part portion recapitulates these extremes of majesty and degradation in a quick demonstration of the cyclical nature of creation. Neither reforming humanity nor repairing the world ever results from a single action. Miracles, no matter how impressive, do not last. Human nature is slower, more gradual. The giving of the Torah was a failure. It's impossible, my dear Lord of the Universe, to impose a Torah – as excellent as it may be – from above. One can only wait patiently until it's absorbed and begins to blossom from below. Sometimes it takes thousands of years, and even then there's still room for improvement.

The last conflict the children of Israel faced in the sweltering desert before the war with Amalek is summed up in these words: "And the name of the place was called Massah [trial], and Meribah [strife], because of the striving of the children of Israel, and because they tried the Lord, saying: 'Is the Lord among us, or not?'" (Exod. 17:7). It follows a series of complaints of hunger and thirst that were answered with various quick fixes, including manna and quail, each accompanied by more grumbling – from above and below.

The language of the Hebrew verse is telling. There seems to be a deliberate echo in the words *nes* (miracle) and *nastam* (their trying [of the Lord]), referring to an incident immediately before, when the people complained that they were thirsty and Moses responded, "wherefore do ye try (*tenasun*) the Lord?" (Exod. 17:2). The first half of the portion was dominated by God's *nes*, his triumphant miracle of the parting of the sea. The second half takes place in the shadow of the people's trying behavior (*nastam*) when they don't get what they want. When God doesn't supply a *nes*, the people respond with *nastam*. If you haven't got a triumph, you're going to get a trial. But God doesn't always pass the test. For evidence, look at the next verse, immediately after the naming of Massah (trial) and Meribah (strife): "Then came Amalek, and fought with Israel in Rephidim" (Exod. 17:8). In this war, the triumph results not from a miracle but from human action, by Joshua and his warriors.

Note, however, that God takes responsibility for his believers' trial of him. This is how the portion concludes:

> And the Lord said unto Moses: "Write this for a memorial in the book, and rehearse it in the ears of Joshua: for I will utterly block out the remembrance of Amalek from under heaven." And Moses built an altar, and called the name of it *Adonai-nissi*. And he said: "The hand upon the throne of the Lord: the Lord will have war with Amalek from generation to generation." (Exod. 17:14–15)

Israel has put God to a new test, one with which he is not familiar. In remembrance of the event Moses puts up an altar and calls it *Adonai-nissi*, which can mean both "God is my miracle" and "God is my banner." But it seems significant to me that this was a trial of God. And God, having apparently failed in his first trial, or at least felt dissatisfied with his outcome, took on an amazing process of self-education. If that were not the case, why would he need this eternal war with Amalek from that moment until the end of time, "from generation to generation"?

From this perspective, the war against Amalek is not only God's way of checking whether Israel is ready to fight and win on its own; it is also a test of God – whether he is ready to let us manage our world on our own without his dazzling, trying, one-time-only interventions. And to make sure he doesn't forget, we remind him periodically through the commandments of memory and remembrance that we have taken upon ourselves as a people of memory.

Week 17

Yitro – Jethro, the Priest of Midian

Exodus 18:1–20:23

The Holy Temple as a Hall of World Peace

T̲he Holy Temple has, in effect, two different histories. One is the factual history, a tale soaked in blood, human jealousy and national trauma. Here you have the tales of the Maccabees and the Hasmoneans, crowned with acts of characteristically Hellenic physical courage. Generations later come the wars of Jerusalem and its zealots, leading to the great bloodbath that culminated in the burning of the Second Temple and two thousand years of fasting and prayer in commemoration of that defining calamity. There are many more stories one could add about temples and synagogues that became centers of unpleasant and even violent dispute throughout our religious history.

Alongside the practical, historical narrative – and in contrast to it – there is a deeply rooted tradition that yearns for a place of peaceful worship. It strives mightily to pose the Temple as an alternative ideal, in contrast to the force and violence that so often accompany extreme piety. Hidden below ground there is an entire world of subversive ideas, neither political nor self-serving, that aspire to build a sanctuary of peace among people, and within people. Sometimes a stream breaks through to the surface and presents itself as a tolerant, universalist alternative to the violence of religious fanaticism. Here is how the ideal is expressed at the end of this brief but fraught portion:

> And the Lord said unto Moses: Thus shalt thou say unto the children of Israel: Ye yourselves have seen that I have talked with you from

> heaven. Ye shall not make with me – gods of silver, or gods of gold, ye shall not make unto you. An altar of earth thou shalt make unto me, and shalt sacrifice thereon thy burnt-offerings, and thy peace-offerings, thy sheep, and thine oxen; in every place where I cause my name to be mentioned I will come unto thee and bless thee. And if thou make me an altar of stone, thou shalt not build it of hewn stones; for if thou lift up thy tool upon it, thou hast profaned it. (Exod. 20:19–22)

A stunning command. Just a moment earlier, the formal ceremony of the giving of the Torah was completed. The thunder is still echoing through the wadis and canyons of Sinai. The people are still a bit euphoric after the astonishing public revelation of God on earth. The sounds and visions haven't even faded, and here is this ultimate commandment of peace: God prefers a humble altar made of earth. Nonetheless, if the worshipper wishes to build something more steady, permanent and perhaps even a bit dignified, meaning a real stone altar, there is a condition: the stone must be raw, uncut stone. The reason is quite simple and very human: "If thou lift up thy tool upon it, thou hast profaned it." Rashi offers the essential logic in the name of ancient Midrash:

> You may learn this: If you lift up iron upon it, you have profaned it. The altar was created to lengthen the days of man, and iron was created to cut them short. It is not right that what shortens our days should be brought against what lengthens them.... We may draw a logical extension [*kal vachomer*].... Stones, which do not see nor hear nor speak, in order that they may bring peace, the Torah forbids lifting iron against them.... How much more so, then, that no harm should be done to one who brings peace between husband and wife, between one family and another or between man and his neighbor. (Rashi on Exod. 20:22)

Where does this come from? And where is it going? Our tradition connects the story of the binding of Isaac to the site of the Temple. It was on the spot where the angel of God prevented Abraham from slaughtering his son that the Temple was built. In my home, God lets us know, there will be no slaughtering of human beings or spilling of blood. At most the blood of animal sacrifice will be permitted as a substitute for the primordial custom of human sacrifice. Later, much later, God prevents David from building the Temple. Not because the king isn't capable of it, not because he doesn't want it enough, but for other reasons entirely. On the one hand, God doesn't really feel like moving, and so he questions the idea, speaking through the prophet Nathan: "I have not dwelt in a house since the day that I brought up the children of Israel out of Egypt, even to this day, but have walked in a tent and in a tabernacle. In all places wherein I have walked among all the children of Israel, spoke I a word with any of the tribes of Israel, whom I commanded to feed my people Israel, saying: Why have ye not built me a house of cedar?" (2 Sam. 7:6–7). The desert God could not be more plainspoken and direct. He has a hard time moving from a tent into a house, from the wide-open spaces of the desert into the alleyways of Jerusalem.

Not only is the tenant uninterested; he doesn't think the developer, David, is right for the job. The Book of Samuel doesn't spell out precisely why he's the wrong builder. It simply states the facts:

> And it came to pass, when the king dwelt in his house, and the Lord had given him rest from all his enemies round about, that the king said unto Nathan the prophet: "See now, I dwell in a house of cedar, but the Ark of God dwelleth within curtains." And Nathan said to the king: "Go, do all that is in thy heart; for the Lord is with thee. And it came to pass the same night, that the word of the Lord came unto Nathan, saying: Go and tell my servant David, saying: Thus saith the Lord: Shalt thou build me a house for me to dwell in?" (2 Sam. 7:1–5)

King David and the prophet Nathan thought the time had come. Nathan even gave his blessing to the project: "Go, do all that is in thy heart; for the Lord is with thee." But at the end of the day, appearing in a night vision, God explained to the prophet Nathan that his own position was completely different. In the morning he sent him to explain to David that he hadn't been picked for the job, without too many explanations. Only at the very end of the Bible, somewhere deep in the Book of Chronicles, we find the truth, as presented by the rejected David himself:

> And David said to Solomon: "My son, as for me, it was in my heart to build a house unto the name of the Lord my God. But the word of the Lord came to me, saying: Thou hast shed blood abundantly, and hast made great wars; thou shalt not build a house unto my name, because thou hast shed much blood upon the earth in my sight." (1 Chron. 22:7–8)

A person whose hands have shed much blood cannot build a Temple whose purpose is so utterly different.

It was the prophet Isaiah who laid out the contours of the true national project:

> The word that Isaiah the son of Amoz saw concerning Judah and Jerusalem. And it shall come to pass in the end of days, that the mountain of the Lord's house shall be established as the top of the mountains, and shall be exalted above the hills; and all the nations shall flow unto it. And many peoples shall go and say: "Come ye, and let us go up to the mountain of the Lord, to the house of the God of Jacob; and he will teach us of his ways, and we will walk in his paths." For out of Zion shall go forth the law, and the word of God from Jerusalem. And he shall judge between the nations, and shall decide for many peoples; and they shall beat their swords into plowshares, and their spears into pruning hooks; nation shall not lift up sword against nation, neither shall they learn war any more. (Isa. 2:1–4)

Again we see the reverse connection between the true Temple and weapons of war. You are either the people of Esau with swords girded on or believers of "the house of the God of Jacob," people of peace who have buried the weapons of death forever in the ground, in principle. There's a broad hint directed at all the armed believers with their broad beards and long-barreled guns in the scolding words of Isaiah: "And when ye spread forth your hands, I will hide mine eyes from you; yea, when ye make many prayers, I will not hear; your hands are full of blood" (Isa. 1:15).

In short, the Temple, God's sanctuary, is intended to be the house and home of world peace, going back to the time of the binding of Isaac and forward to the very end of days. Anyone who does not fit these initial criteria is not worthy of the sanctuary or of sanctity, of home or of peace.

The Ten Commandments: Israel's Earliest Constitution

FROM THE SAYINGS OF MY FATHER and teacher, may he rest in peace: "All that is left of the Ten Commandments in our time is a pair of fragments: 'I am' and 'You shall not have.'"

My father made gentle fun of the egotism and egocentrism of modern-day humanity, but as always, his words had a basis in serious, ancient texts: "Rabbi Ishmael taught: 'I am' and 'You shall not have' were spoken by the Almighty" (Babylonian Talmud, *Horayot* 8a), and the rest were spoken by Moses. And in the Midrash, concerning the second version of the Ten Commandments that appears in Deuteronomy 5 in *Parashat Va'etchanan*, we are told what would have happened if one more commandment had been given to them directly by the Lawgiver. The second, Deuteronomic version, "teaches us that if one more commandment had been added, they would have died." The disciples of Rabbi Ishmael drew a similar lesson, though in a slightly different form, from the verse that follows immediately after the giving of the Ten Commandments: "And they said unto Moses: 'Speak thou with us, and we will hear, but let not God speak with us, lest we die' (Exod. 20:16). This tells us that they did not have the strength to absorb more than ten commandments" (Mechilta of Rabbi Ishmael on *Parashat Yitro* 8).

Other scholars disagree with the idea that the giving of the commandments might have been split, insisting passionately that the entire gift was given to the children of Israel at Mount Sinai in that one gathering at Mount Sinai. In a sense, though, it doesn't matter. The sages were arguing over the method of transmission. My late father was playfully drawing our attention not to the way the commandments were given, but to the way they were received. The question, then, is what was in those commandments that was so difficult to receive?

What are these ten commandments, these ten statements? What is the special status and significance of these ten utterances, and why are these the images that are emblazoned above the Ark of the Torah in every synagogue? Why weren't some other, equally important words or commandments chosen to engage the worshippers' line of sight every morning and evening? A variety of answers have been suggested. In one view, the commandments are the pure, concentrated essence of the Torah as a whole, a sort of distillate containing all the truths of the Torah within it. Another understanding is that they constitute an independent opus, almost a book within a book that presents an inner truth separate from the larger flow of events and commandments that make up the Torah.

For me, the Ten Commandments are a separate unit with its own truth – a truth of faith and spirituality without the overlay of surplus legislation meant to limit and control people. This is the law of the heart, not an obligation of physical and material actions. This is a direct, uncluttered dialogue between the individual human and the great, unseen, mysterious creation to which we are partners, not conquerers or enemies. To my mind, there is a substantive difference between the Torah's elaborate system of rules and the thesis presented in the Ten Commandments.

First, let's consider what the Ten Commandments do not contain. They have no system of governance comparable to the judges, police and kings scattered throughout the Bible. There is no description of any institutions or governing organizations such as Jethro recommended to Moses at the beginning of this week's portion. There is no reference to a nation or people, but solely to individuals whom God addresses in the first person, with the intimacy of a one-to-one conversation, like a father speaking with his children: "thy God," "for thee." There is no mention of a priesthood, Levite class or prophecy. This is a separate set, a direct conversation between the individual and his or her God, with none of the filters that dim so much of the primordial beauty of the scripture. The Ten

Commandments are a pure essence of the beliefs of the heart, without the technical rules of the body.

The last eight of the commandments could form the basic platform of any decent human society. Imagine a world that has agreed without argument not to murder, steal or covet, a world that honors the individual and his or her work and therefore preserves a day of absolute rest, a sacred Sabbath, a day dedicated to soothing the body and pursuing the significance of the soul and the spirit. Imagine a world and a society in which the family in all its permutations is the foundation of the human community – the old traditional family or the new family with its many forms and genders. A family founded on honoring and respecting life and its creators cannot be a place of violence. These commandments are the constitution of the better world for which we strive.

That leaves us with the first two commandments, the commandments of faith. In the Middle Ages, there was a theological disagreement between the ruling Christianity and the stigmatized Judaism over the question of whether punishment and coercion should apply only to the active, behavioral commandments or also to the commandments of the heart. Maimonides, a famous fugitive from religious persecution, declared without hesitation that one who denies the principles of faith should be "hated, rejected and destroyed." Don Isaac Abravanel, who fled from Portugal to Spain, from Spain to Naples and from Naples to Venice because of his Judaism, believed with all his heart that "the commandments apply also to matters of faith, and so the revelation commanded us." And the punishment of the unbeliever? "Annihilation by fire, brimstone and burning furnace." But is there any way to compel a person to believe? Can violence and force really change the leanings of the heart? In my opinion, no – even if many others believe it. The priests of the medieval Inquisition have brothers in spirit whose mission carries on to this very day. They continue even in our time to impose the commandments of faith by coercion and threats. The first two commandments stand in opposition to this path and testify to something different. They invite us to consider an old-new text whose meaning hasn't dimmed, indeed might only now be coming into its own.

"I am the Lord thy God" and "Thou shalt have no other gods before me" (Exod. 20:2–3) are one utterance with two aspects: on the one hand, the positive statement that we have a God, and on the other hand, the negative statement that nothing else can be a substitute god. What is this obsessive, unyielding war against idol worship? Why is it bad to worship several gods? What's the problem with a colorfully mythical pantheon like that of the Greeks? Is one God so much more helpful than many gods? The modern answer is certainly not. Miracles, if they ever existed, are finished and will not return. We're better off with a world of orderly laws of nature in which everything is known, understood and expected. The laws of creation are revealed to us in a slow, never-ending process, like the layers of an onion that becomes transparent as it is peeled.

It seems to me that the emphasis on God, "one and unique in his oneness" (from the Yigdal hymn), is not directed at some divine ego-trip but straight into the human interior – "*you* shall have no other gods." Every person is a complex mix of characteristics, needs and instincts, including impulses such as greed, jealousy, acquisitiveness along with basic needs like food and sex. Deep within this complex mix there has to be a spiritual need. There has to be an inner recess of eternal search for meaning. Out of that inner core come the morality and values that give humanity preeminence above the animals (cf. Eccl. 3:19), because all the rest is vanity. That's why these constitutional commandments are written in the singular and directed to you the reader, to "thee" and no one else.

This is not the pride of a nation or culture looking down on its fellows, but the insight that creates a sense of proportion within each of us. The responsibility to look for the sublime, to give an advantage to the spiritual and moral over the physical, is incumbent on you, the individual. Abstract divinity, having no body, image or appearance, can take any form the seeker might give it when implanting it in the sanctuary of his or her heart. "That I may dwell among them" (Exod. 25:8) is the very essence of the Jewish faith. This is the eternal struggle against the selfishness of the "I," the conquering of desire by directing it constantly upward toward the moral and ethical.

The other eight commandments follow from this, the reining in of the biological and psychological by the spiritual and moral. More than that, in our world, which lacks the elevated and sublime, in which everything is relative and everything is equal to everything else, every arena and field has its own gods – the gods of needs and the divinity of satisfying them. These compete forcefully among themselves and create the callous universe of want and inequality in which we live. The first two commandments, the commandments of the heart, come to establish a hierarchy that gives priority to what is within. They make our bodily and material needs secondary, and thus less cruel. The first two commandments aren't a whim of divine ego, as my father jestingly taught, but a desire of the heart for a better world that comes from within the individual world of meaning.

Week 18

Mishpatim – The Ordinances

Exodus 21:1–24:18

"These Are the Words" or "These Are the Ordinances"

"Now these are the ordinances which thou shalt set before them" (Exod. 21:1). After the giving of the Torah comes a long list of rules and commands, most of which deal with the criminal justice system of the Torah of Israel. A vast array of social organization was spawned by the "ordinances" of this week's portion: laws of violence; limits on slavery and servitude; laws of property, its loss and its responsibilities; relations between the citizen and the government; procedures and rules of courtroom testimony and much more. It is an impressive compendium of fundamentals that evolved over the years into the Jewish people's system of law and order. Almost every verse in the portion acquired its own heaps upon heaps of commentary. But this time, we are going to follow the trail of one single word, one Hebrew letter in the portion. I want to focus on the first word *and*, represented in Hebrew by the single letter *vav*, in the opening phrase, "And these are the ordinances."

Rashi, speaking in the name of several earlier commentators, focuses on that same *vav* and begins his commentary on the portion as follows: "And these are the ordinances – every place where the word 'these' appeared, it canceled what came before, while 'and these' built upon what came before. The earlier decrees came from Sinai, and so did these come from Sinai" (Rashi on Exod. 21:1). Rashi uses that simple *vav* to support a whole system of human laws, the criminal rules of procedure of those who left

Mishpatim

Egypt, and link it to the giving of the Torah and the Ten Commandments. He goes on to interpret the contiguity between last week's portion, with its commandments, and the laws of this week's portion: "And why is the portion describing the laws connected to the following portion [*Parashat Terumah*, beginning Exod. 25:1], which describes the altar? To teach you that the high court of law should be placed next to the Holy Temple" (Rashi on Exod. 21:1). Many other commentators follow in Rashi's spirit and add various layers to the connection between the giving of the Torah in last week's portion and the detailed rules of this week's.

After having considered all these deep connections, I want to suggest a different explanation for that *vav*, the "and" in "And these are the ordinances." This is not actually a *vav chibur*, the connecting *vav* that translates as *and*; this is a *vav hipuch*, the reversing *vav* in biblical Hebrew that changes verbs from past to future tense and vice versa. Normally, the reversing *vav* applies only to the tenses of verbs. I would like to suggest that this *vav* is there to change the experience of standing at Mount Sinai into something else. These two adjacent portions are not a continuation and elaboration of a single line of thought, but two different spiritual and emotional states that are fundamentally opposed to one another. The giving of the Torah is the climax of a singular experience of revelation, while the laws and ordinances represent the day-to-day obligation to build a decent, just and compassionate human society. This is the contrast between passion and routine, between the unusual and the day-to-day.

There are several Torah stories that concern some event of great proportions, something vast and elevated in appearance whose immediate result is to disappoint and turn positive energy into anger and negativity. Here are a few of them: the creation and the expulsion from the Garden of Eden; the parting of the Red Sea and the strife at Marah; the revelation at Sinai and the sin of the Golden Calf. Time after time God tries to manage the world by crashing into daily reality with thunder and lightning, arriving with a bang and promptly disappearing. But humans are only human. They need something permanent, stable, reliable. The exceptional confuses them. After the peak comes the fall, and the higher the elevation of the event, the more painful the reconnection with the hard ground of reality. Real-life experience teaches that a person who falls from a starting place on the floor suffers less than someone who hits the ground from the penthouse level.

In this sense, this week's portion, *Parashat Mishpatim*, is the alternative to the giving of the Torah. God came down from the mountain and left ten sublime commandments behind. This revelation is far behind us by now, and as for the decline of the Ten Commandments, I noted what my father had to say about it. Still, the collection of laws in this week's portion gave rise to a normative and moral system that became the basis for a stable world of Torah, law and binding judicial precedent. The Mishnah and Talmud, the responsa literature and, indirectly, Israeli law all draw from the roots found in this portion. The structures built gradually from below by humans turn out to be far more stable than the palace of wonders brought down by God from heaven above. The process of learning the scriptures and turning verse into law, regulation, instruction and limitation is an alternative way of managing the world. The path of slow, evolutionary development is preferable to the shortcut of revolution that, dazzling though it may be, ends in a painful crash-landing.

"And these are the ordinances" is the traditional Jewish way that won out over the childish religiosity of olden days. In the era of religious childishness, people needed God to be present like a babysitter. But very quickly this presence turned to quarreling that ended in disappointment and destruction. Now we are at a stage in which God has disappeared from our lives, but on the strength of those distant commands, and thanks to God's removal from the process, we're able to manage our world with a measure of stability. True, we no longer have wonderful dramas, and yet the disappointments are easier to tolerate. So what's preferable – *Yitro* or *Mishpatim*? The revelation at Sinai, or a system of law and order? Take your choice.

The Missed Opportunity

THE LATE PHILOSOPHER MARTIN BUBER, it's said, once commented that if we all lived by the biblical rule of an eye for an eye, we would all be blind by now.

Mishpatim

After the giving of the constitution and ethical principles of Hebrew jurisprudence at Mount Sinai in last week's portion, and after Jethro's construction of a social organization for the people leaving Egypt, the time has come for content and minor details. Ordinances and decrees, laws and instructions fill our portion from the beginning almost to the end. Every one of the subordinate laws of Torah in the portion is an invitation to a broader examination, and the Talmud and commentators, both early and late, take full advantage of the invitation. And, as always, when the legalistic arguments fill every empty space, it's hard to make room for other understandings of background, symbolism and significance. As such, few remember the ending of this portion. God invites Moses and the leaders who were with him to come to him. "And unto Moses he said: 'Come up unto the Lord, thou, and Aaron, Nadab, and Abihu, and seventy of the elders of Israel; and worship ye afar off'" (Exod. 24:1). Down below, in the camp, a complicated process develops of preparation for the summit. It's not entirely clear whether this is a different version of the story of Mount Sinai or the same story with some added details that had been left out last week. Let's look at the whole thing as a single package: Jethro comes and advises, the people prepare, Moses and the elders go up to the mountain. Moses steps further forward to receive the Torah, the Golden Calf is born down below and the rest is history.

In any event, after all the various ceremonies of the covenant, something interesting happens: "Then went up Moses, and Aaron, Nadab, and Abihu, and seventy of the elders of Israel; and they saw the God of Israel; and there was under his feet the like of a paved work of sapphire stone, and the like of the very heaven for clearness. And upon the nobles of the children of Israel he laid not his hand; and they beheld God, and did eat and drink" (Exod. 24:9–11). For the average reader of the mysteries and hidden treasures of the Torah, this is what might be called a "Wow" moment. What is "and they saw the God of Israel" supposed to mean? What is "and they beheld God"? Human beings, flesh and blood, saw the creation of the universe? With their own eyes? That's diametrically opposed to the claims of God, who will turn down Moses's request in just a few weeks to see him, or at least his glory.

In *Parashat Ki Tissa*, beginning in chapter 30, verse 11 of Exodus, after the sin of the Golden Calf and God's great anger, Moses asks God, "Show me, I pray thee, thy glory" (Exod. 33:18). And God replies, "Thou canst not see my face, for man shall not see me and live" (Exod. 22:20). All our lives we have been brought up on the understanding that humankind is unable to see God. Perhaps because seeing in ancient Hebrew also meant understanding, and a human who sees and understands God is no longer human but something else. Perhaps because seeing is eyewitness proof, and if God is proven he is no longer an object of faith but something known and recognizable, part of the concrete, natural world – and a culture whose God is proven is a culture of science and knowledge and, perhaps, a culture without faith. And perhaps simply because God's greatness is so vast that the sensory receptors of the mortal human creature are too narrow to contain the proportions of the God whose "glory fills the universe."

All these assumptions are void, however, in light of the sensational revelation lurking at the end of our portion: "And they saw the God of Israel" (Exod. 24:10). It's written explicitly. And don't let them tell you it's simply imagination or a reflection in a mirror. These verses are filled with verbs describing the human senses: they ate, they drank, they saw, they beheld. The eating and drinking were real. The seeing was just as real.

To understand the mystery and explain this opaque passage, let's return for a moment to the Exodus. All of the plagues that befell Egypt were performed in broad daylight. Only the plague of darkness came in darkness. And in the midst of the great darkness, when no one could see or understand a thing, Pharaoh, the divine emperor of Egypt, scolded Moses: "Get thee from me, take heed to thyself, see my face no more; for in the day thou seest my face thou shalt die" (Exod. 10:28). Out of his personal darkness, he commands him not to see. The very same process unfolds in the Book of Esther, which we read on Purim: "All the king's servants, and the people of the king's provinces, do know, that whosoever, whether man or woman, shall come unto the king into the inner court, who is not called, there is one law for him, that he be put to death, except such to whom the king shall hold out the golden scepter, that he may live" (Esth. 4:11). All of Moses's appearances before Pharaoh had the king's authorization.

Mishpatim

The dramatic summit meeting between Esther and Ahasuerus was possible because the king permitted it. Therefore, God's invitation to Moses and Aaron and the elders to come to the mountain was a sort of holding out of the golden scepter, a permit to meet with the king – in this case, the King of kings. That is the custom: kings do not see other mortals. Not the kings of Egypt, nor the kings of Persia and Media and not the King of heaven, the King of kings, the Holy One, praised be he. Only on rare occasions does the king reveal himself, at the time of his desire, in the hour of mercy.

Such a moment, a time of rare desire, was revealed at the time of the elevation of the soul when the Torah was given at Sinai. The revelation at Sinai, the Ten Commandments and the practical laws of *Parashat Mishpatim* are all elements of a complex, celebratory process of forging a covenant – which is to say, an agreement between two parties. In honor of the signing, party A, God, deigned to attend the signing ceremony, and so did representatives of party B, Moses, Aaron, Nadab, Abihu and the seventy elders. At the end of the ceremony, the parties gathered for a conversation about this and that. But then, in that instant of great exaltation, mankind missed the moment. Instead of conversing, clarifying, rising up to the heights of the pure and holy, they sat down to dine, to gluttonize and to party. There is no greater affront. It is an embarrassment to the diners and an insult to the guest.

In the Song of Songs this omission is defined in the most beautiful language of lovers: "Hark! my beloved knocketh" (Song 5:2). The lover knocks on his beloved's door, wishing to enter and make love. He's actually pleading, "Open to me, my sister, my love, my dove, my undefiled" (Song 5:2). But she is busy with trifles, full of excuses – I have a headache, I'm tired, I'm not dressed, "I have put off my coat; how shall I put it on? I have washed my feet; how shall I defile them?" (Song 5:3). She with her mundane excuses and he disappointed, fed up, ready to look elsewhere. And the result: "I rose to open to my beloved.... I opened to my beloved; but my beloved had turned away, and was gone. My soul failed me when he spoke. I sought him, but I could not find him; I called him, but he gave me no answer" (Song 5:6). Precisely the way that missed opportunity played out at the foot of Mount Sinai, when God came ready for love, knocked on the door and was revealed. But our elders were eating and drinking and living it up. And God, like that gentle, disappointed lover, turned elsewhere. He returned to his ivory tower and never, ever came back.

Moses understood the missed opportunity. He tried with all his might to seize the divine presence before it disappeared: "Show me, I pray thee, thy glory" (Exod. 33:18), he pleads. This is not the arrogance of a leader of the people who thinks he's entitled to something to which neither he nor any other mortal is entitled. On the contrary, as our senior representative in a dialogue with the sublime, he's trying to take hold of the edge of the disappearing robe of God. If you're angry with them, then at least show me – only me, he suggests. He negotiates. With all his being he wants God, who has just revealed himself among his people and believers, to stay. But God gives him the same retort that Pharaoh gave him earlier: "Man shall not see me and live" (Exod. 33:20). He had offered his love and gotten back an insult, and so he left for good, with the parting words: "Thou shalt see my back, but my face shall not be seen" (Exod. 33:23). If you want to see my glory, the disappearing God shoots back at him, you can see my back. That is, you can see the past that is behind me, but the future, that which lies ahead, you will no longer be able to foresee. Like so many times in history, the climax is also the end. The moment of God's appearance on earth is also the moment of his disappearance.

What do all these stories of glory, honor and insult have to do with us? In part, they explain the deep background to the breakdown in relations between God and humanity. More than that, they are another way to demonstrate that this world is devoid of God. God left the world of his own free choice, and from now on the world is our responsibility, and ours alone. This responsibility doesn't end with the needs of the body, the eating and drinking of the elders at Sinai, but requires a constant search for the meaning and the hidden presence that lies beyond what we can see. Humankind need no longer search for God's glory. The only place where we can hope to find even shreds of that revealed grandeur is within our neighbors, those who were created in God's image and still preserve it here on earth. From now on we should say: in the place that has been emptied of the glory of the creator, we can now find the glory of the humanity that he created – all of humanity.

Week 19

Terumah – Offering

Exodus 25:1–28:19

God's Ark and God's Smile

THIS WEEK THE THIRD ROUND of creation begins. The first round was at the very beginning – the creation of man and his world and the forging of the first bonds between individuals and families. The second round was the history of one family and its evolution into a chosen people. This Sabbath marks the beginning of the third round of creation, namely, the ritual of sacrifice: the sanctuary, the sacred vessels, the priests and sacrifices. Still ahead is the fourth round, which is the transition from ritual cult to territorial nationhood, and Moses's summations. The book of biblical ritual is divided into two parts that are closely interwoven and scarcely distinguishable: the doctrine of the priests and the doctrine of sacrifice. The difference between them is small but significant. The doctrine of the priests covers the role, mission, character and lifestyle of the priests. The doctrine of sacrifice is an interesting mystery in and of itself: Who is the sacrificial victim, what does the act of sacrifice do to the person who offers it, and most of all, why is it that not all theorists and lovers of Jewish wisdom are pleased with the commandment of sacrifice in the desert, even as no one questions the permanence of the priests as an eternally identifiable tribe within the larger body of Israel?

In this week's portion we will focus our gaze on a single spot: the Ark of the covenant. This is the first implement of the tabernacle that Moses is ordered to build. Above the Ark a pure gold crown was placed, called the *kapporet* or Ark-cover, and at the two edges of the *kapporet* were cherubs.

Their precise form was not as important as the distance between them. Reduced into that space – above the Ark and between the two cherubs with their spread wings – was God's revealed presence on the earth that he created: "And there I will meet with thee, and I will speak with thee from above the Ark-cover, from between the two cherubim which are upon the Ark of the testimony, of all things which I will give thee in commandment unto the children of Israel" (Exod. 25:22). But before God enters the Ark, let's take him out for a moment.

These are some of the biblical names of the miraculous Ark: "the Ark of the covenant," "the Ark of God," "the Ark of the Lord," "the Ark of the Lord your God," "the Ark of the God of Israel," "the Ark of the testimony," "the Ark of the covenant of the Lord of all the earth" and "the Ark of the covenant of the Lord of Hosts who sits among the cherubim." It turns out that the famous Ark had two functions. One was as a holy storage space for the fragments of the tablets of the law that Moses broke when he came down from his first revelation atop Mount Sinai. It apparently also contained the replacement tablets that Moses chiseled. This is a passive role, containing and protecting. The second, more rarified function of the Ark was outside the tabernacle, outside the camp of Israel and sometimes even outside the world. That's why it was called the Ark of the Lord of Hosts. This was the Ark's function of war, of hosts or armies and of salvation.

To this day on Sabbaths, holidays, Mondays and Thursdays, when we take the Torah scroll out of the holy Ark in the synagogue, we sing a verse from the Book of Numbers: "And it came to pass, when the Ark set forward, that Moses said: 'Rise up, O Lord, and let thine enemies be scattered; and let them that hate thee flee before thee'" (Num. 10:35). It appears that the Ark and its contents were the non-conventional weapons of the Jewish people. The prayer reflects the hope for rescue from enemies and oppressors, but the text shows that this prayer was not always fulfilled. The children of Israel went to war against the Philistines when the prophet Samuel was young, and they lost on the battlefield:

> And the Philistines put themselves in array against Israel; and when the battle was spread, Israel was smitten before the Philistines; and they slew of the army in the field about four thousand men. And

when the people were come into the camp, the elders of Israel said: "Wherefore hath the Lord smitten us to-day before the Philistines? Let us fetch the Ark of the covenant of the Lord out of Shiloh unto us, that he may come among us, and save us out of the hand of our enemies." So the people sent to Shiloh, and they brought from thence the Ark of the covenant of the Lord of hosts, who sitteth upon the cherubim; and the two sons of Eli, Hophni and Phinehas, were there with the Ark of the covenant of God. And when the Ark of the covenant of the Lord came into the camp, all Israel shouted with a great shout, so that the earth rang.

And when the Philistines heard the noise of the shout, they said: "What meaneth the noise of this great shout in the camp of the Hebrews?" And they knew that the Ark of the Lord was come into the camp. And the Philistines were afraid, for they said, "God is come into the camp." And they said: "Woe unto us! For there was not such a thing yesterday and the day before. Woe unto us! Who shall deliver us out of the hand of these mighty gods? These are the gods that smote the Egyptians with all manner of plagues and in the wilderness. Be strong, and quit yourselves like men, O ye Philistines, that ye be not servants unto the Hebrews, as they have been to you; quit yourselves like men, and fight." And the Philistines fought, and Israel was smitten, and they fled every man to his tent; and there was a very great slaughter; for there fell of Israel thirty thousand footmen. And the Ark of God was taken; and the two sons of Eli, Hophni and Phinehas, were slain. (1 Sam. 4:2–11)

Why did God lose that war? On the surface, the answer is clear: the Philistines were better fighters, better trained and armed, more experienced and more determined. Add to this their desperation to save their freedom and their homes and you have a perfect recipe for victory. But the significance of that victory for the prophetic narrator is quite different. It becomes evident from this story that in war – as in faith and in law – there is no room for God. He doesn't declare wars and he doesn't have to win them.

In the days of the Second Temple, the sages of the academy were divided on the question of an impurity in a certain oven, and the later sages surrounded the topic like snakes: "Why 'Achnai'? Rabbi Judah said, quoting Shmuel: Because words surrounded this like a snake [*achna*] and made it impure" (Babylonian Talmud, *Bava Metzia* 29b). The debate concerned a certain oven that was brought before the Sanhedrin to determine if it was kosher. A majority said it was not, but one member, Rabbi Eliezer Ben Hyrkanus, known for his conservatism, argued that it was. After failing to sway the majority by logic, he called on heaven to prove that his interpretation of the rules of Torah was correct. He was answered by a series of miracles: a river flowing backward, the chamber's walls leaning inward and finally a voice descending from heaven to affirm that Rabbi Eliezer's view represented God's intent. The chairman, Rabbi Joshua, dismissed the argument, saying that God's original intent no longer mattered, since God has given the Torah to humanity and as such "it is not in heaven" (Deut. 30:12).

Some generations later, so the story is told, Rabbi Nathan met the prophet Elijah and asked how God had reacted to the rebuff. Elijah said, "God smiled and said: My children have defeated me, they have defeated me." God admits he has been defeated by a majority vote of the sages and smiles in satisfaction at their accomplishment.

So it is that the Torah is now on earth. It is in our hearts and on our lips to act upon, not far away in heaven where no one can reach it to bring it down to us. So too, every victory against an oppressor or enemy comes from within the human fighter, from the spirit of the nation and the troops and from the determined leadership of the high command. When these values are not esteemed, victory can't be achieved by holy bombast that stirs up momentary passions but does not change the basic conditions of the conflicting sides.

An oft-forgotten biblical tale from the era of the Judges illustrates the point. Toward the end of the period of the Judges, following a setback in their war against the Philistines, the Israelites decide to carry the Ark into battle, so that God "may come among us, and save us out of the hand of our enemies" (1 Sam. 4:3). Unfortunately, the tactic fails and the Ark is captured by the Philistines. This doesn't work out well for the Philistines, who find their god Dagon falling over (1 Sam. 5:3–4), their people breaking out in hemorrhoids (5:9) and their villages overrun with rats (6:5). After seven months of misery they bring the Ark back to the Israelites, who store it away in the home of a priest (7:1). There it sits until David brings it to its resting place in Jerusalem (2 Sam. 6:3–17), and from then on, as the Israelites themselves note (in 1 Chron. 13:3), it is no longer used as a weapon of war. It seems as if God has asked his priests and believers, "Please, leave me in the Ark, and put the Ark into the Holy of Holies, and don't ever use me again in your flesh-and-blood campaigns. Work out your wars without me." Since then, God's travels abroad in his Ark-chariot are limited to distant realms, very far from here. We even sing about this in the Sabbath afternoon hymn known as "*Baruch El Elyon*": "The King of the world rides on the prairies (*rochev aravot melech olamim*)." Nor are these prairies the windswept ones we usually think of in Argentina, South Africa or the Arava desert south of the Dead Sea, but the scriptural ones that stretch across the heavens.

Let's return from the plains of heaven to daily life on Planet Earth. There is a traditional synagogue ritual in which we open the Ark, take out the scroll and sing the hymn mentioned above, from the Book of Numbers: "*Vayehi Binsoa Ha'aron* (And It Came to Pass When the Ark Set Forward)" (Num. 10:35). But the Ark doesn't really go anywhere. It always stays where it is, in the front of the synagogue. Only the Torah itself is actually moved from its place, carried among the worshippers, showered with kisses and caresses, stripped of its garment, read aloud in public and finally returned to its place. So what could this verse mean? It seems to me that this is another refinement and adaptation of an ancient concept to a new reality. After its fall in the field of the Philistines, the Ark lost its deterrent power in real warfare, and since then its message has changed. Today our weapon is the Torah's moral content. The essential Jewish struggle today is not over territories or battlefield body counts, but rather a battle of ideas and beliefs. This battle is fought on the fields of humankind's education and the repair of the world. This war is fought over meaning, and victory consists not in winning against the other, but winning him over. The Ark of the Sinai desert has changed both form and meaning. From a tangible, sacred object, it has become an abstract idea. From a space between two cherubs out of which God emerges, sword drawn, to bloody the enemy, it has become a teaching of life, change, renewal and abstraction through dialogue and warmth, not war and indifference.

Making Love in the Desert

*I*N THE WORLD OF FUND-RAISERS there is a rule of thumb called "eighty-twenty." According to this principle, 80 percent of the donations come from 20 percent of the donors. A corollary principle is that it pays to devote 80 percent of one's energy and attention to that 20 percent of large donors, because they are more productive. It's a principle borrowed from modern economics. Every business turnaround specialist knows that the first step in saving an ailing company is to institute the Pareto principle, namely to sell 80 percent of your products to the most profitable 20 percent of stores – or to sell only 20 percent of your products and abandon all the others, which don't contribute sufficiently to the company's profitability. It's one of the basic laws driving any modern economy. It is a fundamental element in many different economic approaches, and it's one of the central causes of discrimination and inequality. After all, it pays to invest more in the more productive segments of the population, doesn't it? The high school in the affluent neighborhood and the prestigious university will produce the scientists and engineers who will contribute more to the Gross Domestic Product, the tax base, productivity and overall national efficiency. It makes sense to invest in them and not in the weak and unfortunate. This is the population whose cows produce 80 percent of all the cream from birth through blissful retirement.

The biblical approach poses a social and human alternative to the economic principles outlined above, which underlie many of the negative social trends we see around us today. One of the outstanding expressions of this biblical alternative can be found in the core theme of this week's portion, *Terumah*. The portion opens a series of great national undertakings,

Terumah

a mass mobilization that is in part awesome in its power, and in part – as in the case of the Golden Calf – wretchedly sad. The verses that describe the underlying concept appear at the beginning of our portion: "And the Lord spoke unto Moses, saying: 'Speak unto the children of Israel, that they take for me an offering; of every man whose heart maketh him willing ye shall take my offering'" (Exod. 25:1–2).

The execution appears a few weeks later, in *Parashat Vayakhel*:

> And all the congregation of the children of Israel departed from the presence of Moses. And they came, every one whose heart stirred him up, and every one whom his spirit made willing, and brought the Lord's offering, for the work of the tent of meeting, and for all the service thereof, and for the holy garments. And they came, both men and women, as many as were willing-hearted, and brought noserings, and ear-rings, and signet-rings, and girdles, all jewels of gold…and every man, with whom was found acacia-wood for any work of service, brought it. And all the women that were wise-hearted did spin with their hands, and brought that which they had spun, the blue, and the purple, the scarlet, and the fine linen. And all the women whose heart stirred them up in wisdom spun the goats' hair…. The children of Israel brought a free-will offering unto the Lord; every man and woman, whose heart made them willing to bring for all the work, which the Lord had commanded by the hand of Moses to be made. (Exod. 35:20–29)

Leave aside for a moment the images seared into our minds from childhood of the elaborate desert tabernacle, and picture the reality as described in the plain language of the biblical narrative. This is a poor people's project, a ramshackle desert hut made of bits and patches of whatever was at hand, but all a single piece of one great collective heart, a multitude acting as one. One had a bit of perfumed oil she had received from her Egyptian neighbor; another had some leftover cooking oil from her kitchen. Each of them brought the little that they had, poured it into a big basin and together stirred up a mixture of oil for a lamp. The same process apparently occurred with incense, or with gold that wasn't necessarily top quality.

Someone had some cheap costume jewelry, someone else brought a body adornment, perhaps even a chastity device, and they melted it all together to make the gold for the sanctuary.

The gold in the sanctuary wasn't necessarily fourteen karat. These weren't the precious metals of the nobility. On the contrary, this was poor people's material. The message in all the enumerated details of the offerings is clear, at least to me. The humility of the tabernacle was its greatness. The simplicity of the tools and materials constituted the deep essence of this great national undertaking. What do I mean? A young couple, when getting married and preparing for the wedding ceremony, usually lacks the resources to buy a home. They live in a rented or temporary home, often lacking a lease and moving from place to place, getting by on little. These are days of love, not luxury. These are the days when I live in your heart and you come to live in mine, and who cares what our physical surroundings look like?

Only at a later stage of life does love turn into routine. Then the hearts grow a bit further apart and our bodies need a bit more space. The apartment needs to get bigger, the marital bed becomes a vast field, far outgrowing the bodies it houses, and sometimes the great love we promised each other under the wedding canopy turns to separation and divorce. It's not uncommon in later years of coupledom to find artificial means being used to extend intimacy and create feelings in a way that young lovers never needed when they first took their vows. Expensive jewelry, lavish trips, artworks and interior design become substitutes for the most basic feelings of the heart.

The analogy between stages of marriage and place of residence also applies to the history of places of Jewish worship. In the beginning everything was simple. We loved God everywhere: in fields of flowers, on a mountaintop, in the burning desert – pure, unblemished love.

> And then the Lord said unto Moses: Thus thou shalt say unto the children of Israel: Ye yourselves have seen that I have talked with you from heaven. Ye shall not make with me – gods of silver, or gods of gold, ye shall not make unto you. An altar of earth thou shalt make unto me, and shalt sacrifice thereon thy burnt-offerings, and

> thy peace-offerings, thy sheep, and thine oxen; in every place where I cause my name to be mentioned I will come unto thee and bless thee. (Exod. 20:19–21)

There's no need for a formal meeting place. Any place is good enough for the unfolding of a love of faith. But we had grown up, and it wasn't enough. We needed something tangible to make the relationship real, so we made a Golden Calf. And God said, if you really need something, come on over to my place. And so the tabernacle was built. Then came Solomon's Temple, which was much bigger in spite – or perhaps because – of the distance that had grown up between us by then. As for the magnificent Temple of Herod, which was built in the first century BCE, there's not much one can say (the Babylonian Talmud, *Bava Metzia* 4a, says: "Anyone who has never seen the building of Herod has never seen a building") except to note that the beauty and richness of the external vessel was as great as the poverty of its spiritual content.

The Babylonian Talmud paints a colorful picture to illustrate our point:

> Like the man who came and said, When our love was strong, we slept on the blade of a sword. Now that our love is not strong, a bed of sixty cubits is not enough. Rav Huna compares this to the love between the Jewish people and God, bringing verses that show the ever-larger dwelling place of God in the world. When they build the tabernacle in the desert, He tells them: "And there I will meet with thee, and I will speak with thee from above the ark-cover" (Exod. 25:22).... "And the house which king Solomon built for the Lord, the length thereof was threescore cubits, and the breadth thereof twenty cubits, and the height thereof thirty cubits" (1 Kings 6:2). And in the time of the prophets, he says: "Thus saith the Lord: My seat is in heaven, and the earth is the resting place of my feet. What house can you build for me?" (Isa. 66:1). (Babylonian Talmud, *Sanhedrin* 7a)

To sum up: Love is found in intimacy, and intimacy is in simplicity, and the simple is what is voluntary, spontaneous and comes from the people. And above all, that which is equal, given by all freely and willingly, is what becomes the true Temple.

Week 20

Tetzaveh – Thou Shalt Command

Exodus 27:20–30:10

The Biblical Dress Code

*P*ARASHAT *TETZAVEH* IS ONE of the series of portions dealing with the crafting of the tabernacle. It details numerous pieces of handicraft, sanctuary art and wilderness devotion, all made of materials donated as offerings by the ancient faithful of Israel. One of these aesthetic undertakings was the preparation of ceremonial dress for Aaron and his sons: "And thou shalt make holy garments for Aaron thy brother, for splendor and for beauty" (Exod. 28:2). Anyone familiar with the Avodah service on Yom Kippur, describing the high priest's once-a-year entry into the Holy of Holies, knows that we're speaking of a very elaborate outfit, comprising both outer garments and underwear, some of it majestic and some even more majestic, made of various fabrics, ornaments, jewels and decorations. This portion is always read on a Sabbath close to the holiday of Purim, so it's only natural that we draw a connection between this week's portion and the costumery of Purim and discuss the place of clothing in our culture.

The scripture explicitly teaches us that the purpose of the priestly garments is "for splendor and beauty (*lechavod uletiferet*)," although the Hebrew might just as easily be rendered "for honor and grandeur." This begs the question: If they didn't have the special clothing, would they lack honor or grandeur? Looking at religious ceremonies wherever and whenever they can be observed, the answer seems to be yes: religions always need pomp and splendor to create the necessary distance between the sublime and the ordinary. Rabbis, priests and ayatollahs all wear ceremonial garb.

They don robes, headdress, heavy silver ornaments, prayer shawls, crowns and special scarves. It only takes one look at a member of the clergy to see that the clothes really do make the man. Dress creates distance and shows homage. It demarcates the difference from the masses of believers in their dusty, everyday wear. It is the esteemed exceptionalism that sets the well-dressed man or woman above the common folk in a way they wouldn't be without their clothing. Even the pacifist message of Mahatma Gandhi was wrapped in the famous garment that he wove himself.

The priestly clothes are a sort of costume, which inevitably raises the question of what exactly is the meaning and purpose of a costume. Some would say that the costume is the wearer's true self. All year long I am covered, hidden, putting on appearances, but on Purim, when the boundaries are lowered, I can bring out the real me for a moment and be a police officer, a soldier, Superman. Others, by contrast, argue that on Purim I take on a covering that is the exact opposite of my real inner self – "turned to the contrary" (Esth. 9:1) – and become an Arab, a woman, a gay man or any "other" I choose. Anyone who protests, "This is not really me – it's a joke, okay?" forgets the fact that opposites are revealing, too. I've never seen an Orthodox child dress up for Purim as an Orthodox rabbi, an Arab as an Arab, or a soldier as a military policeman. Whether it's the truth coming out, the opposite or both at once, it's clear that holidays like Purim and costumes in general fill some basic human need. Almost every culture has a holiday, event or festival that calls for costumes, from Halloween to Carnival to Mardi Gras.

This is not the time nor the place to determine whether the high priest in his robes and scarves represents the true inner self of the Jewish soul or our complete opposite. Suffice it to say that the work of the priest is an ongoing, year-round, life-long costume. We can go one step further and show that the opposite of the priest in Judaism is the prophet. Back in 1893, more than a century ago, the essayist Ahad Ha'Am wrote of the structural tension between priest and prophet:

> The Prophet is essentially a one-sided man. A certain moral idea fills his whole being, masters his every feeling and sensation, engrosses his whole attention. He can only see the world through the mirror of his

Tetzaveh

idea; he desires nothing, strives for nothing, except to make every phase of the life around him an embodiment of that idea in its perfect form. His whole life is spent in fighting for this ideal with all his strength; for its sake he lays waste his powers, unsparing of himself, regardless of the conditions of life and the demands of the general harmony. His gaze is fixed always on what ought to be in accordance with his own convictions; never on what can be consistently with the general condition of things outside himself. The Prophet is thus a primal force.

By contrast,

> It is otherwise with the Priest. He appears on the scene at a time when Prophecy has already succeeded in hewing out a path for its Idea; when that Idea has already had a certain effect on the trend of society, and has brought about a new harmony or balance between the different forces at work. The Priest also fosters the Idea, and desires to perpetuate it; but he is not of the race of giants. He has not the strength to fight continually against necessity and actuality; his tendency is rather to bow to the one and come to terms with the other. ("Priest and Prophet," from *Selected Writings of Ahad Ha'Am*, trans. Leon Simon [Philadelphia: Jewish Publication Society of America, 1912])

To put it in more modern, concise terms, the prophet is a man of absolute truths and the priest is a man of compromise and acquiescence, the sort who forges a compact with reality. Inevitably the priest lives with fragments of untruth around him. Here is the essential difference between the elaborate dress of the priest and the simplicity of the prophet, who may appear in simple robes or mere girdle or less. This is how the scripture describes the process of King Saul's prophesy, or, more precisely, the process of his joining the ranks of the prophesiers: "And he also stripped off his clothes, and he also prophesied before Samuel, and lay down naked all that day and all that night. Wherefore they say: 'Is Saul also among the prophets?'" (1 Sam. 19:24).

A prophet apparently cannot be fully dressed, because the full process of prophesy entails a great baring of the absolute inner truth, something that cannot tolerate the covering or filtering of clothes. Clothes hide the truth and may even distort it. The Hebrew words for "garment," *beged*, and "treason," *begidah*, come from the same three-letter root; likewise the words for "coat," *me'il*, and "fraud," *me'ilah*. Prophesy is the basic matter, and priesthood is the add-on, the costume – or, at best, the basic matter plus its covering. Either way, it's clear that the differences between these two spiritual types are deep and substantive. The prophet tries his whole life to aim toward the moment of truth, and frequently at such a moment of truth you have no choice but to tear away the veils, to tear your clothes. For example, here is Mordecai sitting in the king's gate. And when he learned about the approaching disaster, "Mordecai rent his clothes" (Esth. 4:1). But he wasn't the only person or even the first one to react that way when his life came to a moment of truth. Before him was Reuben, the eldest son of Jacob. When Reuben returned to the pit where his brothers had left Joseph and saw that he wasn't there, because the other brothers had sold him, "he rent his clothes" (Gen. 37:29). His father Jacob did the same thing after him when he learned of Joseph's disappearance, as did Joshua after them, Jephtah the Gileadite, King David, King Ahab and many others, good and true.

And here is the paradox: on Yom Kippur and on Purim we bear witness to the ancient Israelite culture of clothing. In the first case, our absolute personal truth is demanded of us, and in the second case we are given license for an absolute loosening of the reins – and both of them are inseparable parts of Jewish civilization. Both of them involve a disclosure of truth. The repentance of Yom Kippur comes from man's elevation from the routine of daily deceptions to the pinnacle of inner truth. As opposed to that, the intoxicating blurring of the senses of the *ad lo yada* – "until you cannot tell the difference" – of Purim effectively allows the exposure and confession of inner truths that do not come out except in situations of loss of self-control.

Moses and Aaron: Prophet and Priest

THIS WEEK'S PORTION, *Parashat Tetzaveh*, is the direct continuation of last week's portion, *Terumah*, a detailed inventory of the issues involved in building the tabernacle and preparing its implements. There are people who attach enormous importance and holiness to every detail. On the other hand, I am one of those who believe that the tabernacle was a spiritual compromise of the distant past, by which God and his prophet Moses understood that if they didn't give the people something concrete to work toward, they would simply lose the people. And so they compromised and temporarily gave up on the principle of abstract faith in God and his values. They gave the people a movable hut – a portable structure in contemporary terminology – with carpets and embroideries so that they could have what all the other believers in the region had. As such, I don't really get excited about all these exhausting stories. All I look for in a portion like this week's is the human dimension and the substantive significance concealed within these sacred vessels. Following the order of weekly portions and the nature of the Hebrew calendar, *Parashat Tetzaveh* is always read in synagogue during the week of the seventh of Adar, traditionally the anniversary of Moses's death. Seekers of hints and secrets have created a connection between the fixed date and the fact that this portion is the only one in the last four books of the Torah, from the beginning of Exodus to the end of Deuteronomy, that does not mention Moses. Unlike the verses themselves, we will devote our examination to Moses – to the man, his character, his significance and his legacy.

Right near the beginning of the portion, Moses is commanded: "And bring thou near unto thee Aaron thy brother, and his sons with him, from among the children of Israel, that they may minister unto me in the priest's office" (Exod. 28:1). The text doesn't divulge Moses's feelings about the command. Did he understand at that point that Aaron, who had always played second fiddle to his leadership, was receiving an everlasting gift that would immortalize him as a part of the sacred service, while he, Moses, would finish his days as one of the great figures of Israel, remembered forever but with no inheritance to leave his own children? And if he understood, what did he feel? We will never know. This week we will enter this breach between Moses and Aaron.

The Torah is known as the Torah of Moses. The secret of the Torah's eternality and essentiality lies in its power of perpetual self-renewal. That which was immediate and relevant three thousand years ago has successfully renewed and refreshed itself over and over, and so has remained significant to multitudes of believers to this very day. The Aggadic legend of the Talmud vividly illustrates the evolutionary process of moral and religious thinking:

> Rav Yehuda said, quoting Rav: When Moses went up to the mountaintop to receive the Torah, he asked the Holy One, praised be he, to fill in the crowns at the tops of the letters. He said to him: Master of the Universe, who or what are you waiting for? God said to him: There is one man who will appear in a number of generations, named Akiba Ben Joseph, and he will find and fill in every point and detail in the laws. Moses said: Show him to me. God said to Moses: Back up a bit. Moses went and found himself a seat in the eighth row of Akiva's classroom, and he didn't know what they were talking about. His strength was exhausted. When Rabbi Akiba began to talk, his students said: Rabbi, where do you get this from? He said to them: This is the law as Moses received it at Sinai. And Moses was satisfied. (Babylonian Talmud, *Minhot* 29b)

Beyond the wonderfully playful tales of time travel, of an ancient figure like Moses hurtling forward in history to sit in an academy of the future, and beyond the wonderful tension of the man who first received the Torah finding himself unable to understand the wisdom derived from his own original teaching, this story offers a peek at the Torah's power of renewal, which has been so diminished in the last few years.

There is a stark contrast between, on the one hand, the eternally creative freedom of the learning process that was taken from God and Moses almost from the first instant and entrusted to the generations of learners and renewers, and, on the other hand, the cage surrounding Aaron. It's true that his sons were privileged to serve in both of the holy Temples and make their living from the sanctuary and its offerings, the cash donations and the flesh of the sacrifice. It's also true that at every morning prayer service the children of Aaron spread their hands and bless the children of Israel with the priestly blessing. This is unquestionably a great honor, to have their presence eternally noted at so many peak moments in Jewish life. But these are the two fundamentally different models of the founding brothers: the priesthood, frozen in time, its ceremonies forever unchanging, versus the Torah, the dynamic teaching that is always being reexamined and renewed. The sons of Aaron versus the students of Moses.

These should not be mistaken for two types that operate independent of and indifferent to one another, like two parallel planes that never meet. On the contrary, they could sometimes clash forcefully, like the Sadducees of the Second Temple era (the descendants of the high priest Saduc, or Tsadok), who barricaded themselves behind the Temple rituals, remained faithful to the literal text of the Torah and fought bitterly against the Pharisees – the sages and students of the Torah that Moses taught, who renewed and reinvented Judaism and created the interpretive tradition of Oral Law for a non-Temple era.

At other times we find the two trends complementing rather than combating one another. In the previous chapter I cited the wonderful words of Ahad Ha'Am, in his essay "Priest and Prophet," and I'd like to return to them for a moment. Here is how Ahad Ha'Am characterizes the two archetypes: "The Prophet is essentially a one-sided man. A certain moral idea fills his whole being, masters his every feeling and sensation, engrosses his whole attention.... His whole life is spent in fighting for this ideal with all his strength," while, by contrast, "it is otherwise with the Priest. He appears on the scene at a time when Prophecy has already succeeded in hewing out a path for its Idea.... He has not the strength to fight continually against necessity and actuality; his tendency is rather to bow to the one and come to terms with the other."

My father-in-law taught me an important insight about this passage of Ahad Ha'Am: taken as a whole, the relationship between the two brothers can be seen as the first and most basic separation of church and state. Aaron is the symbol of routinized, accommodationist religion, while Moses represents the vision that looks far ahead toward both spiritual values and national policy – and he dedicates himself utterly to that vision to the point of giving up his own private life and his children's inheritance.

Moses, then, is the prophet – the master prophet. He is absolutely dedicated to the idea of freedom and justice that burns within him. Moses sought to create a world completely different in values and customs from the pharaonic Egypt within whose palaces he was raised and against which he rebelled. Aaron is the priest. As such he is not obligated to any single idea. Nothing burns within him. The priest is the technical director of Temple rituals. If he needs to go up to a mountain to receive the Torah, he brings along an entourage. If he needs to make an idol to quiet an angry mob, he will forge them a first-class Golden Calf. If he needs to dwell in the tabernacle of the Lord and eat the leg and breast of the sacred offerings, he and his family are ready to go. In that sense, there could be a certain irony in the verse, "bring thou near unto thee Aaron thy brother" (Exod. 28:1). Moses is commanded to bring Aaron close to him because Aaron is so very far away. And at God's command, Moses traps Aaron inside the sanctuary forever and then heads out to wander the world with his wild, creative spirit.

Moses is the symbol of Judaism's never-ending dynamism. He plants himself in the back rows of the boldest academies in Jewish history, collects teachings and insights and spreads them around to anyone who believes in the power of the prophet and will not settle for the passive blessing of the priest. Therefore, may the memory of Moses (who isn't even mentioned in this week's portion) be blessed.

Week 21

Ki Tissa – When Thou Takest

Exodus 30:11–34:35

The Taste of the Divine

THE PORTION KNOWN AS *Ki Tissa* consists mostly of human deeds. A human, Moses, receives the Torah from heaven, a true gift from God that others proceed to annul by their actions. The people make a Golden Calf and enthrone it as a god, whereupon their brothers slaughter them without mercy. After calm is restored, Moses prepares another pair of stone tablets and goes off to receive the Ten Commandments yet again. Our current portion presents this great theological battle, which, as noted, consists entirely of human actions. Even God's resolute decision to vent his anger on his people and wipe them off the face of the earth is modified following the intervention of the portion's most active human, Moses. From among all these matters, we shall focus this week on one detail that is not central to the portion, but appears at the core of almost every religious ceremony.

Moses does his best to remove the stain of the Golden Calf from the face of the earth. In the course of this he takes "the Calf which they had made, and burnt it with fire, and ground it to powder, and strewed it upon the water" (Exod. 32:20). For years I've been asking myself where he found extra water in the middle of the desert. But this question is marginal in comparison to the astounding action that comes next: he takes the mixture of water – a lot of water – and Golden Calf dust and shoves it down the throats of the frenzied believers, "and made the children of Israel drink of it" (Exod. 32:20). What is that about? We've never seen anything like it. In previous and upcoming plagues he and God kill without account.

In another dispute, no less piercing, the earth opened up its mouth and swallowed all of Korah's troublesome, querulous opposition. Here, on the other hand, is something new: the people eat their sin. To be precise, they drink it. Even the Egyptians in Egypt weren't forced to eat their iniquities. During the plague of blood, "the Egyptians could not drink water from the river" (Exod. 7:21). They couldn't drink, and they didn't. I can't remember a single other biblical incident in which the substance of the sin becomes part of the sinner's punishment. So what is behind this?

The traditional commentators, including Rashi, his grandson the Rashbam and others, follow the familiar biblical frameworks. Drinking certain fluids is a sort of litmus test, an ancient lie detector for examining sinners and deviants. A woman suspected of cheating on her husband is forced to undergo the humiliating ritual of drinking bitter, cursed water, a concoction made up of water and dust from the floor of the tabernacle, into which the four-letter name of God has been ground up:

> Speak unto the children of Israel, and say unto them: If any man's wife go aside, and act unfaithfully against him…and the spirit of jealousy come upon him, and he be jealous of his wife…then shall the man bring his wife unto the priest…and the priest shall bring her near, and set her before the Lord. And the priest shall take holy water in an earthen vessel; and of the dust that is on the floor of the tabernacle the priest shall take, and put it into the water. And the priest shall set the woman before the Lord, and let the woman's hair go loose…. Then the priest shall cause the woman to swear with the oath of cursing, and the priest shall say unto the woman – the Lord make thee a curse and an oath among thy people, when the Lord doth make thy thigh to fall away, and thy belly to swell; and this water that causeth the curse shall go into thy bowels, and make thy belly to swell, and thy thigh to fall away; and the woman shall say: "Amen, Amen." And the priest shall write these curses in a scroll, and he shall blot them out into the water of bitterness. And he shall make the woman drink the water of bitterness that causeth the curse; and the water that causeth the curse shall enter into her

Ki Tissa

> and become bitter.... This is the law of jealousy, when a wife, being under her husband, goeth aside, and is defiled. (Num. 5:12–29)

The essence of the law is this: because there aren't two witnesses, as is necessary to prove the infidelity, the woman is given a special examination. They pour her some "water of bitterness that causeth the curse," made up of water, dust and ink. If the woman hasn't been unfaithful, the Torah maintains, she will receive a special reward and become pregnant, but if she has been unfaithful, then her thigh will fall away and her belly will swell up. Drawing on the ceremony of the wandering wife, Rashi says of our current portion about drinking the water of the Golden Calf, "He 'made the children of Israel drink of it' – he meant to examine them as though they were deviant women" (Rashi on Exod. 32:20).

It seems to me that this story contains another fundamental element, something connected not to criminal detection systems but to the digestive system, not to exposing betrayal but to disclosing faith. Let's start out by looking at the principles of the Catholic faith, and then we'll return to our portion. It's customary in Roman Catholicism to count seven sacraments. These are the ceremonies established by the church in the thirteenth century: baptism, confirmation, marriage, Mass, confession, last rites and ordination.

What is a sacrament? A sacrament is a Christian religious ceremony, usually conducted by the priest for his congregants. The word comes from the Latin *sacramentum*, meaning covenant or oath. Catholic and Orthodox Christians believe that through the sacrament God's grace passes to the believer. Protestant Christians, on the other hand, see the sacrament as an external expression of inner grace – that is, a purely symbolic act, not an actual receiving of grace. Accordingly, most Protestant sects practice only two of the sacraments: baptism and the eating of the communion wafer at Mass.

And what is Mass? It is the most important sacrament in Christianity. It is a Christian prayer in the course of which the priest gives the worshippers bread and wine, which are transformed during the ceremony into the body and blood of Jesus. In this way Jesus passes his grace to the faithful. His flesh becomes their flesh and his blood is mingled with their blood. The ceremony is based on Jesus's message to his disciples at the Last Supper: "Jesus took bread, and blessed it, and broke it, and gave it to the disciples, and said, Take, eat; this is my body. And he took the cup, and gave thanks, and gave *it* to them, saying, Drink ye all of it; for this is my blood of the new testament, which is shed for many for the remission of sins" (New Testament, Matt. 26:26–27, King James Version). The ceremony evolved out of the practice of Christians in the early church of holding feasts for all the members of the community. In the face of Roman persecution, the feast became a symbolic meal that took on a deeply magical, mystical significance.

The Catholic Church developed the doctrine of transubstantiation, meaning the transformation of the substance of the bread and wine. As Thomas Aquinas framed it, during the course of the ceremony the substance of the bread and wine is transformed. The bread becomes Jesus's flesh and the wine becomes his blood. But they appear to remain unchanged – their taste, smell, visual appearance and shape all continue to resemble bread and wine. (It should be recalled that Protestant churches reject transubstantiation and consider the ceremony purely symbolic.) Thus there is an element in religious thinking of substantive transformation. The sacrament, the sacrifice and offering are made by the act of consuming, chewing or swallowing something else that sanctifies and elevates the believing consumer.

When Moses makes the sinning children of Israel drink the gold dust, he is trying to prove just the opposite. He doesn't believe in substantive transformation. He is feeding them their gods of yesterday so that they will digest them and expel them as human waste. In essence he is saying to them that a god made by human hands isn't worth much more than anything else you make, including – and especially – the most repulsive human product. A divinity that can end up as part of human excrement is worth precisely that. He is humiliating the Calf and its believers, and using their own bodies to do so. They made themselves a god of metal, and afterwards "they rose up early on the morrow, and offered burnt-offerings, and brought peace-offerings; and the people sat down to eat and to drink, and rose up to make merry" (Exod. 32:6); and he paid them back and

Ki Tissa

pulled up the rug. You were drinking to your god – now drink your god himself and relieve yourselves of him.

Just to be on the safe side, so that no one will be left with overly Catholic thoughts about the slaughtered Calf, he sends out his loyal Levites and says to them:

> "Thus saith the Lord, the God of Israel: Put ye every man his sword upon his thigh, and go to and fro from gate to gate throughout the camp, and slay every man his brother, and every man his companion, and every man his neighbor." And the sons of Levi did according to the word of Moses; and there fell of the people that day about three thousand men. And Moses said: "Consecrate yourselves to-day to the Lord, for every man hath been against his son and against his brother; that he may bestow upon you a blessing this day." (Exod. 32:27–29)

The Aggadah connects the drinking of the Calf to the slaughter of the impious and paints the entire sequence of events in more creative and fanciful colors: "And he made Israel drink, and anyone who had kissed the Calf found his lips stuck together by the gold, and the tribe of Levi killed those people until about three thousand people among Israel had fallen" (Pirkei D'Rabbi Eliezer 44, words of Rabbi Shimon).

This is the faith, this is the heresy and these are their essences: the physical essence of a golden drink and its bitter aftertaste, and the theological essence of a God who cannot be subject to the touch of the human hand or its handiwork.

Moses and God: A Face-to-Face Conversation

WHAT A PORTION – full of drama, awash in complex, convoluted matters of faith. The beginning gives no hint of the drama that is to come. At the beginning of the portion we encounter the final instructions for the building of the tabernacle by Moses and Bezalel, along with the wonderful social commandment: "The children of Israel shall keep the Sabbath, to observe the Sabbath throughout their generations, for a perpetual covenant" (Exod. 31:16). But these lines pale before the dramatic turn of the verses that follow. Moses receives the tablets, but is slightly delayed at God's printing plant – they're still enacting his Torah with letters of black fire on white fire. The people below are agitated and make a Calf. Moses comes down and smashes the tablets, and a deadly religious war breaks out in the camp between the devotees of the Calf and Moses's loyalists. A second set of tablets is given, and Moses is permitted to see God's back. Amid all the ascents and descents and the unconventional revelation of the Torah that Moses received, Moses's skin begins to radiate, and he hides behind a veil that masks his head.

What is there in all this that could speak to the modern person who loves the past only so long as it relates to the present? This Sabbath's portion certainly constitutes a worthy subject. We must acknowledge the body of social and civil matter, including social legislation, that has evolved over time from the germ of the idea of the Sabbath. And perhaps even the broken tablets, as an expression of all the fissures that express the range of our many spirits and identities. But the best of all the stories in this portion is the conversation between Moses and God.

God is angry. He's nervous. "I will destroy them," he says to Moses. His nose is out of joint, his anger is surging and his well-known inclination toward targeted assassination, combined with his famous policy of collective punishment, once again threatens to destroy our ancestors.

Into this place of divine rage steps Moses at the height of his powers, and challenges God's decisions. The conversation between Moses and God is one of the pinnacles of human dialogue with the divine from the very beginning right up to our own time. And here are the annals of the creator's conversations with his creatures. Adam was the first to talk with God. God asked him, "Where art thou?" and he ran and hid in his shame. God wants to know who is responsible, and Adam pins it on his partner: "The woman whom thou gavest to be with me, she gave me of the tree, and I did eat" (Gen. 3:12). Eve, following her husband, passes the hot potato along to the snake: "The serpent beguiled me, and I did eat" (Gen. 3:13). A conversation of cowards and liars that ends in punishment and expulsion,

Ki Tissa

and ultimately introduces death into the calculus of human existence. Adam has left the Garden of Eden a wiser man – he knows how to tell good from bad – but he has paid the highest price: he has lost eternity. His days are numbered. Adam and Eve have been expelled together from the Garden of Eden, accompanied by falsehood and death, and become mortal. Cain, their son, has an interesting conversation of his own with God centering on rebuke and a suggestion from God to the murderer of self-improvement.

But Cain, stuck in his murderous cantankerousness, continues along the path of sin, drunk with his instincts and unable to control them, and he is banished like his parents to the land of Nod, the land wanderers (*na-vadim*) without rest. When God continues to find himself disappointed, he turns to Noah to set up the first emergency rescue service. We have no idea what Noah's voice sounded like. Unlike Adam before him, he does not dodge the assignment, does not argue, does not ask – in fact, he does not react at all. Noah remains silent throughout the duration of his portion, deaf and dumb in the face of the first mass destruction. God spoke and Noah obeyed, and after them, the Flood.

Then God came again in a rage and wanted to wipe Sodom and Gomorrah and their shame from off the face of the earth. He discussed it with Abraham, his beloved friend. Abraham, unlike the others before him, opened his big mouth and talked back to God: "That be far from thee to do after this manner, to slay the righteous with the wicked, that so the righteous should be as the wicked; that be far from thee; shall not the judge of all the earth do justly?" (Gen. 18:25). Abraham assumes as a point of departure that it's possible for God to be unjust, that perhaps God is mistaken and is perverting justice. They begin a process of bargaining that ends up with God's decision unchanged and Abraham's criticism lingering as an echo on the pages of the book, offering no help to the dead of the Valley of Ghosts that is the Dead Sea.

This week's portion has the story that completes the picture. God is so disappointed in his people after they left Egypt that, like a frustrated father who tells his wife, "They're your children, not mine" – "*Deine mishpuche*" my father used to say to my mother about some of his more "interesting" nephews and Chabad Hasidim, who didn't particularly impress him – God complains to Moses, "Go, get thee down; for thy people, that thou broughtest up out of the land of Egypt, have dealt corruptly" (Exod. 32:7). Thy people, not mine. The master prophet, however, isn't thrilled to be the new owner of the stiff-necked congregation, and he throws the ball right back: "Lord, why doth thy wrath wax hot against thy people?" – which is to say, it's your people, God, not mine. Moses then begins his descent, and on his way down he offers God a fascinating argument, pointing to God's ratings in the public relations sphere. "Wherefore should the Egyptians speak, saying: For evil did he bring them forth, to slay them in the mountains, and to consume them from the face of the earth?" (Exod. 32:12). And God listens. Wonder of wonders, God changes his mind! "And the Lord repented of the evil which he said he would do unto his people" (Exod. 32:14). For the first time since the creation of the universe and the beginning of conversations between humans and their creator, a divine decision is changed as a result of the intervention and bargaining skills of a representative of mortal humankind.

This is the most amazing invitation in the Bible. From here on in, relations between God and his creations will never be the same. God has conceded, if only for a moment, some of his almightiness. His place has been vacated. He has made himself just a little bit less all-encompassing and made room for someone else, for humanity. We have learned that we have the power to change the world, to repair the world. From the moment he makes this concession, God is no longer the sole judge of all living things. He has partners, namely us, and we have something to say. In this week's portion another layer is added to God's retreat from the world and the expansion of human responsibility.

As an aside, I'd like to add a family note. Here is how my father loved to read the portion: first he would read the verse and its plain meaning, then the interpretation and Midrash, and finally he would enfold them in historical reality and general wisdom like a warm, enveloping gown. This portion was a living example of his way of reading the Torah. He would say, the chapter is full of variations on the word *evil*: "Wherefore should the Egyptians speak, saying: For evil did he bring them forth"; "repent of this evil against thy people"; "the evil which he said he would do unto his people"; "thou knowest the people, that they are set on evil." And my father used to wonder, what does all this mean? Where does it come from?

Every year on this Sabbath he remembered to direct me back to the Exodus itself, where the root of evil was found. Rashi offered the following Aggadic tale in his commentary on the verse in which Pharaoh warns Moses and the people leaving Egypt:

> "See ye that evil is before your face" – I heard the following Midrash on this: There was a star named Evil. Pharaoh said to them, I see in my horoscope that star rising toward you in the desert, and it is a sign of blood and killing, and when Israel sinned with the Golden Calf and the Holy One, praised be he, sought to kill them, Moses said in his prayer, "Wherefore should the Egyptians speak, saying: For evil did he bring them forth," and this refers to the saying, "See ye that evil is before your face." (Rashi on Exod. 10:10)

My father used to bring his own broad perspective to this Midrash, playing on the Hebrew word for evil, *ra*. Twelve pharaohs of Egypt were named Rameses, which meant that they were the children of the Egyptian sun god Ra. The message is: do not destroy the children of Israel in your anger, because "for evil [*ra*] did he bring them forth" will be the eternal reply of the Egyptian god Ra, who will dwarf the achievements of our God and blot them out from memory. Therefore when Moses soothes God and averts his evil decree, he is framing his argument in the broader context of the Exodus and the battle between the gods that took place there. God had said, "against all the gods of Egypt I will execute judgments" (Exod. 12:12). Moses now reminds him, you may have executed judgments against them then, but if you continue your judgments against your own people, you will end up losing out to your great rival Ra, the Egyptian sun god. And God is convinced. Moses and my father both saw evil as something exceptional that needed to be avoided and warned against. Goodness is the stuff and substance of life, and it needs to be defended fiercely, even at the price of an argument with the creator of good and evil himself.

Week 22

Vayakhel/Pekudei
And Moses Assembled/
These Are the Accounts

Exodus 35:1–40:38

This Is Moses the Man

THE HEBREW CALENDAR, which is a combination of lunar and solar cycles, is forced to add an extra month every few years to keep the months aligned with the seasons. This creates what is known in Hebrew as a "pregnant" year, in a process analogous to the Gregorian calendar's leap year. The extra month, Adar B, ensures that Rosh Hashanah always comes at the end of summer and that Passover always falls, as mandated in Torah, in the "month of spring" (Deut. 16:1). The Muslim calendar, unlike the Hebrew calendar, does not adapt the lunar cycle to the cycle of the sun, with the result that the fast of Ramadan drifts through the seasons from year to year. The believer sometimes has to fast through the long, hot days of summer, and at other times on short winter days. But the Hebrew calendar raises its own difficulty: Where to find weekly portions for the extra weeks of the leap year? It is precisely for this purpose that several portions operate like an accordion, expanding and contracting as needed. Conjoined portions like *Vayakhel-Pekudei*, *Behar-Bechukotai* and *Tazria-Metzora* are generally read as a single unit. When a leap year comes with its extra month of Sabbaths, however, these portions are split up and read separately. This week we have come to the first of these combined portions,

Vayakhel/Pekudei

Vayakhel-Pekudei. We won't stint either one, however; we have something to say about each.

Vayakhel, the first portion, opens with a summary of the tabernacle project:

> And they came, every one whose heart stirred him up, and every one whom his spirit made willing, and brought the Lord's offering, for the work of the tent of meeting, and for all the service thereof, and for the holy garments. And they came, both men and women, as many as were willing-hearted, and brought nose-rings, and ear-rings, and signet-rings, and girdles, all jewels of gold; even every man that brought an offering of gold unto the Lord. And every man, with whom was found blue, and purple, and scarlet, and fine linen, and goats' hair, and rams' skins dyed red, and sealskins, brought them. Every one that did set apart an offering of silver and brass brought the Lord's offering; and every man, with whom was found acacia-wood for any work of the service, brought it. And all the women that were wise-hearted did spin with their hands, and brought that which they had spun, the blue, and the purple, the scarlet, and the fine linen. And all the women whose heart stirred them up in wisdom spun the goats' hair. And the rulers brought the onyx stones, and the stones to be set, for the ephod, and for the breastplate; and the spice, and the oil, for the light, and for the anointing oil, and for the sweet incense. The children of Israel brought a free-will offering unto the Lord; every man and woman, whose heart made them willing to bring for all the work, which the Lord had commanded by the hand of Moses to be made. (Exod. 35:21–29)

At first glance, this is a description of a wonderful public mobilization of everyone for everyone. But this is so only at first glance. The word "every" appears ten times in connection with the donors. In plain language, when the text says "as many as were willing-hearted" brought gifts, the intention is that they were the only ones who donated. Everyone else, those who were not so willing and generous, did not donate. There is no way to know how many there were and what was the size of the other party.

This restrictive use of "every" invites comparison to the other places in the text where everyone volunteered, not just a portion of the people, and the donations were not for good but for evil. The most piercing criticism is found in the Jerusalem Talmud, which offers the following homily: "Rabbi Yehuda Bar Pazi, speaking in the name of Rabbi, asked: Was someone called but did not fear?" He continued, comparing a mobilization "for good: 'as many as were willing-hearted,'" with another mobilization "for evil: 'And all the people broke off [their ear-rings, to forge the Golden Calf]'" (Exod. 32:3). He cites further examples of mobilizations for good and evil:

> For good: "And Moses brought forth the people [to hear the Ten Commandments]" (Exod. 19:17).
>
> For evil: "And ye came near unto me, every one of you [demanding that spies be sent to examine the Promised Land]" (Deut. 1:22).
>
> For good: "Then sang Moses and the children of Israel [after crossing the Red Sea]" (Exod. 15:10).
>
> For evil: "And all the nation lifted up their voice [in alarm at the spies' report]" (Num. 14:1).
>
> (Jerusalem Talmud, *Shekalim* 1b)

To explain: only those who were willing of heart donated to the establishment of the tabernacle and its implements – and it isn't clear whether they were a majority or a minority. For the sin of the Golden Calf, however, which was also forged from the donations of believers, the entire nation without exception broke off their jewelry.

For the sublime moments of receiving the Torah and standing before Mount Sinai, Moses was forced to chase after the people and roust them one by one from their tents. But for evil acts, they approached him in a threatening mob, assembled of their own free will and without encouragement. So too in the last couplet: at the Red Sea, Moses and a few Israelites sang a song of thanksgiving for the miracle, but after the sin of the spies, with their negative report on the Promised Land, all the congregation of Israel lifted its voices in tearful distress. No wonder that this Talmud passage begins with the words, "Was someone called but did

Vayakhel/Pekudei

not fear?" No wonder, too, that it ends with this judgment by Rabbi Abba Bar Acha: "You cannot speak of the character of this nation."

This inward-looking critique, hidden within the words' nuances – the word "every" comes to signify something quite limited – shows up in yet another, equally distressing Midrash. This next one is drawn from the second of our paired portions, *Parashat Pekudei*. There is a sharp difference in style and tone: the Midrash on *Parashat Vayakhel* relies on nuances of language to distinguish between "every one in the nation" who mobilized to do evil time after time and the smaller group of willing, engaged members. By contrast, the Midrash on *Parashat Pekudei* is far more blunt. This time the problem is not confrontations among factions and subgroups but a direct attack on Moses the man, dismissing him in the most personal fashion possible. This attack is exceptional even in the context of subversive Midrash:

> When the work of the tabernacle was completed, he [Moses] said to them [the Israelites]: "Come and I will draw up an account for you." All Israel came together. As he sat and calculated, he forgot one thousand seven hundred and seventy-five shekels that were used to make hooks for the pillars. He began to sit and wonder. He said: Now Israel will decide to claim that Moses took them. The Holy One, praised be he, looked on and saw that they had been made into hooks for the pillars [which were hidden from view and therefore easily overlooked].... Now the Israelites were content with the work of the tabernacle, as it is written, "These are the accounts of the tabernacle" (Exod. 38:21) [suggesting that not everyone was pleased with the national project that Moses had imposed on them]. And why did he draw up an account for them?... Moses had heard that the Israelites were talking behind his back.... And what were they saying? Rabbi Yitzhak said: To praise him – they were saying: Blessed is she who gave birth to him. All his days the Holy One, praised be he, speaks with him and he is perfect before the Holy One.... Rabbi Chama said: To malign him – they were saying: Look at his neck, his thighs, his calves. He is eating and drinking at the expense of the Jews. Everything he has is at the expense of the Jews.

> And his friend replied, fool! Don't you think a man who oversaw the work of the tabernacle should be rich? And when Moses heard this he said to them, By your lives, when the tabernacle is finished I will give you an account! (Yalkut Shimoni, *Pekudei* 415)

The Midrash is the psychological dimension that fleshes out the biblical story. The Torah is terse and frequently opaque, while the Midrash is sensitive and human. It dares to say things that might otherwise be taboo. It's able to hear notes that aren't audible to the ordinary, straightforward reader. Thus the ancient characters take on additional dimensions, sometimes sublime, sometimes laughable, with the generous, insightful assistance of the authors of the Midrash and Aggadah. Our job is to study and learn the scripture, to understand its criticism, to learn Midrash and to love its daring. Together, these make up the culture of the Jewish people of old and, God willing, of today.

His Glory Fills the Universe

*I*ADMIT THAT THESE PORTIONS aren't my favorites, with all their boring details about the central project of the era, the building of the tabernacle in the desert. I draw some comfort from my cousin Hillel, who edited this book and wrote the following about these portions:

> What I like about these portions is precisely the fact that God has a house with a table, a lamp and a comfortable seat of honor. The house is for God, not his believers. After all, even he has to live somewhere. Maybe this sounds pagan and primitive to you, but to me this feels like something with a lot of vital religious energy. As the Christian mystic W.R. Inge wrote, "When, in our anxiety to escape from anthropomorphism, we identify the God of religion with the Absolute of philosophy, we find that a being stripped of all limiting attributes is not a possible object of worship…. But faith must be allowed to speak its own language, which is not the language of

Vayakhel/Pekudei

science" (W.R. Inge, *Mysticism in Religion* [London: Hutchinson's University Library, 1947], 84–88).

Therefore, this week's words will be devoted to discussing the language of faith. It might sound foreign and difficult to the ears of someone who is not a believer, or who tends to identify with the abstract and not dress in the garb of the tangible. Nonetheless, it is impossible to undersand Jewish identity fully without the basic faith that undergirds the relationship between God and his believers.

This Sabbath we conclude the Book of Exodus. Its closing words are as follows:

> Then the cloud covered the tent of meeting, and the glory of the Lord filled the tabernacle. And Moses was not able to enter into the tent of meeting, because the cloud abode thereon, and the glory of the Lord filled the tabernacle. And whenever the cloud was taken up from over the tabernacle, the children of Israel went onward, throughout all their journeys. But if the cloud was not taken up, then they journeyed not till the day that it was taken up. (Exod. 40:34–37)

This is the Book of Exodus and these are its stories. The book opens with Jacob and seventy members of his household descending into Egypt, and it ends with the uplifting of the spirit and the rising of the cloud. Between the descent at the beginning of the book and the rising of the cloud at the end, a wonderful saga of risings and descents unfolds. Man rises to the heavens. During the revelation at Mount Sinai, Moses leaves the bounds of mortal humanity and disappears into a cloud for forty days and nights, swallowed up in the midst of the thunder and lightning, talking with God and receiving the Torah by hand.

But these stories have a way of finding a balance. Just as man penetrates the kingdom of heaven and survives, God comes down to earth and dwells here for a time. At the beginning he lives in a sort of desert shack, and later on he receives his permanent sanctuary in Jerusalem. The sanctuary is for God what Mount Sinai is for Moses: the point of contact between above and below.

The whole story of the relationship between above and below is one great Jacob's ladder with "the angels of God ascending and descending on it" (Gen. 28:12). Some of these angels are mortals heading upward, and some are angels of heaven coming down to earth to learn about the condition of humanity and to link themselves to it. This religious notion of God descending to earth and dwelling here fosters the aura of utmost sanctity attributed to the Temple Mount to this day. Judaism forbids us to go up to the mountain of God's house because of its holiness. What is this holiness? There is the holiness of good actions: "Ye shall be holy" (Lev. 19:2). This is a holiness that is acquired in the course of great efforts of goodly behavior and acts of kindness. But there is no automatic holiness that comes from some sort of touch of a magic wand that makes us good automatically. Everything depends on effort. Everything is bound up in a long process of change, accompanied by falls and failures as well as moments of ascension.

When the text of this week's portion tells us that "Moses was not able to enter into the tent of meeting, because…the glory of the Lord filled the tabernacle" (Exod. 40:35), the significance is plain enough: there is no room for a human beings to live in a place where God is present in all his fullness. In order for humankind to enter the places of God, God needs to withdraw into himself and somehow limit his presence. This is a genuine paradox: only a limited divinity allows the fullness of human faith to flourish. And vice versa: an all-powerful divinity that is fully present is not a divinity we can believe in or worship, because there is no room for us there.

From here it's a simple matter to explain the holiness of the Temple Mount. The whole world is ours, as the psalm says, "but the earth hath he given to the children of men" (Ps. 115:16). We know that when humankind tries to be everywhere and fill every space, as it did at the Tower of Babel, it leaves no room for mystery and the spiritual to be present among us. We pull back some of the totality of our humanness and leave a little spot for what is beyond our ken at the edge of Jerusalem. Giving of ourselves, of our own free will, we say to God: this is your place. By means of that place, where we willingly decline to tread, we reflect to ourselves the ultimately limited nature of human capability – and this space continually attracts the human spirit that seeks contact with what is beyond.

On the same topic, who knows what this wonderful cloud was, and what mechanism kept it in the same place for so many years? What caused it to go up and down? I found a solution to the cloud's mechanism in Jose Saramago's marvelous 1982 novel, *Memorial do Convento*, published in English as *Baltasar and Blimunda* (translated by Giovanni Pontiero [New York: Houghton Mifflin Harcourt, 1998]). In this magical book Saramago created a wonderful tension between Portugal's famous Convent of Mafra, a whim of the hypocritically pious eighteenth-century King Joao V, and the flying machine. The convent was built with the forced labor of thousands of peasants who were taken from their families and made to build a vast, ornate project, chained to their task alongside hundreds of masons, overseers and monks. Posed against the convent is a flying machine called *Passarola* (Big Bird), a symbol of progress and freedom of spirit, built by Father Bartolomeu Lourenco together with a maimed soldier named Baltasar and his beloved Blimunda. Blimunda is blessed with a wonderful quality: she can peer into a person's inner self and see his deepest human longing. And she, the collector of wishes, gathers two thousand human wishes that have the power to lift the flying ship up to the skies, because "it is the human will that sustains the stars" (116).

In my eyes, the tabernacle in the desert expresses a similar tension between the human spirit that longs to soar to the skies and support the stars, and the tyranny of royal undertakings that sink under the weight of their stones while tethering us to the ground below. All the stories of wandering in the desert form a giant arc stretching from the daily quarrels of a nomadic people to the universal visions of the spirit that burst forth from them. One side raises and the other side lowers; one submerges while the other elevates. The children of Israel progressed through the desert, moving forward when their spirit rose upward like a cloud. When their spirit declined, at times of despair and demoralization, they simply sank in place, mired in their quarrels, and didn't move.

Those distant matters gain a surprising immediacy in light of the daringly original interpretation of the fifteenth-century Italian scholar

Rabbi Ovadia Sforno. Discussing the two artists of the tabernacle, Bezalel son of Uri and Ohaliab son of Ahisamach, Sforno wrote that "the heads of the artists of the tabernacle and its implements were connected to the righteous people of the generation, and therefore the divine presence ministered to the work of their hands, and it did not fall into the hand of enemies. But as for the Temple of Solomon, whose craftsmen came from Tyre [in Lebanon]…parts of it were shoddy…and in the end it fell entirely into the hands of enemies" (Sforno on Exod. 38:21).

This is not a polemic on Hebrew labor. It is a very bold observation about the tangled recesses of the soul of the builder. If the mission is a national or social undertaking that arises from a spirit of truth and genuine commitment, it will endure forever. But if it is a product of slave labor, conquest or unjustified oppression, the project will not survive but will fall to an enemy and be destroyed.

In contrast to a restrictive, closed, prohibiting faith, there is always a sun of tenderness shining, embracing all those who seek a sanctuary of the heart whose foundation is truth and whose pillars are justice. We see the same analogy in the Midrash:

> A scoffer came to Rabban Gamaliel and said: You Jews say that among every ten men the divine presence can be found. How much divine presence is there? Rabban Gamaliel called a servant and struck him on the neck. He said to him: Why did the sun enter the home of the scoffer? He said to him: The sun shines on all the world. And if the sun, which is but one of a thousand thousands of suns, can shine on the whole world, how much more so the presence of the Holy One, praised be he? (Babylonian Talmud, *Sanhedrin* 39a)

Encore

Exodus

*T*HE DRAMATIC EVENTS of the Book of Exodus are very close to us. Not only because they are understandable events, the sort that can be achieved or conceptualized with the familiar tools of history and politics. The stories in the Book of Exodus are close to us mainly because over many generations – daily, on Sabbaths, holidays and especially on Passover – Jewish consciousness has been imprinted again and again with the stories of the Exodus from Egypt, and as the Haggadah emphasizes, "the more one elaborates on the story of the Exodus, the more one is to be praised." The Ten Commandments, the defining laws of the Torah, do not begin with the universal event of the creation, but with "our" event: "I am the Lord thy God, who brought thee out of the land of Egypt, out of the house of bondage" (Exod. 20:2). The Exodus from Egypt, the heroic story of the slaves who smashed their chains, shook off the bonds of evil and set out on their way to the land of hope, is the reason that the Book of Exodus is accepted as the book of freedom. In this sense, the Book of Exodus is the natural extension of the Book of Genesis. The first of the Five Books of Moses tells the story of the individuals who established the world and the human cultures that populate it, and from whom the family of Abraham was chosen. The end of the Book of Genesis focuses on the descent of Jacob and his sons to Egypt, which provides the transition to the Book of Exodus. And it is in Exodus that the narrative moves from the lives of individuals to the stories of tribes and nations.

It seems to me that in addition to the emotional story of the Exodus, the text presents a much broader model of conduct. I'm thinking not of the actual historical narrative of the confrontation between two ancient nations, Israel and Egypt, but of the book's invitation to a deeper, broader pondering on history, politics and the human condition. The Book of

Exodus presents the reader with two possible points of view, the Egyptian and the Jewish, and it invites us to ask ourselves to which side we belong. Egypt is not just past history. The Egypt of the Exodus is a paradigm of a certain iconic behavioral model that characterizes many nations. For the residents of Egypt – slaves as well as masters, maidservants as well as mistresses – the Egypt of their day was an all-encompassing experience. For the children of Israel, Egypt was a never-ending present: the present is the past, and the past is both the present and the future. In the Egyptian outlook, there is not and never will be anything new under the sun. The life of any individual is no different from the lives of his ancestors before him or his descendants after him. Nothing changes. Egypt is the highest form of existence, greater than the sum of its people, and unlike them it will always be there and will always be the same. It is slower and more constant than the flow of the Nile on a hot summer day. Parents live out their days dragging heavy stones or wearily laboring in the fields, and their children will do the same thing when they grow up.

As opposed to the Egypt of ideas, which knows nothing of change and permits nothing new, Moses and God present an entirely different approach, avant-garde, upending convention. When Moses meets God at the burning bush, they have a brief discussion about how to present their target audience – the broken-hearted, broken-spirited children of Israel – with the new partnership of redemption:

> And Moses said unto God: "Behold, when I come unto the children of Israel, and shall say unto them: The God of your fathers hath sent me unto you; and they shall say to me: What is his name? What shall I say unto them?" And God said unto Moses: I am that I am; and he said: "Thus shalt thou say unto the children of Israel: I am hath sent me unto you." (Exod. 3:13–14)

"I am" ostensibly represents the present, but in practice it is something else entirely. The Egyptians are in the eternal present, while the revealed God identifies himself with the Hebrew *Ehyeh* (usually read as present tense, though it is actually future tense): I am the God who will come and bring fundamental change. They are oppressed and enslaved to reality as it now exists, and he comes to them from the future.

This is the essence of the Book of Exodus, an ongoing, multifaceted confrontation between the Egyptian present, which looks insuperable, and the hazy, elusive future of Israel – between on the one hand, a regime whose foundations are fixed and unchanging, and on the other, a perpetually vital factor that challenges and threatens the regime while searching for the next ideas that have yet to appear. The kingdom of Egypt is a fixed, deterministic present, rotating in place. The redemption of Israel is an eternal future, driven by the hope of renewal and a gaze always directed forward. Egypt is an armed camp, always in fear of real and imagined enemies. The Egyptians explain that they have to enslave the children of Israel "lest they multiply, and it come to pass, that, when there befalleth us any war, they also join themselves unto our enemies, and fight against us, and get them up out of the land" (Exod. 1:10). In contrast to the innate paranoia of the Egyptian regime and all regimes that follow in its path, the Israelite type is not threatened by the stranger or foreigner; on the contrary, it is enriched by the encounter, never letting itself become an oppressor, because its own redemption frees it from the oppression of kingdoms.

Egypt, which governs, and Israel, the governed, are not necessarily the political entities of history. Within everyone, in every place and in every society, one can find the stagnation of Egypt and the vitality of Israel. It's very comfortable to live with the known, the routine. It's difficult and challenging to be a wanderer in the unknown land of the future. Even someone who is born a child of Israel can be an Egyptian of Exodus, stuck in place, chained to the present, just as a native of Egypt can live the life of the restless Israelite seeker.

The Egypt of Exodus is no longer a physical place but a spiritual state. Likewise the legacy of Israel and Jewishness are a spiritual state that can and must expand beyond the genetic boundaries of who is a Jew and who was a Jewish mother. Tyranny, the Egyptianness of Exodus, must always fall before the spirits of freedom and renewal.

ויקרא
Leviticus

Week 23

Vayikra – And the Lord Called

Leviticus 1:1–5:26

God's Portion and a Piece of Heaven

Every year, when the time comes for the Book of Leviticus, with all its sacrifices and their spattered blood, I raise my spines like a hedgehog, arch my back against this particular religious reality and refuse to accept it. It might be a reaction to changing times and ideologies, or some vision of a vegetarian end of days, or perhaps fear of extremists in our midst who dream of literally rebuilding the Temple. Few synagogue-goers who attend Sabbath services this week will give much thought to the story of the sacrifices, the altars that once were or the songs of rebuilding the Temple. Most of us don't relate seriously to the possibility that these things might actually be in the works, but that's a mistake.

Certain rabbis have an attitude toward the matter that is very serious and very alarming. Some of them pour enormous spiritual (and physical) energy into trying to prove that visiting the Temple Mount is permissible and perhaps even essential in our time. Their aim is to gather support for their campaign to build the Third Temple, as a necessary step toward the messianic redemption of Israel and the world. The second circle of believers and their preachers seeks more up-to-date claims, more rational-sounding arguments in order to market a product that doesn't inherently appeal to the current generation, namely the ancient Temple as the focus of our lives today. The central tension they have to confront is the lack of relevance of the Temple cult. After all, what could such antique religious customs mean in the life of a modern individual in this day and age?

In fact, various thinkers were struggling with this question as far back as the Middle Ages, including Maimonides and others. Maimonides led the school of evolutionary religion, which held that the sacrificial cult was a compromise that Moses and God adopted in order to offer something concrete to a public that found it difficult to accept an abstract faith. It was meant to serve as a bridge between the religious temperament of that era and the supreme, abstract God who "has no form of body nor body has he," as the Yigdal hymn puts it. But modern messianists take it in the reverse direction. They don't live in the here and now, in a modern, progressive ethos as Maimonides did in his generation. On the contrary, they reject modernity, retreat into the recesses of antiquity and seek to go back in time to a lost age before progress emerged with its threatening new values. They wish not merely to freeze time in its place but to roll it backwards.

Here, for example, is a passage by Rabbi Netanel Yosifon of the Bet El yeshiva, who teaches in Yeshivat Mitzpe Yericho:

> Western culture has made the entire world sick. Humanity has become alienated from nature. We have sunk into a world of computers, Internet and games. Our world preserves a central place for the thinking person, but plants and living things are resources to be exploited and nothing more. Likewise our serving of God has become service of the heart, mere prayer and nothing more. By contrast – in the Holy Temple many of the human senses participate in serving God – hearing the songs of the Levites, smelling the incense, tasting the flesh of the sacrifice and seeing the beauty of the most magnificent building in the world. In the Holy Temple the plants and living things and even the inanimate – in the libation of water, in the salt – take their part in the service of God, and when all parts of the universe come together in the service of God, even the service of the heart – prayer – is elevated. Thus the Temple is a place that calls to all the nations as a house of prayer, and with its destruction, the gates of prayer have been locked shut (Mishnah, Berachot 32). Therefore my soul yearns and longs for the courtyards of the Lord, for there not only my soul but my heart and my flesh will

sing to the living God. ("*Ha'idan hachadash – Beit Hamikdash*," http://www.yeshiva.org.il/midrash/shiur.asp?cat=886&id=6284&q=)

In other words, Yosifon claims that returning to the sacrificial slaughter of animals is essentially part of a return to nature. Killing nature as a way of understanding and connecting to it.

I find both of these impulses – the dream of returning to the Temple Mount and the vision of man's return to a simpler, more ancient natural order – to be repellent. Even though we have grown away from the connection between ancient man and nature, and the alienation between humanity and the environment is all too obvious, the fact is that in our society, the days are long gone when people bought chickens in the marketplace and slaughtered them with their own hands. In the same manner, we turn to a professional mohel to perform the ritual of circumcision, even though the scripture commands the father to circumcise his own son. We have matured, become more refined over the years; many of us still eat meat and still observe the commandment of circumcision, but few of us are prepared to spill blood ourselves. As such, it takes considerable marketing effort by the prophets of the Temple's renewal to sell their messianic merchandise.

Hence the following words by my childhood friend Rabbi Yehuda Kreuzer, who took part in the same discussion where Rabbi Yosifon made the remarks cited above:

> The building of the Temple and the renewal of the sacrificial service are the climax of the Jewish state's true rebirth and the redemption of the world, as Rabbi Abraham Isaac Hacohen Kook expressed it: The expectation to build the Temple and the sacrificial service is the noblest and highest of aspirations.... This aspiration is sometimes difficult for one who lives in the modern world, because we have no daily contact with animals. But this is an error that arises from the fact that we are thinking about the Temples of the past, and we are not imagining the future Temple. From the standpoint of *halachah*, of religious law, the Temple can be conducted in a manner appropriate to our way of life.

> Let us travel a bit further on the wings of imagination to the modern Third Temple: Ariel comes to the Temple Mount to sacrifice a peace-offering he has vowed. He goes to the office of sacrifices and libations and pays for a yearling lamb and libations. He gets a receipt stamped with his number in line for sacrifice. He then proceeds to a waiting room and waits until his number comes up on the electronic board. When his number comes up, Ariel goes to the northern courtyard, where he meets a priest who brings him the lamb (with libations), which has been inspected for blemishes by the priestly board of inspection. ("*Beit Hamikdash veha'adam hamoderni – hilchu shneihem yachdav,*" www.yeshiva.org.il/midrash/shiur.asp?id=4959)

You get the idea. Nothing could be simpler: a lovely, proper sacrifice, all done up in gift-wrapping – the Holy Temple as a sacred delicatessen, with prime Jerusalem fillet of a taste and quality that meets the strictest guidelines of the Bureau of Standards of the Modern World. These things are discussed in broad daylight, but nobody seems to be listening or taking heed; both the discussion and the apathy toward it frighten me greatly.

It seems to me that all this calls for some sort of counteraction. When I look at these apocalyptic dreams, arising perhaps from some nightmare of past generations and their horrors, I want to propose an entirely different way of understanding God's presence in our lives. God is present in our lives by the force of his absence. No, this isn't just double-talk or wordplay. This is a fully developed concept. How do we view a painting or other work of art? Is it only the lines and shapes painted onto the canvas that define it, or does the artist work with the entire surface, so that what remains is the image that is crafted out of the whole?

In art, there is a certain type of creation in which the artist draws the background, and the subject emerges out of it. This is known as *negative space*. In Japanese this concept is called *ma* or *mo*, in Chinese *wu*, and the meaning in both cases is *absence*. In Judaism, we might call this concept the Temple Mount, since it is the one place in our lives that is defined by our absence from it. Consider the well-known image demonstrating the power of negative space: the image seems to clearly portray two faces in profile looking at each other, but when the viewer's focus shifts to the negative space between the faces, it is equally clear that the image displays a vase. There are many such images demonstrating the ambiguity of our perception.

Just as in painting or sculpture, in which a small stroke of the artist describes a much larger space within and around it, so it is in my Judaism. God has no place in the world, because "the earth he hath given to the sons of man" (Ps. 115:16). But if the all-encompassing universe is filled with us and with what we are, how will we be able to see and understand what we create? We need a space that is empty of us and filled with something else. And thus, against the backdrop of the contrast between those spaces in which we are ever-present and those from which we are eternally absent, humanity can be understood as a far more significant creation. The Temple Mount is that place. This is the only plot of land on earth where our feet never tread. This is the place we have left for God to contract himself, and so we say: this is yours and yours alone, on this mountain our feet will not step. In between these two – the present and its absence, the mountaintop and the valleys below, humanity and the sublime – is a space where an eternal interaction unfolds, as between raw stone and the hewn sculpture, between the empty canvas and the completed painting. Sometimes we are the canvas and God is the ultimate work of art, and sometimes God in his infinite vastness is the raw material and we are the final product. All this is possible only in a reality in which there is a clear distinction and clear lines between him and us. He doesn't step on our stage and we don't ascend to his platform. We have been warned.

Even Presidents Sin

IT'S SUCH AN INTIMATE BEGINNING, "And he called." Come here, God says to Moses, I want to tell you a few things. Not the harsher "And God spoke," nor the inattentive "And God said." God calls and Moses comes. And why should this be, since only last week we learned from the scripture itself that "Moses was not able to enter into the tent of meeting, because the cloud abode thereon, and the glory of the Lord filled the tabernacle" (Exod. 40:35). In the last section I argued that a place that God fills entirely is likely to reduce the spiritual living space allotted to humans to mark off and attach themselves to. This week we can look back sympathetically and agree that, despite the tender, inviting words, Moses was simply afraid to approach the place of the Almighty.

Even in a friendship as strong as this one, in which God spoke to Moses "as a man speaketh unto his friend" (Exod. 33:11), there are moments of distance, fear and withdrawal. In this case, therefore, God adopts a gentle tone. Only once Moses has approached are the laws of the priests and the details of the sacrifices laid out for him. For generations commentators have tried to find a point to the sacrifices while at the same time trying to bury this archaic notion under layers of excuses about the constraints of time and place. Reading the blood-soaked verses we are led to think about the animals, about the priests, about the rivers of blood flowing all around and about the smell of roasted flesh rising to heaven. It almost never occurs to us to think about the sinner bringing the sacrifice and the process of purification that he undergoes.

Among all the supplicants appearing in our first portion on sacrificial laws, I'd like to focus in particular on the sacrifice of the leader. Most of those offering sacrifices in the portion are referred to as "souls" – that is, without any individual identification. And of all the souls required or permitted to bring a thanksgiving or sin-offering, burnt-offering or peace-offering, the leader suddenly stands out: "When a ruler sinneth, and doeth through error any one of all the things which the Lord his God hath commanded not to be done, and he is guilty" (Lev. 4:22). Here is one of the wonderful distinctions of the Bible: leadership gets no automatic pass. In the Bible everything is subject to the law, everything is open to criticism. The higher your position, the more you are open to criticism. Nothing of the sort existed in other kingdoms of the past, where the fate of the critic or rebel was clear: death.

The sacrifice of the ruler offers us a rare peek at the complicated attitude of Jewish tradition toward leadership, power and authority. Reading the verses on the sacrifice of the ruler, we can begin to understand the courage of the prophet Nathan when he stood before King David, who had murdered Uriah and violated Bath-sheba, and flatly accused him: "Thou art the man" (2 Sam. 12:7) – you are the rich man who stole the poor man's ewe lamb, the man who "deserveth to die."

We don't know of many other systems of government that guaranteed a similar status of immunity and power to the prophet. In Judaism, the place of faith is also the place of ongoing moral criticism of the government and its injustices. The role of the prophet and man of spirit is to stand always at the side of the oppressed and downtrodden, the "average citizen," and defend him or her unreservedly against the designs of the regime. Our tradition understands that there is no government that is without injustice.

No one ever described the tension between power and evil better than Rabbi Abraham Isaac Hacohen Kook, who said in this context, "It is not meet for Jacob [that is, for us, the children of Jacob] to engage in political life at a time when statehood requires bloody ruthlessness and demands a talent for evil" (*Orot* 14, translation from Arthur Hertzberg, *The Zionist Idea* [Philadelphia: Jewish Publication Society, 1997], 422). There is probably no act of governance that doesn't involve some degree of talent for evil. It was out of this understanding that our sages issued this decree: "Don't make yourself known to the authorities, because they do not reach out except for their own needs. They appear as lovers when it serves them, but do not stand by the individual when he is in need" (Mishnah, *Avot d'Rabbi Natan*, version 2, chapter 22).

The truth is that the sages never went so far as to endorse the pure anarchism of permanent revolution against all government. They always sought a balance, which is why a different chapter of the Ethics of the Fathers contains, as noted earlier, the obligation to "pray for the peace of government, for if not for fear of it we should have swallowed each other alive" (Mishnah, *Avot* 3:2). As noted above, this attitude echoes and foreshadows the words of Thomas Hobbes, who wrote in the seventeenth century of human relations without the fear of government as a human jungle in which "man is a wolf to man." Nonetheless, despite the contradictory impulses we can sum up the overall Jewish attitude as critical and suspicious of anything that carries the whiff of power.

This basic attitude toward government creates a perfect foundation for sharp, direct criticism of all public leadership. Let's return for a moment to the earliest days of the Israelite kingdom and the mythological stories that shaped our view of government:

> Rav Yehuda said, quoting Shmuel: Why did the kingdom of the house of Saul not endure? Because it had no faults. As Rabbi Yohanan said in the name of Rabbi Shimon Ben Yehozadak: Do not put a leader above the public unless he has a basket of snakes tied to his behind, so that if his good sense leaves him, they can say to him: Back up. (Babylonian Talmud, *Yoma* 22b)

There is a double meaning behind this saying. On one hand, this is a clear criticism of the character and behavior of those who reach a position of leadership. There are heights that cannot be reached without sharp elbows and an ability to ignore the casualties left piled up by the side of the road that led to the top. On the other hand, there is also a declaration here: this is how we like our leaders, putting their bastardly side to use for our benefit. At the same time, though, they should know that we know they're bastards. If everyone knows the leader's weaknesses, then in the event that he gets a swelled head, becomes arrogant and cuts himself off from the rest of us, then we can simply say to him: look behind and see the basket of snakes tied to you. We know everything, and if we want, we can bring you down.

Unfortunately, it's not always enough to rely on a system of checks and balances and public knowledge of the leader's past misdeeds. Sometimes the temptation of evil and the intoxication of power are overwhelming, and no amount of public criticism can restrain them. If this were not the case, how could we explain the character testimony provided by Maimonides in his commentary on the passage in *Pirkei Avot* that reads, "Shemaya said: Love work, hate domination and do not become too close to the authorities." Maimonides's commentary casts a wide net of analysis and intense criticism over both King Saul and his great rival, King David. Here is what Maimonides said:

> The authorities – this is the government. And these three precepts [love work, hate domination, avoid the authorities] provide a corrective to religion and the world, because without work one's situation will become difficult and one will be driven to steal and oppress. And as one seeks power, attacks and troubles will come upon him, because others will envy him and hate him, and he will lose his religion, as it is said: When a man is appointed from below, he becomes wicked from above. Similarly with closeness to the government, security is far away from it in this world, and it weakens religion, because one remains scrupulous only for that which benefits him. And you know the story of Doeg. (Maimonides on Mishnah, *Avot* 1:10)

Understanding Maimonides's comments requires a brief summary of the history of the monarchy. In the first Book of Samuel, chapter 21, David flees from King Saul and finds refuge in the priestly city of Nob, where the priest gives him the sword of Goliath and a meal of the sacred showbread. It happened that Doeg the Edomite, a follower of Saul, was there at the time. He went and told the king what the priests had done for David. Saul, enraged, slaughtered the city of Nob and nearly all its priests, except for one who escaped. Maimonides brings this story as a proof-text to show that one should not get too close – neither to the king, nor to a claimant to the throne nor to anyone else from the government.

The leader must thread his way between the raindrops with utmost caution, with determination and considerable sensitivity. The public hates his domination, and perhaps envies it. The talents of evil are waiting for him above, prophets and critics watch tirelessly for him to fail and cynics never stop reminding him of the basket of snakes hanging behind him, like a reminder of his sordid past. Is it any surprise that leaders sin now and then? It's fortunate that he has the possibility of correction and contrition such as the sin-offering of the ruler described in this week's portion. For beyond Judaism's endlessly critical attitude toward the sovereign, there is one more fundamental principle: reform is possible. Revolution is not necessary. We don't want perfect leaders, and therefore we offer them and ourselves the possibility of regret and atonement. Political decapitation is not part of the Jewish tradition of governance. On the contrary, we choose someone who has erred, on condition that he and we have the ability to reform and atone. Of such a government and the mechanisms of reform my late father used to say (loosely quoting someone or other) that "democracy is a wonderful thing; it's too bad they ruin it with elections every four years." What can you do, Dad? Sometimes you just have to love that sin-offering.

Week 24

Tzav – Command

Leviticus 6:1–8:36
Haftarah Jeremiah 7:21–8:3; 9:22–23
Alternate Haftarah Malachi 3:4–3:24

The Offering of Judah and Jerusalem

THIS IS ONE OF THE ONLY PORTIONS in the scripture that is directed entirely to a particular group within the Jewish people, namely the priests: Moses commands "Aaron and his sons." It's very tempting to want to enter the private space of the priestly class. But the subject matter – the sacrifices, the priesthood as a genetic inheritance and all the rest – has already been beaten to a fine pulp, so we'll leave it alone and discuss more general issues. In this case the general issue is the general public and in particular, public servants. The priest is undoubtedly the ultimate public servant. He mediates between the Jewish people and their Father in heaven, although the mediation is rather one-sided. He brings our message upward, but there is no clear evidence that he carries a message from above back to us here below. Much has been said about the automatic nature of the priesthood, the sense of God-given mission that actually diminishes the messenger to the point where the mission becomes irrelevant. Against this backdrop, this week's haftarah reading stands out in sharp relief, dealing with a different sort of public servant who actually does bring the word of God on high down to humanity – the prophet. In this week's haftarah the prophets Malachi and Elijah appear. The haftarah is taken from the Book of Malachi, the last of the prophets and perhaps the most complex of them. It's customary to think that this haftarah, which is read when *Parashat Tzav* coincides with the Sabbath before Passover (in other years the haftarah is a passage from the Book of Jeremiah), was chosen because this Sabbath is called *Shabbat Hagadol* (the Great Sabbath), echoing the final verses of the haftarah: "Behold, I will send you Elijah the prophet before the coming of the great and terrible day of the Lord. And he shall turn the heart of the fathers to the children and the heart of the children to their fathers; lest I come and smite the land with utter destruction" (Mal. 3:23–24). That could be, but the placement of this haftarah on the eve of Passover and in conjunction with *Parashat Tzav*, which speaks to the priests, has a deeper significance.

The initial chapters of Malachi deal with severe prophetic criticism of the Temple ritual, which had fallen into routine and lost the passionate faith and holiness of mission. Here is the unique dialogue (Mal. 1:1–12):

God approaches: "Unto you, O priests, that despise my name."

And the priests play innocent and reply: "Wherein have we despised your name?"

God spells it out: "Ye offer polluted bread upon mine altar."

And the priests respond: "Wherein have we polluted thee?"

God presses his case: "In that ye say: 'The table of the Lord is contemptible.' And when ye offer the blind for a sacrifice, it is no evil! And when ye offer the lame and the sick, it is no evil! Present it now unto thy governor; will he be pleased with thee? Or will he accept thy person? saith the Lord of hosts."

And now God gets to the point: "In vain! I have no pleasure in you, saith the Lord of hosts. Neither will I accept an offering at your hand."

He actually gets more satisfaction elsewhere: "For from the rising sun even unto the going down of the same my name is great among the nations; and in every place offerings are presented unto my name, even pure oblations, for my name is great among the nations, saith the Lord of hosts."

Here, on the other hand, "ye profane it, in that ye say: 'The table of the Lord is polluted, and the fruit thereof, even the food thereof, is contemptible.'"

The prophetic criticism of the defiled Temple ritual is nothing new or unusual. Malachi's innovation is not his piercing message about the corrupt priestly establishment or the ritual that has become polluted. His astonishing innovation is the uninterrupted dialogue between God and his priests, between the creator and the public and their servants. This is one of the very rare moments in the Bible where the text presents the spoken positions of the two opposing sides. The text includes the differing viewpoints and gaps in understanding and doesn't simply offer a one-sided human tirade against heaven, or its obverse, a divine tirade against earth and its inhabitants.

Against the backdrop of the prophet's two opening chapters against the priests and their corrupted sacrifices, the placement of the haftarah on the Great Sabbath becomes clear. It begins with the purifying of the priests, the sons of the tribe of Levi, and their transformation from corrupt public servants into people of truth and loving-kindness: "And he shall purify the sons of Levi, and purge them as gold and silver; and there shall be they that offer unto the Lord offerings in righteousness" (Mal. 3:3). And this righteous offering continues right into the next verse, which is the beginning of our haftarah: "Then shall the offering of Judah and Jerusalem be pleasant unto the Lord, as in the days of old, and as in ancient years" (Mal. 3:4). The offering is a sacrifice from the plant world, made of oil and flour. It doesn't involve bloodshed. It is vegetarian, natural and certainly modest. The offering befits the vision of the end of days, when even "the lion shall eat straw like an ox" (Isa. 11:7). This change in the patterns of nature and life is not merely physiological. The inner character of life will change. Life will become a dialogue instead of a series of one-sided monologues. In Malachi's utopia we are offered a life in which humanity has learned to embrace not only itself and its closest neighbors but others who are completely different. Utopian Judaism, in my understanding of Malachi, dreams of a dialogue of all creation.

Of all the Jewish holidays, there is probably none that's more in harmony with this model of the future than Passover. All of the holidays have a recurring routine that entails repeating the frameworks and holiday ceremonies of the past. Passover, by contrast, perpetuates change, almost from the outset. After all, this is the holiday of "Why is this night different?" The real answer is not the familiar four-part refrain, delivered by the children of the family in the traditional melody, but something else entirely. On this holiday we are obligated to share our table with others who are different from us. At the beginning of the Seder we invite the stranger, the poor and the needy, who might be off-putting in their dress and appearance, and include them in our celebration. From there on, the Haggadah is full of various creative formulations through which our conversation is opened to the wise, the wicked, the simple and the one who does not know how to ask. In the final days of the new human order, our ultimate Seder, all our days will look like this, and all our conversations will have this sound. And don't think it will be easy. It's not only we, the good and enlightened, who must sit at our Seder with the scoundrel and the fool. They have their own Seder customs, and they have to include us, converse with us and listen to viewpoints like ours that are completely different from the ones they're accustomed to hearing on all other nights of the year.

Malachi embraces this vision of an expanding conversation and, after including Elijah the prophet to the mix, adds yet another dimension of dialogue. Elijah restores the hearts of the members of the family to one another and so renews the inter-generational connection that is so often lost in the transition from father to son and mother to daughter: "And he shall turn the heart of the fathers to the children, and the heart of the children to their fathers" (Mal. 3:24). Malachi's words at the end of his book are more than just a touching family embrace. His prophecy is of a restoration of the sacred, sublime and transcendental to our broken, boring daily lives. To understand the importance of this verse, we need to return to the beginning of the Book of Malachi and listen to God's bitter complaint: "A son honoreth his father, and a servant his master; if then I be a father, where is my honor? And if I be a master, where is my fear? saith the Lord of hosts" (Mal. 1:6).

This restoring of the hearts we've talked about is also the restoration of God to the human discourse – not as a critic or complainer, but as a partner in dialogue. Malachi delivers this news in the voice of Elijah the prophet, who so powerfully symbolizes the longed-for transformation of the angry, violent, fanatical prophet into the kind, sensitive, attentive messenger of redemption who reunites humanity, brings families back together and reunites the Father in heaven with his children on earth.

Therefore, when we open the door for Elijah the prophet at the Seder this year, let's not recite the traditional "Pour Out Thy Wrath," which invokes a world of confrontation and hostility. Rather, let's pray in the tones of the sixteenth-century German Haggadah brought by my father-in-law, Lucien Lazar: "Pour out thy love on the nations that knew thee and on the kingdoms that called thy name, for the kindness they show to the seed of Jacob and their defense of thy people Israel from its enemies. May they merit to see thy chosen tabernacle and to share in the joys of thy nations." This is Elijah's true public service, and may his kind increase in Israel and the world.

Of Sacrifice and Suffering

*I*T'S NOT AN EASY READ, this portion of ours with all its sacrifices and offerings. There's something deeply frustrating in that huge collection of rules that have no human application in this day and age and have so little perceptible importance or significance. Nonetheless, what can we learn from all these details?

The world of modern jurisprudence seeks to avoid individually tailored or targeted laws. The law must be generally applicable and guarantee equal protection to all persons. The reason is that individualized legislation, targeted at or tailored for a particular person or group, indicates the presence of some form of corruption: either legislation that singles out a person or group for negative treatment, or a law that discriminates in favor of one person or group over others. The modern world considers laws of this sort to be illegitimate, almost without exception. And here we have our portion, which frames a whole series of laws discriminating in favor of the priestly class: "Command Aaron and his sons, saying…every male among the children of Aaron may eat of it, as a due for ever throughout your generations" (Lev. 6:2–11). We have before us a class-based legislation that includes orders and commandments intended explicitly to benefit the males of the priestly class. These will inevitably arouse criticism and discomfort, if only because of the condescension that results from the priests' material privileges.

The most forceful criticism of this discriminatory legislation is expressed by the editor of the weekly portions, who made his opinion clear by linking this priestly portion to the stinging haftarah from the prophet Jeremiah: "Thus saith the Lord of hosts, the God of Israel…: For I spoke not unto your fathers, nor commanded them in the day that I brought them out of the land of Egypt, concerning burnt-offerings or sacrifices" (Jer. 7:21–22). What a splendid dismissal! In one single assessment of just a few prophetic words, the entire Book of Leviticus is made to disappear as though it never were. Jeremiah was the prophet of the destruction of the First Temple. He saw the corruptions of the First Temple just as Jesus saw them at the time of the Second Temple. It's well, too, to remember the hints and allegations that the scripture supplies about Jeremiah, the better to understand his reproof. As the first verse of his book attests, Jeremiah was "of the priests that were in Anathoth in the land of Benjamin" (Jer. 1:1). When a priest says something about the priests and the priesthood, the criticism has far more credibility, coming as it does from an insider. He knows what he's talking about. And so, what did Jeremiah know?

Anathoth was the home for many years of a family of priests descended from Abiathar, who was deposed by King Solomon, the Temple builder himself, as an act of political housecleaning. When Solomon expels him, the scripture offers a religious-historical explanation: "So Solomon thrust out Abiathar from being priest unto the Lord; that the word of the Lord might be fulfilled, which he spoke concerning the house of Eli in Shiloh" (1 Kings 2:27).

What was this historic grievance that led God to depose the house of Eli from the high priesthood and bestow this asset on the house of Zadok? Turning to the original incident in the beginning of the First Book of Samuel, we find the following: "Now the sons of Eli were base men; they knew not the Lord. And the custom of the priests with the people was, that, when any man offered sacrifice, the priest's servant came, while the flesh was still seething, with a flesh-hook of three teeth in his hand" (1 Sam. 2:12–13).

Briefly, the sons of Eli, the high priest in the days before the monarchy, were famously corrupt. They took the best cuts of meat for themselves and left the dregs and worst cuts for God and the supplicant: "And the sin of the young men was very great before the Lord; for the men dealt contemptuously with the offering of the Lord.... And there came a man of God unto Eli, and said unto him...Wherefore kick ye at my sacrifice and at mine offering, which I have commanded.... But now the Lord saith... Behold, the days come, that I will cut off thine arm, and the arm of thy father's house, that there shall not be an old man in thy house" (1 Sam. 2:17–31).

That's where it began – when Eli was the high priest, and his sons Hophni and Phinehas became gourmands at the expense of the sanctuary and the sacrifices. The sons despoiled the common people, robbed the pilgrims bringing their sacrifice, debased their values and kicked the offerings and sacrifices. The punishment was that the house of Eli would be overthrown, which occurred, as noted, several decades later in the days of Abiathar. And so when Jeremiah came centuries later to testify against the ethical shortcomings of sacrificial rituals of his time, he knew what he was talking about. His family had learned its lesson, as Jeremiah hinted: we sinned and were overthrown, but nothing seems to have improved with the new priestly dynasty. Malpractice has taken root, and our successors turn out to be sinners. Jeremiah warns in his prophetic language that unless the temptations of priesthood and sacrifice are ended, there will be no escape from destruction. Just as the family of Abiathar was overthrown in its time, the whole nation will be overthrown.

Anyone who was not part of the Temple establishment in Jerusalem understood that sacrifices amounted to a tax with a kickback for the insiders, the priests and bureaucrats of the sanctuary, who frequently had very little to do with sanctity. The prophetic criticism, and the later criticism of the sages, came out swinging against the tendency to turn the sacrifice into an end in itself, to a technology of faith that comes in place of a genuine religious feeling of spiritual and ethical obligation.

The sages of the Second Temple period, who achieved greatness because of their wisdom, learning, devotion to the public and high standards – and not because of genes or automatic inheritance – never approved of the goings-on in the Temple in Jerusalem, with its corrupt standards. They saw what the prophets saw, and what Jesus saw. For that reason, they worked over and over to undermine the status of the priests and reduce their importance in almost every possible way. In Mishnah *Horayot* they ruled: "A bastard who is knowledgeable in Torah is greater than a priest who is an ignoramus" (3:8). They went even further: "Even a gentile who studies Torah is as great as the high priest" (3:8). In other words, high priest is an honorable, inflated title that doesn't necessarily convey any genuine content.

In part, the criticism stems from the structural tension between the priests, with their guaranteed status as a social elite, and the sages, many of whom were impoverished workers and tradesmen, and all of whom had to earn their places through years of dedicated study. But that competition is not the only source of their criticism. It reflects the social tension between the old priestly elite of Jerusalem and the new class of Torah intellectuals and academicians, some of whom had been born materially poor, but who came to form the spiritual elite by the power of scholarship. The new Torah that was created in the Land against the backdrop of the defilements of the Temple and the dishonesty of the royal palace brought about not just a religious renewal but a social, class and economic transformation. Here is how the Aggadah tells it:

> There was a high priest who went out from the Temple, and all the people followed him. When they saw Shemaya and Avtalyon walking by [two of the greatest sages, both of whom were converts], they left the high priest and turned and followed the pair. In the end Shemaya and Avtalyon took their leave of the high priest. He said to them: May the sons of gentiles go in peace. They replied: Yes, the sons of gentiles who follow the practice of Aaron will go in peace, but as for the son of Aaron, he will not go in peace when he does not follow the practice of Aaron, does not love peace and pursue

peace and does not bring humankind closer in peace. (Babylonian Talmud, *Yoma* 71b)

The sages' message is clear: actions are what matter, not pedigree. The "practice of Aaron" is not simply the sacrificial practice and the rest of the Temple ritual. There are "sons of Aaron" who automatically enjoy a guaranteed living at public expense and are all too likely to be corrupted, like all automatic religious establishments. And then there are "disciples of Aaron," who follow the practice of Aaron, which includes a defined daily agenda as described by Hillel in the Ethics of the Fathers: "loving peace and pursuing peace, loving humankind and bringing them close to the Torah" (Mishnah, *Avot* 1:12).

In the Aggadah quoted above, the sons of Aaron gorge themselves on free meat while the disciples of Aaron meet their obligation to their fellows by teaching equality and human kindness, without regard for origin, economic class or place of dwelling. In place of the burnt-offering, the Aggadah suggests offering oneself in human partnership. In place of the arrogance of the priests and professional religious functionaries, the love of humankind shown by those who have never done to others what is hateful to them; acting with kindness, justice and righteousness. This is the hardest sacrifice of all, and this is how the haftarah in the Book of Jeremiah is ended: "Thus saith the Lord: Let not the wise man glory in his wisdom, neither let the mighty man glory in his might, let not the rich man glory in his riches; but let him that glorieth glory in this, that he understandeth, and knoweth me, that I am the Lord who exercises mercy, justice and righteousness, in the earth; for in these things I delight, saith the Lord" (Jer. 9:22–23).

Week 25

Shemini – On the Eighth Day

Leviticus 9:1–11:47

Kosher: The Fitness of Foods and the Fitness of Eaters

TWO GREAT HISTORICAL EVENTS take place in this week's portion, *Parashat Shemini*: the dedication of the tabernacle and the untimely deaths of two sons of Aaron, Nadab and Abihu, who brought a strange fire before the Lord. It's a curiosity worth exploring that Jewish culture has chosen through the generations to study *Shemini* less for these momentous events than for the portion's rules of daily conduct, which are indelibly imprinted in our people's collective consciousness. *Parashat Shemini* contains one of the most ancient codes in the Jewish genome, the dietary laws of kashrut. Countless people have no idea who Nadab and Abihu were, but pigs? Everyone knows the attitude of Jews and Judaism toward these creatures. Every generation has offered its own explanation for the laws of kashrut. Some generations have sought through the Jewish table and the limitations of its menu to emphasize the separation between Jew and gentile. In other eras the Jewish menu has been seen as a recipe for improved health, contrasted with the gentiles' less-than-hygienic eating habits.

Along with the physiological explanations have come a host of psychological, philosophical and spiritual theories. All of them are correct and sensible – all, of course, depending on the leanings of the listener. As for me, I read the rules of kashrut from a vegetarian perspective. I love the fact that the laws of kashrut forbid the eating of carnivores and permit

Shemini

only herbivores. I love Rabbi Kook's stance on vegetarianism, in which he argues:

> It is impossible to picture the Master of all things, who has mercy on all that he created, imposing such a law on his wonderful creation that the human race would be unable to survive except by transgressing its moral instincts through the shedding of blood, even the blood of animals. (*Ma'amarei HaRoeh* [Essays of Rav Kook], edited by Rabbi Elisha Aviner and David Landau [Jerusalem: Mossad Harav Kook, 1984])

I love this position, because its roots are deep and ancient. Rabbi Kook was preceded by the early fifteenth-century Spanish scholar Rabbi Joseph Albo, who wrote, "In the killing of animals there is cruelty, rage and the accustoming of oneself to the bad habit of shedding innocent blood. The eating of the flesh of animals also gives rise to heaviness, morbidity and dullness of the spirit" (*Sefer Ha'ikarim* 3:15).

In a similar vein, Don Isaac Abravanel of late fifteenth-century Portugal, in his commentary on Exodus 16:4, explained why God fed the children of Israel in the desert with "bread from heaven" (namely the manna) rather than meat:

> The Holy One, blessed be he, said to Moses: Eating meat is not essential to one's nutrition; rather, it is a matter of gluttony, of filling one's belly and of increasing one's lust. Meat also gives rise in human beings to a cruel and evil temperament. Therefore one finds that predatory animals and birds which eat meat are cruel and wicked. But sheep and cattle, chickens, pigeons and doves, which feed off the grass of the field, have no wickedness in them. This was the intention of the prophet Isaiah, that in time of redemption "the lion shall eat straw like the ox" (Isa. 11:7). Therefore the Holy One, blessed be he, did not tell Moses that he would give the Israelites meat, rather bread, which is a fitting food and essential for the human temperament. (Don Isaac Abravanel on Exod. 16:4, quoted in "The Vegetarian Mitzvah," http://www.brook.com/jveg/)

I'd like to quote an innovative interpretation suggested by my son Itai in his bar mitzvah sermon. He argued that in the first days of history, Adam and Eve had eternal life and a vegetarian diet. But events took their own course: they ate the fruit of the forbidden tree, lost eternal life, were subjected to death and as a by-product were permitted to cut short the lives of the animals that until then had been similarly immortal. The ultimate correction to this first failure will come in the end of days, in the resurrection of the dead. In that time immortality will return and the eating of flesh will naturally pass from the world, and vegetarianism will be our way of life, as it was in the Garden of Eden.

I love to follow the twists and turns in the thinking of the sages throughout the generations. Even when it wasn't the Lawgiver's original intention, these meanderings yield creativity and many good thoughts. It seems to me that in our own time we can and must use the analytic tools of past generations and add new ways of explaining the dietary laws. It is not inconceivable that the kashrut laws reflect the economic structure of the biblical era, and point to the desired relationship between the individual and his property. Goat, sheep, cattle and fowl had long since been domesticated and constituted the property owner's primary assets. As for deer, they were familiar from the fields, vineyards and hills around his home. It's possible that the laws of kashrut were intended to systematize the thinning of the flocks in an orderly manner. The message of these laws is that even though these animals are your property, you are not permitted to slaughter them wantonly, torture them for your amusement, eat their limbs while they are alive or engage in other such abuses. It's enough to see how often people beat their animals mercilessly, cruelly force-feed their geese to soften the liver and kill animals randomly for the sheer joy of killing – or for the pleasure of gluttony. How many of us go to a restaurant and order rare steak, dripping with blood? It was to address all these things that the laws of kashrut were introduced. Food is such a basic human need that the primal Lawgiver was compelled to address it. Because everyone eats, every act of eating has its own attendant moral and social marker: what is permitted, what is forbidden and how to proceed. To paraphrase Napoleon, Judaism marches on its belly. In this context,

Shemini

Judaism's vegetarian vision might serve as a potential platform for a new Jewish ecological discourse, as a basic approach to *tikkun olam*, the repair of the world. Here are some facts:

- Every year nearly 100,000 square miles of the world's rainforest is destroyed – 260 square miles per day – to make way for farming, mining or development, but the largest proportion goes to pasture for beef cattle. In Brazil, home to one-third of the world's rainforest, fully four-fifths of the destroyed rainforest goes to raise beef cattle, mostly for export to North America. Two hundred twenty square feet of rainforest are destroyed for every pound of red meat produced, or fifty-five square feet per fast-food hamburger. ("The Cattle Industry Is Destroying the Rainforest," http://priceofmeat.com/2009/02/07/the-cattle-industry-is-destroying-the-amazon-rainforest/)

- Destruction of rainforests is also a major source of global warming. Burning of trees, the main method of clearing land, together with decomposition of the dead plant matter, accounts for 17 percent of global carbon dioxide emission, more than all the cars, ships and airplanes combined. Moreover, through photosynthesis existing rainforests absorb 4.8 billion tons of carbon dioxide per year, 10 percent of global emissions; clearing the forests destroys an essential global defense mechanism. ("Rainforest Destruction," http://www.rainforest-facts.com/rainforest-destruction.html)

- More than half of all water consumed in the United States goes to beef production. Every pound of beef requires 2,500 gallons of water; the same amount of water can produce one hundred pounds of wheat. As beef, that water will provide four hamburgers; as grain, it will feed a family of four for a month. ("Facts about Beef," http://ran.org/fileadmin/materials/education/factsheets/fs_beef.pdf)

- Cattle in the United States produce more than one billion tons of organic waste each year. Most of it goes untreated and forms one of the largest single causes of pollution to rivers, streams, lakes and aquifers. ("Beyond Beef," http://www.mcspotlight.org/media/reports/beyond.html)

- Cattle and other ruminant livestock emit about 80 million metric tons of methane each year, or 28 percent of all human-generated methane emissions, as a result of burping and flatulence, both aggravated by cheap and unhealthy feed methods. One ton of methane has about 33 times more impact on the climate than a ton of carbon dioxide. Methane currently accounts for about one-fifth of all human-generated global warming. ("Frequent Questions," http://www.epa.gov/rlep/faq.html#1; "Methane's Impact on Global Warming Far Higher Than Previously Thought," http://www.timesonline.co.uk/tol/news/science/earth-environment/article6895907.ece)

- Cattle herding takes up about 24 percent of the planet's landmass and is responsible for much of the rapidly spreading desertification in sub-Saharan Africa and the western rangeland of the United States and Australia. The United Nations estimates that 29 percent of the Earth's landmass now suffers "slight, moderate or severe desertification," mostly as a result of overgrazing. ("Excerpts from the Book: Beyond Beef," http://www.gardensofeden.org/G1BeyondBeef.htm)

But facts alone are not the only argument for a more vegetarian world. Both ancient and modern history speak for it. In an era of holocausts, mass murder and widespread, random violence, it makes sense to take another look at vegetarianism as an alternative worldview in opposition to violence.

Today, in a world of growing coarseness and inhumanity, the laws of kashrut constitute an essential educational phase. They form an answer to the worldview, still all too widespread, according to which there are human beings, and there are others – enemies, whose blood, like the blood of animals, is cheap. To them we reply with a system that strictly regulates the shedding of blood, whether human or animal. The shedding of human blood is entirely forbidden. The shedding of animal blood is permitted only under very severe restrictions. Only when these restrictions are understood and observed is any killing allowed.

Strange Fire

QUESTION: WHAT COULD BE WORSE than the dedication of the sanctuary of the Lord, God of Israel, with a surfeit of sacrificed animals and spattered blood? Answer: the dedication of the sanctuary of the Lord, God of Israel, with two sacrificed humans. That is much worse, and that is what happened. Precisely "on the eighth day" of the dedication celebrations, "Aaron drew near...and slew...and Aaron's sons presented...and he slew...and they delivered...and he slew" (Lev. 9:8–15). At the end of a chapter full of sacrifices the ceremony reaches its ritual climax: "And Aaron lifted up his hands toward the people, and blessed them; and he came down from offering the sin-offering, and the burnt-offering, and the peace-offerings. And Moses and Aaron went into the tent of meeting, and came out, and blessed the people; and the glory of the Lord appeared unto all the people" (Lev. 9:22–23).

In plain language: Aaron finished all the slaughtering, roasting and blood-spilling and went into the tent with Moses; then the two of them came out to face the people and blessed them, and at this climactic moment the glory of God was visible. And how did his glory express itself? "There came forth fire from before the Lord, and consumed upon the altar the burnt-offering and the fat," and the natural response among all those observing was ecstasy: "When all the people saw it, they shouted, and fell on their faces" (Lev. 9:24).

Life in the desert was undoubtedly terrifying and astounding, filled with peaks of faith accompanied by expressions of wonder at the presence of God among his chosen (and choosing) congregation. But the peaks were invariably followed by depths of loss and failure. It took many years for the emotional pendulum to slow down and reach an equilibrium that allowed it to swing with the experiences of the believer and not the rages of God. It's obvious that the climactic celebration and the descent of God's glory would leave the experienced Bible reader with a clenched stomach, waiting for the inevitable blow. And sure enough, Moses and Aaron are still out there blessing the people when "Nadab and Abihu, the sons of Aaron, took each of them his censer, and put fire therein, and laid incense thereon, and offered strange fire before the Lord, which he had not commanded them. And there came forth fire from before the Lord, and devoured them, and they died before the Lord" (Lev. 10:1–2).

It's possible to see the late Nadab and Abihu as one link in a hidden chain of human sacrifices interpolated along the length of the biblical text. It's a topic that's almost never discussed, but if we look, we find that most of the major cultural changes of that time involved a human sacrifice somewhere in the background. Abel was murdered with Cain's knife as a sacrifice on the departure of Adam's firstborn to his new life of wandering, launching the journeys of all the world's expelled, innovative and restless. Abraham's faith was forever forged and stamped on the altar of Isaac, who was almost slaughtered by his father. The eternal struggle between the sons of Abraham demanded its own sacrifice, and so Ishmael was left for dead in the desert by his father, the serial offerer of sons, until he was miraculously saved, perhaps by the same angel who saved his brother Isaac. We didn't leave Egypt until after the smiting of the firstborn, which was the ultimate human sacrifice. And now the two nephews of Moses die right on the people's altar, before their very eyes, as a sign and memorial to the dedication of God's first earthly dwelling.

Let's leave human sacrifice aside for now and look for explanations that are closer to our own world. What happened? Why did disaster interrupt the dedication of the tabernacle? It's hard to tell from the brief, enigmatic text. What is "strange fire," and what's wrong with it? No explanation. But as usual, when the text is opaque the Midrash and commentaries aren't shy about looking for imaginative solutions.

We're going to look at two very different explanations for the deaths of Aaron's sons. Between the two readings lies a broad range of nuances and implications that, taken together, point to the heart of the explanation, both historical and theological. The Talmudic Aggadah imagines what happened just before these two flowers of priesthood, Aaron's sons, met their fates:

Shemini

> Moses and Aaron were walking in front, and Nadav and Abihu were walking behind them. Nadav said to Abihu: When will these two old men die so that you and I can lead the nation? The Holy One, praised be he, said to them: "Do not celebrate what is yet to come." We will see who buries whom. Rav Papa said: As the saying goes, many young colts die and their skins become saddles on their mothers' backs. (Babylonian Talmud, *Sanhedrin* 52b)

This is a plainly political reading; what it refers to, in the delicate language of the Aggadah, is a conspiracy. The Aggadah is describing an attempted plot against the elders of the generation, the senior members of the family, the messengers of God. The arrogant youngsters (who couldn't have been all that young, considering that Moses and Aaron were both in their nineties) want to have their share of power and glory. And so God comes to the rescue of his servants' regime. It could be that God assumed, quite reasonably, that Moses and Aaron wouldn't respond firmly enough to rebels from within their own family. They would ignore, rationalize, hold back, reconsider and avoid washing their dirty laundry in public to the point where it wouldn't be washed at all, and in the end they would be lost.

That, after all, is how King David managed to gloss over the brewing rebellion of his son Absalom, until it almost brought him down. The sudden, dramatic annilation of Nadab and Abihu, as a defense of the regime and an attack on subversion, accords well with the instructions of the Supreme Impresario regarding the funeral arrangements and mourning rituals: "Then Moses said unto Aaron: 'This is it that the Lord spoke, saying: Through them that are nigh unto me I will be sanctified, and before all the people I will be glorified.' And Aaron held his peace" (Lev. 10:3). In modern terms, Moses's message from God could be interpreted as follows: I am watching over you; I am your backup, and no one in that crowd out there in the camp must have any doubt on the matter.

And the instructions continue: "Let not the hair of your heads go loose, neither rend your clothes, that ye die not, and that he be not wroth with all the congregation; but let your brethren, the whole house of Israel, bewail the burning which the Lord hath kindled" (Lev. 10:6). You are the government. You are the symbols of authority, my ambassadors and authorized representatives. Ambassadors do not weep and governments do not mourn when rebels fall, even when they are family. Leave the moaning and wailing to the mourners.

Sovereignty imposes certain obligations on Aaron. As God's representative he cannot mourn in public, because that would make him appear to be questioning the decision of his superior, the source of his own authority, and open him to the charge that he had joined his sons' rebellion, with all the implied consequences. Hence the warning: "that ye die not." We will have more to say about this when we reach *Parashat Acharei Mot*.

An alternative to the conspiracy theory was advanced by the nineteenth-century scholar Rabbi Naftali Zvi Yehuda Berlin, the dean of the famed Volozhin Yeshiva in Belarus, who is known to posterity by his Hebrew initials as the Netziv (and after whom Kibbutz Ein Hanetziv, south of Lake Tiberias, is named). His interpretation brings a psychological depth to the discussion that illuminates and even corrects generations of other readings. Nadab and Abihu, he argues, "entered from a fiery, passionate love of God. And the Torah said that even though the love of God is precious in God's eyes, it should not be in a manner that deviates from God's command" (Berlin, *Ha'emek Davar*, on Lev. 10:1). The fire, as the Netziv understands it, is the flame burning in the heart of the impassioned believer. Observing the fiery, urgent, sometimes violent debates that divided the Jewish people throughout the nineteenth century, pitting Hasidim against Mitnagdim, conservatives against modernizers and traditionalists against Maskilim, he knew whereof he spoke.

There are times when the flames of belief, however pure and sincere they might be, are in fact a strange fire. This is not what God commanded. There is a very fine line between the pure fire in the heart of a believer and the strange, deadly fire of the extremist and fanatic. The distinction provides an excellent opening to a discussion about faith and its limits. Nadab and Abihu enter into the Holy of Holies after everyone else has left, and continue in their passion what their father, their uncle and their God have already completed. Their over-enthusiasm cost them their lives.

Aaron and his two surviving sons are called on to exercise the utmost self-control, the exact opposite of the dead sons' unrestrained religious outburst: not to weep, not to protest, not to go out to the mourners' tent and not to desecrate the sacred. The overreaction of children is answered with the supreme restraint of their father, and neither is an appropriate model for the rest of mortal humankind. We need a more balanced reality, neither unrestrained nor frozen, but human.

May their memory be blessed. And may the explanations and lessons in their memory be sanctified and well learned.

Week 26

Tazria/Metzora
If a Woman Be Delivered/
The Law of the Leper

Leviticus 12:1–15:33

The Lepers' Plague of Our Time

OY, WHAT UNPLEASANT PORTIONS. As kids we used to call these, not *parashat hashavua* (the portion of the week), but *"haphrashat hashavua"* – the secretion of the week, all full of infections, blemishes, growths and other extreme disorders the likes of which our most advanced modern dermatologists have probably never seen, even if they've devoted their lives to healing the exotic diseases of the farthest tropical isles.

The most straightforward and widespread interpretation of these portions is to read them as the doctrine of Jewish hygiene. By this interpretation, these portions and their commandments are intended to keep those infected with these contagious diseases outside the general population so as to reduce the threat of epidemic. This interpretation has support in historical fact. It's widely believed that the Jewish rules of bodily cleanliness and family purity, including bathing, hand washing and avoidance of the dead, with all their contaminations, saved countless Jewish lives during the devastating epidemic of the Black Death.

One of the deadliest epidemics in history, the Black Death spread through Europe in several waves between 1346 and 1361 and is believed to have killed between 25 million and 100 million people – up to one-fourth of the population of Europe at the time. Some villages lost four-fifths of their population. The plague also led to one of the most tragic episodes in Jewish history: during the years 1347 and 1348, a rumor spread across the continent that Jews were poisoning the wells and causing the plague in order to destroy the Christian world. The rumor touched off rioting and resulted in a series of mob attacks on Jewish communities, to the point where the pope himself stepped in to protect them. During those years Jews and lepers became linked in the popular mind as being the cause of the epidemic, and both groups suffered mob violence despite their innocence of the charge. Among the Jewish communities that came under attack were those of Toulon, Girona, Strasbourg, Paris, Rouen, Rome, Augsburg, Wurzburg, Freiburg, Frankfurt and Cologne.

In reality, the epidemic was apparently spread through typical channels of pollution – water sources, unsanitary food, sewage and the like – and people who avoided those contact points were likely to be spared. It was precisely for that reason, ironically, that our ancestors were slaughtered by their neighbors. With the passage of time we can look back and be thankful for the hygienic customs that saved them from the plague. For the modern mind seeking meaning in the ancient texts, this is not enough, however. Let's go and find the hidden, long forgotten plagues that might still threaten us.

Modern medical research has greatly reduced the presence of disease in our private and public spaces. There are still people who suffer from leprosy, but these are isolated cases, and their rarity testifies to the efficacy of the methods that have all but eliminated a once-widespread disease. What, then, are we to do with this piece of the biblical world that has lost its immediacy?

Every generation is permitted, perhaps even obliged, to renew and update the Torah's principles so that they are appropriate to the generation and its commentators. The concept of Sabbath, for example, has within it the capacity for constant renewal as a day of rest for both body and spirit, for the individual and the community. Likewise honoring one's parents, loving one's neighbor and upholding the sanctity of life, including the prohibition of murder and the uncleanness of the dead. But what do we do with leprosy? There was a disease, and it is no more. What can we make of the dead letters that form these two portions, *Tazria* and *Metzora*? We can read them as a monument to the diseases of the past, reminding us again and again of our good fortune. Leprosy can serve to emphasize how wonderful this world of ours is, even with all its shortcomings and imperfections, compared to the worlds of the past that so many people long for without really knowing what they're longing for. As my father used to say, "Even nostalgia isn't what it used to be."

The outwardly repellent quality of leprosy encouraged the sages to give it a far-reaching interpretation, fraught with significance. By their lights, leprosy was the punishment for one of the most elusive crimes against one's fellow man: slander. They went so far as to explain the Hebrew word for leper, *metzora*, as a contraction of the familiar phrase meaning slanderer, *motzi shem ra*. That is, one who tried to push one's fellow outside the circle of the community by telling tales will in the end find himself expelled from society, sitting alone "outside the camp," as the text says. This is a charming bit of wisdom, meant to achieve by means of convoluted commentary a community of forgiving souls, a community of the pure of word that banishes like lepers the polluted of tongue. Among the sages of the Mishnaic and Talmudic period, who surely saw their share of lepers wandering the streets, a debate broke out over what to do: banish them and ignore them, as the scripture commanded, or embrace and identify with them as the prophet Isaiah said, "that thou hide not thyself from thine own flesh" (Isa. 58:7) – even when that flesh is exposed, infected and diseased.

The Amora'im Rabbi Ami and Rabbi Asi, Talmudic scholars of the land of Israel, would not enter a street where a leper lived. Rabbi Shimon Ben Lakish would throw stones at lepers he saw wandering in the city and call out, "Go back to your own place and do not contaminate mankind" (Midrash Rabba, *Vayikra* 15). Such was the social attitude of some of our blessed sages:

> Rabbi Yohanan declared: Beware of flies that touch carriers of *ra'atan* [a skin disease from that era], because they transmit the disease. Rabbi Zeira would not sit in a place where the wind was blowing from the direction of a carrier of *ra'atan*. Rabbi Eleazar would not enter the tents of carriers of *ra'atan*. Rabbi Ami and Rabbi Asi would

not eat eggs that came from a street where carriers of *ra'atan* lived. (Babylonian Talmud, *Ketubot* 77b)

In contrast to these healthy and fastidiously cautious role models, one of the most sensitive and humane of the Amora'im of the land of Israel displayed an entirely different attitude toward the sick and infected: "Rabbi Yehoshua Ben Levi used to wrap himself among them and study Torah with them" (Babylonian Talmud, *Ketubot* 77b).

Rabbi Yehoshua Ben Levi's stance, sitting among the sick and studying with them, opens the way to a contemporary understanding of the laws of the leper. We can broaden our definition of "leper" to include any kind of "other." Just as the leper was banished outside the gates, many Others in our own time are not permitted to come inside the gates. The stranger, the foreigner, the differently gendered and the dissenter are all expelled from among us to someplace far beyond the borders of our self-awareness. Let's ask the scholars of our age, in the name of Rabbi Yehoshua Ben Levi: Are you still afraid of virtual leprosy?

The color of a black person's skin is not contagious. The thoughts of an agitator aren't malignant. The troubles of a person with special needs aren't catching. Even the homosexual and the single mother aren't disease-carriers. So where do you stand? Will you continue to throw stones at them, flee from their flies and avoid eggs from their streets, or will you cross the street, join the children of Rabbi Yehoshua Ben Levi of our generation and "wrap yourselves among them"? You would hardly believe how much wisdom and wealth can come to you from that other place, the place of the Other.

If we could convince the pure of body and thought to dirty their hands just a bit by engaging with a different sort of wisdom, to expand their thinking in a new and more contemporary direction, we might be able to offer an alternative to the celebrated Hebrew poetess Rachel, who wrote at the beginning of the last century about this week's haftarah and the tidings of redemption for the besieged Samaria that were brought to the people of the city by "four leprous men at the entrance of the gate" (2 Kings 7:3):

> For a long while the dreadful enemy
> Brought Samaria to siege;

> Four lepers to her brought tidings.
> To her brought the tidings of freedom.
> A Samaria under siege – the entire land,
> The famine is too hard to bear.
> But I will not want news of freedom,
> If it comes from the mouth of a leper.
> The pure will bring news and the pure will redeem
> – And if his hand won't be there to redeem,
> Then I will choose to die from the suffering of the siege
> On the eve of the day of the great tidings.
>
>> (Rachel Bluwstein, "*Yom Besorah*" ["Day of tidings"], Hebrew: www.benyehuda.org/rachel/Rac049.html. Translation posted by Rabbi Alex Israel on his blog, http://thinkingtorah.blogspot.com/2007/04/four-lepers-haftara-for-parashat.html)

To her and many others we could say: Sometimes we desire a tiding of redemption precisely because it comes from the mouth of a contemporary leper, because the "other" of today may well be the collective "I" of tomorrow. The Judaism of the Talmud sanctified the minority opinion and preserved it on the page for all time, understanding that the minority of today could serve as the majority of tomorrow, as opinions change with the times and the circumstances.

This answer to Rachel was given in a different place and in a different context by the philosopher Emmanuel Levinas, whose ideas have played an increasingly important role in Jewish and Israeli discourse in recent years: "The tie to the Other is knotted only as responsibility, this moreover, whether accepted or refused, whether knowing or not knowing how to assume it. Whether able or unable to do something concrete for the Other. To say: Here I am. To do something for the Other. To give. To be human spirit, that's it" (Emmanuel Levinas, *Ethics and Infinity: Conversations with Philippe Nemo*, translated by Richard A. Cohen [Pittsburgh: Duquesne University Press, 1985], 97).

This is the Judaism of our time, and this is its Torah. There are no more lepers. We are all recovered lepers. We have all been the "other" to somebody, and thus we are all commanded.

The Secrets of the Unclean*

*I*N THE PREVIOUS CHAPTER I wrote, "Oy, what unpleasant portions." My nephew Hillel wrote in reply, "Not distasteful portions, but rather the most interesting and enigmatic portions in the whole *Chumash*. These are the portions, more than any other, whose underlying logic is completely inaccessible to us. This is the most complicated puzzle and therefore the most fascinating to me. Every word carries a hint at the riddle's solution."

My nephew pointed to the profound viewpoint of the Midrash, which rises to the challenge posed by the text's repellent detailing of the ugliest infirmities known to humanity. In this way the sages break through the associative entryway, which opens before them. Here is the Midrash commenting on the verse in the Song of Songs that describes the hairdo of the elusive lover: "His locks are curled, and black as a raven" (Song 5:11). The sages fantasize aloud:

> Rabbi Yehuda interpreted the verse to mean Torah scholars. "Curled and black as a raven" refers to the scholars of Torah, for even though they look dark and ugly in this world, in the world to come they will shine like firebrands. Rabbi Shmuel Bar Yitzhak interpreted the verse to mean the portions of the Torah. "Curled and black as a raven" refers to the passages of the Torah that seem too dark and ugly to be recited in public. But the Holy One, praised be he, said: These verses are lovely to me.... Be aware that this is the case in the portion on skin diseases. (Midrash Rabba, *Song of Songs* 5:14)

A brief explanation of the Midrash: Some parts of the Torah might seem unpleasant to study and interpret, such as the matters discussed in our

---

* Translator's note: Standard biblical translations use the words "unclean" and "impure" interchangeably to denote the Hebrew word *tamei*, which has no exact analogue in English. We follow the same practice.

joined portions, *Tazria* and *Metzora*. But God says he finds these seemingly ugly passages to be quite lovely.

Starting from this positive jumping-off point, let's look at one of the aspects of impurity and purification:

> And the Lord spoke unto Moses, saying: Speak unto the children of Israel, saying: if a woman be delivered, and bear a man-child, the she shall be unclean seven days; as in the days of the impurity of her sickness shall she be unclean.... But if she bear a maid-child, then she shall be unclean two weeks, as in her impurity; and she shall continue in the blood of purification threescore and six days. (Lev. 5:1–5)

In plain language, the passage establishes that a woman becomes unclean immediately after giving birth. Here we need to be clear: not every impurity results from sin or transgression. Despite the immediate, negative associations of "impurity," the impurity discussed here belongs in a different category. Why is a woman made unclean during childbirth? It's very easy to argue that these verses perpetuate a discriminatory attitude that demeans women and childbirth. This criticism is further strengthened when we note that a woman's impurity after the birth of a son is briefer than her impurity after the birth of a daughter, as if the verses want to tell us that a daughter's birth is more unclean.

For all that, we might dare to read the matter quite differently. To do so, we must first add the father to the circle of the unclean. According to the text, a man who ejaculates becomes unclean immediately: "And if the flow of seed go out from a man, he shall bathe all his flesh in water, and be unclean until the even" (Lev. 15:16). Why are the organs and fluids of the body connected to birth and fertility, the very core of our humanity, seen as contaminating? We might expect the very opposite. Birth, new life, hope, a newborn infant who has never tasted sin – these are the height of purity, aren't they? Well, they are, and that's the whole point of the story.

In principle, a man becomes a parent by an act of expelling, while a woman becomes a parent by an act of absorbing. In Judaism, the seed becomes an agent of impurity when it is expelled; the same seed fertilizes when it is absorbed. For nine months the woman is clean and pure, and at the moment of birth she is made impure, like the father, by the act of expelling the fruit of her womb. The question, then, is why does the act of expelling make one impure? To answer this question, we need to clarify the notion of impurity. By understanding the most severe impurity we can understand the milder impurities. The dead body is defined in Judaism as the archetype – that is, the highest form – of impurity. A critical component of the laws of purity and impurity lies along the axis of life versus death – not that of permitted versus forbidden nor of sin versus punishment. The concept of impurity defines a clear boundary between the basic human survival instinct and its final expiration. As such, the discussion of the laws of human impurity is in reality a perpetual expression of commitment to the spiritual sanctity of life within Jewish tradition.

A man who expels seed is essentially expelling not only his own completion, but what the sages call the "blood of his seed" for the future, because every seed that does not fertilize constitutes a tiny measure of death. As we've noted, death conveys impurity, so one who expels even a tiny death becomes impure. As for the woman, she has been carrying a new life inside herself for nine months. Now, as that new life departs her womb, leaving an empty space where life had been taking shape, she is left with a certain feeling of loss. Inevitably, then, she is unclean because a life has left her midst, creating a vacuum that must be cleansed because it once contained a life. A woman who bears a daughter is like a person who had two wombs inside her, two frameworks for potential new life – her own and that of her embryonic daughter. Now there are two empty spaces inside her, her newly empty womb and the second womb that has departed from her. That is, the symbolic "death" experienced by the mother giving birth is doubled when she bears a daughter.

Many writers speak of a powerful, mysterious bond between a mother and her daughter, as though deeper than that between a mother and her son or sons. From now on, therefore, we should say: The *tumah*, the so-called impurity brought upon a woman when she gives birth, is not necessarily an indication of intolerable discrimination against women in Judaism, but the opposite. Let us be clear: discrimination does exist and it is intolerable, and is institutionalized in Judaism from ancient times right up to our own time of hoped-for liberation – but these verses are not the evidence. In this case, greater "impurity" testifies to greater responsibility for new life. The greater the impurity, the greater the sanctity of life. After all, the mother of all women was Eve, whose Hebrew name was *Chavah* – "the mother of all life" (Gen. 3:20); motherhood and life are one, and the impurity proves it.

Week 27

Acharei Mot/Kedoshim
After the Death/Ye Shall Be Holy

Leviticus 16:1–20:27

What Is Holy?

A<small>FTER DEALING IN DETAIL</small> with impurities and purifications, it's time for holiness. We've been dealing for several weeks with what goes into the body. We discussed foods, permitted and forbidden, together with the related rules of kashrut. We learned about things that come out of the body and convey extreme impurity – leprosy, skin diseases, male ejaculation and the fruit of a woman's womb. Enough. It's time to move on from negative prohibitions to positive, constructive commandments. And so we proceed from the first of this week's conjoined portions, "After the Death of the Sons of Aaron," to the second – "Ye Shall Be Holy." This takes us out of the realm of religious rules for the body and into the field of personal behavior.

"And the Lord spoke unto Moses, saying: Speak unto all the congregation of the children of Israel, and say unto them: Ye shall be holy; for I the Lord your God am holy" (Lev. 19:1–2). Unlike other concepts in the scripture that are relatively easily understood by readers and commentators alike, the concept of holiness is not clear at all, and it has given rise to mountains of commentary. Here, for example, is one of the best known Jewish debates on the question of holiness. Rashi writes, "Ye shall be holy: Separate yourself from sexual desire and its sins (Midrash Rabba, *Vayikra*), for where you find a restraint on lust you will find holiness" (Rashi on

Lev. 19:2). Relying on Midrashic tradition, Rashi reduces the concept of holiness in our portion to one single aspect of life, the individual's proper sexual boundaries. Both Rashi and the Midrashim that came before him saw a close linguistic and substantive relationship between the Hebrew words *kedusha* (holiness) and *kedesha* (a pagan temple prostitute). A third word that is sometimes seen as marking the distinction between licit and promiscuous sex is *kiddushin* (marriage). *Kedusha*, *kedesha* and *kiddushin*, all in one bundle.

Rabbi Moses Ben Nachman, the great medieval Spanish biblical commentator and kabbalist known as Nachmanides or Ramban, disagrees with Rashi. He goes several steps further and says:

> In my opinion, this is not meant to separate us from sexual desire, as Rashi said.... The point is that the Torah warned us about forbidden desires and foods, but permitted the union of husband and wife and the enjoyment of meat and wine. If a man finds himself uncontrollably passionate with his wife or wives, drunk on wine, gluttonous in his eating, loose with his tongue and behaving in disgraceful ways that are not explicitly forbidden in the Torah, he may be a scoundrel with the Torah's permission.

Ramban's point is that even within the confines of permitted sex and a kosher diet it is possible to reach such a level of debauchery that one becomes a disgrace – with permission. Accordingly, Ramban goes on to present his own alternative definition of holiness:

> Therefore the scripture comes, after detailing the prohibitions that are absolutely forbidden, to command in a general way that we should separate ourselves from permissiveness. One should be modest in sexual activity...so that Torah scholars do not strut among women like roosters.... One should bless wine modestly...and avoid impurity...and guard his lips and tongue.... It is these and similar matters that this general commandment comes to address.... The main purpose of the scripture in such matters is to warn us that we should be clean and pure and separate ourselves from the mass of people who foul themselves with permissiveness and ugliness.

Acharei Mot/Kedoshim

> And the message of the scripture in saying "For I the Lord am holy" is to say that we may be allowed to cling to him by being holy. (Nachmanides on Lev. 19:2)

I'd like to take the direction that Ramban proposes and develop it even further. The commandment "Ye shall be holy" essentially represents the privatization of holiness. Consider: It is here in the Book of Leviticus of all places – amid the laws of the priesthood, right after the priest-centered rules of sacrifice and the laws of leprosy, whose diagnosis and treatment is among the priests' duties – where along comes *Parashat Kedoshim* and essentially offers every individual the possibility of acting like God. Note the commandment's wording: "Ye shall be holy; for I the Lord am holy." It is an invitation to everyone to take part in the godliness of the universe, to rise above daily routine and beyond the limits of the body, with all its hurts and flaws, and reach somewhere far beyond: "Just as I am holy, so you too shall be holy" (Nachmanides on Lev. 19:2).

So how does one become holy? There's nothing here about genetic superiority. It all depends on us. It's behavioral. It's acquired. Hence, immediately after the portion's dramatic opening with the commandment, "Ye shall be holy," the detail begins in a gripping litany of commandments governing our treatment of one another and of ourselves. Some of them are familiar, and those that aren't, should be. Here are a few of them:

> Ye shall fear every man his mother, and his father, and ye shall keep my sabbaths: I am the Lord your God.... And when ye reap the harvest of your land, thou shalt not wholly reap the corner of thy field, neither shalt thou gather the gleaning of thy harvest. And thou shalt not glean thy vineyard, neither shalt thou gather the fallen fruit of thy vineyard; thou shalt leave them for the poor and for the stranger: I am the Lord your God. Ye shall not steal; neither shall ye deal falsely, nor lie to one another. And ye shall not swear by my name falsely, so that thou profane the name of thy God: I am the Lord. Thou shalt not oppress thy neighbor, nor rob him; the wages of a hired servant shall not abide with thee all night until the morning. Thou shalt not curse the deaf, nor put a stumbling

block before the blind, but thou shalt fear thy God: I am the Lord. Ye shall do no unrighteousness in judgment; thou shalt not respect the person of the poor, nor favor the person of the mighty; but in righteousness shalt thou judge thy neighbor. Thou shalt not go up and down as a talebearer among thy people; neither shalt thou stand idly by the blood of thy neighbor: I am the Lord. Thou shalt not hate thy brother in thy heart; thou shalt surely rebuke thy neighbor, and not bear sin because of him. Thou shalt not take vengeance, nor bear any grudge against the children of thy people, but thou shalt love thy neighbor as thyself: I am the Lord. (Lev. 19:3–18)

It seems to me that all these astonishing commands have a certain common denominator, which goes beyond social propriety and public order. I find something internal in this list, something deeply personal. When Rashi interprets "Ye shall be holy" through the lens of permitted and forbidden sex, and Ramban points toward a broader and more encompassing sense of avoidance, they're both heading toward the same place. They, like many others before and since, are speaking of the holiness of restraint, even if they don't say so explicitly.

The concept of holiness can be understood by considering its opposite, and most attempts to define the opposite of holiness touch on places lacking in restraint and filled with the lusts of the human soul: gluttony, sexual profligacy, xenophobia and intolerance, self-absorbed disregard for the troubles of others – these and more. Overcoming these patterns requires both individual and group restraint. A society whose members manage to control their raw impulses achieves a life of holiness, because being holy means being in control. To be holy is to be modest, sensitive and genuinely human. And perhaps when we sanctify ourselves in the holiness of restraint, we can experience the restrained aspects of God. There are situations in which humanity, by its behavior, sanctifies things that are beyond itself. For it is not only God who grants us his holiness; we, by our behavior, add to his holiness and majesty. We are interdependent, we and God – it is an equation contained in the verse "Ye shall be holy, for I am holy."

Acharei Mot/Kedoshim

"After the Death": The Laws of Mourning

*I*N SOME YEARS *Parashat Acharei Mot* is read immediately after the week of *Yom Hashoah* (Holocaust Remembrance Day) and *Yom Hazikaron* (Israel Soldiers' Memorial Day). When that occurs, we pore through the adjacent portions and wonder: What really happens after the deaths of the two sons of Aaron the priest? There is an opening here for a quest, which never ends well, for life after death. And there is a narrative that turns the "After the Death" back on us, the living. It demands that we address the question of how to return to life, to the normalcy of our daily routine, after the tragedy of death.

I'd like to focus our attention on the gap between private and public mourning, between the pain of the individual and the actions of the state.

Several portions ago, in *Parashat Shemini*, when a strange fire consumed Nadab and Abihu, Aaron and his two surviving sons, Eleazar and Ithamar, were ordered to display absolute stoicism. As the text says:

> And Moses said unto Aaron, and unto Eleazar, and unto Ithamar, his sons: "Let not the hair of your heads go loose, neither rend your clothes, that ye die not, and that he be not wroth with all the congregation; but let your brethren, the whole house of Israel, bewail the burning which the Lord hath kindled. And ye shall not go out from the door of the tent of meeting, lest ye die; for the anointing oil of the Lord is upon you." And they did according to the word of Moses. (Lev. 10:6–7)

God forbids Aaron and his family to undertake the normal acts of mourning, "that ye die not." They are not permitted to leave the tent of meeting, nor to receive condolences from the public, "lest ye die." Death is still present in the air. Hence priests in mourning are cautioned.

But a deeper examination will show us that God is drawing a distinction, which will be elaborated later in the scripture into a broader outlook, between the mourning of an individual and the mourning of a nation. Aaron, living the priestly life, is denied the normal trappings of a private life. He is a public figure, an emblem of sovereignty. If he were to follow the natural rhythms of the mourner, he might be moved to ask the natural question that mourners direct at heaven: "Why?" But a questioning, doubting sovereign, a hesitant, wounded, pathetic leadership, risks being seen as defying God's dominion. Authority means, among other things, self-confidence and absolute faith in the rightness of the path, regardless of the bumps along the way. For that reason, the scripture forbids the senior representatives of sovereignty, Aaron and his household, to cast even the slightest shadow of doubt on the fairness of the decisions of him who gave and then took away. If God entertained such doubts about Aaron and his sons, one can only imagine the reaction at the fringes of the camp, which was constantly in ferment, constantly rebellious, always thinking about returning to Egypt. These are the sources of the commandment of silence, the wellsprings of priestly restraint. Hence Aaron's thundering stillness. "And Aaron held his peace" (Lev. 10:3). The intention is not that he weep in private. Even in his most private moments he appeared stoic, though he may have been broken inside.

That same attitude of separation between public and personal also gives rise to the attitude of the sages toward kings and governments. The Babylonian Talmud says, "A king who forgoes his honor will find his honor unrequited" (*Sanhedrin* 19b) – because whatever harms a king harms all of us, the collective whom the king symbolizes. A pathetic king is a symbol and role model for a pathetic collective that he leads. A despised king will ultimately find that he is the leader of "a people robbed and spoiled.... And they are hid in prison-houses; they are for a prey, and none delivereth, for a spoil, and none saith: 'Restore'" (Isa. 42:22).

No one understood that distinction between the grief of the individual and the duties of the sovereign better than King David. He knew many days of mourning of every sort. More than anyone, he knew his share of deaths and murders. David mourned for his friend Jonathan, for his comrades in battle, for Amnon and Tamar, for Absalom and for his first son by Bath-sheba, who died long before his time.

The background to this last story is familiar and colorful. David sinned with Bath-sheba, who was married to another man, a stalwart of David's own army, Uriah the Hittite. David cooked up a plot that ended with the husband meeting his death on the battlefield, and while he was still fighting courageously his commander King David and his wife Bath-sheba were frolicking all the way from her Jerusalem rooftop to his royal bed, with notorious lack of caution. And because they didn't see what was coming, soon enough everyone could see. Very soon her expanding belly began to show the fruit of their sin to all and sundry.

Then the prophet Nathan stood before the king and rebuked him: "Wherefore hast thou despised the word of the Lord, to do that which is evil in my sight? Uriah the Hittite thou has smitten with the sword, and his wife thou has taken to be thy wife, and him thou has slain with the sword of the children of Ammon" (2 Sam. 12:9). David immediately admits his sin, but the price of the sin will be paid by the newborn baby. As Nathan warns, "the child that is born unto thee shall surely die" (2 Sam. 12:14) – and so the story relates: "And the Lord struck the child that Uriah's wife bore unto David, and it was very sick" (2 Sam. 12:15).

The whole time that the child was sick, David fought with God, trying to change the verdict. He fasted, prayed and pleaded. Everyone who visited him tried to comfort him and encourage him, but he would not be comforted: "David therefore besought God for the child; and David fasted, and as often as he went in, he lay all night upon the earth. And the elders of his house arose, and stood beside him, to raise him up from the earth; but he would not, neither did he break bread with them" (2 Sam. 12:16–17). Then the inevitable happened. The child, who was innocent of his parents' sins, died:

> And it came to pass on the seventh day, that the child died. And the servants of David feared to tell him that the child was dead; for they said: "Behold, while the child was yet alive, we spoke unto him, and he hearkened not unto our voice; how then shall we tell him that the child is dead, so that he do himself some harm?" But when David saw that his servants whispered together, David perceived that the child was dead; and David said unto his servants: "Is the child dead?" And they said: "He is dead." Then David arose from the earth, and washed, and anointed himself, and changed his apparel; and he came into the house of the Lord, and worshipped; then he

came to his own house; and when he required, they did set bread before him, and he did eat. (2 Sam. 12:18–20)

David's actions and reactions are utterly at odds with human nature as we know it. When someone dear to us is fighting for his life, we try not to lose hope. We strain to maintain an optimistic attitude. It's important to us to inspire him with some of our own resilience and hope that he draws strength and recovers. But when the worst happens and the patient dies, all our pain and sorrow bursts forth. We sit on the ground and mourn, at least for seven days. Kings and sovereigns behave differently, as David did. With the death of his child David ceases to be the father tortured with guilt and resumes his role as the symbol of the state. And so he rises and returns to his normal routine. Here is how the conversation goes in the inner chambers of the king's house:

Then his servants said unto him: "What is this thing that thou hast done? Thou didst fast and weep for the child, while it was alive; but when the child was dead, thou didst rise and eat bread." And he said: "While the child was yet alive, I fasted and wept; for I said: Who knoweth whether the Lord will not be gracious to me, that the child may live? But now he is dead, wherefore should I fast? Can I bring him back again? I shall go to him, but he will not return to me." (2 Sam. 12:21–23)

And now comes the happy ending: "And David comforted Bath-sheba his wife, and went in unto her, and lay with her; and she bore a son, and called his name Solomon. And the Lord loved him" (2 Sam. 12:24).

And now, back to the business at hand, the cycle of seasons in Israel: Holocaust Remembrance Day, Soldiers' Memorial Day and the day "After the Death." The Holocaust has happened; Israel's soldiers have fallen in war; the child is dead. To be precise, many children, many parents and a great many traditions, customs, memories and sources of national creativity have been burned in fire and gone up in the smoke of the crematoria. They died and they are no more. They will never return. People continue to mourn, and that is as it should be. But we, the collective, the state and the nation, must get ourselves up from the dust of the earth and return to a full life. And so wrote the poet Yehuda Amichai:

> And the land is divided
> into districts of memory and regions of hope,
> and the residents mingle with each other,
> like people returning from a wedding
> with those returning from a funeral.
> . . . .
> And the land's a package-land:
> and it's well-tied and everything is in it,
> and it's tightly bound
> and the strings sometimes hurt.
>
> (Yehuda Amichai, "Love of the Land," in *Shirei Yehuda Amichai*, vol. 3 [Tel Aviv: Schocken, 2002], translated by Linda Zisquit as *The Selected Poetry of Yehuda Amichai*, eds. Chana Bloch and Stephen Mitchell [New York: Harper and Row, 1986])

Holiness Here and Now

A CORRECT READING OF *Parashat Kedoshim* would find, in my opinion, the ultimate Jewish subversiveness at its most beautiful. Here is how it goes: "And the Lord spoke unto Moses, saying: Speak unto all the congregation of the children of Israel, and say unto them: Ye shall be holy, for I the Lord your God am holy" (Lev. 19:1–2). At first glance, this is just one more Torah portion. True, it is chock-full of commandments; it contains some fifty commandments within its lines, out of the 613 in the Torah. But if you don't read it carefully, you might think it is no different from the norm. Indeed, you might easily read it as another portion of typical religious nagging: a bit of Sabbath, a little respect for parents, some agricultural commandments, concern for one's fellows and a few other items that have long since become part of the permanent legacy of our culture. It's no surprise that we've come to dismiss the commandments of *Parashat Kedoshim* as trivial and banal.

Yet there's a larger picture hidden behind the portion's list of commandments, and it's a very interesting one. The deeper theme is that holiness is not by any means a gift from God on high. That is, there is no automatic holiness. Nobody is holier than anybody else. Holiness is not inherited. As such, no nation is superior to any other nation. No people has reason to believe it is above other peoples of the world. The "choosing" of our people as a chosen people does not exempt us from spiritual effort. On the contrary, it is an eternal challenge. Holiness is an endless effort by every individual and every community to improve our character. Therefore, *Parashat Kedoshim* is a textual guide to the shaping of holiness by the hand of humankind – a human holiness that is derived from below, not some automatic bestowal of God's holiness from above. And herein lies the portion's great importance.

Out of this basic determination that there is no automatic holiness, certain fascinating implications follow. Here are a few of them. "Ye shall be holy, for I the Lord your God am holy." Commentators throughout the generations have tried to draw a distinction between human holiness, which is acquired, relative and limited, and the absolute, perfect holiness of God. Some saw it as Sforno framed it: "It is proper that you resemble me as closely as possible in appearance and deed." Others followed Ramban's reasoning: "Just as I am holy, so you should be holy." That is, human holiness should aspire to the perfection of God's holiness. But this equation has a second possible aspect that is never discussed. If human holiness derives from divine holiness and aspires to return to it, then I would argue that it's possible for divine holiness to derive from and aspire to human holiness. It is not a relationship of absolute equality, unfortunately, but a considerable degree of responsibility for the perpetuation of holiness falls on us. Let me explain:

As I noted at length in Week 16, dealing with *Parashat Beshalach*, we have been throughout our lives, individually and as a nation, God's witnesses: "And the people feared the Lord; and they believed in the Lord, and in his servant, Moses" (Exod. 14:31). Our witnessing of the events of history and its revealed and hidden miracles has become evidence; the evidence has become proof, and from proof it's only a short hop to faith. (This is not the place nor time to examine the opposite possibility: What would have happened if a maidservant by the water's edge had not seen what she and her friends saw? Would we never have brought the faith in One God to the world?)

For the moment, suffice it to say that for many of us, God is the God of history. This is his stage, these are his appearances, and we the audience are his character witnesses and his alibi, witnesses to his presence. And now, along comes this week's portion and places a new equation on the table: no longer the God who draws us close to him merely to "resemble him," no longer the faith of the Exodus from Egypt, but a granting of space to us, to humanity, to be a source of holiness. If we respect our father and mother, love our neighbor, do not steal or swear falsely, then a daring new holiness takes hold of us: human holiness. And only then does the new holiness win the approval of God on high, "for I the Lord, who sanctify you, am holy" (Lev. 21:8).

According to this version of holiness, the commandments of this portion and its guidelines for a life of human holiness give us the opportunity to become a community of testimony. That is, our holiness today, forged in never-ending acts of self-correction and improvement of the world, offers testimony about God. If we live up to our potential for goodness, this is the evidence of the goodness of creation and the creator, but if we sin and befoul the world, the face of the creator is darkened, too.

Let's try to develop the idea of automatic holiness a bit further. The underlying notion that "I the Lord your God am holy" appears about fifteen times in various formulations in this week's portion, mainly as an imprimatur to a commandment of social justice. "I am the Lord" doesn't mean merely, I am holy and therefore you should aspire to me and my version of holiness. Rather, what is holy is the "I" within the human. The "I," the ego, is the place where the image and semblance of God dwell within the human. But how is it possible to sanctify the "I"? A world with "I" at its center is a world of dangerous pride, of nihilism that has no limits or boundaries.

Historical experience teaches that whenever a particular "I" achieves governmental power, it turns quickly toward brutal oppression of every other "I" that refuses to become like it or bend to its will. Therefore, one cannot read the Jewish sanctification of the ego separately from the portion's greatest innovation: "Thou shalt not take vengeance, nor bear any grudge against the children of thy people, but thou shalt love thy neighbor as thyself: I am the Lord" (Lev. 19:18). The opening of his verse states firmly that the "I," each one of us as autonomous individuals, may not come to a place of vindictive, violent conflict with other members of the community around us. But that is not enough. Merely committing oneself not to get angry at a neighbor fulfilling his aspirations, even when they come at my expense, is not sufficient. We have a positive obligation to love one another: Thou shalt love thy neighbor as thyself. That is, to love my neighbor, I must first learn to love myself.

The laws of loving oneself are very complicated, because they come dangerously close to narcissism on the one hand and misanthropy on the other. Therefore, in order to let my "I" truly flourish and develop to its full capacity, I am commanded to develop a love of my neighbor in parallel to my own love of self. Love of self creates the possibility of the sanctity of life, the understanding that I may not deprive myself of life, that I am obliged to live a healthy, balanced life. Love of my neighbor as myself gives rise to love of nature and the beauty of creation, to concern for the needy and the environment. Only in a truly human world, a world of equilibrium between the personal interior and the human and natural exterior, can there be a full harmony that allows all to live in peace and friendship with one another. As Rabbi Akiva rightly said, "Love thy neighbor as thyself" is the greatest rule in the Torah. It is a mighty rule, because the Torah is a human Torah – "It is not in heaven." It prefers the holiness of endless human striving, and its pathways are pathways of humanity and the earth no less than the pathways of God in heaven. It is a great rule, and a very great responsibility.

Week 28

Emor – Speak Unto the Priests

Leviticus 21:1–24:23

Holidays and Circles

*P*ARASHAT *E*MOR CONTAINS, among other things, a rundown of the Jewish holidays ordained in the Torah:

> The appointed seasons of the Lord, which ye shall proclaim to be holy convocations, even these are my appointed seasons. Six days… but on the seventh day is a Sabbath of solemn rest…the Lord's Passover…first fruits…a memorial proclaimed with the blast of horns, a holy convocation…on the tenth day of this seventh month is the day of atonement…the feast of tabernacles for seven days unto the Lord. (Lev. 23:2–34)

The Hebrew word for "season," *mo'ed*, has a double meaning that is lost in its English translation: the same word, here meaning "appointed time," is translated as "meeting" in the phrase *ohel mo'ed*, the "tent of meeting" – the place where the human Moses held his appointed meetings with the Eternal God. The biblical holidays and seasons are both sacred points on the calendar and opportunities for reunions between the creator and his creations.

No less revealing is the Hebrew word for "holiday," *chag*. Its root meaning has to do with circles, and it is closely related to the earliest notions of time in the Jewish world. As I pointed out briefly in Week 1, on *Parashat Bereshit*, there are two basic approaches to the understanding of time. One sees time as a linear axis connecting a given point in the past to a different point in the future. Everything advances and develops in a forward motion. Contrast that with the approach of Ecclesiastes, who wrote, "That which hath been is that which shall be…and there is nothing new under the sun" (Eccl. 1:9). In this understanding, time is a recurring cycle that comes back upon itself repeatedly without end. The basic Jewish approach to time is a combination of these two approaches. If we combine the line and the circle, we get a spiral. Jewish time is a circle that comes back upon itself but is never entirely closed. Rather, it constantly unfolds in a rising pattern. Alternatively, it can be seen as a line that need not be saddened by the cutting off of its beginning from its end, because it always has the opportunity to return to its old neighborhood, if not to the precise moments of its past. In any event, this approach asks us to imagine a revolving circle.

And how do we draw a circle? The best way is with a compass. Consider the legends of the first-century sage known as Honi the Circle-Drawer. Here is one story told about him:

> It happened that the people said to Honi the Circle-Drawer, Pray for rain to fall. He replied: Go and bring in the [clay] ovens for the Paschal offerings, so that they do not dissolve. He prayed and no rain fell. What did he do? He drew a circle and stood within it and exclaimed, Master of the Universe, Thy children have turned to me because they believe me to be as a member of Thy household. I swear by Thy great Name that I will not move from here until Thou hast mercy upon Thy children. Rain then began to drip…. [In a later, similar incident of rain coming because of prayer,] Rabbi Tarfon said to them: Go, eat and drink and observe the day as a holiday. They went and ate and drank and observed the day as a holiday, and at evening time they came and recited the Great Hallel." (Mishnah, Ta'anit 3:5)

Children understand the magic of circles; it shows up in endless games and songs like "Round the Mulberry Bush," "Ring Around the Rosie" and "Pat-a-Cake." Cakes, rounds and circles are all connected in the most fundamental way to each other and to special points along the ever-spinning cycle of time. But those moments never reappear in exactly the same point along the spiraling line. Since ancient times, the Jewish holidays have assumed a variety of forms, forever discarding one form and assuming another. Because this portion, *Parashat Emor*, coincides with the holiday of Lag B'Omer, let's take that as an example of the dynamic, cyclical model of our holidays.

Lag B'Omer, which simply means the thirty-third day of the counting of the Omer, does not appear as a holiday in the Bible. Everything we know about the counting of the Omer appears in this week's portion: "And ye shall count unto you from the morrow after the day of rest, from the day that ye brought the sheaf [*omer*] of waving; seven weeks shall there be complete" (Lev. 23:15). From the day after Passover begins, the night following the first Seder, until the festival of Shavuot, we count every night for forty-nine days the counting of the Omer.

The verses don't indicate any reason for the counting, so any explanation will do. It is possible, for example, that there is a connection between the seven cycles of weeks ("seven weeks shall there be complete") that end with the festival of Shavuot (the name itself means "weeks"; it's sometimes known as Pentecost, Greek for "fiftieth day") and the natural rhythms of the climate in our region of the Middle East. Anyone who has lived in a rural area in Israel, close to the land and its crops, knows the hot winds that blow during the month of May as summer approaches. This climatic phenomenon is popularly known as the *chamsin* (Arabic for "fifty") – the dry, hot wind that blows into Israel from the east. The same wind blows into Egypt from the Sahara Desert to the west.

According to Arab folklore, the *chamsin* winds last for fifty days, hence the name. In Jewish tradition we count seven Sabbaths, forty-nine days in all, and on the fiftieth day we celebrate the festival of Shavuot. This is all too familiar to the farmer in our region, who nervously counts the days from the spring wheat planting in Nissan, the month of Passover, until the harvest in Sivan, the month of Shavuot. Just one more day without disaster, he says to himself, with no rain to spoil the crop and no brushfire to destroy it. Only then, after those hard, nervous days, is the final count celebrated with the festival of Shavuot, on which the first fruits of the harvest are brought as thanks for a season that ended well.

But the agricultural explanation for the counting did not stay long with us. From the days of the Second Temple comes this Aggadah:

> It was said that Rabbi Akiva had twelve thousand pairs of disciples, from Gabbatha to Antipatris; and all of them died at the same time because they did not treat each other with respect. The world remained desolate until Rabbi Akiva came to our Masters in the South and taught the Torah to them. These were Rabbi Meir, Rabbi Judah, Rabbi Jose, Rabbi Simeon and Rabbi Eleazar Ben Shammua; and it was they who revived the Torah at that time. A Tanna taught: All of them died between Passover and Pentecost [Shavuot]. (Babylonian Talmud, *Yevamot* 62b)

The explanation: all twenty-four thousand died except for the five famous survivors whom Rabbi Akiva ordained and trained to preserve the tradition of Torah study. This is not the place to explore the meaning of the phrase "they did not treat each other with respect." We'll content ourselves with the historical conjecture that seems most likely. Rabbi Akiva was the great defender of the Bar Kochba revolt, which was brutally repressed by the Roman legions in the year 135 CE. It's not far-fetched to suppose that the disciples mentioned in the Talmudic legend were the rebels who fell. If so, then these forty-nine days of mourning commemorate another one of those marches of folly scattered throughout Jewish history. After all, if not for the revolt, history might never have recorded the final destruction and dispersion of the Jewish society that continued to flourish here sixty-five long years after the destruction of the Temple in the year 70 CE.

Many different customs of mourning are associated with this period. There are those who don't cut their hair, don't get married and don't celebrate. Many individuals find their own combination of rituals. Some get haircuts on the first of the month of Iyar, and others don't. Some shave on Israeli Independence Day, and others let their beards grow from Passover until Shavuot. Where do all these customs come from? From the following layer of historical memory: during the Crusades, Jewish communities

Emor

throughout the Diaspora experienced no small number of calamities. Many communities were utterly exterminated during the weeks of the Omer. Thousands were slaughtered, and countless more suffered. It was during the counting of the Omer in 1096, in a three-week period in May during the First Crusade, that the legendary destruction of the communities of Speyer, Worms and Mainz occurred. The pogroms of 1648 and 1649 in Poland also took place mostly in this season, at the end of harsh European winters. These disasters that befell our brethren of the communities of Ashkenaz gave rise to the variations in customs of mourning.

With the passage of years, new customs grew up around Lag B'Omer that were far from its original spirit. S.Y. Agnon attests to this:

> One who has not seen the festivities of *Lag Ba-Omer* on the grave of R. Shimon bar Yochai in Meiron, has never seen true joy. Jews, in droves, ascend with songs and instruments, and come to this place, from all of the cities of Israel and the lands of Edom and Yishmael and stand there all night and day and learn…and pray and recite psalms. (S.Y. Agnon, "*Elu ve-Elu*," in *Kol Sipurav Shel Shmuel Yosef Agnon* [Complete stories of Shmuel Yosef Agnon], vol. 2 [Tel Aviv: Schocken, 1959])

Agnon's testimony portrays the holiday as it was before the spread of amulets and celebrations that now accompany the anniversary of the death of Rabbi Shimon Bar Yochai, remembered mainly as the mythical author of the Zohar, the seminal work of Kabbalah. The historical Bar Yochai was one of the great zealots of the Bar Kochba revolt, whose zealotry was so great that the sages were afraid to admit him to the Sanhedrin of his day because of his extremism.

Graveside rituals have proliferated in Israel and become an integral part of the expression of modern Israeli Jewish identity – an expression utterly at odds with the biblical source, which wholeheartedly opposes the worship of wood, stone, orchards and graves. Lag B'Omer, originally a date on the farmer's calendar, evolved into a day of mourning for the deaths of rebels, a memorial day marking the end of the plague that killed them, then a memorial day commemorating the victims of many other tragedies; it is now a festive Israeli holiday celebrated at the graves of mystics.

Adding another layer to this spiraling of the Omer season, and particularly its thirty-third day, we can point to the latest incarnation of Lag B'Omer. It follows logically from years of earnest singing of the children's song about Bar Kochba:

> Long ago in Israel lived a man named Bar Kochba.
> Tall and young with blazing eyes, a hero everyone loved.
> He called the people 'round, he went to the battle ground,
> He fought for freedom from the Romans our hero did astound!
>
> ("Bar Kochba," words by Levin Kipnis, music by Mordecai Zeira, English version by Joanie Calem, http://www.joaniecalem.com/Joanie-booklet-print.pdf)

Not surprisingly, Lag B'Omer was selected as the day to celebrate the soldiers of the Israel Defense Forces reserves. The myth demands it. And besides, there's a holiday available, isn't there?

Holiday and Culture

IN THE LAST SECTION I wrote about the Jewish approach to time expressing itself in a spiral. In that regard, I'd like to make a few observations, not about the shape of time or the manner of its flow, but about the substantive points along that spiraling line. When I look at life, I find that universal phenomena are easier to grasp than particular, peculiar events. I can easily grasp the human need for a weekly day of rest; it's harder for me to see the point of burning a red heifer in order to purify someone who has touched a corpse. If the Japanese and the Spanish don't need this, why do we? I don't know.

By the same token, despite the universality of the phenomenon of holidays in various religions and cultures, I don't entirely understand why they exist. True, every people and every culture has holidays and seasons of rejoicing, and they certainly reflect a deep, primal cultural need. But the differences among the various individual holidays are so great that the universal principle is almost lost amid the details. And yet, for all that, I have no doubt that holidays are a good thing, if only because of the levels of happiness, serenity and human interconnections that emerge from their celebration and help to blunt the stings of daily life.

This week's portion has this to say: "Speak unto the children of Israel, and say unto them: The appointed seasons of the Lord, which ye shall proclaim to be holy convocations, even these are my appointed seasons" (Lev. 23:2). This headline is followed by the most detailed enumeration in the entire Torah, all five books of it, of our Jewish holidays. Seasons of the Lord and holy convocations alike. His and ours.

Two concepts are hidden among the details of this portion: *chag* and *mo'ed* (the holiday and the appointed season). Both of them, as we'll see in a moment, stem from the same understanding of time and its importance in Jewish and biblical culture. Let's start with the concept of *chag* (the holiday). The *chag* is a point in time along the circle of life and culture, as we wrote previously. The *chag* is part of a cycle. It is charted with a compass, which traces the circumference around the center, and each of the individual points along circular line of the circumference is a *chag*. Because part of the Jewish concept of time involves circularity, in the sense of "That which hath been is that which shall be" (Eccl. 1:9), the points of time along the circle of life are *chagim*. Every point has its own special meaning; every holiday has its own distinct character.

The *mo'ed* (the appointed season) is both a time and a meeting. On every *chag*, every point in time that is charted and defined in advance, we have a fixed appointment for an encounter. Sometimes it is an encounter with ourselves, sometimes with the Master of the Universe, but always with a rich web of meaning that is distinct to each holiday. There are holidays focused on human sensitivity, and there are others whose emphasis is fear of God. There are agricultural holidays and historical ones; there are long and short holidays, universal ones and particularistic ones. We have many holidays, and many meanings and values within each one. Whenever the time of year rolls around for a given holiday, we are alive with its particular charge, and we carry it forward down the pathway of the year until our spiritual and emotional batteries are drained, and until it comes again and fills us again with its energy. So, for example, from Passover onward we carry the charge of freedom, and from Chanukah the light that dispels the darkness; on Rosh Hashanah we seek and pursue the peace of the world, and on Yom Kippur we try over and over to realign the fragile relationships between man and his neighbor, the Other. The holidays, then, carry the moral valence of the culture. Thanks to them we remember, ponder, commit, renew and carry on.

The manner of celebration varies from family to family and community to community. However, precisely because of the multiplicity of styles, colorations and traditions, it's worth our while to seek a deeper common denominator among all the various formulations for marking the encounter between humanity and time and between society and its traditions. One such common denominator is offered to us this week by Ramban, who says in his commentary on the portion:

> The point of the holy convocations, the sacred assemblies, is that everyone is called together on this day and assembles to sanctify it. Because all Israel is commanded to gather in the house of God on the appointed [mo'ed] day to sanctify the day publicly in prayer and songs of praise of God, in clean garb, and to make a feast that day… and send portions to those who do not have. Because this day is holy to our Lord, and do not be sad, because the joy of God is your fortress. (Nachmanides on Lev. 23:2)

Ramban draws a link by association between *mo'ed* in the sense of time, "on this day," and *mo'ed* in the sense of encounter, "everyone is called together," and in so doing he reveals the special dimension of the holiday. For every holiday is a day that is different from the ordinariness of the other days of the year. The holiday is both a time and a place, man and God in a single breath.

One could expand endlessly on the holidays that appear in our portion and the others that were added later, such as Chanukah, Purim, Tu B'Shevat and so on. To finish off this brief chapter on a current note, let's look at a cultural phenomenon that differentiates the traditional holidays from those of recent vintage. Among all the ancient holidays that have taken root within the Jewish cultural code, there are no holidays of war or victory.

True, on Purim we celebrate a physical salvation, and on Chanukah a saving of the soul and the sanctuary, but we don't necessarily celebrate the victories on the battlefield. We don't celebrate the entry of Joshua into the Promised Land, even though the date is stated in the biblical text. We don't celebrate the conquest of the land of Israel by the tribes that left Egypt. We have no date for the first independence day of the kingdom of Saul, nor for the kingdom of David. We have no day to celebrate the original Jerusalem Day, when David and his troops conquered the city by stealth of night. When pre-nationalist Judaism looked for the special spiritual contents of the days and the seasons, it chose to immortalize spiritual elevation, not the heroism of body, war and bloodshed. These days may be unassailably necessary, but they have never served as a reason for special holidays or solemn assemblies or joyful celebrations, whether with prayers or plastic noisemakers.

Week 29

Behar/Bechukotai
At Mount Sinai/In My Statutes

Leviticus 25:1–27:34

The Life's Breath of the Torah

IDIOMS AND CATCHPHRASES are part of the unseen bridge that connects literary language to its spoken sibling and links the abstract world of values to the concrete world of daily life. One of the most common expressions in Hebrew, both literary and spoken, is "What does *shmitah* have to do with Mount Sinai?" It has a wide variety of uses, among the unschooled no less than the scholarly. It might not be common knowledge, but the phrase comes directly from the explicit text that opens this week's portion:

> And the Lord spoke unto Moses at Mount Sinai, saying: Speak unto the children of Israel, and say unto them: When ye come into the land which I give you, then shall the land keep a Sabbath unto the Lord. Six years thou shalt sow thy field, and six years thou shalt prune thy vineyard, and gather in the produce thereof. But in the seventh year shall be a Sabbath of solemn rest for the land, a Sabbath unto the Lord; thou shalt neither sow thy field, nor prune thy vineyard. That which groweth of itself of thy harvest thou shalt not reap, and the grapes of thy undressed vine thou shalt not gather; it shall be a year of solemn rest for the land. And the Sabbath-produce of the land shall be for food for you; for thee, and for thy servant and for thy maid, and for thy hired servant and for the settler by thy side that

sojourneth with thee; and for thy cattle, and for the beasts that are in thy land, shall all the increase thereof be for food. (Lev. 25:1–7)

The citing of the exact location "at Mount Sinai" drew the attention of the Midrashic commentators ages ago. Why isn't the location at Mount Sinai noted for all the other commandments? Indeed, wasn't the entire Torah given to Moses at Mount Sinai? The indication of the exact place, Mount Sinai, led Rashi to quote the Midrashim and ask, "What does *shmitah* have to do with Mount Sinai? Weren't all the commandments spoken at Sinai?" (Rashi on Lev. 25:1).

This popular question has yielded large numbers of answers, some of which were appropriate to their times, while others were timeless attempts to delve into the deepest, most substantive roots of Judaism. One answer for our time, for example, was offered by my late teacher and rabbi, Professor Yeshayahu Leibovitz, who wrote as follows:

> The aforementioned commandment [*shmitah*] is connected to the promise of the land…and in the world of religious thought this topic is very important…because of the intention to draw inspiration from those religious-nationalist false prophets, who are present among us to this day, and who claim that the promise of the land to the Jewish people is a primary, unconditional religious fact from which all the land-centered commandments are drawn…. The special phrasing of this verse…comes to teach us that all of the promises in the Torah are no more than petitions and objectives…in the hope that we shall be worthy of these promises. (Yeshayahu Leibovitz, *Sheva Shanim shel Sichot al Parashat Hashavua* [Seven years of discourses on the weekly Torah reading] [Jerusalem: Greta Leibovitz, 2000], 582)

I would like to leave the immediacy of Leibovitz's approach and look for a different way of understanding the inner connection between *shmitah* and Mount Sinai. The *shmitah* year is a year of yielding control. The owner effectively gives up possession of his property. Not only is he prevented from working the land, instead letting it rest and recover from its six years of exploitation; everyone, whether pauper or foreigner, slave or woman, is invited to enter his field and vineyard and pluck from his fig tree. In the *shmitah* year everyone is welcome to do with his things as they would with their own. Every man and woman can sit under someone else's vine and fig tree, and no one may bar their way. And if that's not enough, at the end of seven *shmitah* cycles, meaning every forty-nine years, the Jubilee year begins with even more onerous instructions:

> And ye shall hallow the fiftieth year, and proclaim liberty throughout the land unto all the inhabitants thereof; it shall be a jubilee unto you; and ye shall return every man unto his possession, and ye shall return every man unto his family. A jubilee shall that fiftieth year be unto you; ye shall not sow, neither reap that which groweth of itself in it, nor gather the grapes in it of the undressed vines. For it is a jubilee; it shall be holy unto you; ye shall eat the increase thereof out of the field. In this year of jubilee ye shall return every man unto his possession. (Lev. 25:10–13)

The message is clear: all of a person's important property – his land and inheritance, his slaves and maidservants – essentially does not belong to him. Once every fifty years the Torah commands us to push an economic Reset button, and all property returns to its original owners. Once every fifty years, society stands still. The economy stops in its tracks and rewinds. The Torah does not permit unimpeded capitalism. It impedes and delays. It insists on redistributing the wealth of society. The ancient economist understood the meaning of burgeoning social gaps and the danger of the rich chasing after ever-greater riches while the poor steadily decline into the depths of want, shame and need.

The Bible's economic doctrine is basically a social gospel of the highest order. Concern for the individual who has nothing and firm restraint of those who have much are its cornerstones. Making commands such as these effective in the real world requires that both the individual and society possess skills of restraint and self-control. The commandment of *shmitah* is an expression of economic courage in the sense that Ben Zoma describes in the Ethics of the Fathers: "Who is mighty? He who conquers his impulses" (Mishnah, *Avot* 4:1). Not only am I commanded to conquer the impulse that drives me to ever greater profits; I am required to overcome it heroically and relinquish all of my labors to serve the needs of others who haven't worked or achieved.

Restraint, as has been noted repeatedly in this book, is one of the primary foundations of the Ten Commandments. What is the meaning of "Thou shalt not covet" if not restraint? What is "Thou shalt not steal"? The same thing. Even if I can't overcome my greed and continue itching to get my hands on my neighbor's property or spouse, I am forbidden to steal them from him. I must control my appetites and still my material cravings. Parenthetically, it should be pointed out that our weekly Sabbath is a sort of miniature *shmitah*. That is, a day without production and without profit; a day of restraint and calm that enters our lives once a week. And, of course, the Sabbath is an integral part of the Ten Commandments. The commandments to "keep" and "remember the Sabbath day to keep it holy" were given at Sinai, atop the mountain.

In contrast to the brutal rat race, the lusting and acquisitiveness that mark the other six days of the week, this distinctive day brings a shattering of all our normal conventions, and it does so by consent. Sabbath is our personal *shmitah*. It signals to us that we are not the owners of the world around us, that we do not own time, that we need to take a break from our destructive self-centeredness and make time for another – be it God, family or a book. Sabbath is a day of true freedom from the bonds and burdens of the present.

That said, it seems to me that the commandment of *shmitah* is one of the most difficult and demanding commandments in the Torah. It is the life's breath of the revelation at Mount Sinai. The covenant is not merely a covenant, a simple contract between a people and its God. It is first and foremost a social contract whose broad principles were spoken in ten items on the mountaintop and whose details were given to us this week between the clods of fallow earth and the jubilation of the slaves set free with the coming of the Jubilee year and the sounding of the trumpet of freedom in the land.

Do Not Do As the Egyptians

AND THE LORD SPOKE unto Moses at Mount Sinai, saying: Speak unto the children of Israel, and say unto them: When ye come into the land which I give you, then shall the land keep a Sabbath unto the Lord. Six years thou shalt sow thy field, and six years thou shalt prune thy vineyard, and gather in the produce thereof. But in the seventh year shall be a Sabbath of solemn rest for the land, a Sabbath unto the Lord; thou shalt neither sow thy field, nor prune thy vineyard. That which groweth of itself of thy harvest thou shalt not reap, and the grapes of thy undressed vine thou shalt not gather; it shall be a year of solemn rest for the land. And the Sabbath-produce of the land shall be for food for you; for thee, and for thy servant and for thy maid, and for thy hired servant and for the settler by thy side that sojourneth with thee; and for thy cattle, and for the beasts that are in thy land, shall all the increase thereof be for food. (Lev. 25:1–7)

I'd like to suggest another answer to the familiar question, "What does *shmitah* have to do with Mount Sinai?" This answer creates a bridge between the commandment of *shmitah* and the revelation at Mount Sinai, between the abandonment of the Egyptian empire and the transition into the kingdom of God.

To begin with, let's briefly review the underlying principle of the commandment of *shmitah*. Our portion deals with the social dimension of agricultural life. The landowner, the farmer, works his spread for six years. From the land he draws his bread and his family's sustenance by his sweat and labor. But the seventh year "shall be a Sabbath of solemn rest for the land, a Sabbath unto the Lord" (Lev. 25:4). The farmer, the fieldworker, the planter and the vintner take a sabbatical year off, during which the land is not cultivated. The land rests, too. After seven *shmitah* cycles, at the end of the forty-ninth year, comes the Jubilee year, the *shmitah* of *shmitot*. "And ye shall hallow the fiftieth year, and proclaim liberty throughout the land unto all the inhabitants thereof; it shall be a jubilee unto you; and ye shall return every man unto his possession, and ye shall return every man unto his family" (Lev. 25:10). The Jubilee is much more than a rest period for man and the land. The Jubilee is a renewed social order. Every fifty years slaves gain freedom and liberty, the land returns to its original owners and debts are forgiven. The Jubilee is the inner core of a society that continually reinvents itself.

Alongside the social significance of *shmitah* and Jubilee, it seems to me that the principle behind these two wonderful commandments points toward the Bible's first political idea. This is a principle of governance that aims unstintingly toward governmental stability. However, it is a stability of the sort that is not despotic or oppressive and has none of the inherent contempt of a ruler for his subjects. The biblical way to achieve just governmental stability is stunning in its originality and daring; governmental justice is achieved through constant challenging of the foundations of the governing order. It sounds like a contradiction in terms: this concept of stability via challenging the government calls for some explaining.

Political philosophy stands at the foundation of the modern, liberal Western world. It relies heavily on the thinking of Baron Charles Montesquieu and his principle of separation of powers. Montesquieu analyzed the history of governing systems and categorized them as follows: monarchy is rule by a sovereign whose authority is acquired by inheritance; dictatorship is one-man rule by an individual whose power is not limited by law and is maintained by fear and intimidation of the citizenry; and the republic – Montesquieu's preferred option – is a form of government in which the reins of power are held by the people, or by a chosen representative of the people. In his view, the republic governs according to the finest attributes of humanity. He maintained that any government must aspire to guarantee human freedom, and that in order to do so there must be a separation between the different arms of government, secured by a system of checks and balances between and among them. Montesquieu's doctrine was the basis for the constitution of the United States and of many other democratic regimes in our time.

In order to preserve the republic for the people that chose it, and for the individual members of that people, Montesquieu proposed a system of separation of powers, under which a government has three individual branches of authority – the legislative, executive and judiciary – with a constant system of checks and balances among them. Our real-life experience suggests that Montesquieu's checks and balances are largely horizontal and contingent in nature, meaning that their operation is constant and ever-present. The government balances the parliament, which restrains the court, which in turn checks the government and so on. It is a concept of a very active and dynamic reality.

Long before Montesquieu and his separation of powers, the Bible recognized the weakness of the centralized human government of its day and offered us two profound, long-lasting tools with which to balance the power of government and restrain its inherent dictatorial tendencies. The first tool is the rule of God. Biblical theocracy is completely unlike its modern-day counterpart. In the biblical version, the rule of God is meant to review and offset the king's malice and vindictiveness. Thus, for example, the prophet Nathan acted in the name of God to check King David and his violence. So, too, the prophet Elijah and God acted against King Ahab, his queen Jezebel and her greed. God and his prophets, the religious establishment of that era, served as a shelter and shield in the face of governmental cruelty. The sovereignty of God in those days was free and permissive in nature, particularly in granting considerable freedom and responsibility to the individual. The rule of God and its relationship to the sovereignty of the king found expression in the description of kingship voiced by the prophet Samuel, when he was pushed aside by the populace that preferred a flesh-and-blood king: "He will take your sons…and he will take your daughters to be perfumers…and to be bakers…. And he will take your fields…even the best of them…and ye shall be his servants" (1 Sam. 8:11–17). Under the old king, God, this wouldn't have happened.

The second tool for warding off dictatorship is the device of *shmitah* and Jubilee, expressed in the sentence, "He will take your fields." According to the biblical law that appears in this week's portion, no one has eternal ownership of land, not even the king. Impermanence is always hovering over assets and capital. It is not possible to accumulate endlessly. It is not possible to subjugate the poor and sign their inheritance permanently over to the rich. The model of *shmitah* and Jubilee is the Bible's critical response to Joseph in Egypt. Joseph bought all the land in Egypt for Pharaoh, except for the land of the priests, which he left alone in order to secure the priests' blessing and support for the dictatorial regime of Pharaoh, his benefactor. The Torah suggests and commands that we follow an anti-pharaonic social and economic model, a conceptual exodus from Egypt.

In our system, the nation as a whole is the priestly kingdom; therefore, there is no superior priestly class with greater rights. Needless to say, the public's land belongs to everyone and may not be concentrated in the king's hands and subjected to his whims and desires. It was by dint of this commandment that Elijah was able to stand before King Ahab, who had cruelly stolen the vineyard of Naboth, and say to him: "Hast thou killed, and also taken possession?" (1 Kings 21:19). A monarchical regime lacking review and balances is not a genuinely Jewish governing system.

If we were to look more deeply, we would find that God today is a prisoner of his rabbis, and that democracy is thus the closest equivalent of the balanced biblical freedom described in the Torah and rediscovered by Montesquieu.

The physical processes of *shmitah* and Jubilee that govern land reform have a symbolic authority over the intellectual tradition as well. In ancient Judaism there is no one correct or proper viewpoint, but rather a multiplicity of approaches and opinions. There is no central authority. The method of the traditional study house, the *beit midrash*, maintains a tension among opposing opinions and factions. Thus the House of Shammai balances the House of Hillel. Abaye reins in Rava. Rabbi Judah Halevi differs from Maimonides. In our own time, with no less gravity, the storehouse of secular Jews is filled with spiritual and cultural valuables quite unlike the storehouse of religious Jewry. Judaism itself is a spiritual *shmitah* and Jubilee that demands continuous renewal. Only a Judaism that maintains unending intellectual tension can guarantee continuity into the future. The concentration of all knowledge and power in one place, in a sort of orthodoxy of land, labor and Torah, is a likely path to decay and death, heaven forbid.

Encore

Leviticus

Is it possible to look through the smoke of sacrifices, the clouds of incense, the severed doves' heads and all the other details of the Book of Leviticus, often known as the Priestly Code, and discern the outline of a larger picture?

At first glance, a priestly code is precisely what it is: a guidebook for the priest with instructions for sacrificial offerings and definitions of the priests' other duties in the life of Israelite religious society in ancient times. In practice, as in the other books of the Torah, the individual portions cover a substantial tension between the book's visible and unseen heroes. The simple reading of the text shows the priests as a sort of select class that, on the one hand, presides over the sanctuary service, and on the other hand serves as a guild of folk-healers who treat leprosy, skin diseases and ritual contamination, and supervise ritual cleansing and general sanitation of the camp of the children of Israel. Wherever you might turn in the sanctuary or in the camp of the children of Israel, a priest can be found to care for your needs and his own income.

However, without going into the details of every commandment, the Book of Leviticus, which sometimes seems boring, incomprehensible and even repellent to the modern reader, has an unseen confrontation tucked among its lines between the two brothers who sit in the first rank of the people's leadership, Moses and Aaron. Like the characters in the Book of Genesis, here too we are presented with symbolic brothers, two archetypes substantially different from one another, whose confrontation and its repercussions shape our spiritual lives to this very day.

What is the major difference? Upon Moses's return from his encounter at the burning bush, God defines for him, his messenger, the division of roles between him and his elder brother: "See, I have set thee in God's stead to Pharaoh, and Aaron thy brother shall be thy prophet. Thou shalt speak all that I command thee; and Aaron thy brother shall speak unto Pharaoh" (Exod. 7:1–2). Suddenly, in the ninth decade of their lives, the stammering younger brother and his polished older brother are asked to redefine their relationship.

Out of this redefinition their relationship develops into something very complicated. Aaron is shown again and again to be a vessel that can hold any content: Moses speaks "as God" to Pharaoh and Aaron echoes his words into the ears of Pharaoh and his magicians as though he were a parrot lacking any thought of his own. The children of Israel ask for a Golden Calf and he does as they ask almost without a word of criticism. Moses tells him not to mourn his dead sons, and he obeys: "And Aaron held his peace" (Lev. 10:3). In the Book of Leviticus, Aaron and his descendants receive operating instructions for the sacred service down through the generations, and they never deviate from them. Aaron is the very embodiment of the establishment, the ultimate keeper of commandments. He and those like him cannot survive without rules and regulations. Aaron, God's highest functionary on earth, is the perfect square.

It's no surprise, then, that for generations afterward, up to the end of the Second Temple era, his priestly descendants entrenched themselves in their sanctuary and refused to accept any change or reinterpretation of the holy scriptures. In those days Jerusalem was deeply divided between the Pharisee and Sadducee sects, between the sages who emerged from below, from among the people, and the Temple priests and their supporters "up there."

It's hard to ignore the distinctly priestly character of the Sadducees, who took their name from Saduc or Tsadok the high priest, the patriarch of the dynasty. Beyond their Temple service, the Sadducees were known for their fierce loyalty to the literal word of the written law, as handed down through the generations. That put them bitterly at odds with the Pharisees, the Jewish spiritual renewal movement of that era. Not surprisingly, when Rabbi Yohanan Ben Zakkai escaped from besieged Jerusalem in the final days of the Second Temple and appeared before the commander of the Roman legions, he didn't plead for the Temple to be saved, nor beg for mercy for the priestly line. No, Rabbi Yohanan Ben Zakkai ignored Jerusalem and asked only for "Yavneh and its scholars." He wasn't interested in saving the decadent world of the sacrificial functionaries, the corrupt Temple culture and the degeneration of religious thought. Rather, he sought to liberate the spirit from its bonds and let it soar up into the heavens and out over land and sea.

The title of Kohen, held by the priestly descendants of Aaron, is often synonymous with hidebound conservatism and membership in a hereditary elite that never earned its leadership position by virtue of personal achievement. The opposite of Aaron is his brother Moses, the Levite. His children did not inherit his leadership, yet he had no lack of successors and heirs, brothers in spirit rather than blood. The Torah of Moses is spiritual entrepreneurialism at its best, and Moses can be seen as the spiritual father of Rabbi Yohanan Ben Zakkai.

Here is how the familiar Aggadah, mentioned earlier, describes the resourceful, innovative character of the "children of Moses":

> Rav Yehuda said, quoting Rav: When Moses went up to the mountaintop to receive the Torah, he asked the Holy One, praised be he, to fill in the crowns at the tops of the letters. He said to him: Master of the Universe, who or what are you waiting for? [That is, why don't you give both the Written and the Oral Torah right here and now at Sinai?] God said to him: There is one man who will appear in a number of generations, named Akiva Ben Joseph, and he will find and fill in every point and detail in the laws. Moses said: Show him to me. God said to Moses: Back up a bit. Moses went and found himself a seat in the eighth row of Akiva's classroom, and he didn't know what they were talking about. His strength was exhausted. When Rabbi Akiva began to talk, his students said: Rabbi, where do you get this from? He said to them: This is the law as Moses received it at Sinai. And Moses was satisfied [because he understood that the evolutionary process that he initiated had continued to the point where he could no longer follow the results]. Thereupon he returned to the Holy One, praised be he, and said: "Master of the Universe, you have such a man and yet you give the Torah through me?" He replied: "Be silent, for such is my decree." (Babylonian Talmud, *Minhot* 29b)

Encore Leviticus

There are many more Midrashic tales linking Moses, the giver of the Written Law, to Rabbi Akiva, one of the most revered teachers of the Oral Law. Rabbi Akiva was to the dynamic tradition of Midrash, commentary and intellectual daring, what Moses was to the Torah of God. Neither one accepted things as he found them or settled for the obvious; both of them were always wondering and searching for what lay beyond the apparent, the known and the accepted.

In the Book of Leviticus these two sons of Levi, Moses and Aaron, wrestle with the frameworks that will, over the course of generations, come to shape the religion of Israel and the laws of the Jewish people. Aaron brings the concrete, while Moses represents the abstract. The former is always in need of external tools of expression and mediation: a Golden Calf for a god, priestly clothes to make the man, clearly defined duties of office and a long-term commitment to the dynasty's continuation and title. Moses, by contrast, needs nothing except an idea. He lays the abstract on the discussion table, expecting all future generations to come and take part. God is his interlocutor, and all future generations of students are his partners and heirs. His own children disappear from the story. His corporeality, like God's, is without shape or form, and as mysterious as his birth is, so is his death unknown.

Aaron preserves the religion in its natural, familiar frameworks. But Moses does the impossible and unimaginable: he speaks face to face with the hidden God. This God has no physical boundaries around him and hence there is no limit to the imagination and creativity in seeking him and interpreting his words and intentions.

Aaron, the older brother, does not always succeed in rising to the height that is above all heights, to God in heaven. His younger brother Moses does not always succeed in coming down to the people and connecting to their daily troubles. Stretched between the two of them is the slender thread of the priestly code – between the technical holiness acquired through sacrifices and rituals, in Aaron's sphere of authority, and the holiness of constant striving by the individual yearning to reach into the heights of heaven, which belongs to Moses.

במדבר
Numbers

Week 30

Bamidbar – In the Wilderness

Numbers 1:1–4:20

An Illegal Command

Hebrew words live in clusters. That is, they are bound together in groups of meaning, within families of common association. Thus, for example, *har* (mountain) and *herayon* (pregnancy) belong to the same family; both suggest protrusions: the mountain protruding above the flatland and the pregnancy above the stomach of the expectant mother. Likewise the words *sheka* (depression, hollow or electrical outlet) and *hashka'ah* (investment) both implying a sinking into or below the surface. In nearly every case the family of meaning is bound together by a root consisting of three (or occasionally two) consonants that take on varying combinations of vowels, prefixes and suffixes to create individual words. In this week's portion, we get to watch the birth of a cluster of words revolving around the three-letter root *p-k-d* – *miphkad* (census), *pekudah* (order) and *pakid* (functionary) – and the host of associations lying behind them.

This family of words embraces various Hebrew terms of authority and governance. Each individual word expresses a different aspect of authority. The Book of Numbers, which opens this week with *Parashat Bamidbar*, recounts the preparations for entering the land of Israel. Precisely for this reason, to enter the Promised Land, Moses tries to organize his band of nomads into a cohesive nation. He seems to remember the advice of his father-in-law Jethro, and at the same time hasn't forgotten the power of the Egyptian bureaucracy. As a continual reminder, he has been transporting the bones of Joseph, the Hebrew ancestor who established Egyptian's state economic administration. Joseph was also viceroy to the king himself, thanks to his visionary wisdom as well as his management skills.

Moses, in the course of his own efforts to build an orderly regime with well-functioning institutions, does what every state has done on occasion since ancient times and up to our own day: he counts the population. This provides the basis for deciding how much can be raised in taxes, how many soldiers will be conscripted, how many seniors will need care and so on. And so Moses created the first biblical population registry.

> And Moses and Aaron took…and assembled all the congregation together on the first day of the second month, and they declared their pedigrees after their families, by their fathers' houses, according to the number of names, from twenty years old and upward, by their polls. As the Lord commanded Moses, so did he number them in the wilderness of Sinai. (Num. 1:17–19)

Immediately after the general population count, *miphkad* in Hebrew, our *p-k-d* root divides into various other meanings and uses, and specific duties are assigned – that is, the tribe of Levi is left out of the count, and instead is made accountable for the tabernacle:

> And the Lord spoke unto Moses, saying: Howbeit the tribe of Levi thou shalt not number, neither shalt thou take the sum of them among the children of Israel; but appoint thou the Levites over the tabernacle of the testimony, and over all the furniture thereof; and they shall minister unto it, and shall encamp round about the tabernacle. And when the tabernacle setteth forward, the Levites shall take it down; and when the tabernacle is to be pitched, the Levites shall set it up; and the common man that draweth nigh shall be put to death. (Num. 1:48–51)

These verses describe the appointment of the Levites as the aristocrats of the tabernacle of testimony – the nobles and counts, one might say – for all time. Later in the Bible, the Levites will become the administrative arm of the kingdom of David, and will be counted as part of the loyalist core of the Davidic and Solomonic administrations. Indeed, in every

Bamidbar

biblical society that has passed through the first two stages – census and assignment, or counting and accountability – there evolves a third stage, namely the administrative bureaucracy of managers and accountants. So Joseph advises Pharaoh: "Let Pharaoh appoint overseers (*yaphked pekidim*) over the land" (Gen. 41:34), and so too in the kingdom of Ahasuerus, who was advised by his own counselors: "Let the king appoint officers (*yaphked pekidim*) in all the provinces of his kingdom" (Esth. 2:3). So it goes: from a head count to accountability to noble counts and on to bureaucrats and bean counters.

This family of words hints, in both Hebrew and English, at the natural development of the life of a people: from a nuclear family to a community of individuals to a people leaving together from a house of bondage, receiving a constitution at Mount Sinai and thus becoming a nation. Now, after years of coalescing in the desert, the census symbolizes the beginning of the first Hebrew state. But this is no simple matter. A shadow stalks the light of Israelite sovereignty from its first dawning. The children of Israel and their descendants do not readily accept the principle of centralized government with its discipline and rules. The medieval Spanish commentator Jacob Ben Asher, known as Baal Ha-Turim, was quite blunt in his criticism on this point:

> "Appoint thou the Levites" – Compare this to the verse in Psalms (109:6), "Appoint thou a wicked man over him"; this is as it is said (compare Talmud, Sanhedrin 103b) that no man is made an officer below unless he is made wicked on high. And thus when you "appoint the Levites," who were made officers, you "appoint a wicked man." (Baal Ha-Turim on Num. 1:50)

Baal Ha-Turim, following his favorite method of linguistic association, looks for another scriptural use of the word "appoint" in the same imperative form, *haphked*. He finds it linked in Psalm 109 to wickedness, and he immediately identifies the Levites as wicked. Going further, the daring commentator widens his critique to the entire notion of authority, which, he argues, contains an element of inherent evil.

Baal Ha-Turim is not the only commentator to offer such a sweeping critique of government. There have been many others, before and since. Here is one of the best known of them: "Shemayah used to say: Love work, hate mastery and do not bring yourself to the attention of the government" (Mishnah, *Avot* 1:10). Let's interpret his words: Loving work is clear enough. Hating mastery does not necessarily refer to rabbis, who were known as "masters" in their role as spiritual guides and personal role models, but to hatred of domination and coercion. Shemayah preached against state authority because its power to harm and do evil was far greater than its benefit, especially in the case of a hostile regime like the Roman Empire under whose rule Shemayah lived and against which he preached.

The third part of his saying completes the second: "Do not bring yourself to the attention of the government." That is, keep your distance from the authorities. It's better if they know nothing of you and you know nothing of them. The critics of the state and its works can get along without you.

Many years later, at the beginning of the twentieth century, Rabbi Abraham Isaac Hacohen Kook wrote the following:

> We left the politics of the world under coercion that had within it an internal desire, until that happy time when it will be possible to manage the state without wickedness and barbarism; this is the time we hope for…. Our soul despises the terrible sins of the state leadership in a time of evil. But a time is approaching, very near, when the world will be replenished and we will be able to prepare ourselves, because it will be possible to manage the affairs of our state on foundations of good, wisdom, righteousness and clear, divine enlightenment…. There is no value in Jacob engaging in statecraft at a time when it must be drenched in blood, at a time when it demands a talent for wickedness. We received only the root foundation necessary to establish a nation, and because the trunk above it had been torn away we were deposed from governing, scattered among the nations and planted deep in the earth until "the time of singing is come and the voice of the turtledove is heard in our land" (Song 2:12). (*Orot* 14, translated by JJG)

A state, according to Rabbi Kook, requires a "talent for wickedness," which annuls the value of sovereign independence. The words "state," "sovereignty," "wickedness," "police" and "bureaucrats" are the key players on the field of Jewish political thought.

Generations of sages understood that a government without an effective counterweight, or what we call today an opposition, opens the door to despotism, something completely at odds with the character of Torah law. The character of the Torah is expressed in commandments calling for self-discipline and obedience to the creator of the universe, not in discipline imposed violently from the outside by a wicked government. That is why the daily morning prayers quote from the poetry of the Book of Psalms: "Put not your trust in princes, nor in the son of man, in whom there is no help. His breath goeth forth, he returneth to his dust; in that very day his thoughts perish" (Ps. 146:3–4).

The balancing counterweight is what gave Simeon Ben Shetach, chairman of the Sanhedrin, the strength to order King Alexander Jannaeus to remain standing when he faced that body (Babylonian Talmud, *Sanhedrin* 19a; the story is told in Week 43, "Shoftim"). It is what gave the prophet Nathan the strength to confront King David with the parable of the poor man's lamb after David's marriage to Bath-sheba (2 Sam. 12:4). It is what moved Jews throughout the generations to defer to tyrants' laws without ever surrendering their conscience. The spirit of freedom in the Exodus means opposition to unchecked government wherever it is found, because it represents a far greater danger than any absence of government. The spirit of anarchy, the never-ending resolve to challenge and discomfort the forces of government, proves in the final analysis to be the most consistent factor in Jewish political philosophy, and its roots are here in this week's portion.

The very portion that seems to detail the beginning of the coalition of the tribes of Israel turns out to bear the seeds of non-cooperation as an aspect of national character. The simultaneous pursuit of system and anarchy gave the Jewish people a limitless range of flexibility. Nations that are anarchic but lack order and discipline cannot always translate their nationhood into sovereign statehood. On the other hand, those that are too organized and structured cannot withstand the creative drive of human nature and the always surprising imagination of history. But a nation as filled with contradictions as ours, one that can dream of establishing a third commonwealth and do everything possible to sabotage the plan, can survive anything history might throw at it, whatever the cost.

The Wild Wilderness

Numbers? This week's portion is full of them:

> And the Lord spoke unto Moses in the wilderness of Sinai, in the tent of meeting, on the first day of the second month, in the second year after they were come out of the land of Egypt, saying: "Take ye the sum of all the congregation of the children of Israel, by their families, by their fathers' houses, according to the number of names, every male, by their polls; from twenty years old and upward, all that are able to go forth to war in Israel: ye shall number them by their hosts, even thou and Aaron. And with you there shall be a man of every tribe, every one head of his fathers' house." (Num. 1:1–4)

It looks like the annual report of the Sinai Desert Central Bureau of Statistics ended up in the middle of the Bible. In contemporary language, if we say that someone "doesn't count" we mean that he and his opinion need not be taken into consideration. Hence if someone is counted, she is worthy of consideration. It follows that the census carried out in *Parashat Bamidbar* not only counts the people, but also accounts them worthy. I would like to take this insight as a point of departure and place this portion in a broader context that departs from the traditional interpretation.

For me, every story in the Bible combines existential tensions and human decisions. Sometimes the decisions are the right ones, sometimes not, but they are always human decisions. This helps to explain Adam and Eve's dilemma over the fruit of the forbidden tree, Cain's sin and Abraham's attempt to bargain with the Supreme Judge over the destruction of Sodom.

So too can we read all the stories of the patriarchs and matriarchs, their children and their families.

One of the greatest tensions in the Torah, which at times can be enormously fruitful and at other times profoundly depressing, is the tension between Moses and the children of Israel departing Egypt. Moses walked in greatness, while the children of Israel made a virtue of pettiness. He looked forward with vision, while they looked at the ground beneath their noses, thinking only of survival. He was a statesman and they were fugitives in the desert. This is the context in which the stories of the Exodus take place. Moses wanted to create a nation and build its social institutions, while they just wanted to be left alone after so many years of slavery. And so from the moment that Moses and the people first meet in the beginning of the Book of Exodus all the way through to the end of Deuteronomy, we the readers are witness to a growing confrontation between the prince of Egypt and Pharaoh's slaves. The census in this week's portion is one chapter in the ongoing conflict between the culture of governance and the culture of the wilderness.

Census and wilderness are the two opposing models of organization of any people. This is particularly so of the Jewish people. The wilderness is a place of blinding storms and breakthrough departures, of breaking norms and tablets. The wilderness is the existential avant-garde that runs out ahead of the camp. In an organized state, things are supposed to be done differently. In a state we find checks and balances, moderating processes and gradual history, as opposed to instant hysteria. The opening scene of the Book of Numbers is thus something of a charmingly naïve effort to impose order on the chaos of the wilderness, as though the spirit of Jethro were still hovering over this people. *Parashat Bamidbar* includes census takers, princes, officers, flags, camps and marching formations. The reader might confuse this with a description of a European organization setting out. But this was a dream, and as far from reality as Theodor Herzl's dream of the Jewish State was from real life in today's Israel.

From Moses's viewpoint, this was the way to transform a slave rebellion into sovereign national independence. The process had begun with tough diplomacy in Egypt and continued through the logistical planning for departure and the crossing of the Red Sea. It included the production of the greatest show in Sinai, the revelation and giving of the Torah. It required building a judicial and governing system along Jethro's blueprint. It entailed preparing the Tabernacle and its implements. Now came one more important stage before entering the Promised Land: the census. As for the people, they saw the whole thing rather differently. Moses sent out census takers and the people dodged them. Moses created systems and the people ran circles around them.

I think a great deal about the character of Moses. The constant frustration he must have felt, the endless struggles that wore him down. He had been accustomed to the ways of the royal palace, where the ruler spoke and the servants obeyed. This almost never worked with our ancestors in the desert. When Moses first came to the children of Israel with his tidings of redemption, they did not want to leave Egypt. They suffered from the classic syndrome of slaves who fear to trade the security of their masters' home – however degrading and oppressive the security – for the terrifying unknown of freedom. For years after the Exodus, deep into their journey in the desert, they were still wondering aloud about returning to Egypt. And every time that Moses came to them with ideas of bureaucracy and governance, they dismissed him – which is to say, they dismissed his Egyptianness.

Take, for example, Moses's ascent to the top of Mount Sinai at the transcendent moment of revelation. When he came back down, one of the first things he did was to collect money from the people – they called it a *terumah* (donation) – to build a tabernacle as a sanctuary to his God and his vision. In my chapter on *Parashat Terumah* I interpreted the building of the tabernacle as an idealistic, egalitarian social undertaking, a virtual poor people's sanctuary. It could be, though, that the children of Israel understood it differently: as a national monument to one man's vision, more his than theirs. At first they came towards him and gave him their "sealskins, and acacia-wood" (Exod. 25:5), but as the project dragged on, they grew tired of it and rebelled. Perhaps the Golden Calf was a revolt against the tabernacle and the threats of order, discipline and new lifestyles that Moses was proposing. They didn't want law and order. They wanted a Golden Calf born in chaos, a few days of celebrating and drinking, some wildness in the camp and then back to the disorder of desert life.

The wilderness has a volatile, individualistic quality. It has no rules and no borders. Its nomadic inhabitants have little property, sometimes none – certain nothing valuable or orderly. The idea of the wilderness holds a promise of refuge and survival for the individual. The state structure is almost exactly opposite. The children of Israel went to the desert in search of individual freedom, much the way young people today travel to Sinai, India or Brazil. Moses, on the other hand, had a different vision of freedom. He envisioned national freedom, which is to say an organized collective expressing itself through sovereign independence. Moses was looking far off in the distance, but the children of Israel had not yet opened their eyes.

This pattern of Moses's vision and the people's efforts to shake off the burdens and kick the reins repeats itself in this week's portion. In next week's portion, *Parashat Beha'alotecha*, we will read how the entire complicated structure was built on the fly: "And the children of Israel set forward by their stages out of the wilderness of Sinai.... And in the first place the standard of the camp of the children of Judah set forward" (Num. 10:12–14). As they moved, the Ark of the Covenant moved with them: "And it came to pass, when the Ark set forward, that Moses said: 'Rise up, O Lord'" (Num. 10:35). And immediately afterward, the verses inform us: "And the people were as murmurers, speaking evil in the ears of the Lord" (Num. 11:1).

There is no better way to illustrate the gap between Moses and the masses than to cite one opaque verse from the end of this week's portion. Moses is looking off in the distance with the future laid out before him. He is entirely devoted to this vision. But the people, as usual, are grumbling, doubtful and full of complaints. Every single person is caught up in his own affairs, thinking only of his own temporal troubles, and only Moses is reaching up toward heaven. His experience is entirely cut off from the voices in the camp. One piece of evidence: "Now these are the generations of Aaron and Moses in the day that the Lord spoke with Moses in Mount Sinai. And these are the names of the sons of Aaron..." (Num. 3:1–2).

Moses is so cut off, even from his own family, that his own children are not counted as part of his line but included in the line of Aaron his brother. The "generations of Moses" are "the sons of Aaron."

These tensions between Moses and the collective that he leads can be seen in the biblical story whose echoes are heard to this day. We know the tension between ambitions of greatness and an inability to accept a yoke, commit to a system or follow rules. Sometimes this inability leads to groundbreaking successes, but at other times it invites calamity. Our lives are defined by a tension between the wilderness and the census, between anarchy and organization, between individual freedom and freedom of the collective.

Week 31

Naso – Take the Sum of the Sons

Numbers 4:21–7:89

Turn It and Turn It: The Interpretive Revolution

THE REASON I LOVE STUDYING Torah so much is the kaleidoscopic dimension in this wonderful text. In the Bible, the materials and forms remain the same and yet constantly change, right before our eyes. The biblical story is a continual revolution that is nonetheless connected to its own genesis. Learning Torah invites the learner to ask, "Could it be that this isn't correct? Is it possible to understand this text, or the context of this command, in an entirely different way from what I thought until now?" Indeed, it's possible that everything we have learned in the past year is precisely the opposite of what we'll be trying to understand today, and perhaps everything we're extracting this year will look entirely different by this time next year.

The anonymous Mishnaic sage known as Ben Bag Bag speaks of this when he says, "Turn it and turn it again, for everything is contained in it. Gaze at it, grow old studying it and do not abandon it, for you have no greater measure than this" (Mishnah, *Avot* 5:22). Ben Bag Bag (he was probably a child of converts who came to be known by the initials B.G., for *ben gerim*) offers us a useful Torah study guide. There have been those who sought, and unfortunately still seek, to understand this as a restrictive forbidding the study of anything except the Torah, since it contains everything one might need: physics, mathematics, social sciences, practical science, law and ethics. Everything is in the Torah, and therefore there is no need to look outside its walls, whether to universities, to the wisdom of the world or to dialogue with the fruitful, enriching traditions of other nations.

In the spirit of Ben Bag Bag, let's take these words and turn them around. I understand his instruction to "turn it" as a declaration that the Torah actually invites transformation and revolution. Everything is contained in it because it contains both the interpretation and its opposite, both the opinion and its contradiction. In many senses, the position that is rejected today is part of the whole, and it could well turn out to be tomorrow's central, binding interpretation.

A startling example of this sort of interpretative turnabout appears in this week's portion, in the section dealing with Law of Jealousy:

> This is the law of jealousy, when a wife, being under her husband, goeth aside, and is defiled; or when the spirit of jealousy cometh upon a man, and he be jealous over his wife; then shall he set the woman before the Lord, and the priest shall execute upon her all this law. And the man shall be clear from iniquity, and that woman shall bear her iniquity. (Num. 5:29–31)

This portion is not easy to understand. What is the spirit of jealousy, why does it deserve its own separate "law" and why does the Torah place responsibility only on the woman? These are important questions, but we're going to concentrate on the history of this portion's interpretation.

The sages of the Mishnaic and Talmudic era took the Law of Jealousy and removed one of its most important elements. In our portion the Torah requires that the woman be made to drink a magical concoction called "the water of bitterness." The use of this water was an ancient test of fidelity that was meant to achieve one of two results: if the woman had sinned, her stomach would swell and her thigh would "fall away," and if not, the woman would cleared of guilt and even promised future fertility. It could be that this ceremony, more than serving as a fidelity lie detector, is intended to deter people, especially women, from fornicating and betraying their vows.

However, changing historical contexts and social circumstances led the sages of the Talmudic era to recognize that the weapon of force-feeding the

Naso

water of bitterness was no longer deterring anyone. Therefore the Mishnah states: "When murderers became widespread, the beheaded heifer was abolished.... When fornicators became widespread, the water of bitterness was discontinued." That is, as adultery became a common, accepted social norm, there was no longer a point to the mysterious deterrent ceremony of the Sotah, the "wayward wife." The same judgment was applied to the ceremony of the beheaded heifer, which had to do with finding a murder victim in the vicinity of a city. Once murderers became widespread in the society of the Talmudic era and the ceremony of the beheaded heifer was no longer an effective deterrent, as it no longer represented a societal norm that rejected murder, the sages abolished it. Thus the Torah changes and renews itself in accordance with the times and circumstances.

We found a strict prohibition in our portion, on infidelity and waywardness, accompanied by a frightful ceremony, the water of bitterness. We turned it once and found commentary annulling the biblical command as though it had never existed. Let's continue turning the Law of Jealousy. The portion's point of departure appears to be an assumption that the problem stems from a seductive who not only strays from the straight and narrow, but tempts the men she meets into wandering off the righteous path. By this logic, if we frighten the woman and deter women from adultery, we will have solved the problem of private and public morality within our society. Hence the embarrassing, humiliating ceremony, reminiscent of the medieval witch trials:

> And the priest shall bring her near, and set her before the Lord. And the priest shall take holy water in an earthen vessel; and of the dust that is on the floor of the tabernacle the priest shall take, and put it into the water. And the priest shall set the woman before the Lord, and let the hair of the woman's head go loose, and put the meal-offering of memorial in her hands, which is the meal-offering of jealousy; and the priest shall have in his hand the water of bitterness that causeth the curse.
>
> And the priest shall cause her to swear, and shall say unto the woman: "If no man have lain with thee, and if thou hast not gone

aside to uncleanness, being under thy husband, be thou free from this water of bitterness that causeth the curse; but if thou hast gone aside, being under thy husband, and if thou be defiled, and some man have lain with thee besides thy husband – then the priest shall cause the woman to swear with the oath of cursing, and the priest shall say unto the woman – the Lord make thee a curse and an oath among thy people, when the Lord doth make thy thigh to fall away, and thy belly to swell; and this water that causeth the curse shall go into thy bowels, and make thy belly to swell, and thy thigh to fall away"; and the woman shall say: "Amen, Amen."
And the priest shall write these curses in a scroll, and he shall blot them out into the water of bitterness. And he shall make the woman drink the water of bitterness that causeth the curse; and the water that causeth the curse shall enter into her and become bitter. And the priest shall take the meal-offering of jealousy out of the woman's hand, and shall wave the meal-offering before the Lord, and bring it unto the altar. And the priest shall take a handful of the meal-offering, as the memorial-part thereof, and make it smoke upon the altar, and afterward shall make the woman drink the water. And when he hath made her drink the water, then it shall come to pass, if she be defiled, and have acted unfaithfully against her husband, that the water that causeth the curse shall enter into her and become bitter. (Num. 5:16–27)

Missing throughout this detailed ceremony is the role of the jealous husband. He is simply not there. Attention is focused entirely on the woman, the victim of his jealousy and violence. And not only is the accusing husband missing; the mysterious paramour has evaporated, as though he never were. The biblical reader is left with the impression that women have strayed and been unfaithful, but not with real, flesh-and-blood men.

Later on, in the Mishnaic version we cited as proof that the Law of Jealousy had been annulled, someone else goes missing from the equation: the woman. The heroine of the biblical tale disappears, and the responsibility for violating the bounds of communal propriety and uprooting the law of scripture is now the man's – whether adulterer or murderer – along with the larger community of "adulterous" or "murderous" men. Responsibility for changing and abolishing the original biblical law falls entirely on the male of the species. If one wishes to argue that the term "adulterers" used in the Mishnah is a plural that includes both male and female, it must be acknowledged at the very least that there is a 50 percent improvement in the appearance of male responsibility, which had been entirely absent from the original biblical text. Thus, with one more turning of the textual soil of the Torah, new layers of responsibility are uncovered, and it suddenly becomes apparent that the man, who was absent from the first rendition, has been given primary responsibility in the latest rendition. For so it was written: everything is contained therein, both hidden and revealed, both women and men. You need only to look, and you will find.

The Puppet of the Priest

SPEAK UNTO AARON and unto his sons, saying: On this wise ye shall bless the children of Israel; ye shall say unto them:

The Lord bless thee, and keep thee;

The Lord make his face to shine upon thee, and be gracious unto thee;

The Lord lift up his countenance upon thee, and give thee peace.

So shall they put my name upon the children of Israel, and I will bless them. (Num. 6:23–27)

Sometimes the order in which the Bible presents its content is genuinely surprising. What are these gentle, encouraging, flattering verses doing here? This is a strange place to put verses of blessing. Preceding it is a list of pains and troubles of the leper and the man experiencing an emission, along with the place reserved for their quarantine outside the camp. Immediately following these verses of the Priestly Blessing, we are back to the tabernacle and the ceremonial sacrifices of the princes of the tribes on the day that "Moses had made an end of setting up the tabernacle" (Num. 7:1). Who is doing the blessing here, and what is this blessing?

The credit for understanding this strange juxtaposition of portions goes to one of the great modern biblical researchers and commentators, the Italian-born Professor Umberto Moses Cassuto. Cassuto begins his progression of biblical logic in the previous portion, where the order and internal organization of the tribes and camps is established. After the instructions for the ordering of the camp are concluded, the commandment appears to "put out of the camp every leper, and every one that hath an issue, and whosoever is unclean by the dead" (Num. 5:2). That is, after the camp has been cleansed of all the sick and abnormal, and the public domain has been organized along proper health and hygiene standards, the text moves on to the cleansing of the family and systematizes the ceremony for deterrence of adultery and undermining the institution of marriage. Once the family has been purified, the resolution is narrowed still further and focuses on the individual Nazirite, who seeks to purify himself from within by means of monastic asceticism. Cassuto suggests that these portions are connected by a straight line leading from purification of the camp to the internal purification of the individual, and that in each of these the priest has an important part to play. Located in the heart of the Israelite camp, the priests are the interface that links the surrounding mass of humanity to God, who dwells in the tabernacle in their midst.

It is the priest who conducts the ceremony of the wayward wife, as well as the sacrifice for the Nazirite completing the term of his vows. Wherever you might turn, whatever you did, the priest was a partner – in the public spaces, in religious rituals, in relations between a man and his wife, between a man and his neighbor, between the individual and his own inner soul.

Today, too, there are functionaries present in every corner of society. Systems of medicine, communications, justice and law enforcement fall into this category today, as the priests did in their day. But in the Bible there was an unspoken fear, never quite resolved, of an arrogant or dictatorial attitude among the priests as members of a special class. The priests were responsible for body, soul and ritual. This reality could lead them all too quickly to a sense of disengaged superiority that could only end badly, as indeed happened more than once in our history.

In opposition to the dominion of the priests and the dictatorial tendencies of the religious bureaucracy, the priestly blessing quoted above comes as an antidote. A cautious examination of this blessing shows that it is not in any way, shape or form an expansion of the priests' powers into yet another arena of daily life. The priests of Israel never had the power to bestow blessings or charms. They were little more than scarecrows or robots. The substantive limitations imposed on them made them God's servants, not his stand-ins or replacements.

Take a close look at the words: "On this wise [that is, in the following manner] ye shall bless the children of Israel." In other words, you may not deviate left or right, not for a single syllable or punctuation, not a letter or word. "On this wise" and no other. In the prayer service followed in tens of thousands of Jewish congregations throughout the centuries, the priests have repeated this prayer word for word as it has been dictated to them by the cantor. They are not initiators, but followers. And here is how the verses of the blessing are concluded: "So shall they put my name upon the children of Israel, and I will bless them." This is my name, God says, and I give the blessing. I am the Source of the blessing. I am the Lord, and you are not.

The priestly blessing is essentially a priestly restriction. It is a divine blessing, and its sole beneficiaries are us, the masses of the blessed, who do not need to pay the religious establishment for the blessing services bestowed on us through it.

As a marginal note, we might add another word about religious romanticism. At the beginning of the journey, God promised the people, "Ye shall be unto me a kingdom of priests, and a holy nation" (Exod. 19:6). In the interim, the original undertaking has been dimmed by desert storms and dust clouds. Professional priests have taken over the nexus of the relationship between humankind and the creator. And yet, beyond the thick veils and hostile institutional domination, the Supreme Lover manages to communicate his love and his blessing again and again. He turns his kidnappers into his messengers. The priests who reduced his place in the world have become the distributors of his blessing to the public. It is contentious, sly, confusing, but so typical.

Week 32

Beha'alotecha – When Thou Lightest the Lamps

Numbers 8:1–12:16

Moses's Monopoly

AND MIRIAM AND AARON spoke against Moses because of the Cushite woman whom he had married; for he had married a Cushite woman. And they said: "Hath the Lord indeed spoken only with Moses? Hath he not spoken also with us?" And the Lord heard it. Now the man Moses was very meek, above all the men that were upon the face of the earth. And the Lord spoke suddenly unto Moses, and unto Aaron, and unto Miriam: "Come out ye three unto the tent of meeting." And they three came out. And the Lord came down in a pillar of cloud, and stood at the door of the Tent, and called Aaron and Miriam; and they both came forth. And he said: …"Wherefore then were ye not afraid to speak against my servant, against Moses?" And the anger of the Lord was kindled against them; and he departed. And when the cloud was removed from over the Tent, behold, Miriam was leprous.… And Miriam was shut up without the camp seven days; and the people journeyed not till Miriam was brought in again. (Num. 12:1–15)

A bit of tension comes into the first family of Israel, and suddenly the creator of the universe injects himself into the story. Miriam said something to Aaron, spread a bit of gossip about her tanned, dark-skinned sister-in-

Beha'alotecha

law, complained about her successful little brother, and suddenly God is involved and is meting out punishment. The Israelites stage a protest against God and refuse to move until he heals Miriam in his goodness.

What's not being spelled out here, hidden between the lines? My friend and rabbi Dov Alboim teaches this story in his recent book, *A Walk Through the Void*. Dov investigates the words Miriam spoke and brings a Midrash from Sifre Zuta that reads as follows:

> When the elders were appointed, all Israel lit candles and celebrated the elevation of the seventy to office. When Miriam saw the candles, she said: "Do not say, Happy are your women, but Woe to your women, because from the day that the Holy One, praised be he, spoke with Moses, he has not needed me. Then Miriam went to Aaron. (Sifre Zuta 12:5, s.v. "and she spoke")

Another Midrash adds a touch of sadness to the confessions of Zipporah, the beautiful black woman:

> And Miriam and Aaron spoke against Moses: How did Miriam know that Moses had given up the commandment to be fruitful and multiply? She saw that Zipporah was not adorning herself with womanly finery. She said to her: Why do you not adorn yourself with womanly finery? She said to her: Your brother does not attend to the matter. Therefore Miriam knew and she told her brother and the two of them spoke against him. (Sifre, *Parashat Beha'alotecha*, paragraph 41)

Dov, following the Midrash, draws a line between Miriam's conversation and Moses's conjugal behavior. And here is the connection: the previous passage in the portion tells of the ordination of the seventy elders as part of Moses's administration:

> And the Lord said unto Moses: "Gather unto me seventy men of the elders of Israel, whom thou knowest to be the elders of the people, and officers over them; and bring them unto the tent of meeting, that they may stand there with thee. And I will come down and speak

with thee there; and I will take of the spirit which is upon thee, and will put it upon them; and they shall bear the burden of the people with thee, that thou bear it not thyself alone. (Num. 11:16–17)

To elaborate: the seventy elders were appointed to be Moses's spiritual assistants, to help him handle inquiries from the public, especially following the people's ceaseless complaints, the most recent of which had left Moses broken in spirit. They, the people, remembered "the fish, which we were wont to eat in Egypt for nought; the cucumbers, and the melons, and the leeks, and the onions, and the garlic" (Num. 11:5). Among them was a small group of excitable provocateurs: "And the mixed multitude that was among them fell a lusting," and as a result, "the children of Israel also wept on their part, and said: 'Would that we were given flesh to eat!'" (Num. 11:4).

In response, Moses loses patience and hurls all his bitterness at God:

And Moses heard the people weeping, family by family, every man at the door of his tent; and the anger of the Lord was kindled greatly; and Moses was displeased. And Moses said unto the Lord: "Wherefore hast Thou dealt ill with thy servant? And wherefore have I not found favor in thy sight, that thou layest the burden of all this people upon me? Have I conceived all this people? Have I brought them forth, that thou shouldest say unto me: Carry them in thy bosom, as a nursing-father carrieth the sucking child, unto the land which thou didst swear unto their fathers? Whence should I have flesh to give unto all this people? For they trouble me with their weeping, saying: Give us flesh, that we may eat. I am not able to bear all this people myself alone, because it is too heavy for me. And if thou deal thus with me, kill me, I pray thee, out of hand, if I have found favor in thy sight; and let me not look upon my wretchedness." (Num. 11:10–15)

God, in turn, replies to Moses: "If you have no more strength, then you are losing your exclusivity as my representative," and he promptly ordains seventy assistants for him. How does the Midrash manage to stretch these words to cover the amorous behavior of an elderly who has spent his entire life trying to stabilize his repeatedly challenged authority?

I think that the principle linking the portions together is correct, but closer attention should be paid to another story that appears alongside the portion of the seventy elders and Miriam's gossip. Buried within the account of the people's great celebration over the new nominations, there is a story about the opposition of Eldad and Medad. While God is busy devolving his authority onto the seventy elders, these two are separately prophesying:

> But there remained two men in the camp, the name of the one was Eldad, and the name of the other Medad; and the spirit rested upon them; and they were of them that were recorded, but had not gone out unto the Tent; and they prophesied in the camp. And there ran a young man, and told Moses, and said: "Eldad and Medad are prophesying in the camp." And Joshua the son of Nun, the minister of Moses from his youth up, answered and said: "My lord Moses, shut them in." And Moses said unto him: "Art thou jealous for my sake? Would that all the Lord's people were prophets, that the Lord would put his spirit upon them!" (Num. 11:26–29)

Eldad and Medad are prophesying in the spirit of an alternative prophesy that is not part of Moses and God's mainstream. Joshua is jealous of his master's spiritual monopoly and might perhaps have begun worrying about his own role after Moses dies. That's why he wants Moses to throw the opposition in jail: "My lord Moses, shut them in," he pleads. Moses, however, is a bigger man than Joshua. He has room within himself for his opponents. He understands that the spirit of God dwells not only in his supporters but in his opponents as well.

Miriam is very much like Joshua. She, too, is unhappy with the status of the new prophets. "I am a prophet, too," she tells herself. "Hath the Lord indeed spoken only with Moses? Hath he not spoken also with us?" She stirs up Aaron. Joshua's jealousy is in the political realm; hers is different, but it is jealousy nonetheless. She sees the status of the new prophets and understands that it threatens her own status. In previous chapters we discussed the Law of Jealousy and the connection between jealousy and sex. This week's portion presents other dimensions of jealousy. Included here are political jealousy and petty jealousy of others' good fortune. The Midrash judges the various jealousies to be equal, and in so doing it brings the rules of the wayward wife and her sexuality into Miriam and Aaron's conversation about their dark and lovely sister-in-law.

God intervenes in their conversation and punishes her as part of his ongoing support for Moses. The people, however, rebel against God's punishment, line up behind Miriam and refuse to move until Miriam is healed. Moses, modest as always, recuses himself from the power games, leaving God no choice but to heal her leprosy and get back on the road to Canaan. And so it turns out that such affairs have ever and always been the fate of Jewish politics. And so we say again: leaders, be careful what you say, even in private – especially in private.

Moses: A Genuine Leader

THE WRITING OF THIS PORTION was begun early on, shortly after the Exodus from Egypt and the giving of the Torah. Its beginning can be found in the Book of Exodus, in *Parashat Yitro* (Week 17 of this volume, Exod. 18–20). The rumor of the miraculous departure from Egypt has sprouted wings and found its way to to the ears of Jethro, Moses's father-in-law, the priest of Midian. The priestly in-law has come for a wilderness visit with his famous son-in-law, his daughter Zipporah and his two grandchildren. During his visit, Jethro couldn't help noticing how his son-in-law was managing the affairs of the nation of newly freed slaves. Every day it was the same story. Every property owner, every man in trouble, every aggrieved woman would plant him- or herself at the entrance to Moses's tent and inundate him with public inquiries: "And the people stood about Moses from the morning unto the evening" (Exod. 18:13). Moses was already past eighty years old. Obviously, this isn't the optimal age to be dealing with others' woes.

Jethro immediately offers his penetrating critique: "The thing that thou doest is not good. Thou wilt surely wear away, both thou, and this people that is with thee; for the thing is too heavy for thee; thou art not able to perform it thyself alone" (Exod. 18:17–18). Along with the criticism comes a helping of constructive advice: "Hearken now unto my voice, I will give thee counsel, and God be with thee: be thou for the people before God, and bring thou the causes unto God" (Exod. 18:19). He then explains in detail how to build the first civil service in our history. Here is how he describes the classic division of responsibility: "Every great matter they shall bring unto thee, but every small matter they shall judge themselves; so shall they make it easier for thee and bear the burden with thee" (Exod. 18:21–22). The advice is followed in full: "Moses hearkened to the voice of his father-in-law, and did all that he had said" (Exod. 18:24), and wilderness life returns to normal. They handle the squabbles and he handles the vision, he in the holiness of the mountaintop while they breathe in the desert sands of daily life.

After Moses had organized them all, the time came to set out on the road once again. Our portion relates as follows:

> And Moses said unto Hobab, the son of Reuel the Midianite, Moses's father-in-law: "We are journeying unto the place of which the Lord said: I will give it you; come thou with us, and we will do thee good...." And he said unto him: "I will not go; but I will depart to mine own land, and to my kindred." (Num. 10:29–30)

Something in Moses's invitation apparently impelled Jethro back to his own home. He decided to do without the good Moses was offering. While they were setting out on their way, Jethro was hurrying off on his own way. The Ark of the Covenant of the Lord, too, was setting out on its journey, accompanied by these elegant verses: "And it came to pass, when the Ark set forward, that Moses said: 'Rise up, O Lord, and let thine enemies be scattered; and let them that hate thee flee before thee.' And when it rested, he said: 'Return, O Lord, unto the ten thousands of the families of Israel'" (Num. 10:35–36). Where did these enemies come from? This Ark had never known enemies. When the Egyptians came to the sea, the Ark hadn't yet been built and the tablets inside it hadn't yet been given. Who is this bold battle cry directed against, and what does it have to do with Jethro?

What is the juxtaposition of these portions hinting at? The coming verses will provide the answer.

The very next verses of the portion bring an outburst of disturbances: "And the people were as murmurers, speaking evil in the ears of the Lord; and when the Lord heard it, his anger was kindled; and the fire of the Lord burnt among them, and devoured in the uttermost part of the camp. And the people cried unto Moses; and Moses prayed unto the Lord, and the fire abated" (Num. 11:1–2). The unrest continues into the next disturbance: "And the mixed multitude that was among them fell a lusting," and these extremists infect the rest of the Israelite nation with their defeatist attitude, "and the children of Israel also wept on their part, and said: 'Would that we were given flesh to eat!'" (Num. 11:4). The complaints reach Moses's ear: "And Moses heard the people weeping, family by family, every man at the door of his tent; and the anger of the Lord was kindled greatly; and Moses was displeased" (Num. 11:10).

Moses, the great titan who stopped God from destroying the people and planted himself bravely in God's path, is now trading places with the angry God. Now it's his turn, and he rages at heaven: "Wherefore hast thou dealt ill with thy servant? And wherefore have I not found favor in thy sight, that thou layest the burden of all this people upon me?" (Num. 11:11). (And what a theological assertion, that God acts badly!) Moses continues, right up to the verge of threatening suicide: "And if thou deal thus with me, kill me, I pray thee, out of hand, if I have found favor in thy sight; and let me not look upon my wretchedness" (Num. 11:15). Moses, what happened? Could it be that the enemies Moses wants to scatter every which way by means of God and his Ark are internal enemies, his outspoken opposition? Why are these Israelites harder to take than Pharaoh and the plagues, the sea and Amalek?

The real story, it seems, was this: After Moses exploded, God rolled up his sleeves and went to work in the camp. He withdrew some of Moses's authority and burdens, and delegated them to the seventy elders. God set up an alternate personnel structure to replace the one that had collapsed upon Jethro's departure. But at the same time, two opposition figures were allowed to remain in the camp, Eldad and Medad. The holy spirit had come to rest on them, too, since the diminishing of Moses had enlarged the spirits of others, including some who were different or even opposed. As we read in the previous section:

> …There remained two men in the camp, the name of the one was Eldad, and the name of the other Medad; and the spirit rested upon them…and they prophesied in the camp.… And Joshua the son of Nun, the minister of Moses from his youth up, answered and said: "My lord Moses, shut them in." And Moses said unto him: "Art thou jealous for my sake? Would that all the Lord's people were prophets, that the Lord would put his spirit upon them!" (Num. 11:26–29)

Joshua is advising Moses to take the extreme step of imprisoning the two men, but the extremism of his aide actually has the effect of calming Moses and returning things to their proper proportions. He understands that his ill temper has crossed a boundary and is becoming public knowledge, beyond the intimate space between himself and God. For that reason he silences Joshua with a few curt words, "Art thou jealous for my sake?" – or in simpler terms, "Shush, I can handle this without you."

But Joshua apparently hasn't understood this startling lesson in leadership that he has been taught. Accordingly, the Aggadah uses his example to clarify the close connection between weak internal hierarchies and pointless external wars. So a marvelous Talmudic Aggadah relates in describing the period of transition and handover of powers from Moses to Joshua, from the sun to the moons:

> Rabbi Judah reported in the name of Rab: When Moses departed [this world] for the Garden of Eden he said to Joshua: "Ask me concerning all the doubts you have." He replied to him: "My Master, have I ever left you for one hour and gone elsewhere? Did you not write concerning me in the Torah: 'But his servant Joshua the son of Nun departed not out of the tabernacle'?" Immediately the strength [of Moses] weakened and [Joshua] forgot three hundred laws and there arose [in his mind] seven hundred doubts [concerning laws]. Then all the Israelites rose up to kill him. The Holy One, blessed be

he, then said to him [Joshua]: "It is not possible to tell you. Go and occupy their attention in war." (Babylonian Talmud, *Temura* 16a)

In plain language: Moses already has one foot in the world to come. He asks Joshua whether he needs any last guidance on the ways of leadership before he himself takes his final journey. Joshua, seemingly having forgotten the precedent of this week's portion, shows no understanding of what happens to a society when its founding father departs. And so he answers Moses in the arrogance of youth: I know it all. Trust me. It will be fine. In his arrogance he loses sight of his own common sense and forgets what happened to Moses when Jethro departed and his authority was shaken. It's no surprise, then, that when Moses takes his final leave, Joshua's authority begins to collapse. And so, being a pale shadow of the great shining beacon, he is forced to go down the road that vapid chieftains have trod throughout the generations and deflect domestic unrest – the tribes of Israel that "rose up to kill him" – by launching a foreign war, a much easier fight to wage.

"Rise up, O Lord, and let thine enemies be scattered; and let them that hate thee flee before thee" (Num. 10:35). Now it is clear who the enemies are. At least partly they are political rivals within the camp who can be silenced or brought into an emergency unity coalition only by pointing to artificial enemies on the outside. External enemies and domestic tranquility; everything is in our hands, and "peace" be upon Israel.

The sages directed their criticism of the "national security" miracle cure against King David, too:

> A harp was hanging above David's bed. As soon as midnight arrived, a North wind came and blew upon it and it played of itself. He arose immediately and studied the Torah till the break of dawn. After the break of dawn the wise men of Israel came in to see him and said to him: Our lord, the King, Israel your people require sustenance! He said to them: Let them go out and make a living one from the other. They said to him: A handful cannot satisfy a lion, nor can a pit be filled up with its own clods. He said to them: Then go out in troops and attack [the enemy for plunder]. (Babylonian Talmud, *Berachot* 3b)

Oy vey. Today, too, war is the easiest and most readily accessible recourse of leaders who become mired in their own affairs and can't find a better way out than brute force and warfare to create an artificial unity in a divided nation.

Week 33

Shelach Lecha – Send Thou Men

Numbers 13:1–15:41

You Came to Me, to Open My Eyes: On Forgiveness

THE TALE THAT OPENS this portion is a familiar one: Before entering the land, Moses sends spies ahead to scout out the terrain. Part of their mission is to bring back information about the target, but an equally important part is to lift the spirits of the nation that has been beaten down and worn out by the troubles of slavery and the desert. The spies return with psychologically difficult perceptions. They speak ill of the land, creating a serious crisis that leads to a serious punishment – forty more years of wandering in exile, until this despairing, hopeless generation has passed.

This harsh punishment is essentially a compromise. God had wanted to impose a much harsher punishment, not only for this present display of weakness but for all their doubts and ingratitude up to this point: "How long will this people despise me? And how long will they not believe in me, for all the signs which I have wrought among them?" (Num. 14:11). And so he considers ending this chapter in his life – and theirs – and he says to Moses, "I will smite them with the pestilence, and destroy them, and will make of thee a nation greater and mightier than they" (Num. 14:12).

Moses, as he always does in these situations, stands up to God and becomes Israel's defender. With a host of arguments, partially drawn from the world of public relations and partially referring to God's essential qualities of mercy and kindness, he delivers this brilliant statement for the defense:

Shelach Lecha

> And Moses said unto the Lord: "When the Egyptians shall hear – for thou broughtest up this people in thy might from among them – they will say to the inhabitants of this land, who have heard that thou Lord art in the midst of this people; inasmuch as thou Lord art seen face to face, and thy cloud standeth over them, and thou goest before them, in a pillar of cloud by day, and in a pillar of fire by night; now if thou shalt kill this people as one man, then the nations which have heard the fame of thee will speak, saying: Because the Lord was not able to bring this people into the land which he swore unto them, therefore he hath slain them in the wilderness. And now, I pray thee, let the power of the Lord be great, according as thou hast spoken, saying: The Lord is slow to anger, and plenteous in lovingkindness, forgiving iniquity and transgression, and that will by no means clear the guilty; visiting the iniquity of the fathers upon the children, upon the third and upon the fourth generation. Pardon, I pray thee, the iniquity of this people according unto the greatness of thy lovingkindness, and according as thou hast forgiven this people, from Egypt even until now." (Num. 14:13–19)

And again, for the second time in the history of the journey through the desert, just as he did after the sin of the Golden Calf, God changes his mind: "And the Lord said: 'I have pardoned according to thy word'" (Num. 14:20).

This time, the discussion will focus on the concept of forgiveness itself. Without a doubt, forgiveness creates a new web of relations between the forgiving and the forgiven. The question, however, is this: Is forgiveness a wiping away of the past, as though it had never been, or is it a new way of containing yesterday's wounds and pains? It seems as though there are both kinds of forgiveness. Either way, what the process of forgiveness does to the forgiving side remains an open question.

If I were a container filled with good and someone were to wound me, sin against me, insult or damage me, I would take these things to heart, deep inside. Obviously, some of the good that I contain would be spilled out to make room for the anger and negativity that would seek to take its place. Thus, once I have emptied out some of the good within me to make way for the bad that has taken hold of me, once I am filled with rage and the desire to punish and avenge, my container is full once again. Where the insult has removed good, the anger has replaced it with bad.

Now comes forgiveness, which is a concession by the wounded party. All the bad impulses and negative energies have been cleared from the container, and I have an empty space once again. My container apparently is partly empty again. But only apparently, because forgiveness is not only a gift to the forgiven – it is also a great award to the forgiving. He is granted an opportunity to remove the poisonous waste that has polluted his spiritual environment and given the ability to mobilize all that is positive within him and to be filled anew with good. To be renewed. So it is with humanity. So it is with God. This is what Moses means when he says to God: "Let the power of the Lord be great" (Num. 14:17). Anger weakens you, depletes you, and so I am offering you the blessing of removing it from your midst and letting yourself be strengthened by a cleansing forgiveness.

When God says to Moses, "I have pardoned according to thy word," he is really saying two things. First, I am cleansing myself of anger. Second, I am not just cleansing myself – I am doing it thanks to you. It is not for nothing that this sentence has become the key element in Jewish prayers for forgiveness for generations. The annual period known as the Days of Penitence is not merely a plea for God to show mercy to humanity, but an extended effort to change God and help him overcome his anger. The prayer for forgiveness is a plea both for humanity and for God. This background helps to explain a wonderful Talmudic Aggadah that was set to music and is widely sung, and was a favorite of my late father's during his final days:

> It was taught: Rabbi Ishmael Ben Elisha says: I once entered into the innermost part [of the Sanctuary] to offer incense and saw Akathriel Jah, the Lord of Hosts, seated upon a high and exalted throne. He said to me: Ishmael, my son, bless me! I replied: May it be thy will that thy mercy may suppress thy anger and thy mercy may prevail over thy other attributes, so that thou mayest deal with thy children according to the attribute of mercy and mayest, on their behalf, stop

short of the limit of strict justice! And he nodded to me with his head. (Babylonian Talmud, *Berachot* 7a)

This amazing story seems carved from the very material of this portion. The high priest, Rabbi Ishmael Ben Elisha, enters "once," meaning on Yom Kippur, which is the only day on which the high priest is permitted to enter the Holy of Holies. And whom does he meet at the entrance, sitting on a high and exalted throne? None other than the Master of the Universe himself. And here the Aggadah turns tradition on its head. We might easily expect that when a person unexpectedly meets God, or any other superior authority, he would take the opportunity to make a request. But this is not what happens in our Aggadah. No, it is God who turns to the high priest and asks for his blessing. And again we are surprised: any other person who had been asked by God for a blessing would have responded with a superficial pleasantry made up of flattery and empty words. But not our high priest (who is said by some to be an imaginary character, invented for the purpose of teaching lessons). He faces God with courage, not to mention chutzpah, and offers him the wish that he overcome his ill temper and fill his vessel with good. "May it be thy will that thy mercy may prevail over thy other attributes, so that thou mayest deal with thy children according to the attribute of mercy." Ah, where can we find more priests like that one, and where is there a God like that one? Maybe everyone today is angry and filled with a negative faithful energy because they don't know how good it is to forgive.

From the Sin of the Calf to the Sin of the Spies

THE STORY OF THE SPIES has been told countless times, and always ends with the children of Israel condemned for having wept at the most inappropriate moment. The incident of the spies led to the punishment of forty years' wandering in the desert. We remember the spies and retell their tale right up to the present, consciously and even unconsciously. For example, the symbol of the Israeli Ministry of Tourism is an image of two of the spies carrying a cluster of grapes from the Valley of Eshkol (Num.

13:23). Israelis often describe their country in aggravation as a "land that eats up its inhabitants" (Num. 13:32). Indeed, the modern Hebrew term for slander, *hotza'at dibah*, comes directly from this portion, where it is traditionally translated "spread an evil report" (Num. 13:32). And there are other examples. In short, we never let ourselves forget what happened to our forebears on the eve of their first, unsuccessful entry into the land of Israel.

On the other hand, we remember little of God's mood during those difficult moments. So we will spend some time this week discussing the God of the spies' tale. After the events had unfolded – the spies returned from their grueling journey and gave their unflattering description of the Promised Land, causing the people to settle into a general depression – God leaned on Moses's shoulder and vented some complaints of his own: "And the Lord said unto Moses: 'How long will this people despise me?'" (Num. 14:11). And, as usual, he wanted to destroy them. The text reads like a thundering echo of God's response to the sin of the Golden Calf. Consider the comparisons:

The Calf:

God: "Let me alone, that my wrath may wax hot against them, and that I may consume them; and I will make of thee a great nation" (Exod. 32:10).

Moses: "Wherefore should the Egyptians speak, saying: For evil did he bring them forth, to slay them in the mountains, and to consume them" (Exod. 32:12).

Moses: "Remember Abraham, Isaac, and Israel…to whom thou didst swear" (Exod. 32:13).

"And the Lord descended in the cloud, and stood with him there, and proclaimed the name of the Lord…. 'The Lord, the Lord God, merciful and gracious'" (Exod. 34:5–6)

God: "And the Lord repented of the evil which he said he would do unto his people" (Exod. 32:14).

Shelach Lecha

The Spies:

God: "I will smite them with the pestilence, and destroy them, and will make of thee a nation greater and mightier than they" (Num. 14:12).

Moses: "When the Egyptians shall hear…they will say…the Lord was not able to bring this people into the land…therefore he hath slain them in the wilderness" (Num. 14:13–16).

Moses: "And now, I pray thee, let the power of the Lord be great, according as thou hast spoken, saying: The Lord is slow to anger, and plenteous in lovingkindness, forgiving iniquity and transgression, and that will by no means clear the guilty…. Pardon, I pray thee" (Num. 14:17–19).

God: "And the Lord said: 'I have pardoned, according to thy word'" (Num. 14:20).

Before us are two stories about the people's loss of faith. In the first instance, the impact of the revelation at Sinai was lost, and the Golden Calf was born to take its place. In the second instance, the hopes for the Promised Land collapsed, and we remained nothing more than desert nomads. In both cases, God is infuriated to the point of annihilation and Moses reminds him of two powerful claims: first, God's promise to the nation and its forefathers; second, God's public relations, namely, what will the gentiles say, particularly the Egyptians?

The outcome is also similar. Moses the man changes God's mind. But a more careful examination of the text teaches us several new things that slightly change the tone. From the record of the sin of the Calf it is not clear who is describing God's attributes – Moses or God himself. "And the Lord descended in the cloud, and stood with him there, and proclaimed the name of the Lord" (Exod. 34:6). The Lord descended, but who did the proclaiming? God or Moses? The English translation seems to take it as given that God was the proclaimer, but the Hebrew is actually ambiguous: it could be translated "and proclaimed" or "and he proclaimed" with equal ease. The truth is, we don't know the answer. In any event, Moses is thunderstruck by the sight of God's glory passing before him, and he immediately throws himself on the ground in spontaneous genuflection. In the story of the spies the event unfolds somewhat differently. It is Moses who reminds God of his attributes of mercy, and he neither bows nor prostrates himself. He is not portrayed as a loyal believer, but as a proud defender.

The dynamics that unfolded after these two breakdowns are fundamentally different from one another. The breakdown of the Calf gave way to a resurgence. The tablets were discarded and new ones were drawn up. A covenant was forged. Moses's skin was radiant, and the congregation gathered around him. That was the moment, too, when the Sabbath was given and the work of building the Tabernacle commenced, nearly everything in a positive way. After the return of the spies, on the other hand, God says: "I have pardoned, according to thy word," and yet he punishes them with forty years of wandering in the desert, a plague strikes the camp and finally the handful of rebels who try to storm the Canaanite hill country despite all the troubles meet disaster (Num. 14:44–45). This time, everything is negative.

Why are God's reactions so different? Apparently, the difference in reactions depends on the identity of the directly injured party. What do I mean? At the mountaintop, God says to Moses: "Go, get thee down; for thy people, that thou broughtest up out of the land of Egypt, have dealt corruptly" (Exod. 32:7). Thy people, not mine. This is a clear echo of the ritual cries that were heard earlier in the camp. The people had demanded of Aaron: "Up, make us a god who shall go before us; for as for this Moses, the man that brought us up out of the land of Egypt, we know not what is become of him" (Exod. 32:1). In the eyes of the people, it appears, Moses is God! The Calf, it turns out, was not made as a replacement for God, but as a substitute for Moses, and it is against him, Moses, that the protests are directed. Given that the expressions of mistrust are directed at Moses, God's servant, who is hardly his peer, God has no problem yielding on a point of honor and abandoning his plan to exterminate the Jewish people. The way he sees it, the problems are between Moses and his fellows.

Shelach Lecha

In the story of the spies, however, the mistrust is pointed directly at God. The people say explicitly, "Wherefore doth the Lord bring us unto this land…?" (Num. 14:3). God is the immediate address for the public's complaints, and he takes the matters very personally: "And the Lord said…'How long will this people despise me? And how long will they not believe in me…?'" (Num. 14:11). Now that God is insulted, Moses hurries to remind him of his words and his merciful attributes. Moses actually pleads for God's forgiveness, but God is unconvinced. His decision remains unchanged. Contrary to common belief, when he says to Moses, "I have pardoned, according to thy word," he is not saying, "I've changed my mind and I forgive once again." On the contrary, God is saying to Moses: Yes, as you say, I have forgiven in the past. That was then, in the past, during those halcyon days of the Golden Calf. And once is enough. This time I'm not giving in. Back then it was your honor at stake, but this time it's my honor and I am standing firm. And from this point on all of God's negative energy begins to emerge in the wake of the sin of the spies.

Our historic spiritual awareness has refused to absorb this narrow but distinct difference between the two stories. Somebody scrambled them beyond recognition for us. Here is the most glaring example: the Yom Kippur service begins with the moving *Kol Nidre* ceremony. At its climax we call out to God to pardon us and remind him of the historical record: "Pardon the iniquity of this people according unto the greatness of thy lovingkindness, and according as thou hast forgiven this people, from Egypt even until now." Oh really? This quote is taken directly from the story of the spies (Num. 14:19), from the point in the story at which God, as noted, is still intent on carrying out his punishment of the sinners, and plainly has *not* forgiven them.

The scripture has a certain history to it, an accumulation of residual memories from the distant past. Prayer, by contrast, is not a memory of the past but a hope for the future. The author of a prayer, therefore, can allow himself to take citations out of their context and harness them to his own needs. And so the Yom Kippur service can open with a direct quote from God, drawn from the moment of resounding insult in the story of the spies, while the holy day's other pleas for forgiveness, contained in the *Selichot* prayer that is repeated throughout the day – "Lord, thou didst teach us the thirteen attributes of thy divine providence. Remember us.... And the Lord passed before him and proclaimed in the name of the Lord" – are taken from the sin of the Calf, from the moment of God's greatest forgiveness. The words follow the internal logic of Yom Kippur. The sins between man and his neighbor and between man and God are so mixed together that they are no longer distinguishable. It seems to me that the prayer that opens the holy day with "I have pardoned, according to thy word," from the sin of the spies, essentially indicates that God has returned from the sin of the spies to the sin of the Calf. There, as noted, the central relationship is between the people and Moses – between real, living, breathing human beings – or, as the tradition puts it, "between man and his neighbor." There, and only there, can the process of the Day of Atonement begin. And in many senses, that is where it reaches its climax. For as we know well, "the Day of Atonement does not atone for sins between man and his neighbor, unless the injured party has been appeased" (Mishnah, *Yoma* 8:9).

Week 34

Korach – And They Rose Up

Numbers 16:1–18:32

Korah's Agenda

THE DISPUTE OF KORAH and his company against Moses, Aaron and their supporters is one of the important milestones in our culture of ideological-theological debate. There is not much that hasn't been said about it, and the wish that the earth would open its mouth and swallow our rivals and their supporters on the spot remains alive among us.

For many years I looked at Korah the way others see him: as arrogant, elitist, belligerent, heretical, rebellious, self-interested, egotistical and all the other labels that are almost automatically pinned on political rivals. This time, let's try to reframe our understanding of Korah's role.

The Midrash adorns the stories of Korah in bold colors. It greatly expands the simple verses expressing Korah's complaints. According to the scripture, Korah confronted Moses and Aaron with the following: "Ye take too much upon you, seeing all the congregation are holy, every one of them, and the Lord is among them; wherefore then lift ye up yourselves above the assembly of the Lord?" (Num. 16:3). But the Midrash is not content to leave it as a family dispute within the house of Levi, pitting the Levite Moses against the Levite Korah, and adds detail from its imagination: "Korah jumped up and said to Moses: 'If a tallit is entirely blue, is it exempt from having the blue string of the tzitzit?' Moses said: 'It must have tzitzit.' Korah said to him: 'If a house is full of Torah scrolls, is it exempt from having a mezuzah?' Moses said: 'It must have a mezuzah'" (Midrash Rabba, *Bamidbar* 18:3).

Korah challenges Moses with complex questions regarding the basic logic behind the commandments that have just now been given to the people – for example, the commandment of tzitzit, the ritual fringe, which was given only a few verses earlier. According to the commandment, one of the strands of the fringe must be pure blue; Korah asks if this particular strand can be dispensed with if the entire fringe is made with this special dye. And what about a house filled with Torah scrolls: Can the homeowner be exempted from affixing a mezuzah to the door? The mezuzah on the doorpost has four short passages from the Torah. Korah asks the most basic questions of law and ritual obligation: Can the general and all-inclusive nullify the specific contained within it? These questions come up frequently in later Talmudic discussions of biblical concepts. Sometimes they result in far-reaching legal conclusions, including annulling specific commandments and adapting them to the changing social and legal realities of the time and the place. Then why all the anger at Korah? What's wrong with asking legal questions, even if they can be annoying?

On the simplest level, we can say that Korah is trying, by means of the questions put in his mouth, to undermine Moses's legitimacy. He even accuses Moses, later in the Midrash, of giving interpretations that he did not receive from God but invented. In other words, the Midrash, coming thousands of years after the biblical story, is intent on defending the world of the *beit midrash*, the study house, where God has no judicial authority, where everything belongs to the student and the commentator.

Moses represents the evolutionary continuum that begins with God on Mount Sinai and ends with the sovereignty of man over the continued cultural and legal unfolding of God's Torah. Korah, on the other hand, is not ready to let humankind assume authority for religious creation. He doesn't want to let God go. He insists on paying heed only to the revealed truth. He wants every day to be the revelation at Mount Sinai. God, with a certain ironic smile, offers Korah a hint: "The heavens are the heavens of the Lord; but the earth hath he given to the children of men" (Ps. 115:16). And so this earth opens its mouth with a cynical smile and swallows him. According to this reading, the dispute is between the human Torah and the divine. Between the single moment of revelation, with the permanent

Korah

human responsibility that derives from it, and demand for permanent revelation that never happens in practice and leaves humanity in a state of corrupting passivity and anticipation.

On another level, I would suggest that Korah – especially as he is depicted in the Aggadah and Midrash – understood that the new commandments that had been given to the people created a normative ethical structure the likes of which had never before existed. He wasn't necessarily arguing with the commandments as such; rather, he was asking a question that was very much before its time: How long? Will these commandments obligate us forever, or will there come a time when these commandments will in whole or in part be annulled?

Moses is appalled. He understands that if he brings a system of government down from heaven only to have someone inquire about the expiration date in the very first days, then the clock is ticking from day one toward the end of the affair. Korah's inquiring mouth may be shut up within the much larger mouth of the earth, but Korah's question will never die. His seductive anarchism, which demands time limits on laws, endures in the tradition in a variety of forms.

To give one example, the Talmud records: "Rab Joseph said: This suggests that the commandments will be abolished in the future" (Babylonian Talmud, *Niddah* 61b). Out of this opaque declaration, which relates to a different matter entirely, arise whole mountains of commentary, analyses and positions probing the limits of Korah's initial question. When will this future arrive? Does this refer to the death of an individual, which in any event cancels all of his obligations and commandments, or is it a reference to some utopian human future when reality will be so different from what we know today that we will no longer need the superstructures of permitted and forbidden, the value systems of human society? For example, in the following saying: "The years draw nigh, when thou shalt say: 'I have no pleasure in them' [Eccl. 12:1] – This refers to the Messianic era, wherein there is neither merit nor guilt" (Babylonian Talmud, *Sabbath* 151b).

Moses was able to absorb the contemporary prophesies of Eldad and Medad, but he had a hard time accepting Korah's prophesy of the future. Eldad and Medad debated current events with Moses, while Korah debated matters of essence. Eldad and Medad became a footnote in Jewish history, while Korah and his company, who died on the spot, remain a permanent, living alternative, and so the scripture says: "The sons of Korah died not" (Num. 26:11). Could that be the reason that on Rosh Hashanah, the most universalist of Jewish holidays, the birthday of the world, we take a moment before the sounding of the Shofar to sing the Psalm that begins, "For the Leader; a Psalm for the sons of Korah"? This is one of the most universal songs in all of Hebrew literature, a song about the days to come when all peoples will live in peace and kindness and God will sit on his throne of glory:

> For the Leader; a Psalm for the sons of Korah.
>
> O clap your hands, all ye peoples; shout unto God with the voice of triumph.
>
> For the Lord is most high, awful; a great King over all the earth.
>
> He subdueth peoples under us, and nations under our feet.
>
> He chooseth our inheritance for us, the pride of Jacob whom he loveth. Selah
>
> God is gone up amidst shouting, the Lord amidst the sound of the horn.
>
> Sing praises to God, sing praises; sing praises unto our King, sing praises.
>
> For God is the King of all the earth; sing ye praises in a skilful song.
>
> God reigneth over the nations; God sitteth upon his holy throne.
>
> The princes of the peoples are gathered together, the people of the God of Abraham;
>
> For unto God belong the shields of the earth; he is greatly exalted.
>
> (Ps. 47:1–9)

What Is Holiness?

THE STORY OF KORAH'S DISPUTE with Moses and Aaron was told in its day as a bitter, hard-fought struggle for leadership of the children of Israel. Today, in retrospect, the story tells us much more. It should be remembered that in those times, leadership was derived from the inspiration and support of God. Contrast this with national leadership in our own time, which draws its fleeting authority from the power of mortal voters. The generation of the dispute lived with the revelation and continuing presence of God in the midst of its camp. God, having no form or body, was nonetheless the sole electoral body choosing Israel's leadership. Therefore, the dispute between Korah and his company and Moses and Aaron was not merely a dispute over who would lead the people, but whose side was God on, who had his support. It was a struggle over God and his holiness, over the nation and its soul.

Korah assembled a vast company of his generation's embittered leaders and masses of supporters. He stood up to Moses and Aaron and confronted them with the most convincing of claims: "All the congregation are holy, every one of them, and the Lord is among them; wherefore then lift ye up yourselves above the assembly of the Lord?" (Num. 16:3). It is an egalitarian claim, and seemingly democratic. Everyone has equal standing before God. We are all citizens of the kingdom of priests, all children of the holy nation. Why you, the sons of Amram, and not me, Korah, the son of Izhar, the son of Kohath, the son of Levi?

At first glance it seems like a procedural question about the integrity of the electoral system. But Moses is dumbstruck: "And when Moses heard it, he fell upon his face" (Num. 16:4). Moses fell flat, and the system almost came down with him. Afterward the earth opened its mouth and did Moses's talking for him – it simply swallowed up most of the opposition. What was the argument about? The Mishnah, in the tractate known as the "Ethics of the Fathers," calls it a "dispute which is not for the sake of heaven" and "will not ultimately endure" (Mishnah, *Avot* 5:20). The question before us, then, is what was Korah's real position, and why did Moses fall on his face when he heard it?

Korah's claim poses an alternative theology to that of Moses. Korah begins with the assumption that there is an automatic holiness that can be bestowed on an entire population, that "all the congregation are holy." But automatic holiness effectively relieves the believer of responsibility for real life. If it is true that "all are holy," then every one of the children of Israel is holy by birth, even the most debased and evil-minded among them, with no review or control. For Korah, God's choice of the Jewish people is an immutable given that lifts us above all other peoples, friend or foe. Korah's holiness is essentially a Jewish racial holiness: "All the congregation are holy."

Now it's clear why Moses goes into shock. This is the exact opposite of what he stands for. Moses's response is given elsewhere in the Torah, in the Book of Leviticus, in *Parashat Kedoshim*, in words that sound similar but are used entirely differently: "Speak unto all the congregation of the children of Israel, and say unto them: Ye shall be holy; for I the Lord your God am holy" (Lev. 19:2). This is followed by an interesting elaboration of basic laws that reflect the spirit of the Ten Commandments. The commandments that appear there form the cornerstone of biblical social justice, such as honoring one's parents, and just and ethical dealings with the stranger and outsider. They complete the equation of the Bible's commandments of love: "And thou shalt love the Lord thy God" (Deut. 6:5), "Thou shalt love thy neighbor as thyself" (Lev. 19:18) and "The stranger that sojourneth with you shall be unto you as the home-born among you, and thou shalt love him as thyself" (Lev. 19:34). Moses's holiness is a holiness of perpetual, Sisyphean striving to repair oneself and improve the world. It is a holiness that is acquired, not inbred. It is something that is never guaranteed. It requires constant self-criticism to prevent the believer from defiling the name of God the creator of the universe in whose image we were created.

I began thinking about the differences between Moses's holiness and Korah's quite by coincidence. I was headed for an overseas trip one morning when I heard the news on the radio that Saul Bellow, one of my favorite authors, had died. On the spur of the moment I decided to take one of his books with me to re-read on the plane. I bent down to reach the bottom shelf where I keep the old books I've finished reading, shoved a book into my briefcase and headed for the airport. Once the plane took off I leaned back and prepared to begin my private memorial ceremony for the great Jewish author, only to discover that I had taken the wrong book. Instead of Saul Bellow I had grabbed a volume by Heinrich Boell, the German Nobel laureate novelist and human rights advocate. In Hebrew the two names, Boell and Bellow, look almost the same.

The book, *A Soldier's Legacy*, had been sitting on my shelf unread for years, apparently waiting for its moment. It is a brief novella about a German soldier with a sense of morality, Lieutenant Schelling, and his relationship with his corrupt commander during and after World War II. For a while I simply stared at the book's cover, disappointed that it wasn't Bellow. Then something about the cover art caught my eye. It was a picture of a Wehrmacht soldier with a broad leather belt bisecting his torso, in the middle of which was a metal buckle with something written on it. I asked my seatmate, a charming, older Jewish woman, a Holocaust survivor from Miami, to lend me the magnifying glass she was using to read the newspaper. The words on the buckle said "*Gott mit uns*" – "God with us."

Apparently the German troops marched into battle with some sort of god in their midst. The connection between the "God with us" of the jackbooted soldiers of the self-appointed master race and the "all the congregation are holy and the Lord is among them" of Korah's automatically chosen people with its unearned, unexamined spiritual elevation sudden became clear to me, and I understood what Korah meant by holiness. Is this what the biblical narrator meant in the passage later on in Numbers that said "the sons of Korah died not"? Apparently there are individuals, communities and whole nations that have an emotional need to feel this sense of innate superiority, shorn of any responsibility. It stretches from the dawn of humanity right up to our time. My own Judaism is an eternal battle against racism, religious triumphalism and the self-appointed messengers of God who convince themselves that God is exclusively on their side. Yes, Korah's sons did not die. Some lived to wear Nazi uniforms. Some still wear the star of David.

Korah's holiness is endlessly dangerous. It's easy to understand the distinction many people draw between God, to whom everything is permitted, and mortals like us who live in a world of restrictions and prohibitions. Korahism stands in contrast to this clear division between human and divine. It has no limits. Everything and everyone is holy, everything is godly and everything is permitted. Without limitation or control. Without fear of sin or love of humanity.

It's important to remember that everything about God is holy and everything about humanity is earthbound – and in need of constant oversight. The human domain may not operate under the same calculations as God. Ours is a dominion that must do the right thing here and now, even when God in heaven is signaling us that he isn't happy with our decisions. "We do not obey the still, small voice!" (Babylonian Talmud, *Bava Metzia* 59b). Any attempt to expand the sphere of God beyond his borders, to impose him on a secular institution such as the state, amounts to contempt for the Eternal and can only end in spiritual catastrophe. When a state and society do not submit to scrutiny, when the acts of government are made to seem like commandments from on high, when statecraft and politics hide behind the skirts of religious law and claim to be the expression of divine will – then they are truly a mortal threat, as we have seen more than once in our own past and others' as well.

The entire history of Jewish religious thought is marked by a struggle between the moderating influence of law and the exclusivist sense of chosenness that seeks to burst its bonds in every generation on the claim of automatic holiness. From the ancient scriptures to the latest strains of Jewish messianism, the doctrine of Jewish supremacy has built itself many platforms, and we need to beware of all of them, lest the earth open up its mouth and tell us what it thinks of us.

Week 35

Chukkat – This Is the Statute

Numbers 19:1–22:1

To Be a Refugee

MY LATE FATHER loved this week's portion more than any other Jewish text. He saw in it the eternal dialogue between the past and the future. As a child I never understood the structure of biblical time. When Papa used to teach me on Saturday afternoon, he would say, "Rashi had a hard time last week," and I couldn't understand. How could Rashi, who lived and died a thousand years ago, have a bad time last week? When was this last week, anyway? Was it really last week? Or is there some other sort of week that's different from anything I understand about time? And what about this fateful roundabout that brings poor little Joseph back every year on the same Saturday before Chanukah to fall into the same trap that Potiphar's wife lays for him? It wouldn't leave me alone.

This week's portion that's coming around again has been more important to me than ever in the past few years as a basis for a forward-looking national strategy in the here and now, a foundation and roof beam for a moral, non-cynical foreign policy. It brings together past and present, the classic and the contemporary, in an astonishing harmony. Let's let the verses speak for themselves, like this morning's headlines:

> And Moses sent messengers from Kadesh unto the king of Edom: "Thus saith thy brother Israel: Thou knowest all the travail that hath befallen us; how our fathers went down into Egypt, and we dwelt in Egypt a long time; and the Egyptians dealt ill with us, and our fathers; and when we cried unto the Lord, he heard our voice, and

> sent an angel, and brought us forth out of Egypt; and, behold, we are in Kadesh, a city in the uttermost of thy border. Let us pass, I pray thee, through thy land; we will not pass through field or through vineyard, neither will we drink of the water of the wells; we will go along the king's highway, we will not turn aside to the right hand nor to the left, until we have passed thy border."
>
> And Edom said unto him: "Thou shalt not pass through me, lest I come out with the sword against thee." And the children of Israel said unto him: "We will go up by the highway; and if we drink of thy water, I and my cattle, then will I give the price thereof; let me only pass through on my feet; there is no hurt." And he said: "Thou shalt not pass through." And Edom came out against him with much people, and with a strong hand. Thus Edom refused to give Israel passage through his border; wherefore Israel turned away from him. And they journeyed from Kadesh; and the children of Israel, even the whole congregation, came unto Mount Hor. (Num. 20:14–22)

The children of Israel are road-weary. They've been through trauma, oppression, plagues, punishments and exhausting civil strife. They're more than ready to reach the Promised Land. All that remains is to pass through this one place and on to the next. But other peoples stand in their way, strong and well established as kingdoms in their own lands. They have their own interests, fears, policies and borders, and they will not open their gates lightly. And so the children of Israel, the refugees from the desert, do what every refugee would do: they beg, "Please, let us pass." And the states do what states do: they refuse. They have serious security concerns, as noted. Their security agencies are worried about the possible risk to their regime's stability. That was what Rahab the harlot explained to the two spies of Joshua whom she hid from the king's agents in Jericho before the famous assault:

> And she said unto the men: "I know that the Lord hath given you the land, and that your terror is fallen upon us, and that all the inhabitants of the land melt away before you. For we have heard how the Lord dried up the water of the Red Sea before you, when

Chukkat

> ye came out of Egypt; and what ye did unto the two kings of the Amorites, that were beyond the Jordan, unto Sihon and to Og, whom ye utterly destroyed. And as soon as we had heard it, our hearts did melt, neither did there remain any more spirit in any man, because of you; for the Lord your God, he is God in heaven above, and on earth beneath." (Josh. 2:9–11)

Facing fears of this magnitude, there isn't a security chief in the world who would take a risk of a purely moral or humanitarian nature, no matter how small.

The attempts to cross into the Promised Land through the territories of neighboring peoples and kingdoms continued ceaselessly, and fruitlessly. All the refugees' pleas and promises of peace came up empty. The war that was forbidden them was the only solution to the hope and fury of the refugees in search of a homeland:

> And Israel sent messengers unto Sihon king of the Amorites, saying: "Let me pass through thy land; we will not turn aside into field, or into vineyard; we will not drink of the water of the wells; we will go by the king's highway, until we have passed thy border." And Sihon would not suffer Israel to pass through his border; but Sihon gathered all his people together, and went out against Israel into the wilderness, and came to Jahaz; and he fought against Israel. (Num. 21:21–23)

The Torah tells the story briefly, as a historical event with military dimensions. The Book of Judges, by contrast, broadens the story from a simple military encounter to a religious war between our God and other peoples' gods, between the Lord of Hosts and the god Chemosh. The expanded narrative is the work of Jephthah the Gileadite, the "mighty man of valor" who came to liberate the transjordanian tribes from the yoke of their enemies. He begins by laying out the historical background:

> Thus saith Jephthah: Israel took not away the land of Moab, nor the land of the children of Ammon. But when they came up from Egypt, and Israel walked through the wilderness unto the Red Sea, and

> came to Kadesh; then Israel sent messengers unto the king of Edom, saying: Let me, I pray thee, pass through thy land; but the king of Edom hearkened not. And in like manner he sent unto the king of Moab; but he would not; and Israel abode in Kadesh. Then he walked through the wilderness, and compassed the land of Edom, and the land of Moab, and came by the east side of the land of Moab, and they pitched on the other side of the Arnon; but they came not within the border of Moab, for the Arnon was the border of Moab. And Israel sent messengers unto Sihon king of the Amorites, the king of Heshbon; and Israel said unto him: Let us pass, we pray thee, through thy land unto my place. But Sihon trusted not Israel to pass through his border; but Sihon gathered all his people together, and pitched in Jahaz, and fought against Israel. (Judg. 11:15–20)

Then comes the theological rendering, upgrading the confrontation into a full-scale religious war:

> And the Lord, the God of Israel, delivered Sihon and all his people into the hand of Israel, and they smote them; so Israel possessed all the land of the Amorites, the inhabitants of that country. And they possessed all the border of the Amorites, from the Arnon even unto the Jabbok, and from the wilderness even unto the Jordan. So now the Lord, the God of Israel, hath dispossessed the Amorites from before his people Israel, and shouldest thou possess them? Wilt not thou possess that which Chemosh thy god giveth thee to possess? So whomsoever the Lord our God hath dispossessed from before us, them will we possess. (Judg. 11:21–24)

The biblical narrative didn't rest with the event itself, but turned it into a profound historical lesson, albeit a rather forgotten and neglected one. In the Book of Deuteronomy, in *Parashat Ki Tetzeh*, Moses expounds his doctrine of war (Deut. 21:10–14; 23:10–15; 25:17–19), during which he commands Joshua regarding how to fight and against whom, whom to shun for all time and whom not. Amazingly, the two greatest enemies of Israel during its formative years, Egypt and Edom, are not on the blacklist.

Here is what Moses says of them: "Thou shalt not abhor an Edomite, for he is thy brother; thou shalt not abhor an Egyptian, because thou wast a stranger in his land" (Deut. 23:8). This is a huge challenge to a generation of war.

Historical forgiveness is not the same as immediate forgiveness. Today, five hundred years after the fact, we have no problem forgiving Spain for the expulsion of the Jews in 1492, and we have long since forgotten the massacre of the English Jews at the Tower of York during the Crusades. Most of us have even managed to forgive Germany for the most part. But our immediate conflict with our Palestinian neighbors is much more difficult. And it is precisely regarding them, the immediate enemies, still fresh in the memory, that Moses rules: "Thou shalt not abhor."

This is a commandment that demands the utmost national noblesse, an ability to live by almost utopian values, an aspiration to live the sort of patriotism that is directed toward the perfect and ideal. Applying the norms of personal morality to the behavior of the collective. What was hateful to you when we were oppressed and downtrodden, we must not turn into a policy of intransigence and evil, even in the face of yesterday's oppressors or today's enemies. I pray almost every day that the huge moral challenge that Moses left behind will find its way into the hearts of all those people who are beating on our doors these days, trying to escape Gaza, Darfur or Ukraine but turned back on security, religious or psychological grounds. I hope they and their descendants do not abhor us for generations to come.

Death and Mourning, Life and Reality

DEATH ACCOMPANIES US like a shadow throughout our lives. Shadows have only length and width; they have no depth, nor any other dimension. Only the shadow of death has the extra dimension, time. Death is the only shadow that is always with us. Because it so present, human culture has developed a variety of ways of coping with it and incorporating it into our lives. Most of us repress the fact of its existence. We refuse to acknowledge that it is waiting patiently for us to turn a corner in our lives. Others turn death into an obsession. One group tries to push death out of life entirely; the other group makes life revolve around death. Each approach spawns a fundamentally different sort of culture.

The culture of "life first" sees this world as the principal arena. Here is the only reality we know. Here is where our duty lies. We need this world to be good and properly ordered. We are responsible for it in many ways. Here we receive our reward and our punishment. According to this culture, the degree of our success in this world depends on us. Life is our challenge, and perhaps our salvation. True, death sometimes comes for a visit. But even then, we accept it. We accept it with sadness, but we extend it the hospitality due to just such an uninvited guest. We perform the rituals of mourning, take our leave from the deceased who has been taken from us and carry on with our lives. This sort of human sensibility sees the person and life itself as holy. This is the Judaism of the Torah of life and the sanctity of life.

In contrast to this, the culture of death lives life in different cycles. Its members often see the dead as more important than the living, as their source of inspiration and authority. They find the center of their being in those who were and are no longer, and in worlds located somewhere beyond the world we know. You can find them prostrated across the graves of saints, believing in the power of the dead to bless the living. They will bring you candles from someone's grave to promote fertility, as though the dead person were a participant in the act of procreation, and holy water from someone's memorial as a talisman of good health and long life. They will cast lots and appeal to the dead and believe that a thoroughly dead rabbi is a living messiah. They will see death as a tool for bringing a better world, and for that reason they will happily commit suicide in some religions, joyously commit murder in other faiths and sometimes – as in Judaism – see this world as only a dim corridor to the life of plenty in the world to come. For all these sorts, the world beyond is the important world, the source of the authority that binds them. The dead who populate that world, together with the divinity and its angels said to dwell there permanently, are more important to them than life and its holiness here on earth.

This week's portion places an important point of distinction between the two. The portion has a clearly expressed position in regard to the dispiriting complex of death, of who goes with it and who remains among us. The beginning of the portion describes the distinctive biblical process by which the ash of the red heifer is created, providing the only cure for the greatest of all biblical impurities, the impurity of the dead. The commandment of the red heifer has a special status in biblical legislation, because it alone earns the opaque definition: "This is the statute of the Torah law" (Num. 19:2). And here is the matter of the red heifer: "That they bring thee a red heifer, faultless, wherein is no blemish, and upon which never came yoke. And ye shall give her unto Eleazar the priest… and she shall be slain…and the heifer shall be burnt…her skin, and her flesh, and her blood, with her dung, shall be burnt" (Num. 19:2–5). To complete the recipe, several more elements are required: "The priest shall take cedar-wood, and hyssop, and scarlet, and cast it into the midst of the burning of the heifer" (Num. 19:6).

And the purpose of this strange process? To cleanse and purify a person who has been made ritually unclean by contact with the dead: "And for the unclean they shall take of the ashes of the burning of the purification from sin…. And the clean person shall sprinkle upon the unclean…he shall purify him; and he…shall be clean at even" (Num. 19:17–19). The ceremony and overall process are lengthy, complex and quite mysterious. Still, the larger lesson is clear. The ethical roots of the Jewish tradition draw a clear line between the ritually pure and impure. The impure that remains uncleansed and impure can receive only one verdict: "That soul shall be cut off from the midst of the assembly" (Num. 19:20).

It's interesting that despite the long history of intellectual development within Judaism, our predecessors never compromised on the absolute impurity of the dead body. The dead is the "father of fathers," the archetype of all categories of impurity. The biblical Instructor and the readers of all subsequent generations understood and internalized the sharp dividing line between the living and the dead as something far more substantial than a mere physiological condition. Sages throughout the generations tried by means of ceremonies and prohibitions to focus us on this world and not the world to come – to live life, as the prayer says: "A long life, a life of goodness, a life of blessing…a life of vigor and liveliness." In brief, to live life in the here and now.

The Mishnah, in Tractate *Yadayim*, relates in a fascinating way to the connection between impurity and life. There is a fear that the living will make use of the organs of the dead, as a way of expressing their longing for their dear departed. For that reason, the Mishnah specifies: "Proportionate to the love for them, so is their uncleanness, so that nobody should make spoons out of the bones of his father or mother" (Mishnah, *Yadayim* 4:6). The Mishnah fears that a person might make something out of the mummified or stuffed remains of a parent so as never to have to take leave of them. There is also a broad hint here of the Egyptian rituals of death and burial. Jacob, we recall, demands an oath of Joseph that he "bury me not, I pray thee, in Egypt. But when I sleep with my fathers, thou shalt carry me out of Egypt, and bury me in their burying-place" (Gen. 47:29–30). Rashi amplifies this by quoting from the Midrash: "So that the Egyptians do not make me into an idol" (Rashi on Gen. 47:29). Joseph, carrying on the spirit of his father's will, demands the same thing of his brothers and relatives: "God will surely remember you, and ye shall carry up my bones from hence" (Gen. 50:25). And with the Exodus from Egypt several hundred years later, came the fulfillment of the promise: "And Moses took the bones of Joseph with him; for he had straitly sworn the children of Israel, saying: 'God will surely remember you; and ye shall carry up my bones away hence with you'" (Exod. 13:19).

But let's get back to our portion. It's worth reading the words of Rabbi Hezekiah Ben Manoah, known as the "Hizkuni" after the title of his major work, one of the most interesting commentators in the rich rabbinic world of medieval France. He combines the two poles, mummification of parents and the worship of the dead, and explains as follows: "The Torah ruled more strictly regarding the uncleanness of human remains than any other form of uncleanness, so that people would not linger among the dead because of their love for them and become overwhelmed with grief. Or so that they would not begin appealing to the dead and to ghosts" (Hizkuni on Num. 19:16). Echoing the words of the Mishnah, he continues: "Furthermore, out of respect for God's creatures, the Text was strict regarding their uncleanness, so that their skin would not be used to make wineskins or rugs, nor their bones to make hand-tools, for this would be contemptuous of God's creatures" (Hizkuni on Num. 19:16).

In this context, we should add a few words about the drabness of Jewish funeral culture. Observers are often struck by the contrast between the ornateness, even opulence that characterizes non-Jewish and especially Christian funerals and the austere plainness of their Jewish counterpart. Whatever it might seem, this is not a product of helplessness or disregard. It represents a profound, deliberate principle. The cult of death is not part of our way of life. We maintain simple funerals, modest cemeteries, the necessary farewell and nothing more. Let the dead rest so that the living can carry on with life.

Week 36

Balak – Balak Saw

Numbers 22:2–25:9

What Does Moses Have To Do With Balaam?

WHAT DOES JEWISH collective memory have against Balaam? In the end Balaam was a gentile, not a member of the convenant of the Jewish people. His occupation was recorded as "prophet," and he was hired by a local king, Balak of Moab, to transmit messages from a higher authority against the latest enemy on the scene. As a professional prophet, Balaam testified fairly and honestly before the king and his messengers as to his weaknesses and shortcomings: "If Balak would give me his house full of silver and gold, I cannot go beyond the word of the Lord my God, to do any thing, small or great. Now therefore, I pray you, tarry ye also here this night, that I may know what the Lord will speak unto me more" (Num. 22:18–19).

Negotiations between King Balak, the prophet Balaam, God and various intermediaries go through several rounds before agreement is reached: "And God came unto Balaam at night, and said unto him: 'If the men are come to call thee, rise up, go with them; but only the word which I speak unto thee, that shalt thou do.' And Balaam rose up in the morning, and saddled his ass, and went with the princes of Moab" (Num. 22:20–21). That is, it was agreed that Balaam would go with the messengers of the king, but he would prophesy only what he was instructed by the almighty God. In fact, unbeknownst to the king – though we readers are in on the secret – God has already instructed Balaam *not* to employ a curse: "Thou shalt not curse the people; for they are blessed" (Num. 22:12). Balaam is portrayed, to all appearances, as an exemplary prophet, a messenger who obeys his instructions and follows orders. Presented with an official, royal work order, he didn't give a rushed or hasty answer. He turned to God and asked permission to fulfill the order, and permission was given. So why is God angry? Why does he send an angel to waylay him, sword in hand?

Why does the story continue in this manner?

> And God's anger was kindled because he went; and the angel of the Lord placed himself in the way for an adversary against him. Now he was riding upon his ass, and his two servants were with him. And the ass saw the angel of the Lord standing in the way, with his sword drawn in his hand; and the ass turned aside out of the way, and went into the field; and Balaam smote the ass, to turn her into the way. Then the angel of the Lord stood in a hollow way between the vineyards, a fence being on this side, and a fence on that side. (Num. 22:22–24)

It's no wonder that after all this, Balaam gets angry and strikes his ass. He doesn't understand what God wants from him. But he's unable to vent his frustration on God or the angel, so he behaves like frustrated people in every time and place and takes his anger out on whoever is beneath him – in this case, the poor ass.

Who is Balaam? Balaam is one of the most important prophets in the Bible. Despite not being one of the chosen people, his prophetic qualities rise in certain respects above those of Moses, the lord of all our prophets. Moses speaks with God face to face, like one neighbor to another. Balaam, on the other hand, remains outside this friendly circle, having made his own way to the worlds of knowledge and understanding of the Master of the Universe. He "heareth the words of God, and knoweth the knowledge of the Most High" (Num. 24:16). I can't recall another figure in all our sources of whom it was said that he knows "the knowledge of the Most High." This is the highest of all possible rungs, and hence the importance of the gentile prophet Balaam. And this greatness is what begs a comparison with the greatest prophet of Israel, Moses.

As the popular Israeli songwriter Yaakov Rothblit famously wrote, "The things you see from there, you can't see from here." Things that Moses couldn't see from the midst of the Hebrew encampment, Balaam was able to see and envision "from the top of the rocks…and from the hills" (Num. 23:9) outside the camp. On the other hand, there were things Balaam couldn't make out from his high perch that Moses saw clearly from up close. Moses bore the yoke of leadership every day, taking on all the troubles and quarrels of his flock. Regardless of Jethro's advice, Moses involved himself in every passing detail and couldn't always focus on grander visions. As much as Moses and his spirit could be snared in the micro world of daily life, Balaam was free from the yoke and burdens of leadership, free to concentrate on the macro, to look at the big picture. No wonder Moses so often saw the dark side while his fellow prophet Balaam had visions of the inner soul of that nation toward which King Balak had pointed him.

What follows is based entirely on a simple, literary reading of the biblical text and on my own identification as a reader with the great characters.

Moses, the former prince of Egypt, had been trying for forty years to establish a kingdom of his own, an alternative to the Egyptian monarchy that had never been his. He had far-reaching visions and a vast collection of unfulfilled dreams. He dreamt of a finer God, the likes of which had never been seen. He envisioned an astonishing faith and legal system containing original commandments and covenants between the creator of the universe and his creations. For all that, the management of day-to-day reality had sullied the dream with gritty dust of real life.

The very first thing out of Moses's mouth when God first assigned him his mission at the burning bush, "but they will not believe me, nor hearken unto my voice" (Exod. 4:1), was a stunning intuition that would become the central motif in Moses's career over the next forty years. With every new summit that he ascended, the people managed to pull him down to some new pit of doubt. He was climbing mountaintops to talk with his "friend" the Lord and they were frolicking below with their pathetic Calf. He was leading them to the ancient land of their fathers and they were fantasizing about Egypt and its fleshpots. He was building a careful strategy for conquest and they were rushing impetuously up the next mountainside. For Moses, life in the desert was apparently under constant tension between his far-seeing visions and the daily pettiness of his demanding flock. That's why Moses so often expressed the frustrations of a suffering observer from within, while Balaam could exult with the soaring words of an outside admirer.

Under the circumstances, we have to assume that Moses stored up a good number of frustrations that sometimes came to the verge of exploding. Of course, Moses had monumental achievements: the Exodus from Egypt, the revelation at Mount Sinai, the posthumous conquest of the land and the timelessness of the Torah. And yet, the biblical narrative is filled with his despairing, frustrating helplessness. This painful background only highlights the gap between Moses and Balaam. Even more galling is the fact that Balaam's few verses have bequeathed so many classic turns of phrase to Hebrew culture and tradition: "A people that dwelleth apart" (Num. 23:9); "How goodly are thy tents, O Jacob" (Num. 24:5) – this is the first verse that the observant Jew recites in the daily morning prayers, straight out of the words of the "wicked" Balaam; "A star shall step forth out of Jacob" (Num. 24:17); "Let me die the death of the righteous" (Num. 23:10); and even the phrase "the end of days" (Num. 24:14) comes from Balaam. It seems to me (though I haven't counted) that Balaam's contribution to the poetic language of Hebrew and Jewish culture is larger than that of Moses himself.

Moses prophesies frequently in tones of rage, rebuke, preaching and warning, while Balaam prophesies in a blessing that comes in the place of a curse. The difference in prophetic styles of Balaam and Moses is so great that it's hard to believe that Moses, who by tradition wrote the whole Torah, actually wrote those very positive words of Balaam's. The sages, too, were troubled by the stylistic difference. They were sensitive to every fine nuance and variation in tone; they were sensitive to Moses's frustration, and they rushed to his defense:

> The rebukes deserved to be said by Balaam, and the blessings by Moses. But if Balaam had rebuked them, Israel would have said:

"We are rebuked by one who hates us." And if Moses had blessed them, the nations of the world would have said: "They are blessed by one who loves them." The Holy One, blessed be he, said: "Let Moses, who loves them, rebuke them, and let Balaam, who hates them, bless them, so that the blessings and rebukes will be clear to Israel." (Midrash Rabba [Vilna], *Devarim*, chapter 1, page 5)

Therefore, because of the vast stylistic and cognitive gaps, they saw a need to emphasize explicitly: "Moses wrote his book and the portion of Balaam" (Babylonian Talmud, *Bava Batra* 14b), lest critics come and challenge the unity of the Torah of Moses.

Commentators for generations have been pondering these words: "Moses wrote his book and the portion of Balaam." The late Yeshayahu Leibovitz summed them all up when he wrote:

In any event, this opaque statement is meant to say that the portion of Balaam contains something unusual, which differs from everything that is said in the Torah of Moses and does not constitute an integral part of it…and indeed in the later tradition Balaam is presented as a prophet at a very high level…and a sort of counterweight to Moses. (Yeshayahu Leibovitz, *Seven Years of Conversations on the Portion of the Week* [Hebrew, translated by JJG], [Jerusalem: Hemed, 2006], 714)

Leibovitz went quite far, and now it's time to go one more step forward. "Moses wrote his book and the portion of Balaam," not because they counterbalance each other but because Moses and Balaam are essentially two aspects of the same character. Balaam is Moses's pseudonym. Everything that Moses wanted to say to his people but could not, because it was not his style, because they hadn't earned it, because the time hadn't come, he said to them via Balaam. Balaam is the fictional character through whom Moses transmits his true vision.

Not to prove this, but simply to show its plausibility, let us pay attention to the astonishing similarity in the style of their departures. Twice in his book, the Torah, Moses writes words of farewell. The first time the words are of the aged Jacob bidding farewell to his sons: "And Jacob called unto his sons, and said: 'Gather yourselves together, that I may tell you that which shall befall you in the end of days'" (Gen. 49:1). The expression "in the end of days" does not appear frequently. And yet, remarkably, when Moses takes his own leave from the children of Israel, in his final days, when he no longer has any need or reason for masques or camouflage, he returns to a pattern very similar to that of the aged Jacob. Jacob blessed the tribes and Moses blessed their descendants; both blessings were laced with criticism.

How did Moses summon the people to his farewell? "Assemble unto me all the elders of your tribes…that I may speak these words in their ears.… For I know that after my death ye will in any wise deal corruptly… and evil will befall you in the end of days" (Deut. 39:28–29). The words are typical of their author. And here, in this week's portion, these unusual words appear once again. When Balaam takes his leave of King Balak, he says, "And now, behold, I go unto my people; come, and I will announce to thee what this people shall do to thy people in the end of days" (Num. 24:14). The words are identical, because the writer is the same writer – the prophet Balaam is the prophet Moses.

Week 37

Pinchas – Phinehas the Zealot

Numbers 25:10–30:1

The Covenant of Peace

*E*VEN THOUGH THE TALES of the conquest of the land might seem to the modern mind like nothing more than ancient history to be consigned to the archives of the forgotten past, an examination of the ethical aspects of those events points toward certain dilemmas that remain current in our own time. Let's begin with a simple story and its accompanying commandment:

> And the Lord spoke unto Moses, saying: "Harass the Midianites, and smite them; for they harass you, by their wiles wherewith they have beguiled you in the matter of Peor, and in the matter of Cozbi, the daughter of the prince of Midian, their sister, who was slain on the day of the plague in the matter of Peor." (Num. 25:16–18)

The desert wanderings had brought the tribes into a series of powerful confrontations with other faiths and religions. In one of their stops the Israelites made camp at a place called Shittim, which apparently was near the center of the sexual-religious cult worship of a Moabite god known as the Baal of Peor. As related in the final passage of last week's portion, *Parashat Balak*, the religious orgies at the temple of Peor attracted some of the Israelite men. The most prominent was a prince of the tribe of Simeon, Zimri Ben Salu, who became involved with a Midianite woman named Cozbi.

The Lord of hosts reacted with great historic anger. Not only because of the debased fornication, but because of the theological betrayal, the straying from the God of Israel to the Baal of Peor. For this and other reasons, God gives Moses a harsh command: "And the Lord spoke unto Moses, saying: 'Harass the Midianites, and smite them; for they harass you'" (Num. 25:16–18). Moses, who is married to a Midianite woman, whose sons are by descent at least half Midianite, whose father-in-law was the high priest of the Midianites and was devoted to their faith and rituals, is commanded in essence to launch a blatant campaign of ethnic cleansing and extermination against the Midianite people. Does the Midianite precedent turn at this moment into the model for all our future relations with enemy peoples? Does this model truly impose a prohibition on speaking with the Midianites, or the Spanish, the Crusaders, the Cossacks, the Germans or the Iranians? Or are there keys to open the locked siege doors? There are indeed such keys. And one of them is found in this week's portion.

How? The opening of the portion celebrates Phinehas, who killed the fornicating prince and his Midianite bed-partner. God testifies with satisfaction about him: "Phinehas, the son of Eleazar, the son of Aaron the priest, hath turned my wrath away from the children of Israel, in that he was very jealous for my sake among them, so that I consumed not the children of Israel in my jealousy" (Num. 25:11). In return, God grants him a very strange gift: "Wherefore I say: Behold, I give unto him my covenant of peace" (Num. 25:12). Not only to him, but to all those who follow him forever: "And it shall be unto him, and to his seed after him, the covenant of an everlasting priesthood" (Num. 25:13).

The range of interpretations of this covenant of peace is extremely broad. There are those who interpret God's covenant as a defense treaty. Don't worry about the anger of the tribe of Simeon, the creator of the universe says to him, nor about the blood vengeance of the Midianite family, because I am beside you. Others offer professional explanations, according to which he is worried about his priesthood, because a priest who has spilled blood is barred from performing certain ritual functions, and so God says to him, "You are fit and not barred from anything unto eternity." As the Midrash says, "Therefore I shall say, 'Behold, I give unto him my covenant of peace,' so that they will not challenge his priesthood, even though he has not been anointed except with the blood of Zimri" (Midrash Tehillim, *Psalms* 29).

It seems to me, however, that the covenant of peace described here is not merely an expression of God's satisfaction with an act of zealotry, but a balancing response by God, who sentences the quick-tempered zealot to cross over to a tradition of peace and accept the stranger who differs from him. In so doing God essentially says to him and to us, "Perhaps your zealotry was proper for that day and time, but do not turn those hasty characteristics into a national policy." The veiled criticism in the verses is spelled out clearly in the Midrash.

Real life sometimes has a way of eroding the edges of the Bible's unambiguous fiats. Thus, for example, the Bible forbids the mingling of Ammonites and Moabites in "the congregation of the Lord" and requires us to refrain from seeking their welfare: "Thou shalt not seek their peace nor their prosperity all thy days for ever" (Deut. 23:7). Nonetheless, sages throughout the generations have found the loophole through which they could escape that stricture and rule Ruth the Moabite fit to be the matriarch of Judaism's royal dynasty. The sages frequently take what appears in the Bible as clear praise and turn it into condemnation. This is part of the unfinished battle of Jewish tradition against cults of personality and the evils that are derived from them.

The Midrash frequently criticizes Phinehas. For example: "The Holy One, praised be he, said: It is lawful for him to take his compensation. Therefore I shall say: 'Behold, I give unto him my covenant of peace.' Great is the peace that he gave to Phinehas, for the world is not guided except by peace" (Midrash Rabba, *Bamidbar* 21:1). The ancient command to eliminate the Midianites and its implementation are transformed right before our eyes into a divine declaration that the world is guided and conducted only in peace. Moreover, the sages say, one who makes peace with his enemies becomes a man of peace himself.

Among the Generations

I LOVE *Parashat Pinchas*. It has so many layers and meanings, and every year it allows us to look at the same materials and extract different insights and new images of the soul. This portion is unique among all the portions

Pinchas

of the Torah because it includes three patterns of generational change that occurred to Israel in the desert, on the eve of their entry into the land of Israel. Each of the patterns has a significance for generations. The first generational transfer is between Phinehas and his grandfather Aaron. His two uncles, Nadab and Abihu, died under mysterious circumstances that we discussed earlier in Week 25, *Parashat Shemini* (Lev. 10:1–3). His father Eleazar and his surviving uncle Ithamar left no impression on the biblical narrator. Only Phinehas himself proved his character when it was put to the test when "he turned my wrath away from the children of Israel, in that he was very jealous for my sake" (Num. 25:11). A practical, diligent, savvy leader, who unquestionably fit the violent profile of the children of Levi. Simeon and Levi, the butchers of Shechem, who smote their brothers following the Sin of the Calf, had now found a young, promising, representative community spokesman.

The daughters of Zelophehad also tell their story in this week's portion. They stand up bravely "before Moses, and before Eleazar the priest, and before the princes and all the congregation, at the door of the tent of meeting" (Num. 27:2). Their father Zelophehad, we recall, had no male sons and died "in his own sin." They feared that under that era's laws of inheritance their father's property would not remain within the domain of their tribe, Manasseh, but would pass with them after their marriage to the domain of their husbands' tribes. Moses, acting on their behalf, asked God a halachic legal question and received a decisive answer: "The daughters of Zelophehad speak right" (Num. 27:7). Nobody knows who Zelophehad was, but his daughters made his name great. Anyone who could raise daughters to stand their ground and force God himself to issue feminist legal rulings must have been a remarkable father – unless it was his wife who handled all the parenting.

Close by the daughters of Zelophehad, Moses ascends the stage. Moses had children of his own, but as a leader he was childless; none of his natural children were fit to follow him as his heirs and successors. In any event, his special model of leadership could not have been passed down through genetic inheritance, because that would have been fundamentally opposed to his nature and essence. And so, with considerable sadness, Moses ordained Joshua as his successor, for the passage of generations is always tinged with sadness, even when it is filled with promise. Moses, like anyone else, is reluctant to let go of life, but nature is stronger than any of us, and eventually it calls even Moses. A measure of joy can be extracted from the sadness if the coming generations of children and grandchildren carry on and add luster to the family line. Alas, Moses had children – at least two – but except for their mother and their generation itself, nothing is known about them.

Of all the great leaders in the Bible, only Moses, the greatest, has no one to carry on his name. David had Solomon, Abraham had Isaac and Ishmael and so on. Only Moses, who grew up cut off from his parents' home, lived and died alone. Joshua, his direct heir, was not necessarily the best or most talented. The biblical narrator cites only one characteristic about him: "His minister Joshua, the son of Nun, a young man, departed not out of the tent" (Exod. 33:11). He was the ultimate bureaucrat, a public servant who always came to work on time and always turned out the lights after everyone else, and in the final analysis he knew more about more things than anyone else. He was he essential man, and he was the default choice, the least worst, when the founding father moved on.

But what do all these changings of the guard have in common? The legacy of their deeds is passed on to the next generation and to the memories of future generations. The hasty action of Phinehas is paid back in a divine command that creates an eternal reality: "Behold, I give unto him…the covenant of an everlasting priesthood" (Num. 25:12–13). The daughters of Zelophehad create a binding precedent for all generations to come: "And it shall be unto the children of Israel a statute of judgment" (Num. 27:11). And these two are only an introduction to the greatest of legacies, the legacy of Moses: "Moses commanded us the Torah, an inheritance of the congregation of Jacob" (Deut. 33:4). The very fact that Moses had no formal, biological, dynastic heir turned his Torah rather than his family into the principal legacy. His private pain made way for a creation for the ages. His place of burial is left unknown, lest it become a cultic sanctuary. No formal heir was named for him, but rather countless followers, namely, all of us. One trunk can put forth many branches, and one man can give rise to many cultures.

Week 38

Mattot/Masei
The Tribes/The Stages

Numbers 30:2–36:13

The Idols of the Earth

THE TRADITIONAL JEWISH MOURNING PERIOD known as the Three Weeks, or *Bein Hametzarim* (Between the Straits) occurs during midsummer each year, from the seventeenth of Tammuz to the ninth of Av. Those dates on the Hebrew calendar always coincide with the reading in synagogue of the three portions known as *Matot*, *Masei* and *Devarim*, and there is a delicate symbolic connection between the contents of those readings and the calendar period in which they are read. Those two dates are the anniversaries of the days in the year 70 CE when, the ancient historians record, Roman troops first breached the walls of Jerusalem and finally sacked the holy Temple. Tradition marks the period as a time of mourning for a series of other catastrophes as well, including the sacking of the first Temple in 586 BCE and various medieval massacres and expulsions that took place across Europe and the Middle East on those very dates.

In contrast to those far-flung national calamities, the weekly portions deal with the near-at-hand, with homes, borders and inheritances. The effect is to draw a contrast between the ancient promises that were made and the reality of destruction that unfolded. Those two poles give rise to the belief in a hopeful future of redemption through return from afar, from dispersion to ingathering, from punishment to renewed promise.

This week's portion includes the mapping of the borders of the Promised Land. Chapter 34 of the Book of Numbers is a very important chapter, because it defines the terms of Israeli and Jewish politics from that time to this. The Bible contains several different outlines of the Promised Land's borders, but the border defined in this week's portion is one of the most important. On one hand, the land marked off by this border is not vast, like the territory promised in the Book of Genesis that stretches "from the river of Egypt unto the great river, the river Euphrates" (Genesis 15:18). On the other hand, neither are the borders mapped out here narrow and claustrophobic like the governate of Judah in the days of Ezra and Nehemiah, the Persian province that included Jerusalem, the Valley of Ono (the area of today's Ben Gurion International Airport) and…that's it.

Every verse in this portion ripples with the approaching reality of the conquest of the land. Duties and areas of responsibility are divided up, the territories of the tribes are carefully mapped out, the portions of the tribe of Levi are fixed, including their special cities, and Hebrew literature makes the acquaintance of a verb that will gain vastly in importance in our own time: *mitnachel*, "to receive possession of the land" (Num. 34:13), or as we say today, "to settle."

Against the backdrop of all these preparations, let's focus on the following verses:

> And the Lord spoke unto Moses in the plains of Moab by the Jordan at Jericho, saying: "Speak unto the children of Israel, and say unto them: When ye pass over the Jordan into the land of Canaan, then ye shall drive out all the inhabitants of the land from before you, and destroy all their figured stones, and destroy all their molten images, and demolish all their high places" (Num. 33:50–52)

In simple terms, it can be said that conquest has always required absolute victory over the enemy. An enemy that is not destroyed may form the seeds of a future fifth column that can eventually raise its head in rebellion, as Pharaoh said when he enslaved the children of Israel in Egypt: "Come, let us deal wisely with them, lest they multiply, and it come to pass, that, where there befalleth us any war, they also join themselves unto our enemies, and fight against us, and get them up out of the land" (Exod. 1:10). But a closer reading of the command shows that destroying the human enemy is only part of the order. It also calls for war against their gods, their idols and their places of worship: "Destroy all their figured stones, and destroy all their molten images, and demolish all their high places" (Num. 33:52).

Why? What is the inner logic underlying the Torah's obsessive struggle against idolatry? There are many explanations – at least one analysis for every analyst, beginning with theories about the struggles of primeval gods for a place in the pantheon and including some highly complex and sophisticated theological formulations. In the deepest sense, I believe the war against idolatry is a war of the abstract for its place in the world of the concrete. Our God is an entirely abstract idea – not just another giant statue of a Sphinx with a carved face, not another name for the sun shining in the midday sky, not a supreme king of kings sculpted by human hands, not an animal or a demon. The kingship of the God of Israel, the idea of an abstract God, serves in the Bible as a touchstone by which beliefs are defined.

The successes and failures of the Jewish people are measured as a direct function of the relative strengths of belief in the one God versus drifting toward idolatry – which is all concrete body without content, worship of lifeless objects. The challenge of believing in a God with no physical dimension was the first step in a journey toward ideas and meaning. At the same time, it was a pit that ensnared those who were incapable of living a life of the spirit and were forever seeking a godlike religious object they could touch, feel and embrace. So it was then, so it is in our own time of modern Israelite idols.

On the eve of its entry into the Promised Land, the nation is commanded more than once to fight unflinchingly against this very natural yearning of the heart, to resist the primitive, simplistic idolatry that seeks to worship trees, stones and other objects. In this week's portion, though, the order to battle the Canaanite gods takes on a new tone. This time the order is given in conjunction with the detailing of the borders of the land, to prevent us from turning the land itself into an object of worship.

One day during my childhood, a few days after the Six-Day War of 1967, I set out to explore the enchanted precincts of the Old City. I went down the Street of the Chain, *Rehov Hasharsheret* in Hebrew, turned north toward the Christian Quarter and then headed toward the Lions' Gate. Approaching one street corner I came across several local residents: five portly gentlemen, their capacious rumps overflowing their little wicker bench. There was a platter of tea and coffee at their right hand and a smoking hookah to their left. I stood just beyond them with my camera and tried to capture the comic beauty of the moment. Suddenly one of them stood up and rebuked me in excellent Hebrew: "Little boy, get out of here. What do you think, that I'm some holy place for you to photograph?" He was right. At that moment I was part of the frenzied Israeli chase after a piece of authenticity to connect me and us more deeply to the old-new places we had annexed in the wake of that cursed victory. Like everybody else, I thought that anything that was local and authentic had to be somehow sacred, even if it was only a picturesque, overweight smoker.

The old Bible understood me very well. It knew that the new conqueror, however youthful or gray-haired, would see the native inhabitant as an essential link of authenticity in the roots that bind people to their land. That in their eagerness to forge that bond, the newcomers would adopt a Canaanite coloration to erase their Diaspora-tinged immigrant identity. And that it's a very short step from there to adopting the beliefs, gods, rituals and traditions of the original inhabitants. Adopting the ways of the Canaanites would shatter the sublime values of the revelation at Sinai. The nation of wanderers reaches its goal. It's not far-fetched to anticipate that all the impulses that had been bottled up for so long would now burst forth and the Promised Land would become "holy ground," turning ordinary clods of soil without the slightest spiritual or religious valence into an unwilling "first flowering of our redemption" and fashioning a place of residence as part of a new national idolatry.

The biblical commandment stands in the face of all this and says No! We are in the midst of a generations-long war against all those empty superstitions that try to make things of nature, living or inanimate, into something they can never be – God. This means "no" to the graves of saints and bottles of holy water, and "no" to the wonder-rabbis and ayatollahs who peddle them. It means "yes" to the pure, untwisted ideas that have been the heart of Judaism throughout the ages.

Moses's Forgiveness

SOMETIMES IT SEEMS that the Minister of History is standing on the top floor of the Ministry of Current Events and smiling at us through the windows of the portion of the week. Once again we are bogged down in Lebanon and Gaza, as usual, swords drawn, while much of the portion deals with the darker sides of the war: vandalism, assassinations, more assassinations, collective punishment and flames.

I'd like to poke around a bit in the other side of war, beyond the heat of battle, and shine some light on a verse that we looked at in an earlier chapter: "And the Lord spoke unto Moses, saying: 'Avenge the children of Israel of the Midianites; afterward shalt thou be gathered unto thy people'" (Num. 31:1–2). The eye is drawn naturally to the mechanism of self-destruction that God has placed in Moses's hands. Anyone else would have put off preparing for war against Midian, if only so he could stay here among the living. Not Moses. Like Abraham at Mount Moriah, he sets aside his personal considerations in the face of a divine command and wreaks vengeance on Midian, thus beginning the countdown to his own demise. In effect, he commits suicide. I have been thinking about this for years, wondering what Moses could have been thinking at that moment. Why did he turn the divine command he was given, "Avenge the children of Israel" (Num. 31:2), into an instruction to the people to "go against Midian, to execute the Lord's vengeance on Midian" (Num. 31:3)? And on top of everything else, what did God want from him?

In ordering revenge upon Midian, God is ordering Moses to go a step further, psychologically, than he ordered him in bringing the plagues on Egypt. In the plagues, Moses could draw a distinction between those that he himself brought down and those summoned by Aaron. True, Moses struck some merciless blows, but it was Aaron who brought the plague down upon the Nile, as Rashi notes: "Because the Nile had protected

Moses when he was cast upon the water as a baby, therefore the Nile was not struck by Moses's hand, neither with blood nor with frogs, but rather it was Aaron who brought those plagues" (Rashi on Exod. 7:19).

Midian protected Moses no less than the Nile did. When Moses fled from Pharaoh after murdering an Egyptian with his own hand (Exod. 2:11–15) he found personal and political asylum in Midian. It was there that he met his Midianite wife Zipporah; there he learned how to be a shepherd and a leader. It was his father-in-law Jethro, the high priest of Midian, who taught him the meaning of organized government and saved him from chaos in the desert. All this Moses owed to Midian, and yet God ordered him to strike his benefactors. Who knows how many of his wife's relatives Moses slew in that terrible trial. When Abraham bound his son Isaac on Mount Moriah, an angel was summoned at the last minute to stay the old man's hand and prevent him from killing his son. For Moses, however, there was no one to stay his hand and prevent him from carrying out the divine sentence.

Let's go on. That was not an easy time for Moses. Those were his days of farewell and summation, and along with passing on the mantle and forgoing his great dream of entering the Promised Land, he had to accept this bloodshed as the final backdrop to the death of a leader who never thirsted for blood. The emotional devastation must have found some outlet somewhere. What did Moses truly feel? Where did he hide his tortured soul?

Let us search for the answer. Moses's punishing farewell from the earth began earlier. The process began after he struck the rock (Num. 20:7–12) instead of speaking to it:

> And the Lord said unto Moses: "Get thee up into this mountain of Abarim, and behold the land which I have given unto the children of Israel. And when thou hast seen it, thou also shalt be gathered unto thy people, as Aaron thy brother was gathered; because ye rebelled against my commandment in the wilderness of Zin, in the strife of the congregation...." These are the waters of Meribath-kadesh in the wilderness of Zin. (Num. 27:12–14)

Mattot/Masei

Moses, Aaron and God quarreled over the water, and the place was thereafter named the Waters of Meribath-kadesh (Holy Strife). There they parted ways and Moses's doom was sealed.

Against the backdrop of this great strife between Moses and his Master, and with the war against Midian in the background, we can try to reframe one of the blessings Moses gave to the tribes in *Parashat Vezot Haberachah* (This Is the Blessing) at the very end of the Book of Deuteronomy. Like Jacob before him, Moses takes leave of the tribes by describing and blessing them, each according to its character and fate. Between the lines, we can discern Moses's feelings. This is where he let out his anger, where he settled his accounts with God before passing on. His blessing for the tribe of Levi is essentially not the blessing of a leader of the tribe – Moses the Levite – to his brothers and sisters, but an utterly personal message:

> And of Levi he said: Thy Thummim and thy Urim be with thy holy one, whom thou didst prove at Massah, with whom thou didst strive at the waters of Meribah; Who said of his father, and of his mother: "I have not seen him"; neither did he acknowledge his brethren, nor knew he his own children; for they have observed thy word, and keep thy covenant. They shall teach Jacob thine ordinances, and Israel thy law; they shall put incense before thee, and whole burnt-offering upon thine altar. Bless, Lord, his substance, and accept the work of his hands; smite through the loins of them that rise up against him, and of them that hate him, that they rise not again. (Deut. 33:8–11)

Here is our reinterpretation:

"Of Levi he said" – that is, Moses the Levite said about himself, to himself. "Thy holy one" (or, better, "devoted [*hasid*] one") – I have indeed been your devoted one. I was your devout, the one you favored, your intimate. Until the eruption of the strife between us that you, my Lord, blew out of all proportion. You are to blame, because you are the one who "didst prove at Massah" and "didst strive at the waters of Meribah" – yes, those same waters of Strife, which involved only Moses and God. The tribe of Levi was not involved in that strife. Only the head of the nation and the Head of the universe, head to head.

And here is how Moses characterizes himself and his life's frustrations:

"Who said of his father, and of his mother: 'I have not seen him'" – this is Moses's childhood, adopted by the princess and hidden away in the royal palace, far from his suffering people, cut off from the mother who gave him up to save his life and probably never once having seen his own father. "Neither did he acknowledge his brethren" – there is no better way to describe Moses's alienation from his brothers at the beginning of the story. He was a pharaonic prince who discovered his true origins only at this moment: "And it came to pass in those days, when Moses was grown up, that he went out unto his brethren, and looked on their burdens" (Exod. 2:11). With the noblesse that only a prince could muster, he strikes down an Egyptian man, disposes of the body and discovers to his surprise the next day that the commoners are not grateful but merely contemptuous of his pretensions to be better than them, his fellow Hebrews: "Who made thee a ruler and a judge over us?" (Exod. 2:14). Truly, he did not know his brothers.

"Nor knew he his own children" – the traditional, Masoretic pointing of the Hebrew text makes "children" plural, but the plain Hebrew lettering says "child." Moses almost lost Gershom at their "lodging place" in the desert, en route from Midian to Egypt (Exod. 4:24–26), and only quick action by his Midianite wife Zipporah saved the poor lad. Another debt to Midian, repaid by slaughter. Moreover, Moses all but gave up his family to pursue his mission and barely knew his sons; he did not care for them and left them nothing by way of inheritance. All this he did for the sake of heaven.

After this veiled confession, laced with piercing self-awareness, Moses returns the ball to God's court. It's all because of you, he says, "for they have observed thy word, and keep thy covenant" (Deut. 33:9). I kept my end of the agreement, he hints, and what did you do? Summing up his life, Moses does not speak to God of the burning bush, nor the Exodus from Egypt, nor the revelation at Sinai – only the Waters of Strife. That is where you cheated me, he complains. That's where you betrayed me, where you fought with me for no good reason. All my life I have been let down, by my father and mother, by my brothers and children, but no one disappointed me more than you. My whole life has been watered with strife.

And yet, at the end of his painful personal accounting Moses once again shows his greatness. He forgives God. Despite all of God's anger and vindictiveness. After pouring out his pain, Moses still asks, "Bless, Lord, his substance, and accept the work of his hands" (Deut. 33:11). This is the greatness of Moses and his Torah: criticism and continuity, high road and breakthrough.

As a final note, let's return to this week's portion. This is written: "Balaam also the son of Beor they slew with the sword" (Num. 31:8). If Balaam is indeed Moses, as I wrote in my discussion of *Parashat Balak*, and Moses is Balaam, and if we are to take the text at its word when it says, "Avenge the children of Israel of the Midianites; afterward shalt thou be gathered unto thy people" (Num. 31:2), then the sword of war that struck down Balaam is the sword that killed Moses. For Moses is Balaam, and the mechanism that destroyed him is the mechanism of self-destruction.

Encore

Numbers

THE BOOK OF NUMBERS is the story of preparation and movement on the road from the desert of the present to the hazy future in the land of Israel. It is the book of planning for the great national transformation from wandering to sovereignty, from tribalism to nationhood, from impulses to processes and from happenstance to directedness. By the end of the book the Promised Land has come in view. Repeatedly throughout the book we hear the anticipatory phrase, "in the plains of Moab by the Jordan at Jericho" (Num. 26:3; 33:48; 35:1). That is, we are really at the door. According to the Midrash, Jericho is the bolt that locks the gates of the land of Israel. In another moment, Joshua, with his spies and minions, will slip the bolt, the gates will open and we will be inside – without Moses.

This is, then, a book of transition, and nowhere more so than in its final weekly portion, *Parashat Masei*, which details the way stations on the wondrous journey through the desert that began with a rabble of escaped slaves and ended with sovereign new lords of the land. Is there some turning point in the book, a mythic watershed that divides the journey into a before and after? I believe so. The story of Moses's revenge against the Midianites is the transitional moment in the Book of Numbers.

Here is what is written in chapter 31 of the Book of Numbers:

> And the Lord spoke unto Moses, saying: "Avenge the children of Israel of the Midianites; afterward shalt thou be gathered unto thy people." And Moses spoke unto the people, saying: "Arm ye men from among you for the war, that they may go against Midian, to execute the Lord's vengeance on Midian. Of every tribe a thousand, throughout all the tribes of Israel, shall ye send to the war." So there were delivered, out of the thousands of Israel, a thousand of every

tribe, twelve thousand armed for war.... And they warred against Midian, as the Lord commanded Moses; and they slew every male. And they slew the kings of Midian.... Balaam also the son of Beor they slew with the sword. And the children of Israel took captive the women of Midian and their little ones; and all their cattle, and all their flocks, and all their goods, they took for a prey. And all their cities in the places wherein they dwelt, and all their encampments, they burnt with fire.... And they brought the captives, and the prey, and the spoil, unto Moses, and unto Eleazar the priest, and unto the congregation of the children of Israel, unto the camp, unto the plains of Moab, which are by the Jordan at Jericho.

And Moses, and Eleazar the priest, and all the princes of the congregation, went forth to meet them without the camp. And Moses was wroth with the officers.... And Moses said unto them: "Have ye saved all the women alive? Behold, these caused the children of Israel, through the counsel of Balaam, to revolt.... Now therefore kill every male among the little ones, and kill every woman that hath known man by lying with him." (Num. 31:1–17)

The Bible is full of such stories of tribal warfare, slaughter and ethnic cleansing. How does this story differ from all the others? To begin with, while Moses's biographical details are not mentioned here, they will be familiar to any reader. Years earlier, Moses was forced to flee Egypt when his adoptive father, Pharaoh, learned that he had beaten an Egyptian man to death. He found refuge in the home of Jethro, the priest of Midian, married his daughter Zipporah and had two half-Midianite sons with her. God was first revealed to Moses in the burning bush in Midian. It was Zipporah the Midianite who saved Moses and their uncircumcised son from the wrath of the angel of the Lord who sought to kill them in their overnight dwelling-place in the desert on their way back to Egypt. Moreover, before the giving of the Torah, Moses's father-in-law Jethro, the priest of Midian, came to him with Zipporah and their two sons and together Jethro and Moses set up the administrative structure of the newborn nation. Since we are not told otherwise, we can assume that this same Jethro was present with Moses and the rest of the children of Israel at the revelation at Mount Sinai.

In other words, Moses's entire personal and political career is deeply intertwined with Midian. That is where he learned the foundations of governance and where he was first exposed to the principles of faith and priesthood. And yet now, on the eve of the Israelites' entry into the Promised Land, Moses is commanded to exterminate the Midianites. He is commanded to submit them to genocide because they prostituted Israel. In being commanded and in turn commanding vengeance upon Midian, he is essentially exterminating a part of himself, of his essence and identity. Isn't his own wife a Midianite? Didn't she lie with him just like the Midianite women who prostituted the rest of the children of Israel? When Moses ordered the extermination of all the Midianites, did he spare his wife Zipporah? Did the Israelite warriors have mercy on Zipporah, Moses's "dark-skinned woman," because she was the wife of their leader?

It seems so. The verses state explicitly that the warriors had mercy on the Midianite women and "saved them alive" (perhaps out of respect for their own first lady, Moses's wife), but Moses hardened his heart and commanded them to go back and kill the women who were not virgins. Does this imply that Moses ordered the killing of his own wife?

At a deeper level, this hair-raising story reveals a recurring pattern in Moses's biography: every time Moses enters a substantially new stage in his life, he is forced to destroy physically – effectively to murder – his personal connection to the previous stage. In order to depart Pharaoh's palace, to leave Egypt and his own Egyptian identity behind, Moses killed an Egyptian man with his own hands and fled his old self to find a new self in Midian. At the foot of Mount Sinai, forty days after the giving of the Torah, he sent his Levite brethren to kill the worshippers of the Golden Calf. Thousands were slaughtered in order to sever the deep religious connection between the young Israelite cult of the Calf and the traditional Egyptian Bull god Apis that the Calf was meant to recall. Instead, Moses adopted the culture of Midian as the raw material for a new Israelite ethos. Now, with the new identity primed to step forth, he once again activates his self-destruction mechanism and destroys the Midianite part of his identity. It appears that Moses's murders are liberating.

Years ago, writing in his monograph *Moses and Monotheism*, Freud argued that the Hebrews murdered Moses in the desert. But Freud and his two commentators, Yosef Hayim Yerushalmi and Edward Said, who are divided on the matter, ignored Moses's need to kill the Egyptian in order to liberate himself from Egypt and so become a liberating leader. They did not see his need to kill the Midianite men and women in order to break away from his surroundings and immerse himself in the new independent nationhood toward which he had been leading his people for forty years. And in the end, to complete his disengagement from the Midianites, Moses turns his destruction mechanism on himself: "Avenge the children of Israel of the Midianites; afterward shalt thou be gathered unto thy people" (Num. 31:2). From the moment that he attends to the revenge of the Midianites his own death begins to approach, and with his death he frees the new Israelites from his own immediate, physical self, in order to let them connect to the new physical reality of the land of Israel and the new metaphysical reality of his eternally expanding Torah.

This format of erasing the immediate past so as to embark on the new era became a leading format in our people's history. It's not always easy to see it when you are living in a transition period between eras, but a look backward makes the picture remarkably clear. The destruction of the first Temple brought an end to idolatry and focused the national consciousness on the One God and his sanctuary in Jerusalem. The destruction of the second Temple and the elimination of the last traces of Jewish sovereignty freed us from the cultic Judaism centered around the Temple in Jerusalem, ended the sacrificial cult as a medium of communication between humankind and its creator and placed the responsibility for Jewish identity on the broad shoulders of individual Jews throughout their generations. Prayer replaced sacrifice, Torah study replaced the priesthood and the synagogue replaced the Temple.

Despite the complex geopolitical circumstances that brought these destructions about, Jewish historical consciousness never sought to blame the Babylonian or Roman "contractors of destruction" for our misfortune.

We always assumed responsibility on ourselves, as we say in our holiday prayers, "Because of our sins we were exiled from our land." Sin and punishment are the mechanism by which the Jewish people separates itself from the archaic aspects of its identity, much as a snake sheds its skin, to make way for whatever great renewal is to come. So it was with Moses and his Egyptianness, with Moses and his Midianness, and so it is with us. One wonders whether somebody will claim some day in the future that the Holocaust is to be understood as the third destruction, perhaps as constructive in its own way as its predecessors, because it made possible the birth of modern Israeli sovereignty. A murderous bill of divorce from exile to redemption, like Moses in the desert.

דברים
Deuteronomy

Week 39

Devarim – These Are the Words Which Moses Spoke

Deuteronomy 1:1–3:22

Of Destruction and Memory

THIS WEEK'S PORTION, *Parashat Devarim*, is always read on the Sabbath before the fast day of Tisha B'Av, the ninth day of the month of Av. Chanting the portion in synagogue, the reader traditionally follows the standard Torah melody until he comes to the verse, "How can I myself alone bear your cumbrance, and your burden, and your strife?" (Deut. 1:12). This is chanted in the mournful tones reserved for the Book of Lamentations, in a sort of musical overture to the day of national mourning coming in the week ahead.

The observance of the ninth of Av as a national day of mourning for all the destructions of the past goes back to ancient times. The Mishnah has this to say: "Five calamities befell our ancestors…on the ninth of Av: it was decreed against our forefathers that they should not enter into the Land, and the Temple was destroyed the first time and the second time, and Betar was taken, and the City was ploughed up" (Mishnah, *Ta'anit* 4:6). In their great wisdom, the architects of our historical understanding combined a number of collective traumas into this one day of remembrance. In this way they tell us that life is stronger than grief and memory, and that we should not lose ourselves in them. If we were to immortalize the memory of every traumatic event and sanctify the anniversary of every persecution and pogrom, we would have no days left for happiness. The proliferation of memorial days and five- and ten-year anniversaries could fill all of our datebooks and still leave us short of available days to mark all the evils and traumas of our history. Other than those defined memorial days in which we mark the troubles and pain of the past, Jewish life aspires to live in the present. For that reason, the ninth of Av is fixed as a single day in which we mark the many memories of pain, grief and mourning from the past.

We will focus here on just two questions regarding the ninth of Av. First, what is the significance of this day's traditional format? Second, what is the significance of the day's modern ritual? In the beginning, the sorrowful aspects of the day were shaped to a large degree by the chief witness to the destruction of the first Temple, the prophet Jeremiah. Jeremiah wrote about the events in real time in the heart-breaking Book of Lamentations. The brief biblical book is not merely a work of first-hand testimony about the suffering of that time; it also includes a surprising moral claim that is repeated again and again throughout the book. Let's look one of the many examples:

> Jerusalem hath grievously sinned, therefore she is become as one unclean; all that honored her despise her, because they have seen her nakedness; she herself also sigheth, and turneth backward. Her filthiness was in her skirts, she was not mindful of her end; therefore is she come down wonderfully, she hath no comforter. "Behold, O Lord, my affliction, for the enemy hath magnified himself." (Lam. 1:8–9)

According to Jeremiah, the blame is not with the cruel enemy who came to destroy and kill, to torture and expel. The guilty party is Jerusalem herself: "Jerusalem hath grievously sinned." The enemy's guilt is only that he overreached, that he was too passionate in fulfilling the task assigned him: "For the enemy hath magnified himself." But the principal blame falls on Jerusalem for having sinned, not on the enemy who destroyed.

"Let it not come unto you, all ye that pass by! Behold, and see if there be any pain like unto my pain, which is done unto me" (Lam. 1:12). But if Jerusalem nonetheless looks to find someone guilty, or more properly, responsible, for her suffering, here is the culprit: God. "Wherewith the

Devarim

Lord hath afflicted me in the day of his fierce anger. From on high hath he sent fire into my bones, and it prevaileth against them; he hath spread a net for my feet, he hath turned me back; he hath made me desolate and faint all the day" (Lam. 1:12–13). Nor is that all:

> He hath made my strength to fail; the Lord hath delivered me into their hands, against whom I am not able to stand.... He hath called a solemn assembly against me to crush my young men; the Lord hath trodden as in a winepress the virgin daughter of Judah. For these things I weep; mine eye, mine eye runneth down with water. (Lam. 1:14–16)

Finally, after all this, Jerusalem returns to her mourning and desolation, pulls back from pointing a finger at God and takes full responsibility on herself: "The Lord is righteous; for I have rebelled against his word" (Lam. 1:18).

The Book of Lamentations brings out a sensibility in which the Jewish people's most important day of remembrance is observed not as an occasion to memorialize heroic victory, nor yet inhuman suffering, but as a day to remember national failure. Over the next two thousand years we became a culture shaped by the destruction – a culture that made itself into a living memorial to dereliction and misdeed. Many of us find it easy to ignore this dimension of the holiday and to observe only the destruction and our victimhood, leaving out the responsibility that is part of the remembrance. But even after all these years, there is still an immediacy to the understanding that despite the cruelty of the imperial soldiers, despite the horrible pain of the destruction, our sense of guilt, the idea that "because of our sins we were exiled from our land," became a powerful force for self-improvement. Afterward, by means of that improved self, the same force is marshaled toward the goal of improving the world.

In our own time, I propose that Yom Hashoah, Holocaust Remembrance Day, which is currently timed to mark the anniversary of the outbreak of the Warsaw Ghetto Uprising, be abolished. We should mark the destruction of the European Jewry on the ninth day of Av, as one in the series of catastrophes that have befallen the Jewish people through the ages. Why?

"Holocaust" is a new name for an old phenomenon traditionally known as *chorban*, destruction. Jewish and Zionist leaders saw this as a new era in Jewish history, and they gave it a new name – *shoah* in Hebrew, Holocaust in English. The observance of Yom Hashoah and Warsaw Ghetto Remembrance Day were begun by secular Zionists and Diaspora socialists who saw themselves as the vanguard of a new Jewish people for whom events of the distant past, including the destructions of the ancient Temples marked on Tisha B'Av, had little meaning.

But the idea of creating a new Jewish history, separate from the past, has failed, and the failure is palpable in too many aspects of our life. The destruction of European Jewry in the twentieth century is part of the continuum of the Jewish experience. It is time to return this trauma to its natural place in the Jewish and Israeli calendar and life cycle by marking the remembrance of the Holocaust on Tisha B'Av. In rebuilding the bridge between Israel and Judaism, the Shoah should be given its traditional Jewish name and called the Chorban, or Destruction – a vaster and more horrible destruction than we have ever known before, but a destruction nonetheless. In so doing, we can avail ourselves of the means of remembrance, mourning and renewal in which the Jewish experience is so tragically rich.

Today we have a Tisha B'Av observance that is, for many of us, emptied of meaning by the rebirth of the state of Israel and a Holocaust remembrance ceremony that is divorced from the continuum of Jewish history. Lost in the mix is the traditional directive to set aside times for mourning and not let them take over the entire year. If we can harness the traditional to the service of the immediate and make the remembrance of the Holocaust a part of the Jewish people's traditional day of mourning, both Yom Hashoah and Tisha B'Av will gain new dimensions of meaning. Tisha B'Av will regain its immediacy and urgency because it will recall not just the distant past but the recent as well. And it will gain another dimension as well. It will no longer be just a remembrance of our own people's past traumas, but will stand as a witness and warning to civilization as a whole, which failed to protect the Jewish stranger in its midst and must remain ever vigilant lest it fail a stranger, any stranger, now or in the future. So the nations of the world are warned, and so are we, too, at a time when we are responsible for our own fate and for the fate of minorities that now live in our midst, who watch us to see if we have learned the lesson we have sought to teach our tormentors throughout the generations.

The Promised Lands

*I*T CAN BE AMUSING at times to compare the end of Moses's career with its beginning. This week's portion, *Parashat Devarim* ("The Words"), takes its name from the first words of the Book of Deuteronomy, "These are the words which Moses spoke." We can only smile when we think back to the beginning of the Book of Exodus, when Moses tries to shrug off God's mission with the claim, "I am not a man of words" (Exod. 4:10). Amazing! Think of how many words, and with what fluency, this stammering Moses, he of the halting lips and the heavy mouth, was able to speak in his final days, at the end of his mission.

These words of Moses are a reworking of a great many other words, and they constitute in effect the birth of the Oral Law. The Written Law, the heart of the Torah, was given in the revelation at Mount Sinai in this form: "And God spoke all these words, saying…" (Exod. 20:1), which is followed by the Ten Commandments. In this week's portion Moses reworks the words and translates them into the language of his generation, adapting them to his listeners' ability to hear: "These are the words which Moses spoke…unto the children of Israel, according unto all that the Lord had given him in commandment unto them" (Deut. 1:1–3). God is speaking words from his high place, and Moses is transmitting those same words to the human, comprehensible plane. The stammerer, so it would appear, can sometimes be a very fluent translator.

Our portion is characterized by a large number of geopolitical descriptions of conquests on both sides of the Jordan. Sprinkled in among the historical descriptions of familiar names such as Sihon, Og, Moab and the children of Ammon, Moses planted allusions to other peoples and traditions that have disappeared and are less familiar. "That also is accounted a land of Rephaim: Rephaim dwelt therein aforetime; but the

Ammonites call them Zamzummim, a people great, and many, and tall, as the Anakim; but the Lord destroyed them before them; and they succeeded them, and dwelt in their stead" (Deut. 2:20–21).

At this point the reader wishes to protest: Why is he bothering with them? It was God who promised us this land as a conquest. Why is he mixing in other peoples' business and getting involved in their wars and conquests? This involvement is part of a much broader plan that includes dealing with other strange and forgotten peoples: "As he did for the children of Esau, that dwell in Seir, when he destroyed the Horites from before them; and they succeeded them, and dwelt in their stead even unto this day" (Deut. 2:22). And more: "And the Avvim, that dwelt in villages as far as Gaza, the Caphtorim, that came forth out of Caphtor, destroyed them, and dwelt in their stead" (Deut. 2:23). In short, a new world order. As a background narrative to our forefathers' entry into the land of Canaan, we are told that there is someone up there who is shifting peoples and nations hither and yon and rearranging the region, as if to create for himself and us a new Middle East.

There are those who insist on interpreting this reorganization as though its sole purpose were to clear out the promised land of Canaan for us. Others, however, think differently. Here, for example, is a passage that Rashi offers as his opening commentary on the Book of Genesis and the Torah as a whole:

> "In the beginning..." Rabbi Yitzhak said: The Torah should have begun with [the passage from Exod. 12:1] "This month shall be [unto you the beginning of months]," since this was the first law that the children of Israel were commanded. Why does it [the Torah] begin with "In the beginning"? This is because, in the words of the Psalm, "He hath declared to his people the power of his works in order to give to them the inheritance of nations" [Ps. 111:6]. Thus, should the nations of the world say to Israel, "You are robbers, for you have taken by force the lands of the Seven Nations," they [Israel] will say to them: "All the earth belongs to the Holy One, praised be he. He created it and gave it to whomever he saw fit. It was his will

to give it to them and it was his will to take it from them and give it to us." (Rashi on Gen. 1:1)

The idea behind this week's verses is the same as the idea driving Rashi's commentary. There is a divine logic that drives global geopolitics. The earth is the Lord's and the fullness thereof (Ps. 24:1), and he moves peoples and states across the face of it like so many chess pieces on a giant playing board. If he so wishes, he takes from one and gives to another, and vice versa. So it was with the likes of the Zamzummim and the other inhabitants of the land who came before us.

Another political story follows this same line of logic. When God gives Abraham his midnight promise that his seed will be as the stars in heaven, he defers the fulfillment of the promise for four hundred years, explaining, "for the iniquity of the Amorite is not yet full" (Gen. 15:16). In other words, the current inhabitants of the land have an open line of credit that allows them a certain quota of sin. Once they use up their allowance of authorized wrongdoing, the creator's decree goes into effect and he reappropriates the land "to whomever he sees fit."

It's interesting to speculate as to what would have happened if the Amorites had been given the opportunity to repent. Perhaps their iniquity allowance would not have been used up, in which case there would have been no reason to expel them from the land and dispossess them. What would have happened to us? Would we have remained forever outside the Promised Land? We shall leave this question open and simply remind ourselves to take note of the strange connection between a nation's moral conduct and its tenure on its own soil. What is the mechanism that induces such sickness in a land that it vomits up its inhabitants when their behavior does not live up to the moral standard expected of them? We go on to ask discreetly whether this same mechanism is still in operation today, and whether the land is still capable of spitting out those whose personal and public behavior violates the moral standards known collectively as Judaism.

Let's return to the verses of our portion. It seems to me that the message of Moses and God in these verses is directed toward the prospective conquerors of the Promised Land and is meant to be more than just a chronological history of the region. "You are not the first conquerors in history," we are told. "There were conquerors before you and there will be conquerors after you." Don't make the mistake of thinking that your relationship with the land you are about to inherit has some secret, permanent or automatic quality that differentiates it from the relationships of Esau, Ammon, Moab and countless other distant nations with their own lands and homes. Wars and conquests have much in common. "You are hereby warned," Moses informs us, "that if you make enough mistakes, your permanent situation can become temporary, and someone else can come and conquer you."

Rashi's maxim, "It was his will to give it to them and it was his will to take it from them and give it to us," has an unspoken but familiar and painful postscript: it was his will subsequently to take it from us and give it to a parade of other conquerors – Persians and Babylonians, Byzantines and Turks, British and Palestinians, all depending on the will of the creator of the universe. And his will depends on the allowance of sins, mistakes and misdeeds used up by the land's inhabitants. There is no eternal state and no eternal conquest. Everything is conditional, and everything depends on us. That is why *Parashat Devarim* and its historical lessons are affixed to the Sabbath preceding the ninth of Av, to join the warning to the punishment and the conquest of the land to its destruction. We have been duly warned.

Week 40

Va'etchanan – And I Besought

Deuteronomy 3:23–7:11

Leaders as Human Beings

THERE IS AN INTERESTING RULE of thumb regarding the careers of the leaders of Israel, in both ancient and modern times. None of the prime ministers of Israel finished out a term wreathed in glory with banners waving. Ben-Gurion withdrew to the desert; Moshe Sharett was all but forgotten; Levi Eshkol is remembered as a weakling; Golda Meir was forced to resign amid postwar furor; Rabin was cut down; Peres never received the credit he believed he deserved; Begin didn't have the strength to finish out his term, and the younger men who came after them are dismissed as historic failures even before they have left the stage.

It may be of some comfort to note that our leaders of the distant past were much the same. King Saul was defeated at Gilboa and his mutilated body was hung from the walls of Beit She'an, the enemy city. King David ended his reign with a bitter taste of failure, his family estranged, beset by rebellions and the tribes of Israel still not consolidated into a unified kingdom. Solomon greatly enlarged the borders of his kingdom, but his reign saw the beginnings of the kingdom's calamitous division into north and south, between his son Rehoboam and his rival Jeroboam. This nation never had a moment's peace. Indeed, far more than the land ate up its inhabitants, the inhabitants ate up their leaders. Why was this so?

A nation's patterns of leadership are imprinted on its culture long before a leader is ever selected, and the leader is commonly forced to follow the preset path, regardless of his own personality. Israelis are familiar with the example of their powerful labor federation, the Histadrut: none of its members today was alive at the time it was founded in the 1920s by socialist ideologues from Eastern Europe, yet today's members resemble their forgotten forebears far more than they would readily admit. The same is true of countless other institutions, from armies to farming communities to the neighborhood church or synagogue. Every organization and every nation has its own ingrained personality.

One of the distinctive personality traits of the Jewish people is its mistrust of its leaders. This pattern can be traced to the very first meeting between Moses and the children of Israel in Egypt. From that moment, when the people didn't fully accept Moses, a pattern was born that retains its influence to this day. In this week's portion, Moses pleads with God to let him cross the Jordan and see the Promised Land:

> "O Lord God, thou hast begun to show thy servant thy greatness, and thy strong hand; for what god is there in heaven or on earth, that can do according to thy works, and according to thy mighty acts? Let me go over, I pray thee, and see the good land that is beyond the Jordan, that goodly hill-country, and Lebanon." But the Lord was wroth with me for your sakes, and hearkened not unto me; and the Lord said unto me: "Let it suffice thee; speak no more unto me of this matter." (Deut. 3:24–26)

Moses reminds God of their first meeting. "Thou hast begun" – you started it, he says to God, and everything followed from that. At their first meeting in the desert, it was God who reached out to Moses and said, "Come now, therefore, and I will send thee unto Pharaoh, that thou mayest bring forth my people the children of Israel out of Egypt" (Exod. 3:10).

Moses's response was to express doubt about his own qualifications: "Who am I, that I should go unto Pharaoh, and that I should bring forth the children of Israel out of Egypt?" (Exod. 3:11). This self-doubt would become the dominant note throughout Moses's years of leadership. Only in rare instances did he have the full-hearted self-confidence to go it alone and take it to the limit. Too many times at moments of trial he would fall on his face and look back toward God, not inward to himself. The people, for

Va'etchanan

their part, picked up these worrisome signals. Nations are almost always an attentive, fine-tuned, exacting audience that quickly identifies its rulers' true colors. When those colors are muddy, the people vote no confidence. Perhaps that's why the relationship between Moses and the children of Israel never fully solidified. He didn't believe in himself and they didn't believe in him, and from that point on, criticism became an inseparable part of the biblical institution of leadership.

What's more, the leadership model that Moses designed gave preference to the rule of God over the kingship of "the son of man, in whom there is no help" (Ps. 146:3). Perhaps this stemmed from Moses's own weaknesses, or perhaps from his monotheistic faith as it evolved in the Egyptian royal house, where others before him had followed the one God in the form of the sun disk, Aten. Either way, biblical theocracy – the dominion of God – was a system that the late Martin Buber called "holy anarchy." The implication is that rule by Higher Authority prevents mortal hands from acquiring too much concentrated power and bringing on human despotism. According to Buber, the dominion of God was meant to create a more just and equal human society, a biblical ideal society.

But the dominion of God is not enough. It is too abstract and distant from the day-to-day challenges of the ordinary citizen. Institutions are needed that can maintain a constant critique of flesh-and-blood monarchs, lest their power go to their heads. Perhaps the relentless criticism directed at the kings who rose and fell on our national stage is part of a primeval system of checks and balances between the two arms of ancient government – the dominion of God, longed-for and just, and the kingship of man, necessary but corrupt.

The Torah, that fount of unending criticism, is also the wellspring of Judaism's torrent of opposition to the personality cults of its founders and leaders. This is why the great heroes of the Bible are never perfect. Abraham, for example, is weak and flaccid in the face of Sarah's bullying. Jacob lives with the lies, banishment and fear of his sons, who are even more flawed than he is. David's sins are laid out in the Book of Samuel for a public review that spans the generations. As for Moses, his misdeeds draw the most painful punishment of all – seeing his lifelong dream shattered on the very eve of its fulfillment. All of them stand as object lessons in the biblical idea of statecraft. There are no perfect people and no utopias. There is only reality, with all its compromises.

Moses is denied entry into the Promised Land not only as a reflection of his own lifelong weakness, but because the editor of the Bible's mythology wanted to strike him here, where it hurt the most. There, in the depths of the hero's great frustration, is where the most profound message can be found. If we look closely, we'll find that each of these heroes' weaknesses teaches us a very particular lesson. Each one had a great dream that became a rebuke. Abraham desperately wanted sons to carry on his name, and what he got was a family beset by feuding, banishment and a near-murder on the altar. Jacob wanted only to dwell quietly in his tents, and he ended up wandering and struggling throughout his life. Thus were the great heroes of the Bible. May their much-criticized memory be blessed.

The Spiritual Constitution

ONCE, YEARS AGO, I came home late from Friday evening prayers at my favorite synagogue, Congregation B'nei Jeshurun in New York City. The synagogue was a considerable distance from my hotel, more than thirty blocks, and I was walking quickly, spurred on by cold and fear. Suddenly I saw a homeless man lying on a pile of newspapers on the sidewalk, sheltered by cardboard boxes, wrapped in rags. It's a common enough sight in any great city in the world, including the cities of Israel. Common enough that we barely even notice anymore. But this homeless man seemed different. Sitting beneath the light of a store window, he was immersed in reading a book. The sight was so anomalous that I stood for a while and stared at him: the clean, shiny store window, the homeless man bent to his reading, the light, the book. Hundreds of people passed around us and between us, and none turned their heads. Was the whole world destined to exist in this duality – these beautiful surroundings, so overflowing with wealth and comfort, living cheek to jowl with this alternate reality, so shockingly abject?

Perhaps so. Perhaps there is no way back from progress, with all its benefits and cruelties. And perhaps the road forward to the future has to be a strange road that seamlessly combines forward movement with a backward gaze. We have it within our power to chart a course that takes the material passed on to us by tradition, to rework it and refine it in the laboratory of contemporary values and thus to set out on the path of a renewed tradition that is at once deeply rooted and living in real time.

Take the Ten Commandments, for example. I believe that Jewish tradition can be one of the primary bases for Western civilization's renewal and transformation into a truly model society. The Ten Commandments propose a society founded on justice, free of guile and with a modicum of healthy innocence, perhaps even naivete, at its core. True, it remains an open question what value there is in human decency. From a strictly rational point of view, it seems far preferable to be a person of evil and dishonesty – it brings more money, more power and a fuller portion of life's pleasures. And yet, most people are essentially good, or at least try their best to minimize the bad within them. What can be done to make the most of this fact? I have no universal answer that applies to all human societies, but I have a feeling the goal can be achieved with relative ease within the narrower framework of the Jewish people.

As a first step, we must commit ourselves to doing everything possible to ensure that wherever a Jewish community exists, it will not let a homeless person lie in the road while others walk by unheeding. This implies a transformation of society from one of taking, of entitlement, to a society of giving. In a community of giving no human being can be deemed worthless, because it is assumed that economic affluence is only temporary. Today I am giving and another is receiving. Tomorrow, if the wheel of fortune should turn, there will be somebody to care for me. Precisely because we Jews are dispersed across the globe, because we are strangers in so many societies, we are well placed to offer a model of the practice of giving. Every community for its members, and members of every community (those who have) for those who have not.

One of the most important starting points in the process of transforming society and fostering a community of justice is the principle of constitutional obligation. For me, the Ten Commandments are that constitution, a spiritual, eternal, utterly human constitution. The Ten Commandments can serve as a fine example of an ancient ceremonial formula that retains its freshness and potential for renewal to this very day. Here is how we should read the challenge they pose:

"I am the Lord thy God" (Deut. 5:6).

God created man in his image, so we were taught to believe. Accordingly, there must be some reflection of God in human action. It follows that one need not travel far to find God; he is nearby and accessible. All that is needed is to discover the divine within another human being, in a neighbor and a stranger. Discovering the humanity in our neighbor is Judaism's greatest invention, no less than the discovery of God in the heavens above. "I am the Lord thy God, who brought thee out of the land of Egypt, out of the house of bondage." Our ancient constitution begins with a declaration of human freedom, because that is how we memorialize our God: in the victory of freedom over slavery and equality over discrimination, in the elevation of the sublime within humankind over the lowly and bestial.

"Thou shalt have no other gods before me" (Deut. 5:6).

Establishing a hierarchy of human values depends on the presumption that within every human being there dwells a spark of the divine. You cannot find a value more sacred than life, because in sanctifying your life and that of your neighbor, you sanctify the creator and his creation. You are obliged to aspire to a better life, not merely in the material sense, but in a life made holier. And because all human beings are unique and different in thought and appearance, in body and spirit, it is only in the totality of humankind that God's image can find full expression. Hence: "Thou shalt have no other gods before me." Do not delude yourself into thinking that you can be a child of God on your own, the Commandments warn us. Don't delude yourself that you can live a better life on your own, without fellowship or community or – conversely – by destroying other human beings, other children of God like yourself and all of us.

"Thou shalt not take the name of the Lord thy God in vain" (Deut. 5:10).

None of the means of life can be sanctified as an ultimate objective. Land is not holy, graves are not holy, wars are not holy; neither settlements nor even rabbis are holy vessels. Only the soul is holy, and all else pales before its holiness. Every act of oppression, whether religious or secular, governmental or individual, may be defined as taking the name of the Lord in vain. For we learned in the first Commandment that God is revealed in the face of the other, of the neighbor or friend whom I am commanded to love as myself. Therefore, do not send your people to a war of arrogance; do not push yourself into situations where there is a threat of death. Do not presume to be God's spokesman on earth, in vain.

"Observe the Sabbath day, to keep it holy" (Deut. 5:11).

It is interesting to ponder whether God considered starting his creation of the world with Man, rather than leaving him for the end. In the end, though, we were created after God had acquired a good deal of experience, after five exhausting days of work. It was a moment before he broke for a rest that God created man. And what did God do on his day off? "On the seventh day he ceased from work and rested" (Exod. 31:17). The wisdom of resting on the Sabbath is a gift we bequeathed to the world at large long ago. But we largely forgot the full meaning of the day. The original Hebrew text tells us that on the seventh day God "*shavat vayinafash*," which means, roughly, that he "ceased from work and restored his soul." The Hebrew word commonly translated here as "rested" actually implies something more, an enhancing of life that goes beyond satisfying bodily needs or pursuing material gain.

The Commandment of Sabbath appears in two different versions in the books of Exodus and Deuteronomy. In one case we are commanded to "remember" the Sabbath and in the other case to "observe" it. The Commandment to observe is familiar to us from the meticulous (at times obsessive) attention of Sabbath observers to the rules, laws, activities, prohibitions, times and foods. But alongside the command to observe that appears in this week's portion, we are commanded in the Book of Exodus to remember the Sabbath. What do "Sabbath rememberers" look like?

What are their duties? What rules are incumbent on them? Perhaps this is the place where we can renew the concept of Sabbath for those who do not observe every stricture but love the additional soul granted to us on the weekly day of rest.

"Honor thy father and thy mother...that thy days may be long" (Deut. 5:16).

Why did the drafter of the Commandments decide to attach this promised reward – the hope of long life – to the Commandment of honoring father and mother? Perhaps because this command marks the transition from the Commandments of God to those of humanity.

The Talmud teaches: "There are three partners in man, the Holy One, blessed be he, his father and his mother" (Babylonian Talmud, *Niddah* 31a). Thus by honoring one's parents one also honors their senior partner, the creator. The son and daughter who give proper honor are thereby giving honor to the family representatives of the creator of man. God delegated to them – to our parents – the ability and responsibility to continue the work of creation. They, like him, are granters of souls and creators of life. Whoever honors his parents receives their legacy and then bequeaths it to his own children, forging a new link in the chain that goes back to Adam and Eve, God's own creations. Length of life is not a reward beneficently granted, but a natural result of family life. Whoever invests in his sons and daughters earns the right to reap the fruits of his life and finds the value in the lives of his children and their children after them.

"Thou shalt not murder" (Deut. 5:16).

This sweeping command is based on the difference between God and man. If there is a God, creator of the universe, he can breathe life at any moment into any matter. Man, his creation, resembles him but is not exactly like him. Man can take the life of his neighbor at any moment, but can only give life at the moment of sexual communion. Whoever cannot repair a life that was cut short or restore life to one he has killed may not take a life. It follows, then, that the death penalty is impermissible, since the taking of life is a privilege reserved to God alone.

But this Commandment is not meant simply to prohibit action. A person who seeks to fulfill the image of God within him must learn to heal, to extend the human life expectancy and do whatever is possible to forestall death. This is the positive, active side of "Thou shalt not murder." That is, the other side of the prohibition is the command to do good and prevent murder and the semblance of murder in our lives. Go and fight against violence. Oppose racism with all your might, because it too is a form of murder, like its sibling, hatred. Trading in arms, even when done by Jews, is aiding and abetting in murder. Trading in drugs is trading in death. All of these come under the heading of "Thou shalt not murder." Religious faith is innately legitimate, regardless of the name one gives to God, but any religion that crosses the red line of the sanctity of life is illegitimate. Even if the killer is a Jew who kills in the name of his religion, like Yigal Amir, who assassinated Yitzhak Rabin, or Baruch Goldstein, who killed twenty-nine Muslim worshippers in a Hebron mosque, he is still a murderer, and his name enters the black list of the enemies of humanity and God.

"Neither shalt thou commit adultery" (Deut. 5:16).

In the logic of community life, in which the family is the very foundation of human existence, adultery is a sort of small-scale murder. When human life is filled with betrayals between and man and a woman, it creates a society without the underpinning of family. But the family is the cornerstone of community and society. When one undermines the foundation, one threatens the stability of the entire communal structure.

"Neither shalt thou steal" (Deut. 5:16).

Property is not a dirty word. One might even describe property as a concrete expression of God's blessing. We want a home equipped with all the trappings: food, appliances, media of entertainment and relaxation. The home is our refuge from all the injuries and dangers that lurk outside in the wide world. Nonetheless, there are those to whom the sanctuary of our home represents a target to rob and vandalize. They break in, steal and violate the things we hold sacred. When the Jewish constitution tells us

"Neither shalt thou steal," it is commanding us not to violate the property, privacy or rights of our neighbor.

"Neither shalt thou bear false witness against thy neighbor" (Deuteronomy 5:16).*

"Every violation of truth," the nineteenth-century poet and philosopher Ralph Waldo Emerson once said, "is not only a sort of suicide in the liar, but is a stab at the health of human society." My entire web of connectedness to my surroundings is based on honesty. Suppose that one day I discover that my friend, my partner in human society, has deceived me and lied to me. Has he hurt only me? Certainly not. He has threatened the health of the entire society in which we live. The ancient biblical ideal, which retains its power to this day, holds that a society unable to distinguish between truth and falsehood is a sick, rotting, suicidal society.

"Neither shalt thou covet" (Deut. 5:17).

Here again, the text offers two different versions. In Exodus, the commandment begins, "Thou shalt not covet thy neighbor's house" (Exod. 20:13), while the Deuteronomy version begins, "Neither shalt thou covet thy neighbor's wife." Each version goes on to include the other, and then both go on to list servants, livestock and more. The reversal of emphasis, however, drives home an important point: that this commandment combines the concepts of theft and adultery. In effect, this commandment reinforces the prohibitions in the two earlier commandments by prohibiting not just the action but the intention as well. A constitution whose central prohibition is on the act of sin can slide quickly into a cruel, vindictive theocracy of the Saudi type. On the other hand, a society in which intention can be criminalized is a cruelly inquisitorial or totalitarian society. A Jewishly giving society strives for something more. It seeks to educate a person from within, to influence his intentions without threatening violent, intrusive measures to attempt to control his thoughts. "Thou shalt not covet" is

---

* In Hebrew, the Exodus version says "*ed sheker*" or "false witness," while the Deuteronomy version reads "*ed shav*," which could also be translated "vain witness."

a call to self-improvement and courage – the courage to conquer one's impulses.

These Ten Commandments can be part of a traditional, yet contemporary response to the ills of modern humanity. It's not always necessary to invent something new or destroy old worlds in a fit of ideological passion. Sometimes it's better to renew the old – to renew and sanctify. Acting out of free will – and at the same time, from a lack of any alternative – we must harness the values we find rooted in God-centered religion to the needs of a human-centered society. It need not matter to me whether my neighbor believes in God, or what his God is called, so long as I can find an ethical and behavioral common language with him. Then and only then can we live together in a shared community of commandment and communication.

Perhaps this is what Moses meant in this week's portion, *Parashat Va'etchanan*, when he pleaded with the people time after time and warned that survival in the Promised Land was conditional on a life of law and morality. Only such a life can guarantee the Jewish people's distinctiveness within the family of nations, as Moses said:

> And now, O Israel, hearken unto the statutes and unto the ordinances, which I teach you, to do them; that ye may live, and go in and possess the land which the Lord, the God of your fathers, giveth you…. Behold, I have taught you statutes and ordinances, even as the Lord my God commanded me, that ye should do so in the midst of the land whither ye go in to possess it. Observe therefore and do them; for this is your wisdom and your understanding in the sight of the peoples, that, when they hear all these statutes, shall say: "Surely this great nation is a wise and understanding people." For what great nation is there, that hath God so nigh unto them, as the Lord our God is whensoever we call upon him? And what great nation is there, that hath statutes and ordinances so righteous as all this law, which I set before you this day?" (Deut. 4:1–8)

Unfortunately, our history has proven repeatedly, to our grief, that the opposite is also very true. A life of immorality shortened our collective presence in the land of Israel and led us to a long and painful exile and to worldwide humiliation and isolation.

The choice between the two paths is in our hands.

Week 41

Ekev – Because Ye Hearken

Deuteronomy 7:12–11:25

Land and Food

As religious Jews we recite *Birkat Hamazon*, the grace after meals, countless times in our lives, and yet rarely do we pay attention to the contents of this lovely and uplifting blessing and the contexts from which its words are drawn.

Children are taught that the blessing is simply a way of thanking God, the creator of the universe, for giving us the sustenance of life. But *Birkat Hamazon* has many more levels to it, and it is to them that we devote the following words. In the desert, far from the Promised Land, the Israelites received this command: "And thou shalt eat and be satisfied, and bless the Lord thy God for the good land which he hath given thee" (Deut. 8:10). This original command became a multi-layered prayer – actually a series of individual prayers – that stands on its own today as an independent work of sacred literature. This is its history, as related by the Talmudic Aggadah:

> Rabbi Nahman said: Moses instituted for Israel the benediction "Who feeds" [the first blessing in *Birkat Hamazon*, "Blessed art Thou, O Lord, our God, who feeds the whole world in his goodness"] at the time when manna descended for them. Joshua instituted for them the benediction of the land [the second blessing] when they entered the land. David and Solomon instituted the [third] benediction, which ends: "Who buildest Jerusalem." [Within that third benediction,] David instituted the words "For Israel thy people and for Jerusalem

thy city," and Solomon instituted the words "For the great and holy House." The [fourth] benediction, "Who is good and bestows good," was instituted in Yavneh with reference to those who were slain in Betar. For Rabbi Mattena said: On the day on which permission was given to bury those slain in Betar, they ordained in Yavneh that "who is good and bestows good" should be said: "is good" because their bodies did not putrefy, and "bestows good" because they were allowed to be buried. (Babylonian Talmud, *Berachot* 48b)

Explanation:

Level one: Moses took advantage of the miracle of manna to establish the custom of giving thanks for food and sustenance and "instituted for Israel" the blessing that begins *Birkat Hamazon*, "Blessed art thou, O Lord, our God, who feeds the whole world in his goodness..."

Level two: Joshua, who led the conquest of the Promised Land, expanded the basic blessing over food to include the soil in which it is grown, and so he "instituted for them" the second blessing in the series, "Blessed art thou, O Lord, our God, for the land and the food."

Level three: Before David conquered Jerusalem and made it his capital, it would hardly have made sense to thank God "for Israel thy people and for Jerusalem thy city." Therefore, the Talmud says, it's only logical that David himself must have "instituted the words" in question.

Level four: Solomon, as the great builder of the first Temple, was able to add his own layer to the prayer and thus to be memorialized for all time, and so "Solomon instituted the words" within David's blessing that say: "For the great and holy House that bears thy name."

Level five: "Who is good and bestows good." *Birkat Hamazon* does not commemorate only history's great deeds and miracles, but also its great catastrophes, in particular the destruction of the ancient city of Betar in 135 CE, which ended the three-year Bar Kochba rebellion against Rome. The sages at the yeshiva of Yavneh instituted the blessing that includes the words "the King who is good and bestows good to all" to recall "those who were slain in Betar."

There is virtually no record of the discussion that took place at the revered academy when the terrible news arrived from Betar. Betar was

Bar Kochba's last stronghold, and the Midrash tells ghastly tales of what happened there: "Eighty thousand Roman battle trumpets entered the city of Betar when it was taken and they slew men, women and children in it until their blood ran into the great sea" (Babylonian Talmud, *Gittin* 57a). "The Romans went on killing until a horse was sunk in blood up to its nostrils. The flowing blood was turning over boulders the size of forty *se'ah* [seventy-one gallons, the amount needed to fill a kosher mikvah], and the blood flowed four Roman miles into the sea" (Jerusalem Talmud, *Ta'anit* 68d). "Rabbi Yohanan said: The brains of three hundred children were found dashed upon one stone" (Midrash Rabba, *Lamentations* 2:4). Who wept for their slain kin, and who celebrated the death of the false messiah who had brought such carnage on Israel? We will never know.

Ever since then, however, the blessing "who is good and who bestows good" is included in the daily grace after meals. In that first generation, this was the blessing that expressed respect for the dead, as Rabbi Mattena said: "On the day on which permission was given to bury those slain in Betar, they ordained in Yavneh that 'who is good and bestows good' should be said: 'is good' because their bodies did not putrefy, and 'bestows good' because they were allowed to be buried." Afterwards, that blessing came to be a prayer of thanks for any bit of good we find in life around us, unrelated to those particular horrors.

In addition to all these, there is another important historical level to the prayer, found in this week's portion. The verses immediately preceding the command to bless the food describe the good land that the Israelites have entered:

> For the Lord thy God bringeth thee into a good land, a land of brooks of water, of fountains and depths, springing forth in valleys and hills; a land of wheat and barley, and vines and fig-trees and pomegranates; a land of olive-trees and honey; a land wherein thou shalt eat bread without scarceness, thou shalt not lack any thing in it; a land whose stones are iron, and out of whose hills thou mayest dig brass. (Deut. 8:7–9)

We are commanded to bless and say thanks every day for this land, its bounty and its sustenance. But the biblical Commander is quite familiar with the souls of his servants. He knows that wherever there is plenty and bounty, the dangers of arrogance and complacency lurk nearby.

> Beware lest thou forget the Lord thy God, in not keeping his commandments, and his ordinances, and his statutes, which I command thee this day; lest when thou hast eaten and art satisfied, and hast built goodly houses, and dwelt therein; and when thy herds and thy flocks multiply, and thy silver and thy gold is multiplied, and all that thou hast is multiplied; then thy heart be lifted up, and thou forget the Lord thy God, who brought thee forth out of the land of Egypt, out of the house of bondage…and thou say in thy heart: "My power and the might of my hand hath gotten me this wealth." …And it shall be, if thou shalt forget the Lord thy God, and walk after other gods, and serve them, and worship them, I forewarn you this day that ye shall surely perish. (Deut. 8:11–19)

In its origins, then, *Birkat Hamazon* is a plea against national arrogance. The land is indeed promised, and its produce is tasty and good. But it waits lovingly for the modest among us. Power is the key that comes back to turn the lock and expel us from here every time we forget the true source of our beneficent plenty. From now on, therefore, when we recite the grace after meals, let us remember not only the "good and bestowing good," but also the caution: "I forewarn you this day that ye shall surely perish. As the nations that the Lord maketh to perish before you, so shall ye perish" (Deut. 8:19–20). *Birkat Hamazon* is the daily preventive medicine that the Jew is commanded to take for that deadliest of national illnesses: chauvinistic arrogance and the exile that follows.

Culture and Memory

WE HAVE BEFORE US the two sides of the coin of our national condition: on one side, "that ye may live, and multiply, and go in and possess the land" (Deut. 8:1), and on the other side, "ye shall surely perish" (Deut. 8:19). What determines the difference, according to our portion, between destruction and a joyous, optimistic reality? Worldview and perspective. The balance between these two outcomes depends on our relationship with time. Someone who lives with the lessons of memory and history may look forward to a good and even a very good future. But someone who lives only in the present, without drawing on the experience of the past, is doomed to pay the price of repeated error.

There probably isn't another portion in the Torah that deals at such length with the obligation of memory and the prohibition on forgetting. "And thou shalt remember all the way which the Lord thy God hath led thee these forty years in the wilderness" (Deut. 8:2); "Beware lest thou forget the Lord thy God, in not keeping his commandments" (Deut. 8:11); "But thou shalt remember the Lord thy God, for it is he that giveth thee power to get wealth" (Deut. 8:18); "And it shall be, if thou shalt forget the Lord thy God" (Deut. 8:19); "Remember, forget thou not, how thou didst make the Lord thy God wroth in the wilderness" (Deut. 9:7). In the view of the portion, the proper way to live in the world is with full knowledge and understanding that human wisdom is cumulative, and woe to him who begins learning each day anew as though his predecessors had not erred and paid the price to bring us this far.

One who forgets the past is doomed to repeat his mistakes over and over, and every time history repeats itself the cost goes up. These repeated commandments of memory call humanity to live a life of depth and remembering. When a person looks around and sees the present as a reality that is somehow guaranteed and not subject to change, he can easily come to see himself as a product of that reality, shaped by events rather than shaping them. He doesn't know where things came from, and it really doesn't matter to him.

Judaism, however, is not a religion of the present, but a culture of memory. When we accompany someone to his final resting place, we reflect continually on the wise words of Akavia Ben Mehalalel, "Know where you come from and where you are going" (Mishnah, *Avot* 3:1). The past and the future are all that matters, while the present is an elusive reality formed by the combining of the other two. At times this approach can lead to a stifling conservatism and a stringency in observing commandments that have no contemporary meaning. Sometimes the future we imagine can be so utopian that it leads to a steady deterioration of the present while we wait passively for the coming of perfect redemption in a tantalizing endtime. Still, attention to the past brings great benefits to a society and its legacy. Someone who has been burned by Amalek will not readily become entangled with Edom, and someone who remembers his adventures as a slave in Egypt will not harass the inhabitants of the land or spread lies about the strangers and aliens living there.

The late Columbia University historian Yosef Hayim Yerushalmi devoted one of his most important books, Zakhor, to this elusive commandment:

> The Hebrew Bible seems to have no hesitations in commanding memory. Its injunctions to remember are unconditional, and even when not commanded, remembrance is always pivotal. Altogether the verb zakhar appears in its various declensions in the Bible no less than one hundred and sixty-nine times, usually with either Israel or God as the subject, for memory is incumbent upon both. The verb is complemented by its obverse – forgetting. As Israel is enjoined to remember, so it is adjured not to forget. Both imperatives have resounded with enduring effect among the Jews since biblical times. Indeed, in trying to understand the survival of a people that has spent most of its life in global dispersion, I would submit that the history of its memory, largely neglected and yet to be written, may prove of some consequence. (Yosef Hayim Yerushalmi, Zakhor: Jewish History and Jewish Memory [Seattle: University of Washington Press, 1982; New York: Schocken 1989], 5. Citation refers to the Schocken edition.)

Let's digress for a moment from the pathways of memory and ponder another mystery: the human need for the passing thrill of victory as a reminder of one's own value. Where does this feeling lead? To a people consistently choosing war as the way to experience their own strength. The Midrash offers a different answer to that need, at once compelling and challenging. Jewish Aggadah prefers spiritual and moral victories over physical and military ones.

The Midrashic expression "my children have defeated me, they have defeated me" – which appears in the Aggadic tale as God's response when the sages of the academy expel him from their deliberations (the story is told at greater length in our chapter on *Parashat Terumah*, Week 19) – is God's invitation to his believers to contend with him. It shows his willingness to be defeated by his children. The children have the right and the ability to defeat their Father in heaven, and he has the ability to smile and take pleasure in it. The children also have the right to contend for partnership with their creator in repairing the world that he created; this competition too is within their power to win. The Talmud makes this point playfully in a lesser-known Midrash, playing on the dual meanings of the word *menatzeyach*, which means both victor (or winner, conqueror or to defeat) and orchestra leader (or conductor). It is in the second sense of the word that many of the Psalms begin, "*Lemenatzeyach shir mizmor* (For the leader, a song, a Psalm)." It seems, however, that there was a tradition among some sages in Babylonia to read it differently:

> Rav Kahana said on the authority of Rabbi Ishmael, the son of Rabbi Yose: What is meant by "For the leader [*lamenatzeyach*] a Psalm of David"? Sing praises to him who rejoices when they conquer him. Come and see how the character of the Holy One, praised be he, is not like that of mortal man. The character of mortal man is such that when he is conquered he is unhappy, but when the Holy One is conquered he rejoices. (Babylonian Talmud, *Pesachim* 119a)

Elsewhere in the Midrash, the point is made even more strikingly:

> If I have defeated you, I am the One who loses. If you defeated me, I profit. I defeated the generation of the Flood, yet I lost. I was victorious at the Tower of Babel and at Sodom, yet did I not lose? I defeated Jeremiah, and did I not lose? And when I destroyed my Temple and exiled my children? And yet, at the sin of the Golden Calf, Moses defeated me, and I profited from it. It is my wish that you defeat me! (Midrash, *Pesikta Rabbati* [Ish Shalom], chapter 40)

The Midrash has a double message. On the one hand, every time God defeats us and a calamity ensues, we are not the only victims or losers. Our vanquisher is himself a victim. On the other hand, there is no point in stoking ourselves with bravery, for on the human battlefield both the victor and the vanquished lose in the end. True victory lies in vanquishing anger, for God and man alike.

May it be his will that our days be peaceful, and that light comes to our leaders and ministers and shows them the path of peace, which is the true victory, for it has no vanquished and no grief.

Week 42

Re'eh – Behold

Deuteronomy 11:26–16:17

Therefore Choose

WHAT IS THE MEANING of this decision set before me: "See, I have set before thee this day life and good, and death and evil" (Deut. 30:15)? For many people, living within a religious framework means choosing a life of meaning and coercion, in a system of commandments with many prohibitions and few allowances. For others, life within a religious community feels stifling, implying not just the burden of the commandments but the informal disciplinary tools of threats, ostracism and gossip. In the religious world of our day there is very little room for leniency, as the forces of constraint and inflexibility grow ever more powerful. It's no coincidence that in Jewish parlance, the opposite of "religious" was for many years "free," since the religious person's prohibitions keep him tethered to his home while the free-thinker wanders wherever he wishes.

The opening of this week's portion speaks of a different approach. It declares that the siege mentality that characterizes religion is not inevitable. An important component that's too often missing in the defensive posture of modern religious life is the ability of the individual believer and community to think, to wonder and to choose among options. The very idea of free choice has become all too rare in today's religious communities. Too many things have become axiomatic, absolute and beyond question. This week's portion, like some others across the expanse of Moses's immortal books, offers us a way to faith through doubt.

The portion's opening hints at an interesting line of thought that runs like a scarlet thread through all of biblical faith, namely free choice. At first glance the entire Torah appears to be one big collection of prohibitions and restrictions – but only at first glance. Eve was the first to violate a commandment and open the gate into the paradise known as curiosity. Abraham flouted the religion of his family and his homeland and discovered the creator of the universe. Moses did not follow the straight path, and he brought freedom into the world. This week's portion offers contemporary believers the right to choose and decide for themselves, with all the challenges that this path implies.

To understand the concept of choice, let's digress for a moment to the Middle Ages and Maimonides's concept of *teshuvah* (repentance).

> Freedom of choice to follow the laws of God or not to follow them, is granted to all men. If a person wants to follow the path of virtue, becoming a righteous person, that is his choice. Similarly, he can choose to follow the road of evil, becoming a wicked person. After Adam sinned, the Bible says, "Man is become as one of us, to know good and evil" (Gen. 3:22). Meaning, mankind has become unique in the world. Only man, with his knowledge and thought, can distinguish good from evil and choose between the two, and no one can stay his hand from doing good or evil. (Maimonides, *The Laws of Repentance* 5:1)

Maimonides connects the choice between good and evil, and between blessing and curse, to the first moment of the birth of human consciousness in Adam and Eve in the Garden of Eden. Free choice is a divine attribute ("as one of us"). As such, choice is certainly an appropriate element in the religious makeup of man as the guardian of God's image on earth.

Maimonides continues:

> Do not even contemplate the notion held by gentile fools, and ignorant Jews, that God decides at birth whether a person will be righteous or wicked. This is not true. Each person has the potential to become a righteous person like Moses our teacher, or to be an evildoer like the wicked king Jeroboam. He may acquire wisdom or

foolishness, be compassionate or ruthless, miserly or generous, or have any other character trait. There is no higher power that compels, persuades or decrees which path one must choose. He freely chooses of his own accord the road he wants to follow. (Maimonides, *The Laws of Repentance* 5:2)

Finally, the great sage closes the circle that we opened with our first verse:

> The principle of freedom of choice is a basic concept and a pillar on which the entire Torah and its commandments rest, as it is written, "See, I have set before thee this day life and good, and death and evil" (Deut. 30:15). And it is further written, "Behold, I set before you this day a blessing and a curse" (Deut. 11:26), meaning that the choice is in your hands. Whatever a person wishes to do among human actions, he will do, whether good or evil.... That is, God does not force people or decree that they do good or evil. It is all up to them. (Maimonides, *The Laws of Repentance* 5:3)

What is the importance of free choice? Its importance lies in the fact that choice opens the way to questioning, doubt and uncertainty. A person who has no doubts, to whom everything is clear, often adopts an absolutist, uncritical attitude. This mentality can frequently give rise to fanaticism and bloodthirstiness. Certainty is one of the greatest constraints on the exercise of choice. The human tendency toward absolute faith, insensitive to other views and inattentive to conflicting truths, can lead to disastrous religious arrogance. A community or religious assembly that does not practice open deliberation will lack balance, because they are more fearful of alternatives than faithful to the truth. Such people are a danger to themselves and those around them.

For this reason our portion offers humankind the road of doubt, of pondering every truth. Everything is open to choice and decision. There is no nature determined in advance, no faith that comes without the pain of uncertainty. But if you travel down this road, you will gain something wonderful. You will gain a life of imperfection, of modesty without arrogance, a life of contentment with less, of concern for the neighbor who just might be in the right. Not surprisingly, this week's portion contains one of the Bible's most compelling collections of rules to show care for a neighbor, from the setting aside of tithes for the orphan and widow (Deut. 14:29) to the sabbatical year of forgiveness of loans (Deut. 15:2) and freeing of slaves (Deut. 15:12) and the outright prohibition against tolerating poverty (Deut. 15:4). The neighbor who looks like a pauper or slave might turn out to be the one who is truly free, while I am the real prisoner, trapped in my mistaken beliefs.

What Enters the Mouth is What Pollutes the Soul

"BEHOLD, I SET BEFORE YOU this day a blessing and a curse" (Deut. 11:26). Moses's final days weigh heavily upon him. He can already see the big picture. He looks into the distance and pays less attention to details. As he sees it, this is the right and proper context in which to speak about the struggle against idolatry, about moral values and the need to keep away from the enemies' abominations. So what is a list of forbidden and permitted animals doing in the middle of these great things? Is there something in the biblical laws of kashrut that is somehow connected to the great choice between blessing and curse, between life and death?

The vast number of commentaries and theories seeking to explain the doctrine of forbidden foods is testimony to the fact that there is no one clear, simple answer. Some have claimed that the forbidden animals are those used in the cultic worship of other peoples and religions. Other commentators claim that these animals actually appeared in the ancient ceremonies of our ancestors. To my mind it would have been better if the Torah had stated straight out that the list is arbitrary, with no reason or logic. The message of the listed foods is not found among the items that appear there, but in a commandment pronounced earlier in the portion, which is one of the foundations of the Jewish rules of slaughter:

Re'eh

> Thou shalt say: "I will eat flesh," because thy soul desireth to eat flesh; thou mayest eat flesh, after all the desire of thy soul.... Only be stedfast in not eating the blood; for the blood is the life; and thou shalt not eat the life with the flesh. Thou shalt not eat it; thou shalt pour it out upon the earth as water. Thou shalt not eat it; that it may go well with thee, and with thy children after thee, when thou shalt do that which is right in the eyes of the Lord.... Observe and hear all these words which I command thee, that it may go well with thee, and with thy children after thee for ever, when thou doest that which is good and right in the eyes of the Lord thy God. (Deut. 12:20–28)

There are very few commandments of which it is said explicitly that they reflect what is right and good in the eyes of the Lord. In what way do the commandments of kosher slaughter and the list of forbidden and permitted animals reflect what is right and good?

Let's go back to the very beginning. In the Garden of Eden we ate fruit and spoke with snakes, and toward the end we wore fig leaves. We were banished from the garden because our father and mother ate from the fruit of the tree of knowledge, and thus they learned the meaning of good and bad. "See, I have set before thee this day life and good, and death and evil" (Deut. 30:15), which is to say, good is equal to life and death is equal to evil. In *Parashat Bereshit*, the beginning of the beginning, God did not want humans to be capable of distinguishing between life and death. He wanted a human consciousness in which there was only life and goodness, in which death and evil had no dominion. Therefore he warned Adam: "In the day that thou eatest thereof thou shalt surely die" (Gen. 2:17). That is, on the day that Adam became aware that he could choose the option of evil and death, death would become an integral part of the world. But the incident of the fruit occurred, and the first family was banished from the Garden of Eden. Eternal life was snatched from us. Then the firstborn of the human race, Cain, laid his hand on his brother Abel, and so death entered human culture and has not yet left.

From Cain the biblical culture of death evolved forward. During the time of Cain and Abel and their sacrifices only God was allowed to eat meat while everyone else was vegetarian. Only much later did he permit us to eat meat, but forbade us to murder. From the creation of Adam until after the Flood the human race was vegetarian. Only after leaving the Ark was eating meat permitted, with this restriction: "Only flesh with the life thereof, which is the blood thereof, shall ye not eat" (Gen. 9:4). And immediately after the permitting of eating meat, murder was strictly forbidden: "And surely your blood of your lives will I require…at the hand of man, even at the hand of every man's brother, will I require the life of man. Whoso sheddeth man's blood, by man shall his blood be shed; for in the image of God made he man" (Gen. 9:5–6). Thus we learn that slaughter and murder are inextricably linked.

Kosher slaughter, Rabbi Kook taught us, is an attempt to refine the murderous nature of the human. Every human being is a murderous beast who has been domesticated and refined. In order to lighten our struggle with our inherent murderousness, we have been permitted as a compromise to shed some animal blood. The logic of the forbidden foods is an educational logic that tells us: you may not put anything in your mouth until you have checked its kashrut (literally, its fitness). You must be aware at every moment of the lethal dimension of your appetites, and always ask whether the animal is permitted or forbidden, whether its slaughter was kosher or improper. In other words, the question of kashrut serves at any given moment as a reminder that the slaughter that is permitted to us is merely a concession by God to the flawed soul of his creation. In a sense, a person who observes the laws of kashrut voluntarily limits his participation in the permitted act of killing and eating animals. What is more, anyone who rises to the next level and refrains from eating animals returns, as it were, to the initial phase in the Garden of Eden, where there was no death and no permission to kill.

The conceptual broadening of kashrut into a general awareness of the distinction between good and evil is very much in line with this week's portion. There is no doubt that the road to God's blessing passes straight through the territory of death and evil. By broadening the concept of kashrut, we can see it as part of a much wider moral universe. Not only kosher food, but also relationships within society may be judged through the lens of life and good versus death and evil. Naama Harel, a

Hebrew literature scholar at Emory University who has written extensively on literary notions of species, published the following on the website of Anonymous for Animal Rights, an Israeli activist collective:

> I will only review the actualization of metaphors according to which the man is a hunter and the woman is the hunted animal and his or her flesh, even though there is also a lot of truth to metaphors between men and animals, such as the image of the "stud." The Hebrew language, both the standard as well as slang is filled with expressions taken from the field of meat and game and transferred into the sexual field. In fact, the entire field of sex is called "flesh lust" or "flesh pleasures."
>
> "Sexual hunger" is a passion for sex. A man seeking a woman for a night is a hunter and is armed with his "weapon," the organ of manhood. If the woman gives in easily then she is "easy prey." Events in which women present their bodies (beauty contests, for example) are compared to meat markets and are often nicknamed "the butcher shop."
>
> The Hebrew language also borrows expressions from Arabic, as well as from Yiddish: The word "Freha" in Arabic means a spring chicken, a chick, and a girl's thighs are called Pulkes" in Yiddish – chicken legs. A good-looking girl is a chick, meaning – "a piece, a cut"; and a full-figured woman is "juicy."
>
> The Hebrew language pictures women not only as meat, but also as farm animals prior to their being turned into a product: so, for instance, a "Ketchka" – a goose in Yiddish – means a "light-headed girl, a giggler, a racket raiser." Common nicknames for a fat woman are "cow" or "beast," and "bunny" is a nickname for a girl who is easy to get sexually. (Naama Harel, "Vegetarianism as Feminism," http://anonymous.org.il/art494.html)

One more citation, if you'll bear with me. Not long ago I met a young woman waiting tables in Efrat. In between ordering my coffee and paying my check we chatted for a moment about vegetarianism. Some time later she wrote me a letter with her thoughts on the topic, which captured precisely my own thoughts on vegetarianism. Here is what she wrote:

> One of my objections to eating meat is that it removes us from nature. We're no longer a part of it. We have turned eating meat into an industry of growing by abuse and fattening for murder. We are no longer part of the food chain, but above it. If we were part of nature and hunted for survival, I would look at the whole matter differently.

So who says kashrut is no longer relevant today?

Week 43

Shoftim – Judges

Deuteronomy 16:18–21:9

Who Needs a King?

THREE GOVERNMENTAL STRUCTURES appear in this week's portion that remain as fresh today as they were when they were written. And the order of their appearance is no coincidence: first judges, then police officers, then kings.

First, Moses institutionalizes the system of social justice, and within it the consensual mechanisms of power: "Judges and officers shalt thou make thee in all thy gates, which the Lord thy God giveth thee, tribe by tribe; and they shall judge the people with righteous judgment" (Deut. 16:18). And what is righteous justice? "Thou shalt not wrest judgment; thou shalt not respect persons; neither shalt thou take a gift; for a gift doth blind the eyes of the wise, and pervert the words of the righteous. Justice, justice shalt thou pursue" (Deut. 16:19–20). And the goal is clear: "that thou mayest live" (16:20).

Even though the expression "judges and officers" refers to something quite different from the judicial systems familiar to us today, nonetheless we can recognize an impressive vision of statecraft. On the one hand a system of justice, and on the other hand enforcement mechanisms that were expanded and elaborated over the course of generations. Commentators in various generations drew themselves mental pictures of the systems and their practical implementation, as they imagined them.

Here is one example from Rashi, drawing on earlier Midrash and translations: "Judges: magistrates who render legal decisions. Officers:

who compel the people to abide by their instructions by administering corporal punishment with cudgels and whips, until they accept the judge's decision" (Rashi on Deut. 16:18). Later in the portion, Moses enables the people to choose a king. The delay suggests that only after the communal structure has been organized and an awareness of civil justice has been developed can the coalition of tribes, the confederation of ancient Israel, become a monarchy.

Thus Moses imagined the first state of Israel with a stable judicial system: "And the man that doeth presumptuously, in not hearkening unto the priest that standeth to minister there before the Lord thy God, or unto the judge, even that man shall die; and thou shalt exterminate the evil from Israel. And all the people shall hear, and fear, and do no more presumptuously" (Deut. 17:12–13). And he continues immediately in the very next verse:

> When thou art come unto the land which the Lord thy God giveth thee, and shalt possess it, and shalt dwell therein; and shalt say: "I will set a king over me, like all the nations that are round about me"; thou shalt in any wise set him king over thee, whom the Lord thy God shall choose; one from among thy brethren shalt thou set king over thee. (Deut. 17:14–15)

This is a monarchy that grows up from below, resting on systems of justice. It is not a dictatorship imposed from above by kings motivated by power, ego and the conniving of their intimates.

The passages on kingship are written in an original style that is not widespread in the scripture. "And [thou] shalt say" – that is, the commandment's operational mechanism is to be determined by the decision of the people. If they want a monarchy, a monarchy there will be. If they don't want one, none will arise. This is a proposition that gives considerable latitude to public opinion. Many commentators took note of it. One of the latest, Rabbi Naphtali Tzvi Yehuda Berlin of Volozhin, known as the Netziv, was cognizant by the beginning of the nineteenth century of the democratic winds stirring in Europe. Here is what he wrote in his commentary on the Torah, *Ha'emek Davar*:

> We can see that the leadership of a state changes, and it may be governed by the will of the monarch or by the will of the people and their representatives. There are states that cannot tolerate governance by royal decree. Other states behave without a king like a ship without a captain. This is not a matter that can be ordained by positive commandment, because the quality of public leadership affects matters of life and death, which may in the worst case result in the suspension of commandments in any case. Therefore it is impossible to command categorically that a king be appointed…where public opinion is hostile to monarchical rule, seeing that neighboring states are governed in better ways. (Netziv on Deut. 17:14)

The Netziv's comments are far-sighted. First, he understands that governance does affect matters of life and death. Second, because lives can be at stake, this is not a place for absolute, arbitrary commandments like those in the rest of the Torah. Rather, it must be left to the discretion of the public to take responsibility for managing its own affairs according to its own preferences. Some will choose monarchy and some will choose other, more egalitarian forms of leadership. This verse deems both options legitimate.

Thinkers in earlier generations also pondered the laws of kings. Maimonides flatly declared that the command "Thou shalt in any wise set him king over thee" was a positive commandment, binding on the children of Israel at the moment that they entered the land, despite the seemingly conditional intention of the text, and despite the fact that in the Talmud this view was held by a minority of one. The opposing view was laid out by the Iberian Jewish philosopher-statesman Don Isaac Abravanel (1437–1508), the greatest Jewish leader of the late Middle Ages. A high-ranking financier and adviser to the royal courts of Portugal and Castile, he was also a biblical scholar and commentator, outspoken philosopher and multi-talented author whose influence extended far beyond the Jewish community. Abravanel's philosophy evolved against the backdrop of that tumultuous century that saw the expulsion of Jews from Spain and the decisive showdown between Islam and Christianity on the Iberian Peninsula. Even though Abravanel was a mystic who believed in the literal truth of the Torah, his views on the origins and development of culture and the history of the state and various systems of governance (especially monarchy and democracy) are remarkable for their modern approach:

> "I consider this opinion about the indispensability of a king to be false. [As to the value of unity,] it is not at all impossible for a people to have many leaders conducting the state and its laws in unison and concurrence. [As to continuity,] I know of no reason why their leadership should not be temporary, changing from year to year, or at other intervals, and thus making their actions subject to control and, if need be, to the punishment of those who follow them in office. [As to the benefit of absolute power,] I do not see any reason why their power should not be limited and regulated according to established laws and customs. Common sense dictates that one man in the position of a monarch is more likely to do wrong than many people acting together. For if any one of them is inclined to commit a crime, his colleagues will prevent him from doing so, knowing very well that all of them will be called to account after a short while and will be subject to the punishment meted out by their followers and to public disgrace" (Abravanel's Commentaries on Deuteronomy 17:14 and 1 Samuel 8:4, in Benzion Netanyahu, *Don Isaac Abravanel: Statesman & Philosopher* [Ithaca, NY: Cornell University Press, 1998], p. 173ff)

And regarding this week's portion, the great statesman and renaissance philosopher wrote, "If a king is righteous, a government of many righteous persons is far preferable." Abravanel is an old but very relevant commentator. The lack of a single Jewish approach toward government and its nature creates an opening for a broader and more dynamic potential system of governance.

The Power of the Law

THE DEVELOPMENT of the Israelite bureaucracy is well documented in the Bible. In the beginning the administration consisted of one big, corrosive mess. Everyone descended daily on Moses, the only person who knew what to do and how to do it: "Moses sat to judge the people; and the people stood about Moses from the morning unto the evening" (Exod. 18:13). The first outside observer, Moses's father-in-law Jethro, commented to him after his arrival at the camp about the inefficiency of the operation. Moses was an inexperienced leader of an untested people. He had been a prince up to age eighty, and then came the Exodus. Jethro sets up an improvised mechanism for Moses and saves him from premature collapse:

> Thou shalt provide out of all the people able men, such as fear God, men of truth, hating unjust gain; and place such over them, to be rulers of thousands, rulers of hundreds, rulers of fifties, and rulers of tens. And let them judge the people at all seasons; and it shall be, that every great matter they shall bring unto thee, but every small matter they shall judge themselves; so shall they make it easier for thee and bear the burden with thee. (Exod. 18:21–22)

Nowhere does the Bible specify who these able men were, what they did or how they operated. Still, we might be able to guess. They are described as "fearing God," and yet at the first opportunity, at the sin of the Golden Calf, when Moses could have used a few God-fearing men with him, he cries out, "Whoso is on the Lord's side, let him come unto me" (Exod. 32:26). And who comes? The entire tribe of Levi, God-fearing, able and out for blood:

> And when Moses saw that the people were broken loose – for Aaron had let them loose for a derision among their enemies – then Moses stood in the gate of the camp, and said: "Whoso is on the Lord's side, let him come unto me." And all the sons of Levi gathered themselves together unto him. And he said unto them: "Thus saith the Lord, the God of Israel: Put ye every man his sword upon his thigh, and go to and fro from gate to gate throughout the camp, and slay every man his brother, and every man his companion, and every man his neighbor." And the sons of Levi did according to the word of Moses;

and there fell of the people that day about three thousand men. (Exod. 32:25–28)

It seems evident that Moses had initially appointed his loyalists, members of his own tribe, as the people's judges and his accessories. But now that Moses was passing from the world, it was clear to him that the personal system he had established could not continue to function without a strong central hub like Moses himself. Equally clear to him, apparently, was the people's hostility toward the cold-blooded Levites. He understood that the time had come for the fragmented tribes to take on the shape of an organized nation. Therefore, in this week's portion Moses upgrades the private system he had established and expands it into a fully articulated vision of governance: judges, officers and a king. Moses's legacy of political theory is more complicated than a monarchical system, with all its limitations, or a judicial system and its values.

> Judges and officers shalt thou make thee in all thy gates, which the Lord thy God giveth thee, tribe by tribe; and they shall judge the people with righteous judgment. Thou shalt not wrest judgment; thou shalt not respect persons; neither shalt thou take a gift; for a gift doth blind the eyes of the wise, and pervert the words of the righteous. (Deut. 16:18–19)

When the people began their path through the desert, the judges had to be able-bodied men – or to put it slightly less delicately, tough guys, muscular types who could break up fights and defend Moses. It also wouldn't hurt if they were the sort who knew how to enjoy the job just a little. As the years passed, there was a growing appreciation that law and order were preferable to the existing system of rough and ready discipline that brought neither social unity nor equality. From the moment that the universal benefits of justice were universally understood, the judges and officers no longer needed weapons. The public's interest in legal justice and the growing confidence in the system were now the best defense. The armed Levite militias were disarmed; they now changed their mission and became sacred servants. The Israelite legal system was placed on a single foundational principle: justice – justice that included a prohibition on favoritism, an obligation to investigate thoroughly before passing sentence and, above all, a prohibition on accepting bribes.

Only after the institution of a functioning judicial system, and only on the basis of broad popular consent, might a king be appointed. The portion discusses three principles for choosing a king. First, the king is appointed by the people. Second, the king is subservient to the constitution, which restrains him from turning his monarchy into a dictatorship and making his appointment a hereditary legacy. His constitution is the Torah:

> And it shall be with him, and he shall read therein all the days of his life; that he may learn to fear the Lord his God, to keep all the words of this law and these statutes, to do them; that his heart be not lifted up above his brethren, and that he turn not aside from the commandment, to the right hand, or to the left; to the end that he may prolong his days in his kingdom, he and his children, in the midst of Israel. (Deut. 17:19–20)

Third, there can be no king without a judicial system. Moses, with all his experience, understood that a monarchy must be stable, and stability means dynasty. But dynasty contains the seeds of dangerous moral erosion. For that reason he built a remarkably daring system of separation of powers and mutual oversight. The king is subservient to the Torah. The Torah institutionalizes legal justice under the administration of the judges of Israel, treating every person equally. In other words, not only do the people appoint their king and judges, but the judges oversee the king to defend all of us.

Two of the best-known stories in our tradition concerning the tension between the monarchy and the legal system are built upon Moses's three-legged structure. The first is the story of King Ahab and Naboth of Jezreel. Ahab and his wife Jezebel coveted Naboth's vineyard, so they used every underhanded legal trick to frame him, indict him and ruin him. The details are not very important here; what is important to note is that even in the era of the strongest of all the kings of Israel, Ahab of the house of Omri, a king could not simply expropriate land he desired without going through the biblical legal process, if only for appearance's sake. This is the incident that gave rise to the immortal cry of Elijah the Prophet, "Hast thou killed and also taken possession?" (1 Kings 21:19) – that is, did you murder him and then inherit his property? – and ultimately led to the fall of the house of Ahab. Even under the most despotic of monarchies, due process of law had the power to bring down the corrupt.

The second story concerns the Hasmonean king Alexander Jannaeus (103–76 BCE), known in the Talmud as King Jannai or Yannai. The story encapsulates the biblical principle of separation of church and state as interpreted by the later Talmudic sages. It is important to note that the king was an ally of the majority Sadducee faction among the sages of the Sanhedrin. The chairman of the Sanhedrin, Simeon Ben Shetach, was the leader of the minority Pharisee faction.

> It happened that a slave of King Jannai killed a man. Simeon Ben Shetach said to the Sages, "Set your eyes boldly upon him and let us judge him." So they sent the king word, saying: "Your slave has killed a man." Thereupon he sent him to them [to be tried]. But they again sent him a message: "Thou too must come here, for the Torah says, 'If warning has been given to its owners' [Exod. 21:29, referring to an ox that gores and causes death; if the same ox has gored before and the owner has been warned, the owner may then be tried and executed. The same principle is applied here to the owner of a slave].... The king accordingly came and sat down. Then Simeon Ben Shetach said: "Stand on thy feet, King Jannai, and let the witnesses testify against thee; it is not before us that thou standest, but before him who spoke and the world came into being, as it is written, 'Then both the men between whom the controversy is, shall stand' and so on" [Deut. 19:17, referring to the procedural rule that if two witnesses contradict each other, both "stand before the Lord" while the judges interrogate them]. "I shall not act in accordance with what thou sayest, but in accordance with what thy colleagues say," the king answered. (Babylonian Talmud, *Sanhedrin* 19a)

Shoftim

Here the king is invoking his royal privilege and trying to intimidate the other members of the Sanhedrin, most of whom are his allies, into supporting him. Simeon, the chairman, "then turned first to the right and then to the left, but they all looked down at the ground. Then said Simeon Ben Shetach unto them, '"Are ye wrapped in thoughts? Let the Master of Thoughts come and call you to account!' Instantly, the angel Gabriel came and smote them to the ground, and they died" (Babylonian Talmud, *Sanhedrin* 19b).

Thus, as the Torah nears its end it summarizes its biblical concept of governance. Here it is in a nutshell: the priesthood is genetic, and therefore its role and its power are limited and minimized. The politics of monarchy are human in nature, which implies considerable danger; therefore, limits are imposed on royalty by the power of God in heaven. This power is represented on earth by the legal justice system of the Torah as implemented by the judges of Israel, the representatives of the people.

Week 44

Ki Tetzeh – When Thou Goest Forth

Deuteronomy 21:10–25:19

The Logic of the Commandments

THIS WEEK'S PORTION contains more individual commandments than any other portion in the Torah. This is the crossroad where laws and commandments come together from a variety of the Bible's thematic realms.

The portion opens with a discussion of the legal rights of a woman taken captive as a prize of war and then claimed by her captor as a wife. It continues with the obligations of a husband toward multiple wives and their children (in a case where he loves one wife more than another), the obligations of a finder of lost property, the rights of a condemned convict, rules of interest and debtors' rights, cruelty to animals, fair weights and measures, employee rights and much more. More than seventy individual commandments out of the famed six hundred thirteen can be found among this week's verses. Strangely, it is very difficult to discern any logical or systematic order among the commandments that appear here. Some express the most sublime values, while others seem utterly mundane.

The debate over questions of the commandments' logic and meaning is lengthy and unresolved. Some commentators say humanity should not seek to find meaning in the commandments, but simply accept them as dictates from the All-Knowing. God knows the reasons. We are too puny to understand, nor do we need to know. These commentators see a certain grandeur in unexplained commandments that exist to prove the faith of a believer who obeys without understanding. Other commentators seek the

Ki Tetzeh

meaning of each individual commandment, whether in a genuine quest to understand, in hopes of endearing it to the faithful or to add a new, updated explanation to replace an older one that has become obsolete.

There is a wise saying in the Talmud by the fourth-century Palestinian Talmudic sage Ulla, attesting to the wisdom and the complexity of the commandments' authority: "Ulla said: When rules are decreed in the land of Israel, their reasoning should not be revealed until twelve months after their decree, lest a person who does not agree with the reasoning should come and belittle it" (*Avodah Zarah* 35a). The educational intent of the practice is clear: first let the injunction become habitual, let people grow accustomed to its observance as part of their daily routine, and only then let them know the reasons for the legislation. On the other hand, if an injunction does not successfully establish itself as standard practice, then the following rule takes effect: "A rule is not imposed on the public unless a majority of the public can accept it" (Babylonian Talmud, *Bava Batra* 60b). A sophisticated process takes place, balancing those who impose rules and those who receive them.

Yet a third view sees the observance of the commandments as a contractual expression of the partnership between God and humanity. This is expressed in a Talmudic Aggadah, one of a long series of tales that are told to communicate ideas in the form of a debate between a prominent Jew and a prominent gentile:

> The Roman procurator Turnus Rufus once asked Rabbi Akiva, "Whose actions are finer, those of God or of man?" R. Akiva answered him: "Man's actions are finer." Turnus Rufus responded: "The heavens and the earth – could man create their equal?" Rabbi Akiva said to him: "You cannot make your case by citing something that is beyond man's realm. Bring me something that is within man's capabilities." Turnus Rufus then asked him: "Why do you practice circumcision?" Rabbi Akiva responded: "I knew that you would ask me this. That is why I said that man's actions are finer than God's." Rabbi Akiva brought sheaves of wheat and cakes, and said to Turnus Rufus: "These sheaves are the work of God, while these cakes are the work of man. Aren't the cakes finer than the sheaves?"

Turnus Rufus returned to his previous argument and said: "If God wants children to be circumcised, why doesn't he produce the child circumcised from the womb?" Rabbi Akiva responded: "And why does his umbilical cord come out with him, with the child hanging by his stomach until the mother cuts it? And so, regarding your question as to why the child is not born circumcised, this is because God gave the commandments to the Jewish people in order to refine them. This is why David said [Ps. 18:31]: The word of the Lord is refined." (Midrash Tanhuma, *Tazria* 5).

Whether or not Rabbi Akiva actually ever met Turnus Rufus and debated him, the message of the story is clear: God gave the commandments to the Jewish people so that they can refine themselves, in the way that a goldsmith refines a raw material and shapes it into a precious object of his own design. According to Rabbi Akiva, God is the artist, man is the raw material and the commandments are the hot kiln.

Still, reading through some of the commandments can be an uncomfortable experience. How, the reader might ask, can one subscribe to a religion that requires a rapist to marry his victim without inquiring as to the victim's feelings on the matter? The days of male dominance are over, and women's rights cannot permit a rule of this sort. The Torah of the past fails in too many areas to answer the challenges of the present, undermining its meaning and urgency to a generation like ours. Discussing the meaning of the commandments, therefore, becomes far more crucial, if no less difficult.

It seems to me that for some commandments, their very banality is the heart of their message. Yes, there are groundbreaking rules and brilliant legislative innovations in the Bible. Among these are the Sabbath as a day of physical and spiritual rest, restrictions on slave labor, the continual social revolution of the Sabbatical and Jubilee years, and the concept of the stranger with its accompanying obligations to accept him as an equal. On the other hand, the scripture is filled with things that were greatly important in their day but now evoke nothing more than faint echoes of a forgotten meaning.

Ki Tetzeh

What, for example, can we make of the commandment barring the entry of Ammonites and Moabites into the congregation of the Lord? It's not even clear just who this congregation of the Lord might be, since there is no longer a single definition that encompasses all the Jews who consider themselves Jewish. And nobody knows who the Ammonites and Moabites are today. Another example is the execution of adulterers who perform the act of love outside the formal marriage framework. Would any member of modern civilization even dream of such a punishment? Heaven forbid. Half of our society would meet an untimely end under a hail of stones.

In my way of understanding, the observance of so many commandments that were relevant in their day transmits a very important message precisely because of the fact that they are no longer relevant. The Torah is not a fixed system of unchangeable laws – quite the opposite. Reality is stronger than any commandment. It is clear from tradition that commandments whose logic and foundation have lost their power will fall by the wayside unless they gain a new significance that may not have been visible when the commandment was first given. It thus falls to the reader, the believer and practitioner to separate the wheat from the chaff. To know what does and does not make sense in his time, and leave the things that have become meaningless to some future time when they may acquire a new meaning.

Those who acknowledge the obligation to annul commandments that have lost their meaning will include, I would hope, the atrocious commandment that concludes this portion, or else give it a radically new meaning that accords with the moral temper of our time:

> Remember what Amalek did unto thee by the way as ye came forth out of Egypt; how he met thee by the way, and smote the hindmost of thee, all that were enfeebled in thy rear, when thou wast faint and weary; and he feared not God. Therefore it shall be, when the Lord thy God hath given thee rest from all thine enemies round about, in the land which the Lord thy God giveth thee for an inheritance to possess it, that thou shalt blot out the remembrance of Amalek from under heaven; thou shalt not forget. (Deut. 25:17–19)

The law requires that we relate to those Amalekites the same way we do to the Moabites and the Ammonites. Because their memory has been lost, so too has the actual command been lost that we exterminate them and blot them out. We must not attach Amalekism, as it were, to any other nation or individual of any given religion, faith or race. The only Amalek that we may go to war against is the Amalek of the heart, that which dwells within each of us – what the Hebrew poet Leah Goldberg called "the wicked child in me." Every person has a small Amalek, and every nation has a great Amalekism. Amalek is no longer a nation or people but a psychological state. The commandment to blot out the remembrance of Amalek – if it can or should be given new meaning – calls us to blot out evil from the world, beginning within each of us.

The Other and Myself

THERE ARE COMMANDMENTS that are directed at the sublime and moral in people and cultures. Other commandments, by contrast, are earthbound and human, and their purpose is to compromise with the dark side of human nature. This week's portion moves between these two extremes: on the one hand, a vast broadening of the concept of national belonging by means of the commandments regarding the stranger and our obligations toward him, and on the other hand, almost embarrassing reflections on the reality of biblical family life. Our current task is to find the bridge between the abandoned depths and the sublime peaks.

The text repeatedly emphasizes our noble obligation toward strangers:

> Thou shalt not pervert the justice due to the stranger, or to the fatherless; nor take the widow's raiment to pledge. But thou shalt remember that thou wast a bondman in Egypt, and the Lord thy God redeemed thee thence; therefore I command thee to do this thing. When thou reapest thy harvest in thy field, and hast forgot a sheaf in the field, thou shalt not go back to fetch it; it shall be for the stranger, for the fatherless, and for the widow; that the Lord thy God

Ki Tetzeh

> may bless thee in all the work of thy hands. When thou beatest thine olive-tree, thou shalt not go over the boughs again; it shall be for the stranger, for the fatherless, and for the widow. When thou gatherest the grapes of thy vineyard, thou shalt not glean it after thee; it shall be for the stranger, for the fatherless, and for the widow. And thou shalt remember that thou wast a bondman in the land of Egypt; therefore I command thee to do this thing. (Deut. 24:17–22)

However, in contrast to this collection of commandments regarding the stranger, the portion is chock-full of commandments touching on relations between man and woman. A minority of them deals with the beautiful, intimate aspect of family life, while the majority is devoted to the unusual and perverse. The portion repeatedly returns and focuses in varying ways on the topics of sex and impulse gratification, of daily conflicts that spin out of control and familial dysfunctions that call for repair. The portion begins with the cycle of connections between war and violence and family dysfunction: the Israelite warrior went out to battle and brought home captives and booty – including "a woman of goodly form, and thou hast a desire unto her, and wouldest take her to thee to wife" (Deut. 21:11). No good can possibly come from this tale.

Rashi looks for a sequence of associations, and here is how he explains the connections between the portion's opening incidents: A husband comes home from the battlefield with an attractive woman captive. Suddenly he has two wives in his family – the beautiful, new one and the old, hated one. Inevitably, conflicts and tensions arise, and the inescapable result is a collapse of household child rearing. Their son becomes unmanageable, a "stubborn and rebellious son" (Deut. 21:18). In Rashi's own words:

> And you take her to be a wife: The Torah speak of this only because of the evil inclination. For if the Holy One, praised be he, would not permit [him to marry] her, he would live with her illicitly. However, if he does marry her, in the end she will be hated, as it says afterward: "If a man have two wives, the one hated, and the other hated, and they have borne him children" [Deut. 21:15], in the end he will sire

a stubborn and rebellious son. That is why these passages adjacent to one another. (Rashi on Deut. 21:11)

But the portion's sequences of associations on the topic do not end there. Here are some more:

> If any man take a wife, and go in unto her, and hate her, and lay wanton charges against her, and bring up an evil name upon her, and say: "I took this woman, and when I came nigh to her, I found not in her the tokens of virginity"...the damsel's father shall say unto the elders: "I gave my daughter unto this man to wife, and he hateth her...yet these are the tokens of my daughter's virginity."...And the elders of that city shall take the man and chastise him.... But if this thing be true, that the tokens of virginity were not found...the men of her city shall stone her with stones that she die; because she hath wrought a wanton deed in Israel. (Deut. 22:13–21)
>
> If a man be found lying with a woman married to a husband, then they shall both of them die, the man that lay with the woman, and the woman; so shalt thou put away the evil from Israel. (Deut. 22:22)
>
> If there be a damsel that is a virgin betrothed unto a man, and a man find her in the city, and lie with her...ye shall stone them with stones that they die: the damsel, because she cried not, being in the city.... But if the man find the damsel that is betrothed in the field... then the man only that lay with her shall die.... For he found her in the field; the betrothed damsel cried, and there was none to save her. (Deut. 22:23–27)

And there are more of these strange, disconcerting stories, all of them revolving around sex, power and lust.

What does this bounty of injunctions show us? Piety or wantonness? Over-strictness or utter lack of basic values? We can't know the answer. And yet, we cannot avoid the question: What is the connection between the commandments regarding the stranger and the passages about lust that we find bound together in the same portion?

Ki Tetzeh

I believe there's a common denominator between the wonderfully humane commandments regarding the stranger and the elaborate licentiousness detailed elsewhere. The portion's real subject is the walls that surround us, both overt and unseen. We find it comfortable to be among those who resemble us. It is difficult to live with strangers, and with those who differ from us and threaten us by their very otherness and mysteriousness. To break down the walls of spiritual isolation the Torah commands us to open ourselves up to the stranger the way we once expected the Egyptians to open themselves to us, the nation of slaves in their midst, only to find our hopes dashed. Jewish civilization permits conversion, accepts the newcomer and remains alert to his complicated relations with his new surroundings. Biblical conversion is one of the most compelling tools there is for preventing the racism and xenophobia that threaten a culture as ethnically based as ours. The portion's sexual scenarios also touch on areas of human weakness, but here the Torah tries the opposite approach: rather than blowing a hole in the fence of isolation, it tries to repair the breaches in the wall, lest the whole family break out.

Here are two Midrashic tales that highlight the contrast between the two commandments. On human weakness and passion the Midrash Aggadah says this:

"Why did the Holy One, praised be he, permit taking a gentile woman captive in war? So one would not lie with her dead body. And why would that be? Because of the evil impulse. He said it is better to eat the flesh of slaughtered animals than to eat carrion" (Midrash Aggadah [Buber], *Deuteronomy* 21). The attractive gentile woman is described here as slaughtered, presumably in a kosher manner, and not carrion, which would be absolutely forbidden. How blessed to defined as slaughtered and not carrion. The commandments concerning the attractive captive who becomes her captor's wife constitute a compromise between the giver of the commandment and its recipient. If not for the stopgap offered here, the man would follow his instincts and lose his whole moral and personal world. The compromise of permitted sex is one of the few compromises that the Torah makes with the Israelite who has not yet reached the higher level of commandment and pure faith, rather than partial. It is much like the compromises over animal sacrifice and kosher meat versus vegetarianism that we discussed previously.

If the commandments are a ladder leading up to heaven, these were its base, planted on the muddy soil of earth and the worst of human pollution. The following Midrash offers the opposite: the top of the ladder, reaching upward. Years after the Torah was canonically sealed, the sages counted the number of times stranger is mentioned. They found thirty-six references, and the significance they deduced from this is explained by Rashi: "If there is a case of hanging in a man's family record, do not say to him, 'Hang this fish up for me,' for any mention of hanging will insult him" (Babylonian Talmud, *Bava Metzia* 59b). The modern version of this is the proverb "Don't mention rope in the home of a hanged man."

The sages almost always looked at real-time affairs in the context of history and tradition. We are a people that is eternally in flight from Egypt, and we may never forget what was done to us as slaves and strangers, weak and helpless. A person who attains the proper level of sensitivity to the helpless, the stranger, the orphan and the widow has by definition passed through many stages in the refinement of his love for those closest to him. He will not give free rein to his aggressive impulses in a pointless war. He won't give in to avarice nor humiliate a prisoner. He won't allow his worst instincts to take control of him and thus destroy his loving family. One who loves the stranger and outsider will love his intimates no less. Love of the stranger is one of the Bible's hidden keys to preventing war and loving peace. One who loves the stranger will be attentive to the people and culture from whom that stranger emerged. In the opposite corner stands the oppressor, the rapist and abuser of women, who is condemned to never-ending war abroad and the destruction of his society and family at home.

Week 45

Ki Tavo – When Thou Art Come In

Deuteronomy 26:1–29:8

Cursed Be the Staff of Judgment of the Stranger, the Orphan and Widow

Let's admit the truth: life is an ever-growing series of compromises between desires and abilities, between the dream and the possible. Few things in life are perfect. Even the Torah, the teaching that God gave through Moses, is a teaching of life and not theory. Its laws are directed at a life that contains a measure of imperfection. It is possible and proper to live by the Torah's commandments, but one can and must aim higher. Everything depends on us. And yet, having said all that, we occasionally find absolutes jumping out at us from Moses's words. Sometimes he loses hold of the moderating reins of real life and hurls his binary thinking at the people: either life or death, either blessing or curse, either my way or the highway to destruction. This week's portion falls into that category. It is filled with long, weighty passages dealing with rebuke and punishment. On the surface, there is no apparent middle ground between the two opposing absolutes.

After a brief opening, containing the commandment to bring the first fruits, interwoven with a history of the children of Israel from Egypt up to this point, comes a dramatic ceremony of blessing and curse. It takes place on two mountains overlooking the city of Shechem, Mount Gerizim and Mount Ebal, the mountains of blessing and curse:

> And Moses charged the people the same day, saying: "These shall stand upon mount Gerizim to bless the people, when ye are passed over the Jordan: Simeon, and Levi, and Judah, and Issachar, and Joseph, and Benjamin; and these shall stand upon mount Ebal for the curse: Reuben, Gad, and Asher, and Zebulun, Dan, and Naphtali. And the Levites shall speak, and say unto all the men of Israel with a loud voice…" (Deut. 27:11–14)

Here we come to an interesting elaboration of the actions that make a person cursed:

> Cursed be the man that maketh a graven or molten image, an abomination unto the Lord, the work of the hands of the craftsman, and setteth it up in secret. And all the people shall answer and say: Amen.
>
> Cursed be he that dishonoreth his father or his mother. And all the people shall say: Amen.
>
> Cursed be he that removeth his neighbor's landmark. And all the people shall say: Amen.
>
> Cursed be he that maketh the blind to go astray in the way. And all the people shall say: Amen.
>
> Cursed be he that perverteth the justice due to the stranger, fatherless and widow. And all the people shall say: Amen.
>
> Cursed be he that lieth with his father's wife; because he hath uncovered his father's skirt. And all the people shall say: Amen.
>
> Cursed be he that lieth with any manner of beast. And all the people shall say: Amen.
>
> Cursed be he that lieth with his sister, the daughter of his father or the daughter of his mother. And all the people shall say: Amen.
>
> Cursed be he that lieth with his mother-in-law. And all the people shall say: Amen.
>
> Cursed be he that smiteth his neighbor in secret. And all the people shall say: Amen.

> Cursed be he that taketh a bribe to slay an innocent person. And all the people shall say: Amen.
>
> Cursed be he that confirmeth not the words of this law to do them. And all the people shall say: Amen.
>
> (Deut. 27:15–26)

Many of these cursed prohibitions pertain to actions that a person would be ashamed to perform in public. Therefore one is forewarned in a public curse not to perform them in private. In the words of the sages: "Wherever the Sages forbade something for appearance's sake, it is forbidden even in the innermost chambers" (Babylonian Talmud, *Shabbat* 146b). Anyone who worships another god "and setteth it up in secret," or whose sexual appetites are forbidden by societal norms, is warned not to enact the forbidden relations – with gods, his mother-in-law or a neighbor's cow – in some hiding place where he thinks he is safe from society's watchful eye.

Among all these prohibitions, two stand out at variance with the landscape described here: "Cursed be he that maketh the blind to go astray in the way" and "Cursed be he that perverteth the justice due to the stranger, fatherless and widow." There is no real secrecy in these actions. Unlike most of the other misdeeds detailed above which take place without a witness, a blind person is a reliable witness to any misdirections or stumbling blocks placed in his way. Judgment takes place in public view, including the trial of the widow and the sentencing of the orphan and stranger. Each of these acts involves more actors than just the sinner acting in the privacy of his own thoughts or in concert with a few co-conspirators. So why are these two included here?

These two commandments show us that we need to rethink our understanding of the biblical concept of secrecy. There are things that might appear to be public but actually involve factors that are still secret. How so? Society does not notice the poor and helpless. It discounts them, ignores them and turns them into non-people, and the things that are done to them in plain sight become non-events. It is a sort of evil human wizardry that makes the uncomfortable disappear and treats the irregular as if it never existed, even though it sits before our very eyes, asking to be seen.

Here is how the medieval Spanish poet and Torah commentator Abraham Ibn Ezra described these invisible people: "For they have no helper, and they are hidden. The stranger, the orphan and the widow are mentioned here because if the judge subverts the case of others, they will protest and make the matter known. However, the stranger, the orphan and the widow do not have the ability to do so" (Ibn Ezra on Deut. 27:19). In other words, to be taken into account in society requires power and influence. Those who are denied access to the centers of power and influence become part of a secret humanity, the invisible people, and suddenly there is no difference between the cow that is helplessly, unwillingly inseminated and the widow whose life is ended by her husband's death, or the orphan and stranger who are erased from human consciousness.

To emphasize his words and give the force appropriate to an absolute prohibition, Moses promises horrific punishments to anyone who would dare to violate the oaths: "But it shall come to pass, if thou wilt not hearken unto the voice of the Lord thy God, to observe to do all his commandments and his statutes which I command thee this day; that all these curses shall come upon thee, and overtake thee" (Deut. 28:15). In principle, the punishments are conceived as a tit-for-tat response: "And thou shalt grope at noonday, as the blind gropeth in darkness, and thou shalt not make thy ways prosperous; and thou shalt be only oppressed and robbed alway, and there shall be none to save thee" (Deut. 28:29).

Moses speaks in absolute terms of blessing and curse, but the actual content of his words is sensitive and open, extending a hand to those who need it. The Torah was fortunate that the man who received it from heaven was "slow of speech and of slow tongue," someone with disabilities and limitations who nonetheless set out on his mission and managed against all odds to succeed. Who would know better than he that the next redeemer might emerge from hardship and disability.

Late Reconciliation

*I*F THE TORAH WERE WRITTEN TODAY, the last portions of the past few weeks would have been dedicated to the colorful aspects of Moses's departure. We would be reading about gossip, calculations, angry words and a few

Ki Tavo

crocodile tears for the sake of appearances. To our good fortune the Torah was written then and is interpreted today, and not the opposite. Thus we have the opportunity almost every week to understand the present through the lens of the past. Tradition and its interpretation serve as limitless ammunition for a permanent revolution.

Woven through this week's portion like a minor theme is the phrase "this day," the day on which Moses is to die. Almost 10 percent of the times the phrase "this day" appears in the Torah are in this one portion. The phrase appears only twice in telling of the creation of the world, compared to twelve times in this portion, *Parashat Ki Tavo*. Moses, the slow of speech, does not stop talking, instructing, summing up and commanding. On his last day, the elderly, dying leader seems to be full of energy, particularly focused and fully cognizant of the human condition from which he is taking his leave. With "this day" as our backdrop, let's try to add another level of understanding to the commentary on the blessings and the curses.

Parashat Ki Tavo is a portion of extremes, with blessing and curse and almost no moderate middle. At one extreme, many of its verses are filled with harsh rebuke, while at the other extreme, blessings are promised as well. On one side, we are warned that anyone who transgresses will be cursed in various ways, and on the other side, anyone who keeps the commandments will be blessed. In contrast to other portions in this genre of blessing and curse, *Parashat Ki Tavo* is spoken in its entirety by Moses personally and at his own initiative. The curses and blessings that appear at the end of the Book of Leviticus in *Parashat Bechukotai* begin with God speaking in the first person: "If ye walk in my statutes…. But if ye will not hearken unto me" (Lev. 26:3; 26:14). In this week's portion, though, everything comes from the mouth of Moses: "And Moses…commanded…"; "And Moses…spoke…"; and again "And Moses charged the people the same day" (Deut. 27:11). Let's examine this "day" and Moses's place in it.

First, what is the significance of "this day"? "But the Lord hath not given you a heart to know, and eyes to see, and ears to hear, unto this day" (Deut. 29:4). Rashi expresses a very personal and unusual thought:

> I have heard that on the day that Moses gave the Torah scroll to the children of Levi…all Israel came before Moses and said to him:

"Moses our teacher, we too stood before Sinai and received the Torah and God gave it to us, so why do you give the members of your tribe control of it? Tomorrow they will say to us, he did not give it to you, he gave it to us." And Moses was happy to hear this, and he said to them: "This day thou art become a people unto the Lord thy God [Deut. 27:9], on this day I have learned that you are faithful and desirous of the Lord." (Rashi on Deut. 27:9)

We have discussed the arrogance of the children of Levi looking down their noses at the rest of the people and telling them, "He did not give it to you, he gave it to us." Today we will look at the positive, original aspect.

On the face of it, all this sounds like a wonderful dialogue between a leader and his followers. They are asking him to apply the law equally on everyone, saying, "We too stood before Sinai." In the Torah of Moses, so the children of Israel claim, knowledge belongs to all and there are no hierarchies. But a question emerges between the lines of this Midrash: Why was it that Korah and his congregation, who were making the very same request – "All the congregation are holy, every one of them…wherefore then lift ye up yourselves above the assembly of the Lord?" (Num. 16:3) – were swallowed up by the earth, while here the arrogance of the children of Levi is forgiven and all Israel receives a dismissive pat on the head from Moses? What does Moses understand now that he didn't know back then at the time of Korah's rebellion?

In *Parashat Korah* Moses heard the demand for equality delivered with an insult – "Wherefore then lift ye up yourselves above the assembly of the Lord?" – and fell on his face. This made it clear that two different concepts of holiness were facing off against each other: God's, presented through Moses, and Korah's. Korah claimed an inherent holiness, since "all the congregation are holy," while Moses made holiness an obligation of the individual human heart in his efforts at improving the self and the world.

It took Moses forty long years to convince the people that he was right and not Korah. Forty years of exhausting arguments and squabbles (as the Psalm documents: "For forty years was I wearied with that generation" [Ps. 95:10]) had brought Moses and the people at long last to a meeting point. The people now say, according to Rashi and the Midrash: "We too... received," and Moses for his part "was happy to hear this." Finally they have become active and motivated to carry on his legacy. Maybe this is what the Mishnaic sage Judah Ben Tema meant when he said, "At age forty a man is ready for understanding" (Mishnah, *Avot* 5:21). When they had reached the collective age of forty, they reached an understanding of nationhood. They came to understand what was expected of them. They key phrase is "we received," which is to say, we have absorbed it, we understand it and we are ready to join you in carrying on your work in the effort to uplift humanity and improve the world.

Hence the differences in language between God's previous rebukes in Leviticus and Moses's rebukes here. Is this merely a stylistic difference between the Book of Leviticus, in which God speaks, and Book of Deuteronomy, told in Moses's voice, or is there something deeper? Why, of course it is deeper. *Parashat Ki Tavo* is read in synagogue each year shortly before Rosh Hashanah and the solemn Days of Awe in the month of Tishrei. These are holy days of ennoblement of the soul, of standing before God to seek atonement and renewal. They are distinct in that one cannot approach the holy days without first atoning for sins against one's neighbors, without seeking and receiving the neighbor's forgiveness. And so it is with Moses and the children of Israel at the end of their journey through the desert. Between the lines, he and they are seeking mutual forgiveness. They do so in the proper way, speaking in the first person, directly and without mediation. After long years of struggle, Moses can now take his leave of the world reconciled. They have asked for his Torah and received it. Wisdom and knowledge now belong to everyone.

Anyone who wishes may come and learn. No one has a monopoly on the Torah or its interpretation, not even its attendants, the Levites. The melding of the people's readiness and Moses's happiness has brought about a reversal of roles, as we recite in the *Shofarot* verses on the fast approaching holy day of Rosh Hashanah: "When the voice of the horn waxed louder and louder, Moses spoke, and God answered him by a voice" (Exod. 19:19).

Why Was Moses Punished?

ONE OF THE GREAT PUZZLES of the biblical narrative is the question of Moses's punishment. What sin did this greatest of our heroes commit that could justify such a punishment – the denial of his most burning desire, to enter the Promised Land? From age eighty until he reached one hundred twenty, he gave his all. He worked day and night, sacrificing his family life, paying the exorbitant price of the loss of all privacy, enduring endless criticism, grievance and complaint. He didn't deserve to enter the Promised Land?

It might be argued that these are the laws of nature. He wasn't young anymore. Perhaps his old heart couldn't stand the emotion, the pressure and expectation. But no. At the beginning of the Book of Deuteronomy Moses makes clear that he will not enter the land because God is punishing him on account of Israel's behavior: "The Lord was angry with me for your sakes, saying: Thou also shalt not go in thither" (Deut. 1:37). What had the children of Israel done – and what had Moses done with them – that could evoke such terrible divine anger?

It does not make sense to me that the punishment is because Moses struck the rock to draw forth water in the wilderness of Zin (Num. 20:11). Yes, God had told Moses to speak to the rock, and Moses "spoke" to it with a stick instead of words. But Moses had defied God on other occasions far more harshly and resolutely than this nervous tap on an inanimate rock somewhere in the forsaken wastes of the Sinai Peninsula. Striking the rock could not be the reason. The truth lies elsewhere, buried deep in the text and waiting to be discovered.

One of the most painful truths in the biblical narrative has been lying hidden for years under a cloak of words. Moses was punished by God for the same reason that the generation who left Egypt were punished. They and he sinned in thinking that Moses was God. They forgot for a moment how fleeting is human life and they turned a mortal born of woman and man, Moses son of Jochebed and Amram, into an independent divinity. For this there is no forgiveness, and there can never be absolution.

Ki Tavo

Where is this written? In the Torah! Moses climbs Mount Sinai to receive the Torah. He stays there more than forty days and forty nights, right through the awesome pyrotechnic display of the giving of the Torah. Toward the end of the forty days the people start to lose their grip. As they lose count of the days that have elapsed, tension rises in the camp and a movement emerges to press for a new god. They turn to Aaron the priest, who goes spineless when they confront him, and they demand: "Up, make us a god who shall go before us; for as for this Moses, the man that brought us up out of the land of Egypt, we know not what is become of him" (Exod. 32:1). In their view, it was Moses who brought them out of Egypt, not God. Moses is the god who redeemed them from Egypt, and they are simply demanding a replacement for the god who disappeared on the mountaintop. The children of Israel have not grasped the sublime abstraction behind the Lord of prophets. They have not distinguished between the messenger and the Sender. Moses was God to them. This was their sin.

The sin was so great and the punishment so terrible that some have compared it to Adam's sin and expulsion from the Garden of Eden. God's initial response to the sin of the Golden Calf, we recall, was to destroy them all, and he only relented in the face of Moses's pleading. The next time he decides to destroy them is after the sin of the spies who brought an evil report of the Promised Land, and of him, and here again he contents himself with merely denying them entry into the land. The parallel between the two sins and punishments is striking.

And what about Moses's sin? It is very hard to enter the mind of a such a person. It is hard to understand the moods of someone who stood up to Pharaoh and defeated him, who brought plagues down on the superpower of the ancient world, split the sea, spoke with God, crossed the desert, sent out spies and stopped plagues. No one before him had accomplished anything like this. Could it be that at some point he became confused? Did the voices rising from across the camp about his supposed divinity somehow break through his protective wall of modesty and lull him into thinking of himself as a god? If so, did he then stand equal before the law with his people? Anyone who ever committed the sin of replacing God in heaven with a human god was denied entry into the Promised Land. The land was intended to be a place where no person was worth more than another. This place of ours is holy because all people are equal here. No one can think of another as god, nor can anyone consider himself worthy of worship.

Here is how Moses reveals his inner turmoil in this week's portion:

> And Moses called unto all Israel, and said unto them: Ye have seen all that the Lord did before your eyes in the land of Egypt unto Pharaoh, and unto all his servants, and unto all his land; the great trials which thine eyes saw, the signs and those great wonders; but the Lord hath not given you a heart to know, and eyes to see, and ears to hear, unto this day. And I have led you forty years in the wilderness; your clothes are not waxen old upon you, and thy shoe is not waxen old upon thy foot. Ye have not eaten bread, neither have ye drunk wine or strong drink; that ye might know that I am the Lord your God. (Deut. 29:1–5)

At first glance, this appears to be Moses's historical review, regaling his people with their history and the miraculous nature of their great journey through the desert. However, a more exacting reading reveals a shocking inner truth. Here is how that passage reads when it is broken down:

Narrator: "And Moses called unto all Israel, and said unto them."

Moses, to the people: "Ye have seen all that the Lord did before your eyes in the land of Egypt unto Pharaoh, and unto all his servants, and unto all his land; the great trials which thine eyes saw, the signs and those great wonders."

Moses, to God: "But the Lord hath not given you a heart to know, and eyes to see, and ears to hear, unto this day."

Moses, to himself: "And I have led you forty years in the wilderness."

Moses, to the people again: "Your clothes are not waxen old upon you, and thy shoe is not waxen old upon thy foot. Ye have not eaten bread, neither have ye drunk wine or strong drink."

To whom, then, does Moses address these words: "That ye might know that I am the Lord your God"?

This entire passage is a conversation (albeit one-sided) between Moses and the people. Some of the words are statements about God and his deeds and some are about the people and its history. Neither the people nor God are speaking in this passage, only Moses. Accordingly, what we have here is Moses's personal testimony, first hand and unmediated. Moses concludes his sermon with these unequivocal words: "I am the Lord your God."

It is hard to escape the plain language of the text. The passage immediately preceding this one ended with these words: "These are the words of the covenant which the Lord commanded Moses to make with the children of Israel in the land of Moab, beside the covenant which he made with them in Horeb" (Deut. 28:69). The passage under discussion begins, as we noted, quite differently: "And Moses called unto all Israel, and said unto them." The biblical author was perfectly aware of the difference between a text that comes from God and a text representing a solo performance by Moses.

In this solo text, Moses turns to the people and addresses them directly as the party immediately present, as "you," while God is referred to in the third person, as a party not immediately present. Suddenly a message jumps out from the text: "I have led you forty years in the wilderness" – I, Moses, addressing you in the first person singular – "that ye might know that I am the Lord your God." It is hard to imagine, unpleasant to consider, and certainly has not been addressed by any of the traditional commentators throughout the generations, but a careful reading of this conversation does not leave much room for imagination as to whom Moses had in mind when he concluded his address with the words: "I am the Lord." This is his sin, one more possible solution to the age-old riddle of why Moses was punished and denied entry to the Promised Land.

Week 46

Nitzavim/Vayelech
You Are Standing/And Moses Went

Deuteronomy 29:9–31:30

This Song

THE NEW YEAR IS ALREADY PEEKING through the lengthening shadows of earlier sunsets. The skies of Israel are cloudier, and everywhere the crisp air and sunlight of these special days await the coming of autumn and the New Year, Rosh Hashanah. The double portions of *Nitzavim* and *Vayelech* are another sign that the year is coming to an end. These two brief portions will always be the last portions read in the outgoing year. The yearly cycle of Torah readings ends and begins again on the holiday of Simchat Torah, the "Rejoicing in the Torah" that comes three weeks after Rosh Hashanah, but the last portion of the year's regular Sabbaths is always *Parashat Vayelech*, which ends with the words: "And Moses spoke in the ears of all the assembly of Israel the words of this song, until they were finished" (Deut. 31:30).

In the verses that precede this gentle finale, Moses details his warnings and curses, but then, suddenly, all the curses that Moses has been reciting turn into an uplifting song. How can this be? What song is this? Are we speaking of the sublimely rhythmic couplets of the next portion, *Parashat Ha'azinu*? Or perhaps of the entire Book of Deuteronomy, Moses's epic retelling of the life, history and destiny of the Jewish people? Perhaps the entire Torah is one great song? There are as many interpretations and

Nitzavim/Vayelech

commentaries as there are commentators. Today we shall search in a slightly different direction.

The song that Moses recites into the ears of the assembly is mentioned earlier in the portion. It refers to what is essentially Moses's spiritual will, the mystery of mysteries of the Torah. "This song" is the scorched memory of Jewish consciousness, the root source of the grief and optimism that dictates the Jewish people's destiny throughout the generations from destruction to redemption and back again. "This song" is that something that always comes to mind at moments of great crisis. This is the song of this week's portion:

> And the Lord said unto Moses: "Behold, thy days approach that thou must die; call Joshua, and present yourselves in the tent of meeting, that I may give him a charge." And Moses and Joshua went, and presented themselves in the tent of meeting. And the Lord appeared in the Tent in a pillar of cloud; and the pillar of cloud stood over the door of the Tent. And the Lord said unto Moses: "Behold, thou art about to sleep with thy fathers; and this people will rise up, and go astray after the foreign gods of the land, whither they go to be among them, and will forsake me, and break my covenant which I have made with them. Then my anger shall be kindled against them in that day, and I will forsake them, and I will hide my face from them, and they shall be devoured, and many evils and troubles shall come upon them; so that they will say in that day: Are not these evils come upon us because our God is not among us? And I will surely hide my face in that day for all the evil which they shall have wrought, in that they are turned unto other gods.

> "Now therefore write ye this song for you, and teach thou it the children of Israel; put it in their mouths, that this song may be a witness for me against the children of Israel. For when I shall have brought them into the land which I swore unto their fathers, flowing with milk and honey; and they shall have eaten their fill, and waxen fat; and turned unto other gods, and served them, and despised me, and broken my covenant; then it shall come to pass, when many

evils and troubles are come upon them, that this song shall testify before them as a witness; for it shall not be forgotten out of the mouths of their seed; for I know their imagination how they do even now, before I have brought them into the land which I swore." So Moses wrote this song the same day, and taught it the children of Israel. (Deut. 31:14–22)

Six of the eight references to the word *song* in the Torah appear in this passage. What is this hinting at?

These verses in the above passage are among the most emotionally fraught in the entire Bible. This is the summary of our fate and destiny. It contains a built-in pessimism and an eternal seed of hope. These verses are the key to the cycle of Jewish survival. Here is how I read them:

Leaders arise and save the people, but they are temporary and mortal. Every leader goes through what Moses went through and ends up sleeping with his fathers. After his death the people fall apart. The path is lost, the direction is hidden in clouds, the purpose suddenly disappears into secrecy and the people are left to grope in the dark in search of its path and its mission. In its search it goes whoring after other gods – gods of wood and stone, silver and gold. And all the while the true divinity, with all its nobility and sublime meaning, is so near and accessible that it is easily ignored. Error and doubt bring on great ruin, and with it come troubles in triplicate: "many evils and troubles." Characteristic of these periods is a great hiding of God's face. God is no longer discernable, salvation is nowhere to be seen and despair grows and spreads.

And humankind does not call itself to account until disaster hits; it does not examine its failings or correct its ways. But when trouble and failure come knocking at the door, a process of correction emerges out of the corruption. And who can reawaken optimism and hope? Why, "this song." It plants itself before the punishing Father in heaven and casts its plea in his face, as if to say, "I come to bear witness that you were right. Yes, you told us. Sometimes, though, it is better to be wise rather than right." Then it goes down below, stands before the suffering people and transforms itself from song into memory, and from memory into recollection, and from recollection into revival, renewal and return to the milk and honey of life – and back again. This is the song of the Jewish people's secrets, the soul of a nation that alternately reveals and hides itself.

We encountered the hope borne by this song once before, during the troubles in the Book of Numbers. Moses and Aaron were striking the rock instead of speaking to it, and for this heresy God says to them, "Because ye believed not in me, to sanctify me in the eyes of the children of Israel, therefore ye shall not bring this assembly into the land which I have given them" (Num. 20:12).

After this, the people of Edom refuse our ancestors permission to pass through its borders en route; Aaron dies; the Canaanite king of Arad makes war on the Israelites and takes captives; and a plague of "fiery serpents" descends on the people, biting them and killing many of them. This was a bad period. The face of God was largely hidden, and what little could be seen of it was angry and punishing. And then a change occurred, beginning at the initiative of the battered people themselves and continuing with the charmed song:

> And the people came to Moses, and said: "We have sinned, because we have spoken against the Lord, and against thee; pray unto the Lord, that he take away the serpents from us." And Moses prayed for the people. And the Lord said unto Moses: "Make thee a fiery serpent, and set it upon a pole; and it shall come to pass, that every one that is bitten, when he seeth it, shall live." And Moses made a serpent of brass, and set it upon the pole; and it came to pass, that if a serpent had bitten any man, when he looked unto the serpent of brass, he lived. (Num. 21:7–9)

And with the decree of life came the song: "Then sang Israel this song" (Num. 21:17).

Of this song that transforms worlds and softens God's decrees the Midrash has this to say: "Then sang Israel this song: This is one of the three things that Moses said to God to which God replied: You have taught me something" (Midrash Rabba, *Bamidbar* 19:33). The song of Moses and Israel is the song of humanity taking its fate in its own hands. Prayer and willingness to change are the song that teaches God how to come out of hiding and show his face once again. God the student is hidden in the inner core of "this song."

"This song" has the power to transform whole destinies, to turn exile into redemption, punishment into blessing and eternal curse into a resurrection of humanity. This is the song of Moses that accompanies us as we enter the new year, with its hopes and prayers that are never in vain.

Week 47

Ha'azinu – Give Ear

Deuteronomy 32:1–32:52

Return, O Israel

THE SABBATH OF PARASHAT HA'AZINU is commonly spoken of affectionately as *Shabbat Shuvah* (Sabbath of Return) after the opening words of the haftarah, the passage from Prophets that accompanies the Torah reading: "Return, O Israel" (Hos. 14:2). The name has a double meaning, since this Sabbath falls between Rosh Hashanah and Yom Kippur, during the Ten Days of Repentance. The Hebrew word *teshuvah* (repentance) comes from the same root as *shuvah* (return), and means essentially the same thing: return to the right path. But that gives us only the meaning of the word. What does the act mean? What is *teshuvah*?

Many look at the concept of *teshuvah* as a fairly simple matter, captured in the first verse of this week's haftarah reading: "Return, O Israel, unto the Lord thy God; for thou hast stumbled in thine iniquity" (Hos. 14:2). On the face of it, this is the official invitation to return to the fundamentals of faith. Some of us understand this as an instruction to head for some Jewish equivalent of the confession booth, to unburden ourselves of the sins within our hearts and then, as is customary, to head right back out and sin some more. There are many who sin and confess in a constantly recurring cycle without any substantive change in themselves or their surroundings, without uprooting the source of the sin that necessitated the *teshuvah*. But is this really *teshuvah*?

It isn't always easy to return to the same familiar God. Anyone who reads the plain language of the scriptures will be hard pressed to see the creator of the universe as a kindly, forgiving father. The Flood swept the earth clean, Sodom was overthrown and the sea drowned Pharaoh's soldiers along with their horses. Catastrophes have continued straight on down through the generations, including the Holocaust and beyond. The waves of God's anger do not quickly recede. Why should we expect him to show any greater forgiveness in our own personal cases? And so we content ourselves with a far more limited discussion, and assume that *teshuvah* is probably a purely human doctrine with no connection to anything occurring on a higher plane in response to our actions.

The penitent, the returnee, is unquestionably someone who wishes to retrace his steps and correct them. Whether he has sinned on a large scale or small, he seeks repair, improvement and self-renewal. Not everyone can reach this level. How often have you said to yourself, "It's too late – at this age a person can't change"? How many times have others said it about you? Quite a few, no doubt. In the face of all this, the Torah comes to tell us: no one is ever too old to change, whatever their past habits or behavior. The High Holy Days and the Season of Repentance are not merely warnings against stubbornly persisting in following the wrong path. More than anything, they offer encouragement and positive reinforcement to a person who decides to leave one path and head down another.

Jewish culture believes in the never-ending human power of self-renewal and rededication. We wait for a person to find renewal until his last day. Just as every tree, no matter how old, brings forth new greenery with the coming of spring, every person can blossom with new leaves of soul and spirit when the season of repentance arrives. For that reason, the Torah of *teshuvah* and renewal is based neither on persistent feelings of guilt nor on cheap, easy gestures of absolution, but rather on uncompromising faith in the positive within humanity. There is only one condition: one who seeks to return and be renewed must work hard at it. There is no free atonement or easy *teshuvah*.

Give Ear to the Song of the Shepherd and the Flock

"Give ear, ye heavens, and I will speak; and let the earth hear the words of my mouth. My doctrine shall drop as the rain, my speech shall distil as the dew; as the small rain upon the tender grass, and as the showers upon the herb" (Deut. 32:1–2).

The writer, apparently Moses, was very familiar with nature. Not merely as a casual consumer of weather reports but as a true and intimate lover of the beauty of the universe and all its secrets. The heavens above and the earth below were his audience. The rain and dew, the grasses and shrubs of the field were his conversation partners, his witnesses and his students. They all listened to the song of his life, attentive to every dot and dash in his work, especially now, nearing the conclusion of the book and the end of the marvelous career of the greatest of the great of all time. The tension of these last days is astonishing: a mixture of petty, everyday detail and timeless truth – a will and a legacy, a final closing of accounts and an opening of new spiritual horizons. With all this as a backdrop, the introduction of nature into Moses's world of imagery and narration is a pleasant surprise.

As noted, Moses was very familiar with nature. He had been shepherd of sheep as well as of Israelites. He had wandered through the desert and knew the pathways of the eagle through the sky as well as its nest atop the cliffs. He knew where the honeycombs were hidden in the clefts of the rock and could drink the juice of the grape until he was satiated and drunk. His song rose from his life experiences, and this is the secret of its charm. He loved creation in all its manifestations and sometimes he would sing to it, with all the feeling and precision of a lover. He sang on the edge of the sea and he sang on the brink of his death. We have no better way of sharing in Moses's song of farewell than to say a few words about the Green Torah bursting forth from between its lines and breathing new life into so many aspects of today's world.

There was a time when humanity was an inseparable part of nature. People were born and died no differently from the beasts of the field and the birds in the sky. Even when humans occasionally damaged their environment in their quest for food or while on the move, it was almost never malicious or catastrophic. Everything took place within tolerable limits; nothing was irreparable. All of nature was at humanity's service, even if it occasionally exploded in incomprehensible anger in a flood or an earthquake, a plague, a disease or an infestation of snakes.

The wrath of nature was seen in those days as the work of an angry God, at least partly because humanity was still in its infancy and had not yet learned the laws of nature and physics that govern the world. The people of the past lacked the tools of destruction that are available to us today. They did their best to tame their immediate surroundings while at the same time blending in naturally. Humanity was smaller, death was closer and more immediate, life expectancy was shorter and mortality among adults and children was more commonplace. Now times have changed beyond recognition. Relations between man and nature have deteriorated drastically. We damage nature and cause it pain, and nature in turn rages out of control and strikes us mercilessly, whether with a hurricane in New Orleans or a tsunami in East Asia, earthquakes that destroy entire cities or epidemics like AIDS that our ancestors could not have imagined. These are days of raging war, and peace between the creator and his creations is nowhere in sight.

In this difficult and dangerous time we ask: Can we propose a moral, spiritual, human vision to counter the destruction of nature going on all around us? I believe – more precisely, I think and feel – that the environment is the most compelling religious issue of our time. Over the course of recent centuries the West has changed beyond recognition. Once it was a culture that was entirely religious (notwithstanding all the variations and complexities of religion), but religion has now yielded its place and secularism has moved in to fill the vacuum. There is no lack of explanations for the gulf between religion and secularism. I would like to offer just one of them. Religion rests on the certain knowledge that there is another world beyond this world, waiting for us at the end of our days. We have many names for it: "the world to come," "paradise," "the netherworld," "hell," "the realm of the angels," "the immortality of the soul" and "the heavenly tribunal" are just a few of them.

Secularism by definition cannot accept any claim, faith or description that is not based on facts, ethics or justice. After all, secularism has its roots in rationalism, and in its worldview whatever is beyond the rational simply does not exist. It follows that the worldview of secularism focuses on the here and now, on what exists in defined places at known times, with the common denominator being empirical knowledge. That which lies beyond the empirical might be a wonderful belief, legend or soothing of the soul, but it has no factual basis and so in secular wisdom it is as nothing.

Secularism limits itself to this world. Whatever happens here is real, and anything beyond it is outside the realm of secular wisdom, somewhere between illusion and utopia, faith and superstition. This what gave birth to modern industry. Pursuing success and fulfillment in our own lifetimes, because after I die nothing will be left of me but worms and maggots. So it was that religion became the mistress of the future with all its worlds, while secularism gained dominion over the expanses of the present.

Throughout the years of secularism's existence there have been many who felt something was lacking in it. There is something hollow in the constant pursuit of success, something threatening in the great emptiness that awaits us after life itself. Facing this despair, many have turned and are turning back to the religious path to find answers. They are looking for higher meaning beyond the day-to-day. They want spiritual horizons that run deeper than the sensory and concrete. They're willing to defer the rewards of this world in order to merit a greater and more lasting compensation in the world to come.

Into the empty space between the immediacy of the secular mindset and the eternity of the religious perspectivity comes Green Torah. To my mind, there is no other agenda in modern society that is as profoundly religious as the green agenda.

The hollow place seeks to be filled. Environmental responsibility is the necessary content. The new spirituality and the old are connected by a bridge built out of Midrash:

> When the Holy One, praised be he, created Adam, he took him and let him pass before all the trees in the Garden of Eden and said to him: See my works, how fine and excellent they are. Everything that I have created, I have done for your sake. Take care that you do not corrupt and destroy my world, for if you corrupt it, there is no one to restore it after you. (Midrash Rabba, *Ecclesiastes* 7:28)

The countless people worldwide who fear for the health of the planet are partners with the creator and his creation. They are the environmental activists who care for the integrity of their own physical surroundings, who work to purify sewage and watersheds, who toil diligently to protect God's creation from human ruin.

Those who live healthy lives for themselves and for the planet are doing something that goes beyond the narrow confines of the secular experience. In fact, they are caring for the world to come. They are laying the foundations for something that will continue after their own death – namely, the world. They are repairing the corruption of the world in which they live so that their children and all the generations that follow will have a better world – for that matter, so that they will have a world at all. This is where religious thought and green thought come together.

Green faith is still young and has not yet produced its own dogmas and structured theologies, and yet in many ways it resembles the older worlds of religion. Its believers are committed to it with all their soul and with all their might. They scrupulously observe both minor and major obligations. They have their own dietary laws as well as positive and negative commandments. Most important, it takes no great effort to see the connections between Green thought and Moses's own Ten Commandments: "Thou shalt not murder" nature or its creatures. "Thou shalt not steal" or "covet" those things that cannot be uprooted without threatening their extinction. "Thou shalt not bear false witness against thy neighbor" by living in luxury on the sweat and suffering of someone on the other side of the world. "Give ear…and let the earth hear."

Week 48

Vezot Haberachah
And This Is the Blessing

Deuteronomy 33:1–34:12

The End...and a Beginning

Many leaders have a single, defining moment in history, for good or ill, by which they will be remembered for generations to come. Harry Truman's time on the stage was defined by Hiroshima and Nagasaki. Mikhail Gorbachev's singular day was the day the Berlin Wall came down. David Ben-Gurion's moment was the birth of the State of Israel in May 1948. One could name countless other examples.

By this measure, it is very hard to find one singular moment of Moses, who passes into history with the completion of this, the last of his five books. Which of his moments was not important? We credit him with the first revelation of Sinai at the burning bush, the striking of the rock, the crossing of the sea, the plagues of Egypt and appeasing God after the sin of the Golden Calf.

And yet, if it is hard to name Moses's defining moment, we can guess what Moses believed was the defining moment of the children of Israel. During his farewell, in his last days or perhaps on his final day, he said to them: "This day thou art become a people" (Deut. 27:9). Somehow, amid all the anger and quarrels, it happened. They ceased being a complaining rabble of individual ex-slaves and became one nation. From this moment on, amazing adventures awaited them as a nation of Hebrew slaves that renounced the fleshpots of Egypt and turned its face toward the Promised Land.

On this day, Moses, the retiring leader whose strength was still in his loins, whose "eye was not dim, nor his natural force abated" (Deut. 34:7), leaves behind one more mark on history that stands in almost complete contradiction to all the rest of his life's work. Throughout the four books that lay out the history of Moses and the Israelites, he never addresses them as individual tribes. For Moses, the children of Israel are always an assembly "standing this day all of you before the Lord your God" (Deut. 29:9), the crowd that Jethro observed: "All the people stand about thee" (Exod. 18:14). True, Moses had set the tribe of Levi apart, but he treated all the others as a single mass. Now, in his last moment, Moses breaks Israel down again into its tribal components and rolls the wheel backward to its starting point as a family in the Book of Genesis.

"And there was a king in Jeshurun, when the heads of the people were gathered, all the tribes of Israel together" (Deut. 33:5). Suddenly he is not relating to them as "the children of Israel," as he has called them so many times throughout the scripture. Moses sets aside his leader's scepter for a moment and takes on the voice of the mythic patriarch Jacob at his moment of death: "All these are the twelve tribes of Israel, and this is it that their father spoke unto them and blessed them; every one according to his blessing he blessed them" (Gen. 49:28). Each of the tribes now receives individual attention in a separate blessing. Why is there no general blessing for all the tribes together? Even Balaam was able to see the Israelite whole and bless it. Not Moses?

And one more question is worth asking, regarding Jewish tradition. Our tradition does not dedicate special days of mourning for the deaths of its patriarchs. Why do we celebrate the death of Moses, which is identified with the festival of Simchat Torah? He is dead and we celebrate, literally dancing on his unknown grave.

"Moses commanded us a law, an inheritance of the congregation of Jacob" (Deut. 33:4). The story of the Torah is the story of a coalescing of a national consciousness with two lobes, as it were. One is the national side, dedicated to the collective, to joint action and to unity of deed and purpose. Fulfilling the concrete, physical goals of a nation seeking a territorial inheritance requires cooperation among the tribes, which no individual tribe may shirk. Moses has an heir for his nation-building in Joshua, and many more to continue the work afterward. By dint of this unity Sihon and Og were defeated, the walls of Jericho were brought down and a land was inherited. As for the second lobe, the Torah of Moses, this is an entirely different story. Here there is no one heir, no unity of action, indeed no unity at all. On the contrary, what is called for here is a multiplicity. Moses gave one Torah, but many people received it. Many tribes, many blessings.

"Moses commanded us a law, an inheritance of the congregation of Jacob." A new people is knocking on the gates of the Promised Land and intimidating the kings and nations all around. The tribes are almost unified in the face of the outside, but Moses insists on blessing them separately. The various blessings express the itemization of the collective identity according to its separate, independent components. On his final day Moses draws a line between the nation of immediate conquest and the interpreters of the Torah who are yet to come. He separates the nation's disciplined, united warriors from its independent, individualist, innovative and sometimes revolutionary students. By breaking out the separate tribes Moses guarantees that all their voices will be preserved forever.

Moses's blessing is a blessing of the riches to be found in pluralism, in making room for the tribes, the schools, the congregations and the traditions all creating together the spiritual tapestry – the mosaic that he commanded us on his last day. Therefore we celebrate on the anniversary of his death, because even then he was thinking about us today. This day, on which everyone is called to the Torah and bears a part of it, is the everlasting day of Moses, whose body died but whose soul lives on in his letters.

Encore

Deuteronomy

My beloved father's passing from the world was slow and quite orderly. Over the course of many months we sat with him every morning and conversed. We spoke of old memories that had to be refreshed one last time, about topics he wanted to emphasize before his departure, about final questions that awaited his response and clarification. He looked after Mother, his partner and spouse, went over the arrangements for the funeral and even decided the inscription on his gravestone. One day he turned to Ada, my beloved sister, and asked her, "Do you have a pen and paper?" "Yes," she said. "Then write something down. Write down the words I'd like you to say at my funeral."

The days and weeks passed and Father was called to the heavenly court. When the time came, we stood together with a great many loved ones and admirers, bereft and weeping, and bade farewell to a wise and much-loved man. Eulogies were offered by Israel's leaders. Then my sister, the only woman among the otherwise all-male eulogizers, rose and shocked everyone with these words:

> Father asked that I say a few words. He explained that in his opinion the most important revolution to occur in the last century, the greatest of revolutions, was the entry of women into the world of action and creation. This was a greater revolution than the French or communist revolutions, because in its wake the world added vast new numbers to its active, creative life. Wherever this revolution has run its course, society enjoyed a 100 percent increase in people who became full partners in the life of that society. Father also said that he feared not all segments of our society were aware of the importance of this revolution.

Encore Deuteronomy

From the depths of his grave Father challenged the orthodox thinking of our day and days to come. I well remember the thought that entered my mind in the midst of my grief: this is Father's legacy, his spiritual will – a bequest of equality and justice. I've thought about that moment many times since then. I try to understand the lives of people who are still alive by the words they would want to leave behind when they die. It is in this spirit, the spirit of my father's farewell, that I try to understand Moses's final will. Yes, this entire book is devoted to his legacy and life story, but how can we sum up the essence of Moses's legacy? What words could encapsulate the overall theme of his teaching?

In my view, it would not be his past deeds, not his easy passage from conversing with God to speaking with humanity, not the revelation at Sinai nor even the Exodus from Egypt that form the pinnacle of Moses's achievement. The greatest and most enduring of his gifts is presented in these verses:

> For this commandment which I command thee this day, it is not too hard for thee, neither is it far off. It is not in heaven, that thou shouldest say: "Who shall go up for us to heaven, and bring it unto us, and make us to hear it, that we may do it?" Neither is it beyond the sea, that thou shouldest say: "Who shall go over the sea for us, and bring it unto us, and make us to hear it, that we may do it?" But the word is very nigh unto thee, in thy mouth, and in thy heart, that thou mayest do it. (Deut. 30:11–14)

Moses takes his leave. As he departs, he does not ask that he be remembered as a mortal who met God in heaven. His advice to us is: do not seek another Moses, "that thou shouldest say: 'Who shall go up for us to heaven, and bring it unto us?'" There is no need for another Moses. The Torah of Moses is enough.

We should not seek the meaning of these things outside the realm of human existence. We should not believe in magicians, fortune-tellers, frauds and mystics. Everything is right here – not in heaven, not beyond the sea. What is more, this is a protest statement against charismatic leadership that bedazzles and blinds the eyes of its devotees. There is no rabbi, holy man, sage or rebbe who can do the work for us. There is no one to decide for us. The responsibility begins and ends with us.

With his final breath our teacher Moses charged full-force against the beliefs of the pious fools and robots. Moses leaves behind a will whose essence is a spirituality of personal responsibility: "In thy mouth, and in thy heart, that thou mayest do it." The Torah speaks in human language. These are the principles of a faith with humanity at its core. A spirituality of responsibility does not decree mere obligation to the written word, but opens the way to a fruitful, dynamic culture of debate and interpretation, perpetually enriching itself and "every happy one that holdeth her fast" (Prov. 3:18).

The spirit of Moses has no room for reliance on the authority of anyone who has been "beyond the veil" and witnessed hidden signs and wonders, so to speak. Moses demands that everyone rely on his own authority of knowledge, morality and values that rise up from here below rather than descend upon us as a gift from above. This authority cannot be bequeathed, but we can play a role in it as equals. This is the spirit of that humanity for whom the world was created, in which even God cannot divert the flow of discourse from its human course. This legacy was translated many generations later into the defining Talmudic Aggadah of the oven of Akhnai. This tale has been mentioned more than once in this volume, and there is no better way to end it:

> On that day [during a debate between Rabbi Eliezer and the other sages over the ritual purity of a certain oven] Rabbi Eliezer brought forward every imaginable argument, but the sages did not accept them.
>
> Said he to them: "If the *halachah* agrees with me, let this carob-tree prove it!" Thereupon the carob-tree was torn a hundred cubits out of its place. Others affirm, four hundred cubits.
>
> "No proof can be brought from a carob-tree," they retorted.
>
> Again he said to them: "If the *halachah* agrees with me, let the stream of water prove it!" Whereupon the stream of water flowed backwards.
>
> "No proof can be brought from a stream of water," they rejoined.

Again he urged: "If the *halachah* agrees with me, let the walls of the academy prove it," whereupon the walls inclined to fall.

But Rabbi Joshua rebuked them, saying: "When scholars are engaged in a halachic dispute, what have ye to interfere?" Hence they did not fall, in honor of Rabbi Joshua, nor did they resume the upright, in honor of Rabbi Eliezer; and they are still standing thus inclined.

Again he said to them: "If the *halachah* agrees with me, let it be proved from Heaven!" Whereupon a Heavenly Voice cried out: "Why do ye dispute with Rabbi Eliezer, seeing that in all matters the *halachah* agrees with him!"

But Rabbi Joshua arose and exclaimed: "It is not in heaven" [Deut. 30:12]. What did he mean by this? Said Rabbi Jeremiah: That the Torah had already been given at Mount Sinai; we pay no attention to a Heavenly Voice.

(Babylonian Talmud, *Bava Metzia* 59b)

This is an astounding story. The greatest sages of that generation were debating a matter that had come before the academy – the majority, led by Rabbi Joshua, against the lone voice of Rabbi Eliezer. When Rabbi Eliezer saw that he was not convincing his colleagues by force of logic and the traditional reading of the Torah, he called on higher forces to help him. Assistance came in the form of repeated signs: a carob tree torn from its roots, a stream of water flowing backwards and the very walls of the academy threatening to collapse on the heads of Rabbi Eliezer's opponents. When all these had failed to convince the majority, the Holy One, praised be he, delivered a personal, explicit message in his own heavenly voice. But even this failed to sway the majority, because according to the Torah of Moses, the Torah and its interpretation belong here on earth. The Torah belongs to humankind, and they rule on the basis of majority decision without reliance on miracles, heavenly voices or even the Master of the universe, the Father of all voices. "It is not in heaven" – this is the essence of Moses's legacy.

But the story did not end there. Later the Aggadah relates, "Rabbi Nathan met the prophet Elijah and asked him: What did the Holy One, blessed be he, do in that hour? 'He laughed,' the prophet replied, 'and said, my children have defeated me, my children have defeated me!'" Moses's legacy calls on us to defeat God on the field of his Torah. When humanity takes on personal responsibility for the legacy and tradition, along with the decisions of the future, we repair the world and become God's partners in the act of creation. We defeat God by the power of his own Torah.

This is the essence of the Torah: to give him, the giver of the Torah, endless reasons to smile. It is the smile of a father seeing his children defeat him as they grow and mature. The smile of God.

Chazak, chazak venitchazek – be strong, be strong and may we be strengthened.